Lecture Notes in Computer Science   10014

Commenced Publication in 1973
Founding and Former Series Editors:
Gerhard Goos, Juris Hartmanis, and Jan van Leeuwen

More information about this series at http://www.springer.com/series/7410

Billy Bob Brumley · Juha Röning (Eds.)

Secure IT Systems

21st Nordic Conference, NordSec 2016
Oulu, Finland, November 2–4, 2016
Proceedings

 Springer

Editors
Billy Bob Brumley
Tampere University of Technology
Tampere
Finland

Juha Röning
Computer Science and Engineering
University of Oulu
Oulu
Finland

ISSN 0302-9743   ISSN 1611-3349   (electronic)
Lecture Notes in Computer Science
ISBN 978-3-319-47559-2   ISBN 978-3-319-47560-8   (eBook)
DOI 10.1007/978-3-319-47560-8

Library of Congress Control Number: 2016953314

LNCS Sublibrary: SL4 – Security and Cryptology

Printed on acid-free paper

This Springer imprint is published by Springer Nature
The registered company is Springer International Publishing AG
The registered company address is: Gewerbestrasse 11, 6330 Cham, Switzerland

Preface

The NordSec conferences were started in 1996 with the aim of bringing together researchers and practitioners in the field of computer security in the Nordic countries, thereby establishing a forum for discussions and cooperation between universities, industry, and computer societies. Over the years, NordSec has developed into an international conference that takes place in the Nordic countries on a round-robin basis. It has also become a key meeting venue for Nordic university teachers and students with an interest in security research.

These proceedings contain the papers presented at NordSec 2016: the 21st Nordic Conference on Secure IT Systems held during November 2–4, 2016, in Oulu, Finland. The venue was the University of Oulu, co-located with the 10th International Crisis Management Workshop and Oulu Winter School.

Of the 49 total submissions received by the July 8 extended deadline, 43 met the requirements for peer review. After a brief manuscript bidding process, the review period spanned July 12 through August 10, during which the 29-member Program Committee along with 20 external reviewers produced a total of 151 reviews. With an average of 3.5 reviews per manuscript, this strong effort brought us quite close to our goal of four reviews per manuscript.

Based on the reviews and following a brief yet active discussion phase, we notified authors on August 15 that 16 manuscripts were accepted for presentation at NordSec 2016. Amongst these papers, five clear themes emerged: system security, network security, software security, cryptography, and authentication. Furthermore, the accepted papers suggest cyber-physical system security is currently an active academic research area.

We were honored to have three brilliant invited speakers: (1) Shay Gueron, University of Haifa, Israel, and Intel Corporation (Intel Development Center, Haifa, Israel); (2) Jan-Erik Ekberg (Trustonic); (3) Daniel Komaromy (Comsecuris).

As NordSec 2016 chairs, we extend our sincerest gratitude to everyone involved in making this year's instance a success, including but not limited to: the authors who submitted their hard work, the Program Committee and external reviewers, the invited speakers, Christian Wieser (Conference Ops), and our generous sponsors Ericsson and Intopalo.

September 2016

Billy Bob Brumley
Juha Röning

Organization

General Chair

Juha Röning   University of Oulu, Finland

Program Chair

Billy Bob Brumley   Tampere University of Technology, Finland

Conference Operations

Christian Wieser   University of Oulu, Finland

Program Committee

Magnus Almgren	Chalmers University of Technology, Sweden
David Bernhard	University of Bristol, UK
Billy Bob Brumley	Tampere University of Technology, Finland
Mads Dam	KTH Royal Institute of Technology, Sweden
Nicola Dragoni	Technical University of Denmark, Denmark
Danilo Gligoroski	Norwegian University of Science and Technology, Norway
Eric Xu Guo	Qualcomm, USA
Kimmo Halunen	VTT Technical Research Centre of Finland, Finland
Chris Hankin	Imperial College London, UK
Rene Rydhof Hansen	Aalborg University, Denmark
Daniel Hedin	Mälardalen University, Sweden
Marko Helenius	Tampere University of Technology, Finland
Kimmo Järvinen	Aalto University, Finland
Frank Kargl	Ulm University, Germany
Svein Johan Knapskog	Norwegian University of Science and Technology, Norway
Hanno Langweg	Norwegian University of Science and Technology, Norway
Peeter Laud	Cybernetica AS, Estonia
Samuel Marchal	Aalto University, Finland
Fabio Martinelli	IIT-CNR, Italy
Chris Mitchell	Royal Holloway, University of London, UK
Hanne Riis Nielson	Technical University of Denmark, Denmark
Valtteri Niemi	University of Helsinki, Finland
Andrew Paverd	Aalto University, Finland

Kai Rannenberg   Goethe University Frankfurt, Germany
Heiko Roßnagel   Fraunhofer IAO, Germany
Juha Röning   University of Oulu, Finland
Ben Smeets   Lund University, Sweden
Seppo Virtanen   University of Turku, Finland
Xueyang Wang   Intel, USA

Additional Reviewers

Fatma Al Maqbali	Hugo A. López	Angelo Spognardi
Zaruhi Aslanyan	John Mattsson	Fatbardh Veseli
Fabina Dietrich	Flemming Nielson	Luca Viganò
Per Hallgren	Andrea Saracino	Shuzhe Yang
Daniel Hausknecht	T. Schafeitel-Tähtinen	Artsiom Yautsiukhin
Kekai Hu	Christopher Schmitz	Ahmed Seid Yesuf
Sebastian Kurowski	· Alexander Sjösten	

Sponsors

Ericsson
Intopalo

Contents

Cryptography

Authentication

System Security

Event-Triggered Watermarking Control
to Handle Cyber-Physical Integrity Attacks

Jose Rubio-Hernan[1]([✉]), Luca De Cicco[2], and Joaquin Garcia-Alfaro[1]

[1] SAMOVAR, Telecom SudParis, CNRS, Université Paris-Saclay, Evry, France
{jose.rubio_hernan,joaquin.garcia_alfaro}@telecom-sudparis.com
[2] Politecnico di Bari, Dipartimento di Ingegneria Elettrica e dell'Informazione,
Bari, Italy
luca.decicco@poliba.it

Abstract. The use of control-theoretic solutions to detect attacks against cyber-physical systems is a growing area of research. Traditional literature proposes the use of control strategies to retain, f.i., satisfactory closed-loop performance, as well as safety properties, when a communication network connects the distributed components of a physical system (e.g., sensors, actuators, and controllers). However, the adaptation of these strategies to handle security incidents, is an ongoing challenge. In this paper, we analyze the use of a watermark-based detector that handles integrity attacks. We show that (1) the detector is able to work properly under the presence of adversaries using non-parametric methods to escape detection; but (2) it fails at detecting adversaries using parametric identification methods to escape detection. We propose a new strategy that complements the watermark-based detector in order to detect both adversaries. We validate the detection efficiency of the new strategy via numeric simulations.

Keywords: Cyber-physical security · Critical infrastructures · Attack detection · Adversary model · Networked Control System

1 Introduction

As an evolution of traditional industrial control systems [9], cyber-physical systems [11] combine feedback control technologies with novel computing and communication capabilities. The recently coined cyber-physical security term refers to mechanisms that address security issues associated to these environments. The use of inadequate cyber-physical security mechanisms can have an adverse effect in critical infrastructures, either national or private ones [6]. These issues place the study of cyber-physical security mechanisms as a hot research topic.

Given the control-theoretic nature of cyber-physical systems, the control community is actively working to adapt traditional control strategies to detect faults and errors, towards detectors of malicious attacks [7,8,17]. Motivated by the same objectives, we present in this paper a solution that combines two different control strategies to handle integrity attacks against cyber-physical systems.

© Springer International Publishing AG 2016
B.B. Brumley and J. Röning (Eds.): NordSec 2016, LNCS 10014, pp. 3–19, 2016.
DOI: 10.1007/978-3-319-47560-8_1

The contributions of this paper can be summarized as follows. First, we analyze the effectiveness of a challenge-response detector based on control-theoretic watermarks, under the assumption of integrity cyber-physical attacks. We reexamine the security of an existing contribution by Mo et al. in [13], and revisit its security effectiveness under a new adversarial scenario. We show that under the new assumptions, the original contribution presents some weaknesses. We then propose a new detection strategy that combines event-triggered control strategies with the previous watermark-based detector, in order to cover the new adversaries. Finally, we validate our proposed approach via numerical simulations. Our results show the effectiveness of our novel proposal.

The paper is organized as follows. Section 2 provides the necessary background. Section 3 reviews the watermark-based detector scheme by Mo et al. [13], provides a new adversary model and reexamines the security of the detector under the new adversary model. Section 4 presents the new detection strategy to handle the uncovered limitations, and validates the approach via numerical simulations. Section 5 reviews related work. Section 6 concludes the paper.

2 Background

2.1 Cyber-Physical Attacks

The use of communication networks and IT components in traditional control systems paves the way to new vulnerability issues. Attacks against these setups are named cyber-physical attacks. These attacks target physical processes through the network. In [19], authors propose a taxonomy of cyber-physical attacks based on the resources of the adversaries. Such resources are mainly measured in terms of adversary knowledge (e.g., *a priori* knowledge of the adversary about the system and its security measures). For instance, the knowledge of the adversary about the system is the main resource used to build up complex attacks, and to make them undetectable. Based on the degree of the adversary knowledge, the attacks may succeed at violating system properties, e.g., availability and integrity, as well as at obtaining operational information about the system to make the attacks undetectable.

Based on the adversary knowledge, cyber-physical attacks related to integrity can be classified as: (i) the replay attack where the adversary does not need knowledge about the system model [13]; (ii) injection attack, where the adversary injects false data or deviation of the legitimate data. These attacks are not detected if the data are compatible with the dynamics of the system [19], i.e., the adversary must to know the physical processes; and, (iii) covert attack, where the adversary knows perfectly the cyber-physical system behaviour. This attack is defined in [18] where the authors conclude that it is not possible to be detected.

Several techniques exist in the literature to counter these attacks. For instance, (a) signal-based detector methods [1]; (b) statistical detection mechanisms [5]; and (c) stationary watermark-based detectors, adapting failure detector mechanisms [13]. In the following sections, we re-examine the watermark-based technique, and some control strategies, in order to propose an improved security technique against integrity attacks. The new detection strategy handles cyber-physical adversaries which are not detected with the aforementioned techniques. Such cyber-physical adversaries use a parametric technique to obtain the knowledge about the system model.

2.2 Control Strategies

Control theory is a well-known topic, where the evolution of the technology has been the main motivation to create new control policies to manage these systems, keeping the control features. Among these new technologies, we can mention the networked control systems (NCSs), where the loop between the different components of the system is closed through the network. A wide range of research has been reported in the literature focusing on managing these new technologies in order to preserve the control properties of the systems. They have generated new challenges in control/estimation, signal processing, and communication in order to solve the new performance problems as limited power transmission, bandwidth constrains, packet drop, delay or security. The networked control systems have motivated to consider control/estimation and communication in a unified way [10], in order to solve problems as performance or security. Among all control strategies in NCSs, we have focused on the strategies depending on the transmission policy; sampled-data control, or event-triggered control. Into the sampled-data policy, we find mono-frequency sampling, i.e., the same sampling frequency for all the channels, or multi-frequency sampling, i.e., different sampling frequencies depending on the channel (sensor/controller or controller/actuator) [17]. Event-triggered control (ETC) has been also studied depending on the policy to send the events, Periodic event-triggered control (PECT) [8] or stochastic events-triggered schedule [7]. This topic is inline with our research since the security in NCSs includes the management of the control properties through the network to avoid that an external entity, an adversary, has the capacity to control these properties and harm the system.

2.3 Watermark-Based Attack Detection

The watermark-based detector is proposed in [13], with the goal of detecting replay attacks against cyber-physical systems. To analyze the watermark-based detector, the authors use an industrial control system modeled mathematically as a discrete linear time-invariant (LTI) system. This mathematical model is used to describe the dynamic behaviour of the system. The system can be represented as follows:

$$x_{t+1} = Ax_t + Bu_t + w_t \tag{2.1}$$

$$y_t = Cx_t + v_t \tag{2.2}$$

where $x_t \subset \mathbb{R}^n$ is the state's vector, $u_t \in \mathbb{R}^p$ is the control signal, $y_t \in \mathbb{R}^m$ is the system output, and $w_t \in \mathbb{R}^n$ and v_t are the *process noise* and the measurement noise respectively. The noises are assumed to be a zero mean Gaussian white noise with covariance Q, *i.e.* $w_t \sim N(0, Q)$ and R, *i.e.* $v_t \sim N(0, R)$ respectively.

Moreover, $A \in \mathbb{R}^{n \times n}$, $B \in \mathbb{R}^{n \times p}$ and $C \in \mathbb{R}^{m \times n}$ are respectively the *state* matrix, the *input* matrix end the *output* matrix.

Let us now define the well-known *Linear Quadratic Gaussian* (LQG) approach used as a control technique in [13]. This technique has two independent components:

1. a *Kalman filter* producing an optimal state estimation $\hat{x}_t$ of the state x:

$$\hat{x}_{t|t-1} = A\hat{x}_{t-1} + Bu_{t-1}$$

$$\hat{x}_t = \hat{x}_{t|t-1} + K_t(y_t - C\hat{x}_{t|t-1}) \tag{2.3}$$

where K_t denotes the Kalman gain, and $\hat{x}_{t|t-1}$ is the *a priori* system state estimation.

2. a *Linear Quadratic Regulator* (LQR) providing the control law u_t.

$$u_t = L\hat{x}_t \tag{2.4}$$

where L denotes the feedback gain of a linear-quadratic regulator.

After describing the model of the plant, hereinafter we present the detection scheme proposed in [13] against replay attacks. The idea is to superpose a watermark signal $\Delta u_t \in \mathbb{R}^p$ to the optimal control law $u_t^\diamond$. The new control input u_t is given by:

$$u_t = u_t^\diamond + \Delta u_t \tag{2.5}$$

Note that the watermark signal is independent from the process noise w_t and the output noise v_t. To detect the adversaries, the watermark-based detector employs a well-known χ^2 detector [3]. The *alarm signal* g_t generates by the detector is defined as:

$$g_t = \sum_{i=t-w+1}^{t} (r_i)^T \mathcal{P}^{-1}(r_i) \tag{2.6}$$

where w is the size of the detection window, $\mathcal{P}$ is the co-variance of input signals from the sensors and $r_t = y_t - C\hat{x}_{t|t-1}$ is the residues generated from the estimator at each t-th time step.

To verify if the system is under attack, g_t is compared with a threshold γ. If g_t is equal or greater than the threshold, $g_t \geq \gamma$, the detector generates an alarm.

3 Watermark-Based Attack Detection Against a New Adversary Model

Let us assume the system employs the detector described in Sect. 2.3, so that the controller superposes its output with an authentication watermark Δu_t. At steady-state, i.e. after the transient has been exhausted, the output of the system can be considered as the sum of its steady-state value and a component that is due to watermark signal that shall be only known by the controller.

Hereinafter we denote the adversary proposed in [13] as a cyber adversary [16]. This attacker has the ability to eavesdrop all the messages sent by the sensors y_t and to inject messages with a signal y'_t to conduct malicious actions without any knowledge about the system model. Let us also define a cyber-physical adversary as the attacker who is able to eavesdrop the messages with the intention of improving its knowledge about the system behaviour, in order to conduct malicious actions [16].

Based on the way to model the system's behaviour, two different cyber-physical adversaries can be defined.

Definition 3.1. *An attacker that, only uses the previous input and output of the system to obtain a system behaviour is defined as a non-parametric cyber-physical adversary.*

Remark 1. This adversary can use a Finite Impulse Response (FIR) identification model [20].

Cyber and non-parametric cyber-physical adversaries can be handled using a non-stationary watermark detector scheme [16]. However, if the cyber-physical adversary is able to acquire the parameters of the system, a non-stationary watermark detector scheme is not able to detect the attack.

Definition 3.2. *An attacker able to estimate the parameters of the system using input and output data to mislead the controller detector is defined as a parametric cyber-physical adversary.*

The signal injected by the parametric cyber-physical adversary cannot be detected by the χ^2 detector (cf. Eq. (2.6)), using a non-stationary watermark-based scheme.

Remark 2. This adversary can use an ARX (autoregressive with exogenous input) or an ARMAX (autoregressive-moving average with exogenous input) approach in order to estimate the model of the system [14].

We assume that the main constraint of this adversary is the energy spent to eavesdrop and analyze the communication data, i.e., the number of samples eavesdropped to obtain the system model parameters.

Proof. If the system uses a watermark-based detector, the system control inputs are represented by Eq. (2.5), and the outputs are represented by:

$$y_t = C(Ax_t + B(u_t^\diamond + \Delta u_t) + w_t) + v_t \tag{3.1}$$

note that the watermark can be defined as an independent and identically distributed Gaussian distribution or a stationary Gaussian distribution. Using the ARX approach we can define the system defined in Eqs. (2.1) and (2.2) as follows:

$$Y(z) = H(z)U(z) + V(z) \tag{3.2}$$

where $U(z)$ and $Y(z)$ represent the inputs and the outputs of the plant respectively. $V(z)$ represents the external noise which affects the outputs of the plant. And $H(z)$ is another way to describe the model of the system presented in Sect. 2.3, using frequency domain.

$$H(z) = \frac{Y(z) - V(z)}{U(z)} = \frac{\mathcal{N}(z)}{\mathcal{D}(z)} = \left(\frac{n_0 z^m + n_1 z^{m-1} + \dots + n_m}{d_0 z^n + d_1 z^{n-1} + \dots + d_n} \right) \quad (3.3)$$

where $\mathcal{N}(z)$ and $\mathcal{D}(z)$ are the polynomial functions which build the model of the system. We prove that under the attacker model of Definition 3.2, the adversary is able to know exactly the watermark signal and thus $\Delta u_t = \Delta u_t'$.

Proposition 1. *A parametric cyber-physical adversary is able to obtain the system model, $H(z)$, and mislead the controller, eavesdropping the control inputs and the measurements of the sensors. The probability to be detected, is equal to the probability to obtain an erroneous model. This probability, is directly proportional to the order of the system, i.e., the order of $\mathcal{D}(z)$, and inversely proportional to the window size to eavesdrop the data channel.*

Proof. If the adversary knows all the control inputs, and the measurements of the sensors, then the model obtained by the adversary can be defined as; $H_{at}(z) = (Y(z) - V(z))/U(z)$. Comparing the adversary model of the system and the real model system, it is straightforward to prove that both system models are equal, $H_{at}(z) = H(z)$. Nevertheless, the adversary has an error that depends on the order selected to create the model and the number of samples eavesdropped to compute the parameters of the model, the window size. Following the Mean Square Error (MSE):

$$MSE = \frac{\mathcal{H}(\zeta)}{\hat{T}} \quad (3.4)$$

where $\mathcal{H}(\zeta)/\hat{T}$ is the error variance, since the system model used in this paper (cf. Sect. 2.3) contains no bias error [2]. This error is directly proportional to system complexity (flexibility), ζ, and inversely proportional to the samples eavesdropped by the adversary. It is worth to note that the complexity is directly proportional to the system order. Indeed, for a system with a small order is easier to obtain a good approximation model by the adversary.

To summarize, these adversaries look at the real system like a black box. They can increase the order (complexity) of their model to improve the possibility to go into the order's range where the real system could be identified. Nevertheless, they need to use a larger window size to minimize the MSE value. For this reason, the computation cost of the attack increases for a high order of the system, since the adversary needs to increase their order model, as well as, the window size in order to minimize the MSE. It is worth mentioning that the number of samples eavesdropped before the attack, as well as the order system of the adversary, are the main parameters to avoid detection.

3.1 Numerical Validation

In the previous sections we have seen that the watermark detector proposed in [13] and the improvement proposed in [16] are not able to detect parametric cyber-physical adversaries. We have validated both watermark detector against the parametric cyber-physical adversary presented in Definition 3.2. Hereinafter we present only the detection ratio with respect to this adversary using the detector improvement proposed in [16] due to space constraint. Nevertheless, we have obtained the same detection ratio using the detector proposed in [13]. This adversary is able to identify the system model parameters from the input and output plant signals. To validate the watermark detector against the parametric cyber-physical adversary, we define three different use cases:

1. First use-case: the adversary knows only a subset of control inputs and measurements of the sensors. This adversary will be detected by the watermark-based detector proposed in [13].

Proof. Assuming, on the one hand, a system defined as $H(z) = (Y(z) - V(z))/U(z)$, where $U(z) = U_1(z) + U_2(z)$; and, on the other hand, an adversary whose model can be defined as $H_{at_1} = (Y(z) - V(z))/U_1(z)$, since this attacker only knows a subset of inputs $U_1(z)$ [21]. Then, if all the inputs and outputs are correlated, the adversary will be detected by the system, since:

$$H_{at_1} = \frac{Y(z) - V(z)}{U_1(z)} \neq \frac{Y(z) - V(z)}{U(z)} = H(z) \qquad (3.5)$$

proves that the model used by the adversary, H_{at_1}, is different to the real system model.

2. Second use-case: the adversary has access to all the control inputs and measurements of the sensors. In this case, the parametric cyber-physical adversary could be able to obtain the model of the system with great accuracy. To do so, the adversary has to use the order of the unknown system, p, and to use a large window size, $\hat{T}$, to eavesdrop the data in order to get the correct system model.

Figures 1(a) and (b) show the detection ratio of the watermark detector against a parametric cyber-physical adversary. Figure 1(a) shows the results of 200 Monte Carlo simulations using systems of order ten, against this adversary. The results present the ratio of detection if the adversary uses a window size equal to 200 and different system orders for the model. If the attacker chooses the correct system order for the model, the ratio of detection is around 7%. Nevertheless, if the adversary order varies in the range [8, 12], the detection ratio is not higher than 10%. Out of this range, the ratio of detection increases drastically. Figure 1(b) shows the ratio of detection for 200 Monte Carlo simulations using systems of order 25, against seven different parametric cyber-physical adversaries. The assumed window size is settled to $\hat{T} = 300$. If an adversary uses a

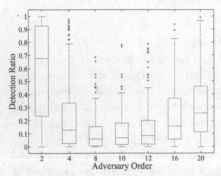
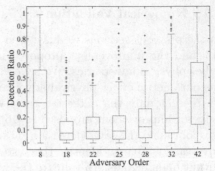

(a) Detection ratio with respect to the adversary order for systems of order 10

(b) Detection ratio with respect to the adversary order for systems of order 25

Fig. 1. Detection ratio function with respect to the adversary order. (a) For systems of order 10 against a parametric cyber-physical adversary with a window size equal to 200. And (b) for systems of order 25 against a parametric cyber-physical adversary with a window size equal to 300

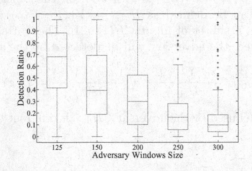

Fig. 2. Detection ratio function with respect to the adversary windows size. The order used by the parametric cyber-physical adversary is the correct systems order, $p = 25$

model of the system with the correct order, the ratio of detection is around 8 %. The range of orders where the ratio of detection does not increase drastically is [18, 28]. If an adversary uses an order in this range, the ratio of detection is not higher than 10 %. Otherwise, the likelihood to detect the adversary is high.

Figure 2 shows the ratio of detection of the same system, against a parametric cyber-physical adversary with different window sizes (125, 150, 200, 250, and 300), and the correct system order. The results confirm that the adversary needs a bigger window size in order to attack a system using a higher order, with a ratio of detection less than 10 %. From these results we can conclude that a parametric cyber-physical adversary, who is capable to eavesdrop and analyze a large number of samples from the communication channel, and using an equivalent order system, is capable of evading detection.

3. Third use-case: This is a particular case of the second use-case, where the adversary knows a subset of inputs (control inputs) and outputs (measurements of the sensors). These inputs and outputs are independent of any other inputs and outputs. For this reason, the adversary is able to attack this subset of the system. In this use-case, the adversary has all the knowledge about a subset of the system since it is independent of the other subsets of the same system.

4 PIETC Watermark-Based Detection Strategy

In the previous section we have seen that the watermark-based schemes are able to handle attacks carried out by adversaries with limited knowledge about the system dynamics, f.i., the ones defined in our work as either cyber adversaries or non-parametric cyber-physical adversaries (cf. Definition 3.1). Nevertheless, it fails at detecting those adversaries with enough knowledge about the system dynamics, defined in our work as parametric cyber-physical adversaries (cf. Definition 3.2). In this section we present a new detector scheme, hereinafter denoted as periodic and intermittent event-triggered control watermark detector (PIETC-WD). This new detector aims at detecting the three adversary models defined in our work.

Our scheme consists of a local controller located in the sensors and a remote controller creating a distributed controller. The cooperation between the local and the remote controller allows us to create an intrusion detection policy to capture integrity attacks. The local controllers manage the dynamics of the plant, and the remote controller manages the system closed-loop in order to ensure the system against integrity attacks. Notice that our new scheme requires an additional controller together with the sensors, that must have enough computation power to process data estimations, e.g., to predict errors between environmental and estimated data. The actuators do not require additional computational power. Nevertheless, during the time between two consecutive events, they must keep the last data received from the remote controller.

To carry out with our scheme it is necessary to define communication policies among the sensors, the actuators and the remote controller. We define two communication policies for ensuring the system: (i) *periodic communication policy*, which the communication from the sensors to the remote controller is periodical, with a T_{sc} period, and also from the remote controller to the actuators, with a T_{ca} period; and, (ii) *intermittent communication policy*, which allows for sending data from the sensors to the remote controller if the local controller produces an alarm. Notice that T_{sc} cannot be equal to T_{ca} to avoid that an intermittent communication takes place while the periodic communication is being sent.

Definition 4.1. *Periodic and intermittent event-triggered control watermark detector (PIETC-WD) is a detector strategy with distributed control tasks. On the one hand, the sensors control the system periodically, using their local controllers and a local watermark-based detector* [13]. *On the other hand, the remote* *controller uses the estimation error received from each sensor to periodically generate the control inputs. The remote controller also controls the closed-loop communication with an intermittent watermark.*

We provide more information about the controllers and the communication policies in the following subsections.

4.1 Local Controller Design

The local controller is located in the sensors and uses a watermark in order to verify that the dynamics of the system is correct. Each sensor has a local controller with a LQG approach (cf. Sect. 2.3). We denote the local controller in each sensor by $i \in \{0, 1, ..., N - 1\}$, where N is the number of sensors in the system. This controller adds a watermark to the sensor measurement before sending the residue to the remote controller:

$$y_t^{(i)} = y_t^{\diamond(i)} + \Delta y_t^{(i)} \tag{4.1}$$

$$r_t^{(i)} = y_t^{(i)} - C_i \hat{x}_{t|t-1}^{(i)} \tag{4.2}$$

where $y_t^{\diamond(i)}$ is the sensor measurement, $\Delta y_t^{(i)}$ is the watermark added by the local controllers, and $r_t^{(i)}$ is the residue sent to the remote controller to compute the control input $u_t^{(i)}$. Notice that the new sensor measurement $y_t^{(i)}$ is computed after verifying that $y_t^{\diamond(i)}$ is the correct sensor measurement.

4.2 Remote Controller Design

The remote controller receives periodically the residue of each sensor, $r_t^{(i)}$, and computes these residues using the LQG approach (cf. Sect. 2.3) to obtain the state estimation:

$$\hat{x}_t = \hat{x}_{t|t-1} + K_t(r_t) \tag{4.3}$$

where r_t is a vector generated by all the residues of the sensors. We can define the control inputs vector, u_t, as follows:

$$u_t = L(\hat{x}_{t|t-1} + K_t r_t) = L(\hat{x}_{t|t-1} + K_t(r_t^* + \Delta y_t)) \tag{4.4}$$

where r_t^* is the residues' vector before adding the watermark, and Δy_t is the vector generated by all the sensors' watermarks.

The watermark used intermittently by the remote controller is added to the control inputs. The controller adds a watermark with probability β. Denoting $\lambda_t = 1$ or 0 as indication function whether the watermark is added or not, we assume that $\lambda's$ are iid. Bernoulli random variables with $E[\lambda_t] = \beta$.

The intermittence of the watermark communication allows us to define the watermark behaviour as a non-stationary distribution. This watermark, Δu_t (cf. Eq. (2.5)), permits us to detect if the closed-loop is being manipulated. It is worth noting that Δu_t is a stochastic signal with the same variance as Δy_t.

4.3   Periodic Communication Policy

The periodic communication policy is managed by the sensors. The sensors add the watermark in the measurements received by the plant and send the residue r_t to the remote controller. The remote controller uses these residues to generate the control inputs sent to the actuators. The actions of these actuators produce change in the state of the plant that are captured by the sensors. If the real state differ from the state estimated by the sensors, then the sensors will switch from periodic communication policy to intermittent communication policy (cf. Sect. 4.4).

In order to validate the proposal, let us assume that an attack is started at time T_0 and we compute the residue $r_t^{(i)}$ for $t \in [T_0, T_0 + T - 1]$:

$$r_t^{(i)} = y_t'^{(i)} - C_i \hat{x}_{t|t-T}^{(i)} \tag{4.5}$$

where $y_t'^{(i)}$ is the sensor measurement sent to the controller by the adversary. Moreover, it is easy to show that the following holds:

$$\hat{x}_{t|t-T}^{(i)} = \hat{x}_{t|t-T}'^{(i)} + \mathcal{A}_i^{t-T_0}(\hat{x}_{T_0|T_0-1}^{(i)} - \hat{x}_{T_0|T_0-1}'^{(i)})$$
$$+ \sum_{j=0}^{t-T_0-1}(\mathcal{A}^j(A_i + B_iL_i)K_i(\Delta y_{t-1-j}^{(i)} - \Delta y_{t-1-j}'^{(i)})) \tag{4.6}$$

where $\hat{x}'^{(i)}$ is the local estimated state for each sensor when the system is under attack and $\mathcal{A}_i = (A_i + B_iL_i)(I_i - K_iC_i)$ is a stable matrix [13]. Substitution of (4.6) in (4.5) yields:

$$r_t^{(i)} = \underbrace{y_t'^{(i)} - C_i\hat{x}_{t|t-T}'^{(i)}}_{\text{First term}} - \underbrace{C_i\mathcal{A}_i^{t-T_0}(\hat{x}_{T_0|T_0-1}^{(i)} - \hat{x}_{T_0|T_0-1}'^{(i)})}_{\text{Second term}}$$
$$\underbrace{- C_i \sum_{j=0}^{t-T_0-1}(\mathcal{A}_i^j(A_i + B_iL_i)K_i(\Delta y_{t-1-j}^{(i)} - \Delta y_{t-1-j}'^{(i)}))}_{\text{Third term}}$$

Let us consider separately the three terms in the equation written above: the first term follows the same distribution of $(y_t - C_i\hat{x}_{t|t-1}^{(i)})$; since $\mathcal{A}_i$ is asymptotically stable – i.e. all its eigenvalues are inside the open unit disk of the complex plane – the second term converges exponentially to zero. In fact, the entries of $\mathcal{A}_i^{t-T_0}$ converge exponentially fast to zero. The third term, under attack, is not equal to zero, since $\Delta y_t^{(i)} \neq \Delta y_t'^{(i)}$, and the adversary is detected; from a cyber adversary viewpoint, the measurements of the sensors change all the time and replay measurements are not accepted; likewise, a cyber-physical adversary is not able to obtain the system model using the methodology proposed in Sect. 3. For instance, the parametric cyber-physical adversary model, using the ARX approach [14], is computed as follows:

$$H_{at_2} = \frac{f(R(z), Y(z)) - V(z)}{U(z)} \tag{4.7}$$

where f is a linear function of the residue $R(z)$, and the output $Y(z)$.

Assuming that the real model is $H = (Y(z) - V(z))/U(z)$, we can see that $H_{at_2} \neq H$, and the adversary is not able to obtain the model of the system.

4.4   Intermittent Communication Policy

The aforementioned periodic communication policy is managed by the sensors. The sensors produce an alarm if $g_t \geq \gamma$. When a sensor produces an alarm, this information is sent immediately to the remote controller. The affected sensor sends the real sensor measurement to the remote controller in order to carry out a second verification. An alarm happens if the control input has been manipulated by an external entity, a problem occurs in the system or the remote controller adds the watermark in the control input.

When the remote controller receives a measurement from a sensor, if a watermark Δu has not been sent, then the remote controller creates an intrusion alarm. Otherwise, if a watermark has been added to the control input, the controller verifies if this alarm is produced by the watermark. If the residue generated between the real measurements of the sensors and the estimation is under the threshold, the remote controller sends the control input generated before adding the watermark. However, if the residue is over the threshold, it means that an external entity is into the closed-loop, and an alarm is activated.

In order to validate our claims, let us assume the following attack in the communication channel between the sensor and the controller after the controller sends a control input with a watermark. It is started at time T_0 and we compute the residues r_t for $t \in [T_0, T_0 + T - 1]$:

$$r_t = y'_t - C\hat{x}_{t|t-T} \tag{4.8}$$

Moreover, it is easy to show that the following holds:

$$
\begin{aligned}
\hat{x}_{t|t-T} = \hat{x}'_{t|t-T} + \mathcal{A}^{t-T_0}(\hat{x}_{T_0|T_0-1} - \hat{x}'_{T_0|T_0-1}) \\
+ \sum_{j=0}^{t-T_0-1} (\mathcal{A}^j B(\Delta u_{t-1-j} - \Delta u'_{t-1-j}))
\end{aligned} \tag{4.9}
$$

Substitution of (4.9) in (4.8) yields:

$$
r_t = \underbrace{y'_t - C\hat{x}'_{t|t-T}}_{\text{First term}} - \underbrace{C\mathcal{A}^{t-T_0}(\hat{x}_{T_0|T_0-1} - \hat{x}'_{T_0|T_0-1})}_{\text{Second term}}
$$

$$
- \underbrace{C\sum_{j=0}^{t-T_0-1} (\mathcal{A}^j B(\Delta u_{t-1-j} - \Delta u'_{t-1-j}))}_{\text{Third term}}
$$

The first term follows the same distribution of $(y_t - C\hat{x}_{t|t-1})$; the second term converges exponentially to zero. Since the third term is not equal to zero, $\Delta u_t \neq \Delta u'_t$, the adversary is detected; from a cyber adversary viewpoint, the measurements of the sensors change all the time and replay measurements are not accepted; likewise, a cyber-physical adversary is not able to obtain the system model using the methodology proposed in Sect. 3.

4.5   New Parametric Cyber-Physical Adversary

In this section we present a new parametric cyber-physical adversary with the knowledge about the new detector strategy, in order to evaluate the new detection strategy. This attacker has knowledge about the new communication policies and the existence of the local and the remote watermarks. Nevertheless, the new adversary does not know the watermark co-variances, the controller's parameters used to obtain the correct error between data, and neither the moment when the remote controller forces an intermittent communication.

The new adversary could be able to detect the correlation model between the inputs and the outputs of the plant. This adversary can force the sensors' intermittent communication with malfunction control inputs, and mislead the controller with replay error data to obtain the model. Nevertheless, this adversary is not able to know when the communication is periodic or intermittent, since the attacker does not know when the remote control sends the watermark added to the control inputs which generates the intermittent communication. The intermittent communication does not change the communication between the remote controller and the actuators, but produces an intermittent communication between the sensors and the remote controller, necessary to verify the closed-loop.

Briefly, the new adversary is able to attack the integrity of the system. Nevertheless using the PIETC-WD strategy, the adversary is detected by the controllers of the sensors. The remote controller detects the attack when the remote controller verifies the behaviour of the closed-loop. The adversary cannot avoid the alarm in the sensors (local controller). Nevertheless, the attacker can cut off the communication between the sensors and the remote control misleading the remote controller with correct residues (e.g. replay residues). Moreover, in order to avoid the alarm in the remote controller, the adversary can switch between sending the measurements of the sensors or the residues, but the adversary has a great probability to be detected. We validate the PIETC-WD strategy against the new parametric cyber-physical adversary in the next section.

4.6   Numerical Validation

This section validates through numerical simulation the PIETC-WD strategy proposed in previous sections. We validate this strategy using a use case of a chemical plant. This plant has multiple sensors with local controllers, actuators and a remote controller, which manage all the measurements of the sensors and actuators. The sensors used in this use case send information about pressure, temperature, and density. This information is produced when there is an alarm, and also periodically to indicate the behaviour of the system to the controller. This plant has to be controlled periodically since, if during ten consecutive periodical samples, the system receives wrong or malicious control inputs able to disrupt the system, a critical state might be reached.

To avoid that an adversary gets the system into a critical state, we use our detector strategy (PIETC-WD), with a policy for the remote controller's watermark defined as follows:

– The controller's watermark uses a policy based on a probability to add the
watermark in a specific window of samples. In this use case, the windows
of samples is assumed equal to five. For each sequence of five control input
samples, the probability to add the watermark at each sample is $\beta = 50\%$. The
system is able to produce $2^5 = 32$ different sequences with the same probability
to be generated, $\theta = 1/2^5$. Nevertheless, if among these five samples, the
system does not send any watermark, three more samples are used to add a
watermark to the control input until a new control sequence starts. These three
samples added to the original control sequence add $2^3 = 8$ more sequences
where the five first samples have not watermark, and the three last samples
have the following probability to add the watermark:

- The probability to add the watermark in the sixth sample is 60 %.
- The probability to add the watermark in the seventh sample is 50 % if
  the watermark is added in the sixth sample. Otherwise, if the watermark
  is not added, the probability is 60 %.
- The probability to add the watermark in the eighth sample is 50 %, if
  the watermark is added in the sixth or seventh sample. Otherwise, the
  probability is 60 %.

Figure 3 shows the results of 200 Monte Carlo simulations using the above
use case and controller's watermark policy, against the cyber and the cyber-
physical adversary. These results present that the ratio of detection is around
97 % against the new parametric cyber-physical adversary and more than 99 %
against the other cyber and cyber-physical adversaries using the PIETC-WD
strategy with a correct policy for the remote controller's watermark.

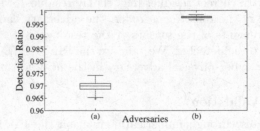

Fig. 3. Detection ratio function with respect to the PIETC-WD strategy with a defined
controller's watermark policy; (a) against the new parametric cyber-physical adversary;
and (b) against cyber or other cyber-physical adversaries

5   Related Work

Security of cyber-physical systems (CPS) is drawing a great deal of attention
recently [4]. Solutions focusing on control approaches for the detection of cyber-
physical attacks is the research axis more closely related to this paper. This axis
is the one that explicitly considers the interconnection between cyber and physical control domains in networked control systems. Recently, the control system

community started to study security of cyber-physical systems both under the methodological point of view and from a more technological standpoint by looking at particular problems arising in, e.g., smart grids. Concerning the methodological aspects, several studies have proposed to adapt classical frameworks to handle security issues in networked control systems.

Among cyber-physical attacks handled in the literature, replay attack is the only attack that the adversary is able to carry out without knowledge about system model. To carry out the rest of the attacks, it is necessary some system knowledge. For example, to execute a dynamic false-data injection attack, handled by Mo *et al.* [12], the adversary has to have a perfect knowledge of the plant's behaviour, or to execute a covert attack, handled by Smith *et al.* [18], is necessary to have the knowledge about the plant's and controller's behaviour. Otherwise, the adversaries defined in this paper are able to obtain the knowledge of the plant's behaviour in order to attack the system. Concerning the detection mechanism, one line of research has considered the adaptation of fault detection systems to detect a class of attacks [13,15,19]. In particular, Mo *et al.* show in [13] that it is possible to detect replay attacks by properly watermarking control inputs. Teixeira *et al.* propose in [19] a mathematical framework to model several attack strategies. An alternative modeling approach is taken by Pasqualetti *et al.* in [15], where the authors propose to employ the theory of geometric control to model cyber-physical systems attacks. In this paper we focus on the interconnection between control strategies and watermarking detectors to handle the integrity attacks.

6 Conclusion

In this paper, we have addressed security issues in cyber-physical systems. We have focused on designing a robust distributed control strategy, in order to detect parametric cyber-physical adversaries. These adversaries are able to acquire the knowledge of the system needed to compromise the control inputs and the measurements of the sensors to attack the system.

We have reviewed the watermark-based detector proposed in [13]. We have shown that the detector fails at properly handling attacks carried out by parametric cyber-physical adversaries. In particular, we have shown that an adversary that learns about the system model is able to model the watermark from the control signal and succeeds at attacking the system without being detected. We have also shown that the watermark-based detector works against a parametric cyber-physical adversary who knows only a set of control inputs, [21]. Nevertheless, if the adversary knows all the control inputs and sensor measurements of the system, and uses the correct orders range with a window size sufficiently long, the watermark-based detector fails.

Finally, we have presented and validated our strategy. This strategy is capable to detect cyber and cyber-physical adversaries with a great detection ratio, even if the adversary finds the correct model of the system.

Acknowledgements. The authors acknowledge support from the Cyber CNI Chair of Institut Mines-Télécom. The chair is held by Télécom Bretagne and supported by Airbus Defence and Space, Amossys, EDF, Orange, La Poste, Nokia, Société Générale and the Regional Council of Brittany. It has been acknowledged by the Center of excellence in Cybersecurity.

References

1. Arvani, A., Rao, V.S.: Detection and protection against intrusions on smart grid systems. Int. J. Cyber Secur. Digit. Forensics **3**, 38 (2014)
2. Barenthin Syberg, M.: Complexity issues, validation and input design for control in system identification (2008)
3. Brumback, B., Srinath, M.: A chi-square test for fault-detection in Kalman filters. IEEE Trans. Autom. Control **32**(6), 552–554 (1987)
4. Corman, D., Pillitteri, V., Tousley, S., Tehranipoor, U.: Lindqvist: NITRD cyber-physical security panel. In: 35th Symposium on Security and Privacy (2014)
5. Do, V.L., Fillatre, L., Nikiforov, I.: A statistical method for detecting cyber/physical attacks on scada systems. In: Proceedings of IEEE Control Applications (2014)
6. Falliere, N., Murchu, L.O., Chien, E.: W32. stuxnet dossier. White paper, Symantec Corp., Security Response, 5 (2011)
7. Han, D., Mo, Y., Wu, J., Weerakkody, S., Sinopoli, B., Shi, L.: Stochastic event-triggered sensor schedule for remote state estimation. IEEE Trans. Autom. Control **60**(10), 2661–2675 (2015)
8. Heemels, W., Donkers, M., Teel, A.R.: Periodic event-triggered control for linear systems. IEEE Trans. Autom. Control **58**(4), 847–861 (2013)
9. Hespanha, J.P., Naghshtabrizi, P., Xu, Y.: A survey of recent results in networked control systems. Proc. IEEE **95**(1), 138 (2007)
10. Ke-You, Y., Li-Hua, X.: Survey of recent progress in networked control systems. Acta Autom. Sinica **39**(2), 101–117 (2013)
11. Kim, K.-D., Kumar, P.R.: Cyber-physical systems: a perspective at the centennial. Proc. IEEE **100**(Special Centennial Issue), 1287–1308 (2012)
12. Mo, Y., Garone, E., Casavola, A., Sinopoli, B.: False data injection attacks against state estimation in wireless sensor networks. In: 2010 49th IEEE Conference on Decision and Control (CDC), pp. 5967–5972. IEEE (2010)
13. Mo, Y., Weerakkody, S., Sinopoli, B.: Physical authentication of control systems: designing watermarked control inputs to detect counterfeit sensor outputs. IEEE Control Syst. **35**(1), 93–109 (2015)
14. Natke, H.: System identification: Torsten Söderström and Petre Stoica. Automatica **28**(5), 1069–1071 (1992)
15. Pasqualetti, F., Dorfler, F., Bullo, F.: Cyber-physical security via geometric control: distributed monitoring and malicious attacks. In: 2012 IEEE 51st Annual Conference on Decision and Control, pp. 3418–3425. IEEE (2012)
16. Rubio-Hernan, J., De Cicco, L., Garcia-Alfaro, J.: Revisiting a watermark-based detection scheme to handle cyber-physical attacks. In: 11th International Conference on Availability, Reliability and Security, Salzburg, Austria. IEEE (2016)
17. Salt, J., Casanova, V., Cuenca, A., Pizá, R.: Sistemas de control basados en red modelado y diseño de estructuras de control. Rev. Iberoamericana de Autom. e Informática Ind. RIAI **5**(3), 5–20 (2008)
18. Smith, R.: Covert misappropriation of networked control systems: presenting a feedback structure. IEEE Control Syst. **35**(1), 82–92 (2015)

19. Teixeira, A., Shames, I., Sandberg, H., Johansson, K.H.: A secure control framework for resource-limited adversaries. Automatica **51**, 135–148 (2015)
20. Tripathi, S., Ikbal, M.A.: Step size optimization of lms algorithm using aunt colony optimization and its comparison with particle swarm optimization algorithm in system identification (2015)
21. Weerakkody, S., Mo, Y., Sinopoli, B.: Detecting integrity attacks on control systems using robust physical watermarking. In: Proceedings of Decision and Control (2014)

Detecting Process-Aware Attacks
in Sequential Control Systems

Oualid Koucham[1]([✉]), Stéphane Mocanu[1], Guillaume Hiet[2],
Jean-Marc Thiriet[1], and Frédéric Majorczyk[3]

[1] Univ. Grenoble Alpes, CNRS, Gipsa-lab, 38000 Grenoble, France
{oualid.koucham,stephane.mocanu,
jean-marc.thiriet}@gipsa-lab.grenoble-inp.fr
[2] CIDRE/Inria, CentraleSupélec, Cesson-sévigné, France
guillaume.hiet@centralesupelec.fr
[3] DGA/Inria, Rennes, France
frederic.majorczyk@supelec.fr

Abstract. Industrial control systems (ICS) can be subject to highly
sophisticated attacks which may lead the process towards critical states.
Due to the particular context of ICS, protection mechanisms are not
always practical, nor sufficient. On the other hand, developing a process-
aware intrusion detection solution with satisfactory alert characterization
remains an open problem. This paper focuses on process-aware attacks
detection in sequential control systems. We build on results from runtime
verification and specification mining to automatically infer and monitor
process specifications. Such specifications are represented by sets of temporal safety properties over states and events corresponding to sensors
and actuators. The properties are then synthesized as monitors which
report violations on execution traces. We develop an efficient specification mining algorithm and use filtering rules to handle the large number
of mined properties. Furthermore, we introduce the notion of activity and
discuss its relevance to both specification mining and attack detection
in the context of sequential control systems. The proposed approach is
evaluated in a hardware-in-the-loop setting subject to targeted process-
aware attacks. Overall, due to the explicit handling of process variables,
the solution provides a better characterization of the alerts and a more
meaningful understanding of false positives.

1 Introduction

Cyber attacks represent a growing concern for industrial control systems (ICS)
[1]. On one hand, ICS are increasingly connected to traditional information systems. This trend has been spurred, among other reasons, by the adoption of commodity hardware and software components, as well as the convergence towards
TCP/IP solutions [11]. On the other hand, a majority of industrial systems
lack security mechanisms, having historically relied on isolation from traditional
information systems. In the singular context of ICS, protection mechanisms are
not sufficient, nor always practical. For instance, hardware constraints hinder the

B.B. Brumley and J. Röning (Eds.): NordSec 2016, LNCS 10014, pp. 20–36, 2016.
DOI: 10.1007/978-3-319-47560-8_2

use of measures such as encryption to ensure confidentiality or integrity [5]. Any latency within the low layers of industrial systems can affect the real-time constraints and perturb the functioning of the control loops. Despite recent efforts geared towards developing suitable protection mechanisms [15], ICS remain particularly vulnerable, highlighting the need for appropriate detection measures. In this paper, we are concerned with developing such a detection solution.

As opposed to traditional information systems, ICS are cyber-physical systems interacting with a physical process. Taking into account this aspect is paramount to the detection of targeted attacks relying on advanced knowledge of the process [17]. Noteworthy examples include the highly sophisticated Stuxnet attack [12]. ICS are characterized by a duality between continuous behavior as traditionally represented by differential equations, and sequential behavior where control follows sequences of discrete steps. Our focus is on the latter aspect. This paper presents an anomaly-based intrusion detection approach to detect process-aware *sequence* attacks targeting a particular class of systems, namely sequential control systems. Sequence attacks aim to put the process in a critical state by a malicious temporal ordering of commands or messages [6]. Examples of such attacks include *exclusion* attacks where two states should not happen simultaneously (an open valve and a running motor at the same time for instance), or *wear* attacks where components' lifetime is reduced through malicious manipulations (by, for example, repeatedly opening and closing a valve) [17]. We restrict ourselves to *qualitative* sequence attacks where only the temporal ordering matters.

General overview. We build on results from runtime verification and specification mining to automatically infer and monitor process specifications. The specifications are represented by sets of temporal safety properties [2] over states and events corresponding to sensors and actuators. The properties are synthesized as monitors which report violations on execution traces. Filtering rules allow handling the large number of mined specifications. Mining and monitoring can also be done per *activity*, a notion which captures the different subprocesses and functioning modes of a sequential system. A subprocess refers to a phase in the operation of the system. For instance, a sequential system might go through a start phase, a shutdown phase, and several intermediate phases. An activity can also distinguish between manual or automatic modes of functioning. Compared to prior work on process-aware intrusion detection [4,22], this work focuses on the sequential aspect of control systems, covers more expressive properties through a suitable formalism, and discusses a solution to alleviate the effort of manually writing process specifications. In contrast with sequence-aware solutions targeting communication patterns within ICS [6,29], the proposed approach explicitly handles process variables. This leads to improved alerts characterization, and a better understanding of false positives.

Contributions. All in all, we make the following contributions:

- We propose an approach to detect process-aware sequence attacks targeting sequential control systems by leveraging results from runtime verification and specification mining

– We suggest a number of filtering rules to handle the large size of inferred specifications, and introduce the concept of activity while discussing its relevance
within sequential control systems
– We evaluate our solution in a hardware-in-the loop setting and analyze its
performance and limitations

The paper is organized as follows. Section 2 provides an overview of prior work
on intrusion detection within ICS. Section 3 discusses background concepts pertaining to ICS, runtime verification and specification mining. Section 4 presents
our approach including our specification mining algorithm Sect. 4.2 and filtering
rules Sect. 4.3. Section 5 evaluates the approach and discusses its limitations.

2   Related Work

Intrusion detection work in ICS can be classified into two broad categories: (i)
approaches which seek intrusion manifestations solely in the cyber part [7,21,30],
and (ii) approaches which take into account the physical process [4,14,22]. We
are interested in attackers whose objective is the disruption of the underlying
physical process. These attacks represent a challenge to traditional intrusion
detection approaches. Thus, we argue that a knowledge of the physical process
is essential to the detection of sophisticated process-aware attacks, and to the
understanding of false positives. In this paper, we present a process-oriented
intrusion detection solution.

A majority of the approaches found in the literature are anomaly-based, i.e.
they try to detect any significant deviation from a reference behavior. These
solutions often rely on assumptions about the simplicity of ICS protocols, the
stability of the network's structure, or the regularity of the communications.
Compared to signature-based intrusion detection, anomaly-based approaches
have the crucial advantage of potentially detecting novel attacks. However, while
ICS exhibit certain regularities relative to traditional systems, investigations on
real-world data show that these assumptions are not always justified [6]. Moreover, anomaly-based approach, especially when relying on machine learning techniques, exhibit some drawbacks [26] such as the number of false positives, and
the poor characterization of the alerts. This can lead to wrong reactions by the
operators, or to a loss of confidence in the IDS alerts. As a result, some effort is
needed to better characterize the alerts and handle false positives. Our approach
attempts to address some of these issues.

Within the literature, the work closest to ours include the sequence-aware
approaches developed in [6,29], and the process-aware approaches developed in
[4,22]. Caselli et al. [6] adopt a Markov chain-based solution relying on communication patterns to detect *sequence* attacks. Sequence attacks are defined as
malicious/erroneous ordering or timing of commands or messages. We argue that
such attacks, in the scope of sequential control systems, are better detected by
focusing on process variables instead of network communications. In the same
vein, Yoon et al. [29] propose a probabilistic suffix tree-based approach to model
communication patterns under a high predictability assumption. Mitchell et al.

[22] rely on manually written behavior rules to detect process-aware attacks. Carcano et al. [4] develop ISML, a language for describing critical states. While similar to our solution in terms of process awareness, both approaches require manual expression of the behavior rules and are not suitable for detecting all malicious ordering of events. This is because both approaches rely exclusively on propositional logic formulae to express behavioral rules or critical states. Such formalism cannot represent general ordering constraints. Schumann et al. [25] propose R2U2, a framework for the runtime monitoring of security properties in unmanned aerial systems. Our approach focuses on sequential control systems and discusses the automatic generation of properties.

3   Background

This section discusses the necessary background concerning ICS, runtime verification and specification mining.

3.1   Industrial Control Systems

ICS are hierarchical systems consisting of multiple components which interaction achieves an industrial objective [27]. Among these components, Programmable Logic Controllers (PLC) are of particular interest to our approach. Operating at the cyber-physical frontier, PLC execute *control logics* to regulate the physical process. This is realized through a scan cycle that includes: (i) reading inputs from sensors, (ii) executing the control logics, (iii) transitioning to new stable states, and (iv) writing outputs to actuators. Due to their critical role, PLC constitute an ideal target for process-aware attacks.

The IEC61131-3 standard [16] defines five programming languages for programmable controllers: (i) Ladder diagram, (ii) Function Block Diagram, (iii) Sequential Function Chart (SFC), (iv) Instruction List, and (v) Structured Text. In this paper, we focus on SFC which is a graphical language representing the control logic as a series of steps and transitions. SFC is especially suitable for processes exhibiting a step by step behavior [16]. This is the case of sequential control systems which are the focus of our approach.

3.2   Runtime Verification

Runtime verification [19] is a verification technique which aims at checking whether a run of a system satisfies or violates a given correctness property. In our case, a run of a system consists of a possibly infinite sequence of sets of logical propositions. Each position in the sequence represents the current state of sensors and actuators. In practice, during runtime, we only have access to finite prefixes of runs. Monitors are devices which take as input such a finite prefix, and yield verdict belonging to a truth domain, indicating the status of the property on the trace. Using a monitor, we would like to check whether an execution satisfies a given correctness property. Thus, our aim is to detect sequence attacks using monitors synthesized from high-level correctness properties, and expressed in a formalism suitable for representing ordering constraints.

States. Let AP be a finite set of atomic propositions about sensors and actuators in the process. A state s is an element of 2^{AP}.

Linear temporal logic. Our main goal is the detection of sequence attacks involving the ordering of messages or commands. To formally represent the normal ordering relationships between states, a suitable formalism is required. Linear temporal logic [23] augments propositional logic with operators able to express ordering relationships. The syntax of LTL over the alphabet $\Sigma = 2^{AP}$, which we write $LTL(\Sigma)$, is defined as follows:

$$\varphi :: p \mid \neg\varphi \mid \varphi \vee \varphi \mid \varphi U \varphi \mid X\varphi, \ p \in AP$$

We define Σ^{ω} (resp. Σ^*) as the set of infinite (resp. finite) sequences over Σ. Let $\varphi, \varphi_1, \varphi_2 \in LTL(\Sigma)$ be LTL formulae, $i \in \mathbb{N}$ a position, and $w(i)$ the ith element of the infinite sequence $w \in \Sigma^{\omega}$. LTL formulae can be inductively interpreted over elements in Σ^{ω} as follows:

$$
\begin{aligned}
w, i &\models p \in AP & &\Longleftrightarrow & p &\in w(i) \\
w, i &\models \neg\varphi & &\Longleftrightarrow & w, i &\not\models \varphi \\
w, i &\models \varphi_1 \vee \varphi_2 & &\Longleftrightarrow & w, i &\models \varphi_1 \vee w, i \models \varphi_2 \\
w, i &\models \varphi_1 U \varphi_2 & &\Longleftrightarrow & \exists k &\in \mathbb{N}, k \geq i. \ w, k \models \varphi_2 \wedge \forall i \leq j < k. \ w, j \models \varphi_1 \\
w, i &\models X\varphi & &\Longleftrightarrow & w, i+1 &\models \varphi
\end{aligned}
$$

We also define $\Diamond\varphi \equiv true U \varphi$ and $\Box\varphi \equiv \neg\Diamond\neg\varphi$. Here, $\neg$ and $\vee$ are, respectively, the negation and logical OR operators. The remaining logical operators $(\wedge, \Rightarrow, \Leftrightarrow)$ can be derived as usual.

Events. In sequential control systems, we are often interested in expressing properties involving *events* such as *rising* ($\uparrow$) or *falling* ($\downarrow$) edges. Such events can be expressed in LTL [24]:

$$a^{\uparrow} \equiv \neg a \wedge Xa \qquad a^{\downarrow} \equiv a \wedge X\neg a$$

Monitoring and finite semantics. As discussed above, monitors only have access to finite but expanding prefixes. However, LTL formulae are interpreted over infinite sequences. This mismatch restricts the class of *monitorable* LTL formulae [2]. Monitorability refers to the capacity of a monitor, after any finite number of observations, to still detect the violation/satisfaction of a property after, at most, a finite number of additional observations. Formally, an LTL formula φ is monitorable if for every finite word $u \in \Sigma^*$, there exists a finite word $v \in \Sigma^*$ such that for any infinite word $w \in \Sigma^{\omega}$, uvw either satisfies or violates φ [2]. In this work, we are interested in a particular class of monitorable formulae called safety properties. Informally, a safety property states that "something bad should never happen". The formula $\Box\neg(valve_1 \wedge valve_2)$ is a safety property stating that $valve_1$ and $valve_2$ should never be simultaneously open.

In practice, monitors can be synthesized as finite state automata from LTL formulae. Such an automaton recognizes minimal bad prefixes of a safety property. Minimal bad prefixes are finite sequences which cannot be extended to satisfy the safety property, and which do not contain any other bad prefix [8]. If a safety property is violated on an infinite sequence, then it has already been violated on some finite prefix. In our case, a monitor is a finite state automaton which recognizes, as early as possible, such a prefix and reports a violation. Constructing a monitor usually requires translating the LTL formula into a Büchi automaton which accepts all infinite sequences satisfying the formula (see [28] for a formal definition). A nested depth-first-search allows the identification and removal, from the Büchi automaton, of all states which cannot initiate an accepting run. The resulting automaton can then be treated as a finite state automaton with all states accepting, and used as a monitor [8].

3.3 Process Specification Mining

Specification patterns. While LTL provides a suitable formalism to characterize safety properties pertaining to states and events ordering, expressing specifications directly in terms of formulae remains tedious. As properties grow in complexity, writing accurate and correct formulae becomes a difficult task. Thus, several works [10,24] have looked at *specification patterns* that express commonly occurring properties. By relying on such specifications patterns, we can give meaning to properties and, in our particular case, to violations of safety properties. Another advantage of using specification patterns is controlling the nature of properties to be monitored to the class of safety properties.

We base our work on a subset of Dwyer's patterns augmented with events [10,24]. Dwyer's patterns and classification are the result of an extensive review of the literature for recurring specifications. We restrict ourselves in this paper to *absence*, *universality*, *precedence* and *response* monitorable patterns. Absence patterns state that a certain event or state never occurs during the execution of the system. Universality patterns state that a certain event or state always holds during the execution of the system. Precedence and response patterns express relationships between two events or states where the occurrence of one is a necessary condition for the occurrence of the other.

Moreover, we can specify *scopes* which restrict the portion of the execution where the pattern should hold. Five scopes are defined: (i) a *global* scope, (ii) a scope starting *after* an event/state, (iii) a scope ending *before* an event/state, (iv) a scope *between* two events/states, (v) a scope starting *after* a first event/state and lasting *until* the eventual occurrence of a second event/state. All scopes are left-closed and right-open. Readers are referred to [10] for more details. In the rest of this paper, we will express specification patterns as predicates over events/states. The predicate name captures the nature and scope of the pattern. For instance, the predicate $absence\_between(X, Y, Z)$ refers to the absence pattern concerning event/state Z between events/states X and Y. An instantiation of a pattern is a mapping of placeholders to propositions.

Mining specifications. The problem of specification mining can be expressed as follows: given a finite set of specification patterns and a finite set of execution traces of a system, find all instantiations that are valid on the traces. Several works have explored this issue based on a variety of patterns [18,20]. Usually one is required to explore the space of all possible instantiations (permutations) and test the validity of each instantiation on the traces. While the size of the search space can be significant, recent work [18] has shown that using memoization and selective treatment of the traces can significantly reduce the complexity of the task even when dealing with general LTL formulae. However, the number of valid mined specifications can still remain significant, especially due to the introduction of events. Section 4 presents our mining algorithm and filtering rules to handle this issue.

4   Attack Detection Approach

4.1   General Overview

Our approach proceeds in two stages: a *mining and filtering* stage, and a *detection* stage. In the first stage (Fig. 1), specifications expressed as a set of temporal properties ($\{Spec^1_{LTL}, \ldots, Spec^m_{LTL}\}$) are mined from execution traces of the system by relying on specification patterns. When using activities, execution traces are divided depending on the current activity using the activity recognizer, and mining is done per activity. In all cases, the resulting raw specifications undergo a set of filtering rules to reduce their number.

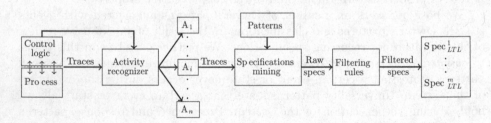

Fig. 1. First stage: mining and filtering the specifications

The traces are assumed to be free of malicious activity and representative of the normal behavior of the system. However, the representativeness is not guaranteed as the mining operates on a finite window. This can be an important source of false positives. While this limit is common to all approaches based on a learning phase, we would like to better characterize false positives (and alerts in general) by giving them meaning with respect to the process behavior, i.e. higher semantics in terms of the process. For instance, for a given alert, we would like to report on the concerned actuators/sensors, the process stage during which the alert was raised, and the reason why a violation represents an illegitimate action with respect to the process's normal behavior.

A first level of characterization is achieved by relying on specification patterns which reflect common safety properties expressed directly in terms of sensor/actuator states and events. A second level of characterization is attained by the means of activities. An activity corresponds to a subprocess or to different modes of functioning within the sequential system. Activites can distinguish between different normal behaviors within the process, while reducing the complexity of the mining phase. To define and distinguish the activities in the traces, we require a high level expression of the control logic. In our work, we derive the activity recognizer from control logic expressed as SFC. In practice, steps in the SFC are assigned to activities, and the activity recognizer interprets the SFC using its formal semantics [3]. The task of assigning activities to steps is left to an expert or a developer. As future work, we intend to explore heuristics which can guide the expert and automatically suggest activities assignments.

The monitors, synthesized from the mined and filtered properties, report violations during the detection phase (Fig. 2). When using activities, the activity recognizer dynamically identifies the current activity, and only the relevant property monitors (i.e. those pertaining to the current activity) read the trace to detect the violations and output their verdicts.

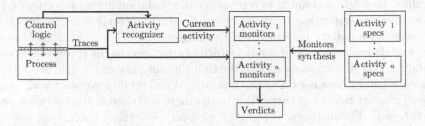

Fig. 2. Second stage: detecting specification violations

Threat model. We assume that the attacker's objective is the disruption of the physical process using qualitative sequence attacks. We also assume that the measurements sent by the sensors are correct. This means that we do not handle false data injection attacks i.e. injection of bad measurements. As we rely directly on process variables, no assumptions are made on the trustworthiness of the PLC if a proper logging mechanism is available at the field level. However, we still require the presence of a secure channel for sending alert notifications.

4.2 Mining Process Specifications

In this section, we present our mining algorithm which carefully walks through the search space to find valid properties which could have been violated on the mining traces. This constraint is captured by the notion of *falsifiability*. A falsifiable property with respect to a trace is a property which can be violated on the trace. Falsifiability is especially relevant with regards to pattern scopes. Execution traces arising from sequential control systems are highly structured due to the execution of specific control logics. As such, they contain a relatively limited number of scopes. All properties which refer to non-existent scopes are not falsifiable. Since they specify constraints on non-existent scopes, one cannot check their violation. Consider for instance the property $universality\_after(valve1, motor1)$. It corresponds to the following LTL formula: $\Box(valve1 \Rightarrow \Box motor1)$. The antecedent of the implication refers to the scope. If $valve1$ is not true at any position on the trace, the implication becomes vacuously true and the formula is not falsifiable. In addition, properties such as $absence\_before(valve1, motor1)$ and $absence\_between(valve1, valve2, motor1)$ will also be vacuously true on the trace since all these formulae involve implications with false antecedents ($\Diamond valve1$ for the first formula and $valve1 \land \Diamond valve2$ for the second formula). By checking the falsifiability of the initial property, we can ignore other scope-related formulae.

Thus, the main idea is to partition the space of possible instantiations in terms of scopes, then check their falsifiability with respect to their scopes in order to potentially bypass other scope-related properties. In practice, for each type of scope, we instantiate a monitor called an *auxiliary monitor* which checks whether the property is falsifiable on the traces. An auxiliary monitor essentially makes sure that the scope pertaining to a property instantiation actually occurs on the traces. As an example, for the property $universality\_after(valve1, motor1)$, we synthesize an auxiliary monitor from the formula $\Diamond end \rightarrow \neg(\neg valve1\ U\ end)$. Here, end represents a special symbol which is appended to the traces and is used to adapt LTL's infinite semantics to the finite mining traces [9]. The property is violated if $valve1$ does not occur on the trace. When mining, we start with single scopes (*after* or *before*) as they affect both single and double scopes (*after until* and *between*). For instance, if an *after* property involving $valve1^\uparrow$ as a scope is not falsifiable on the execution traces, then all *after*, *before*, *after until* and *between* properties involving the $valve1^\uparrow$ scope will not be falsifiable.

Typically, we have many traces at our disposal. When running the auxiliary monitors, we can enforce several policies depending on the number of violations recorded. In all of our scopes, except for the *after until* case, we require that the auxiliary monitors report no violations on all the traces, i.e. that the properties are falsifiable on all the traces. This has the advantage, with regards to our notion of activity, to naturally restrict the scopes to the variables pertaining to the activity for which the mining occurs. For the *after until* case, we require the property to be falsifiable in at least one of the traces. The goal is to limit the cases where an *after* property is valid, and which lead to several corresponding scope-irrelevant *after until* properties to become valid.

Algorithm 1 outlines our mining procedure. For each instantiation, we retrieve the verdicts of the main and auxiliary monitors (line 7). If the main monitor reports a violation, then the property is false (and falsifiable), so we move to the next instantiation in the same scope. Else if the auxiliary monitor raises a violation, we blacklist the current scope and all related scopes before moving to

---

ALGORITHM 1. Specification mining

Data: Tr : Finite set of execution traces, I : Finite set of property instances
Result: Set of valid properties
1   $\Pi = partition\_by\_scopes(I)$;
2   $blacklisted\_scopes = \{\}$;
3   $valid\_properties = \{\}$;
4   **foreach** $type \in \{after, after\_until, before, between, global\}$ **do**
5   **foreach** $scope \in \Pi(type) \setminus blacklisted\_scopes$ **do**
6   **foreach** $instance \in scope$ **do**
7         $(verdict\_inst, verdict\_aux) = check\_instance(instance, Tr, type)$;
8   **if** $verdict\_inst = \bot$ **then** $instance \leftarrow invalid$;
9   **else if** $verdict\_aux = \bot$ **then**
10           $blacklisted\_scopes \cup = \{scope\} \cup affected\_scopes(type, scope)$;
11   break;

12   **foreach** $type \in \{after, after\_until, before, between, global\}$ **do**
13   **foreach** $scope \in \Pi(type) \setminus blacklisted\_scopes$ **do**
14   **foreach** $instance \in scope$ **do**
15   **if** $instance$ is $valid$ **then** $valid\_properties \cup = instance$;

16   **return** $valid\_properties$;

---

the next scope. The function *check_instances* returns a verdict depending on the falsifiability policy on the set of traces and the type of the instantiation.

4.3 Specifications Filtering Rules

In order to deal with the important number of specifications generated after the specification mining phase, we use a set of filtering rules. These rules are based on the semantics of Dwyer's patterns as discussed in Sect. 3.3. The idea is to find logical dependencies between mined properties based on their scopes and events/states relationships. The general form of these logical dependencies is:

$$\frac{\psi_1, \quad \psi_2, \quad \forall \sigma \in \Sigma^\omega, \sigma \models \psi_2 \Rightarrow \psi_1}{filter(\psi_2)}$$

In this rule, ψ_1 and ψ_2 are valid properties on the traces. The premise $\forall \sigma \in \Sigma^\omega, \sigma \models \psi_2 \Rightarrow \psi_1$ represents the fact that, for all infinite sequences σ, whenever property ψ_2 is satisfied, then property ψ_1 is also satisfied. In other words, by keeping track of violations of ψ_1, one can indirectly detect violations of ψ_2.

Logical dependencies arise in the case of Dwyer's patterns due to the interplay between scopes and states/events. Suppose we have mined the properties $universality\_after(valve_1, motor_1)$ and $absence\_after(valve_1, motor_1^\uparrow)$. The first property states that "motor$_1$ stays on after a state where valve$_1$ is open" while the second property states that "motor$_1$ is never started after a state where valve$_1$ is open". On all infinite sequences when the first property is satisfied, the second property will be satisfied. This is due to the fact that for $motor_1$ to be started after $valve_1$ is on, it needs to be off at some point. However, this is impossible due to the first property. Note that the converse is not true. There exists an infinite sequence where the second property is satisfied but not the first: a sequence where, after a state in which $valve_1$ is on, $motor_1$ goes off but never on. Note also that the second property is informative. The violation of the second property, in conjunction with the violation of the property $absence\_after(valve_1, motor_1^{\updownarrow})$, can be symptomatic of a *wear attack* on $motor_1$. The case sketched above generalizes to the following rule:

$$\frac{absence\_after(X, Y^{\uparrow}), \quad universality\_after(X, Y)}{filter(universality\_after(X, Y))}$$

We can formally prove that $\forall \sigma \in \Sigma^{\omega}, \sigma \models \psi_2 \Rightarrow \psi_1$ for given LTL properties ψ_1 and ψ_2 by referring back to their semantics defined in Sect. 3.2. In our case, to systematically verify such logical relationship, we build the Büchi automaton corresponding to the formula $\psi_1 \vee \neg \psi_2$, and check that it accepts all possible infinite words i.e. the formula is valid [28]. We have identified and verified a non-exhaustive set of 20 rules which represent logical dependencies between patterns. Their identification relies on observations about: (i) inclusion relationships between scopes, and (ii) the interplay between events and states within the same scope such as in the example above.

5   Evaluation

In order to evaluate our solution, we have implemented the process shown in Fig. 3 in a hardware-in-the loop setting including a real PLC and a simulation of the process. We acknowledge that a thorough evaluation would require real data from an operational plant. However, getting such data is difficult due to the particularly sensitive context of ICS. Publicly available datasets[1] are often too simple, including few sensors/actuators. Studies which use real datasets are often limited to network trace files, while we require the availability of control logic for a comprehensive analysis. Yet, we believe that this evaluation can shed some light on the advantages and limitations of the proposed solution.

5.1   Process Description

The process [13] in Fig. 3 represents a typical sequential system. The goal is to produce a mixture of products following a certain recipe. The process involves two stages. In the first stage, two weighted products are introduced successively in the tank *T1* via the valves *vp1* and *vp2*. The required weights are indicated by sensors *p1* and *p2*. A mixer actuated by motor *m1* performs the primary mixing. After 50 s, and if *TP* is empty as indicated by the sensor *tpvid*, the mixture can be cleared out from *T1* through the valve *vt1*. In a second stage, a

---

[1]   https://sites.google.com/a/uah.edu/tommy-morris-uah/ics-data-sets.

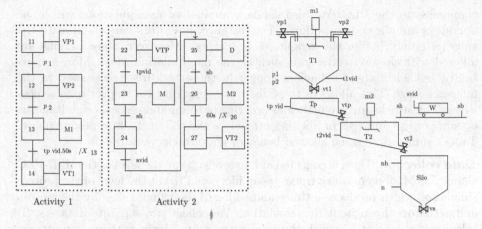

Fig. 3. Example of a sequential process and its control logic expressed using SFC [13]

product carried by the wagon W is added to the primary mixture. Sensors sb and sh indicate the position of the wagon. Actuators m and d (not shown in the figure) are responsible for the wagon's movement. A mixer actuated by motor $m2$ performs the secondary mixing, which lasts for 60 s. Finally, the end product is drained to the *silo* through valve $vt2$. The valve vs allows emptying the *silo*. We would like to keep the final product level in the *silo* between the levels indicated by nb and nh. When the level reaches nb, a new production cycle is started until the level reaches nh. Figure 3 shows part of the SFC implementing the control logic for this process. In total, the process contains 20 actuators and sensors.

Activity decomposition. Following the process description, we can identify two main activities as shown in Fig. 3. We also use a default activity to mark all the coordinating steps which are outside these activities.

5.2   Experimental Setup

We evaluate our approach in a hardware-in-the-loop setting. The process is simulated in OpenModelica[2] while the control logic is implemented in a Schneider M580 PLC. A Human-Machine Interface (HMI) allows monitoring the process status and send commands. The HMI-PLC communication relies on the Modbus protocol. The monitors, the specification miner, and the activity recognizer are implemented in C++. To synthesize the monitors from LTL formulae corresponding to patterns, we use the Spot library[3]. Filtering rules are implemented in Prolog and take as input the predicates resulting from the mining phase.

Attacks. We perform a total of 15 process-aware sequence attacks during the simulation to test our solution. The attacks are carried by sending malicious

---

[2] https://www.openmodelica.org.
[3] https://spot.lrde.epita.fr.

commands to the PLC. We also define a number of manipulations which the operators are allowed to perform. For instance, operators can manipulate the valve *vp1* only before the weight *p1* is reached. Moreover, some actions are allowed without any restrictions such as the manipulation of *vs*. More importantly, not all of these behaviors appear in the attack-free traces used in the inference stage. This allows us to evaluate our solution with respect to false positives. The attacks involve malicious ordering of commands such as simultaneous opening of *vp1* and *vp2*, or opening *vt1* before the end of the first mixing phase. Table 1 summarizes some allowed behavior and attacks performed.

Data collection. Data is collected at two levels: (i) at the level of the HMI-PLC channel as Modbus network traces (pcap files), and (ii) at the level of the process simulation which produces a timestamped log of the values taken by the sensors and actuators throughout the simulation. We collect two separate datasets: (i) a legitimate dataset in which the process runs for 20 min without any attacks but with manual intervention of a human operator who performs actions within the allowed behavior, and (ii) a dataset spanning 40 min with interventions of a human operator and containing process-aware sequence attacks. The parameters of the simulation, such as the flow rates, are chosen so that the process completes several times the various stages during the recording window. All our tests are run offline using the recorded datasets.

Table 1. Examples of allowed behavior and sequence attacks performed on the process

Allowed behavior	Performed attacks
• Manipulating *vp1* before *p1* is reached	• Manipulating *vp1* after *p1* is reached
• Manipulating *vp2* after *p1* is reached and before *p2* is reached	• Manipulating *vp2* before *p1* is reached or after *m1* is started
• Manipulating *vt1* after *m1* is stopped	• Opening *vt1* before *m1* is stopped

5.3   Results

Process specification mining. We apply our proposed specification mining algorithm on traces per activity. Inference is performed on an Intel Dual Core i5 2.4 GHz machine with 4 GB of RAM running Linux kernel 4.4.5. We evaluate the mining algorithm in terms of 3 measures: (i) the monitors overhead, (ii) the runtime efficiency, and (iii) the number of mined properties.

Monitors overhead. As mentioned in Sect. 3.2, the monitors are derived from Büchi automata which can lead to a double exponential space blow-up with respect to the formula's size [2]. The monitors we generate do not represent pathological cases. All the monitors we synthesized have a size less or equal than 25 states. This is in fact another motivation for using patterns: we can control the patterns in terms of monitorability and size of the associated monitor. Moreover, only the mapping differs between instantiations of the same pattern. This reduces the memory-overhead required for the mining task.

Runtime efficiency. We measured the runtime efficiency of our specification miner for both activities. Our proposed algorithm spends on average 45 s for the first activity, and 55 s for the second activity. This is reasonable as mining is performed once on the training traces. We notice however that our solution performs worse on the second activity compared to the first one. This is mainly due to the presence, in the second activity, of more sensor and actuator variables. Another remark is that the algorithm's performance deteriorates when faced with unstructured execution traces such as randomly generated traces. However, this does not apply to sequential control system as they follow specific control logics.

Number of properties. Out of 407820 possible instantiations, the mining algorithm returns 7206 properties for the first activity, and 16269 properties for the second activity. We also apply our filtering rules to the mined properties. The filtering rules take into account: (i) the logical relationships identified in Sect. 4.3, (ii) the actual sensors and actuators involved in each activity. With regards to the second set of rules, an interesting feature of the mined properties is that their scopes involve sensors/actuators which are specific to the activity in question. This is due to the falsifiability policy we impose which naturally restricts the scopes. The filtering results in 719 properties for the first activity, and 1908 properties for the second activity.

Comparison with Texada. We also experimented with Texada [18], an efficient general LTL specification miner. We mine the patterns using its map mapper. It is worth noting that although Texada can omit vacuous properties, the runtime overhead becomes significant (over 10 min for both activities using the linear mapper). Texada's map miner spends little over 1 min for both activities. In contrast, the number of properties returned by Texada is an order of magnitude bigger. When comparing the mined properties, in the cases where our notion of falsifiability matches that of Texada, the mined properties are similar.

Attack detection. We evaluate the detection capabilities of our solution by running the inferred monitors on the malicious execution traces. Table 2 reports some violations recorded and their interpretation. All 15 performed attacks were detected by the monitors. Their interpretation relies on two key elements: (i) the activity during which the violation is reported, and (ii) the pattern corresponding to the property violated. However, as expected and discussed in Sect. 4.1, we obtain some false positives. The main recorded case of false positives was relative to the manipulation of *vt1*. As the operator does not manually interfere with *vt1* during the learning phase, we infer properties such as *absence_global(vt1↓)*. This property holds in the absence of manipulations, since *vt1* is the last action performed in activity 1, and *t1vid* signals the end of the activity. Knowing that an operator is allowed to manipulate *vt1* at some point during the activity, this property is too restrictive. Note that we also mine properties such as *absence_before(p2, vt1)* which violations would correspond to an attack.

In addition to delivering high semantics in terms of alerts' understanding, we can also deactivate monitors which do not correspond to properties we want to ensure. For instance, the property *absence_global(vt1↓)* which causes a false positive can be deactivated, as it clearly concerns a legitimate action. The easiness

Table 2. Examples of raised alerts and their corresponding interpretation

Alert	Type	Properties violated	Interpretation
Alert 1 (act. 1)	TP	$absence\_between(m1^\uparrow, p1^\downarrow, vp2^\uparrow)$ $absence\_between(m1^\uparrow, p2^\downarrow, vp2^\uparrow)$	$vp2$ opened after starting $m1$ (attack)
Alert 3 (act. 1)	FP	$absence\_global(vt1^\downarrow)$ $absence\_after\_until(m1^\downarrow, p1^\downarrow, vt1^\downarrow)$	$vt1$ closed after $m1$ is stopped (legitimate action)
Alert 5 (act. 2)	TP	$absence\_before(m2^\downarrow, vt2^\uparrow)$	$vt2$ opened before the end of the mixing task (attack)

* TP: True Positive, FP: False Positive

with which one can alter the learned behavior is due to the inference of multiple properties which individually concern a limited set of sensors/actuators. Note also that one can analyze a priori the inferred properties by performing queries over variables which might cause false positives. For instance, since the valve vs can be opened any time during the execution of the system, one can query the inferred properties to ensure that no property restricts the usage of vs.

One issue we encounter when running our monitors is the possibly consequent number of violations raised for each attack. In our experiments, some attacks can produce as much as 30 violations. While these violations do not represent false positives, their number can render their analysis arduous. Moreover, some properties are more pertinent. Further work is needed to handle this issue through a correlation stage which can summarize and prioritize pertinent violations.

6 Conclusion

In this paper, we presented an approach for the detection of process-aware sequence attacks in sequential control systems. We used runtime monitors to report violations of process specifications expressed as sets of safety temporal properties. We also developed a mining algorithm to alleviate the cost of writing specifications. The notion of activity within sequential systems was introduced to improve mining and attack detection. Finally, we evaluated our approach in a hardware-in-the-loop setting subject to process-aware attacks. The evaluation results show that we are able to detect such attacks while achieving a good understanding of false positives. Our main goal for future work is the addition of a correlation stage to deal with the important number of raised violations.

References

1. Common cyber security vulnerabilities in ICS. Technical report, U.S DHS (2011)
2. Bauer, A.: Monitorability of omega-regular languages. CoRR abs/1006.3638 (2010)

3. Bauer, N., Huuck, R., Lukoschus, B., Engell, S.: A unifying semantics for sequential function charts. In: Ehrig, H., Damm, W., Desel, J., Große-Rhode, M., Reif, W., Schnieder, E., Westkämper, E. (eds.) Integration of Software Specification Techniques for Applications in Engineering. LNCS, vol. 3147, pp. 400–418. Springer, Heidelberg (2004). doi:10.1007/978-3-540-27863-4_22

4. Carcano, A., Coletta, A., et al.: A multidimensional critical state analysis for detecting intrusions in SCADA systems. IEEE Trans. Ind. Inf. **7**(2), 179–186 (2011)

5. Cárdenas, A., Amin, S., et al.: Challenges for securing cyber physical systems. In: Workshop on Future Directions in Cyber-physical Systems Security, July 2009

6. Caselli, M., Zambon, E., Kargl, F.: Sequence-aware intrusion detection in industrial control systems. In: Proceedings of the 1st ACM Workshop CPSS, pp. 13–24 (2015)

7. Cheung, S., Skinner, K.: Using model-based intrusion detection for SCADA networks. In: Proceedings of SCADA Security Scientific Symposium, pp. 127–134 (2007)

8. d'Amorim, M., Roşu, G.: Efficient monitoring of ω-languages. In: Etessami, K., Rajamani, S.K. (eds.) CAV 2005. LNCS, vol. 3576, pp. 364–378. Springer, Heidelberg (2005). doi:10.1007/11513988_36

9. De Giacomo, G., Masellis, R.D., Montali, M.: Reasoning on LTL on finite traces: insensitivity to infiniteness. In: Proceedings of AAAI 2014, pp. 1027–1033 (2014)

10. Dwyer, M.B., Avrunin, G.S., Corbett, J.C.: Patterns in property specifications for finite-state verification. In: Proceedings of ICSE (1999)

11. Dzung, D., Naedele, M., Von Hoff, T.P., Crevatin, M.: Security for industrial communication systems. Proc. IEEE **93**, 1152–1177 (2005)

12. Falliere, N., Murchu, L.O., et al.: W32.Stuxnet Dossier-Symantec security response. https://www.symantec.com/content/en/us/enterprise/media/security_response/whitepapers/w32_stuxnet_dossier.pdf. Accessed June 2016

13. Foulard, C., Flaus, J.M., Jacomino, M.: Automatique pour les classes préparatoires, 1st edn. Hermés-Lavoisier, Paris (1997)

14. Hadziosmanovic, D., Sommer, R., et al.: Through the eye of the PLC: towards semantic security monitoring for industrial control systems. In: Proceedings of ACSAC (2014)

15. ISO/IEC 29192 - Information technology - Security techniques - Lightweight cryptography. Standard, ISO, Geneva, Switzerland (2012)

16. John, K.H., Tiegelkamp, M.: IEC 61131–3: Programming Industrial Automation, 2nd edn. Springer, Heidelberg (2010)

17. Larsen, J.: Breakage-Black Hat (2008). https://www.blackhat.com/presentations/bh-dc-08/Larsen/Presentation/bh-dc-08-larsen.pdf. Accessed June 2016

18. Lemieux, C., Park, D., Beschastnikh, I.: General LTL specification mining. In: Proceedings fo ASE 2015, pp. 81–92 (2015)

19. Leucker, M., Schallhart, C.: A brief account of runtime verification. J. Logic Algebraic Program. **78**(5), 293–303 (2009)

20. Li, W., Forin, A., Seshia, S.A.: Scalable specification mining for verification and diagnosis. In: 47th ACM/IEEE DAC, pp. 755–760 (2010)

21. Lin, H., Slagell, A., Di Martino, C., et al.: Adapting bro into SCADA: building a specification-based intrusion detection system for the DNP3 protocol. In: Proceedings of CSIIRW 2013, pp. 1–4 (2013)

22. Mitchell, R., Chen, I.R.: Behavior rule specification-based intrusion detection for safety critical medical cyber physical systems. IEEE Trans Depend. Sec. Comp. **12**(1), 16–30 (2014)

23. Pnueli, A.: The temporal logic of programs. In: Proceedings of SFCS 1977, pp. 46–57. IEEE Computer Society, Washington, DC (1977)

24. Puaun, D.O., Chechik, M.: On closure under stuttering. FAC **14**, 342–368 (2003)
25. Schumann, J., Moosbrugger, P., Rozier, K.Y.: R2U2: monitoring and diagnosis of security threats for unmanned aerial systems. In: Bartocci, E., Majumdar, R. (eds.) RV 2015. LNCS, vol. 9333, pp. 233–249. Springer, Heidelberg (2015). doi:10.1007/978-3-319-23820-3_15
26. Sommer, R., Paxson, V.: Outside the closed world: on using machine learning for network intrusion detection. In: 2010 IEEE S&P, pp. 305–316 (2010)
27. Stouffer, K., Falco, J., Scarfone, K.: Spp. 800–82 Rev 2. Guide to Industrial Control Systems (ICS) Security. NIST (2015)
28. Vardi, M.Y.: An automata-theoretic approach to linear temporal logic. In: Banff Higher Order Workshop 1995 (1996)
29. Yoon, M.k., Ciocarlie, G.F.: Communication pattern monitoring: improving the utility of anomaly detection for industrial control systems. In: SENT (2014)
30. Zimmer, C., Bhat, B., et al.: Time-based intrusion detection in cyber-physical systems. In: Proceedings of First ACM/IEEE International Conference on CPS, pp. 109–118 (2010)

Towards an Automated and Dynamic Risk Management Response System

Gustavo Gonzalez-Granadillo[1]([✉]), Ender Alvarez[1], Alexander Motzek[2],
Matteo Merialdo[3], Joaquin Garcia-Alfaro[1], and Hervé Debar[1]

[1] Institut Mines-Télécom, Télécom SudParis, CNRS UMR 5157 SAMOVAR,
9 Rue Charles Fourier, 91011 Evry, France
{gustavo.gonzalez_granadillo,ender.alvarez,joaquin.garcia_alfaro,
herve.debar}@telecom-sudparis.eu
[2] Institute of Information Systems, Universität zu Lübeck,
Ratzeburger Allee 160, 23562 Lübeck, Germany
motzek@ifis.uni-luebeck.de
[3] RHEA Group, Avenue Pasteur 23, 1300 Wavre, Belgium
m.merialdo@rheagroup.com

Abstract. Achieving a fully automated and dynamic system in critical infrastructure scenarios is an open issue in ongoing research. Generally, decisions in SCADA systems require a manual intervention, that in most of the cases is performed by highly experienced operators. In this paper we propose a framework consisting of a proactive management software that aims at anticipating the occurrence of potential attacks. It conducts an initial evaluation of reported proactive evidences based on a quantitative metric of monetary return on response investment. The framework evaluates and selects mitigation actions from a pool of candidates, by ranking them in terms of financial and operational impacts. The purpose of this process is to select an optimal set of mitigation actions from financial and operational perspectives and propose them to reduce the risk of threats against the monitored system, without sacrificing an organization's missions in favor of security. A real world case study of a SCADA environment shows the applicability of the model, from the analysis of the input data to the selection of the response plan.

Keywords: Dynamic response system · RORI · Operational impact · Automatic response · Critical infrastructures

1 Introduction

Critical infrastructures are systems and assets, whether physical or virtual (e.g., a company, an institution, an organization), which if disrupted, damaged, or destroyed, would have a serious impact on the health, safety, security, or economic well-being of citizens or the effective functioning of governments and other infrastructures depending on it [1]. Critical Infrastructures include sectors that account for substantial portions of national income and employment,

© Springer International Publishing AG 2016
B.B. Brumley and J. Röning (Eds.): NordSec 2016, LNCS 10014, pp. 37–53, 2016.
DOI: 10.1007/978-3-319-47560-8_3

such as energy (including nuclear), ICT, finance, healthcare, food, water, transport, safety, government. Most of these sectors use industrial control systems (ICS) in order to provide control of remote equipment [2].

Achieving a fully automated system in critical infrastructure scenarios is an ongoing research area. Generally, decisions in SCADA systems require a manual intervention, that in most cases is performed by highly experienced operators. However, it is possible to automate incident handling. For some threats, a system should be able to automatically select mitigation actions that provide the most suitable response possibilities to reduce identified risks below an admissible level while minimizing potential negative side effects of deliberately taken actions.

In this paper, we propose a dynamic risk management response system (DRMRS) that evaluates, ranks and selects optimal mitigation actions based on financial, operational and threat impact assessment functions. The selected actions are transformed into response plans that are automatically enforced by the system's policy enforcement points (PEPs). These latter are defined as security components that work as gateways or front doors to digital resources. PEPs are capable of applying security rules (e.g., permission, prohibition, obligation) over the triplet {subject, action, object}. Examples of PEP are web servers, portals, firewalls, LDAP directories, SOAP engines, and similar resources [3].

The contributions on this article are summarized as follows: (1) A model that automatically computes the input parameters of the financial impact metric and provides an indication of the feasibility of each evaluated action. (2) A process that dynamically generate and validate response plans. (3) The implementation and validation of the model. (4) The deployment of the model over a real scenario to perform automated responses in a critical infrastructure system.

The remainder of the paper is structured as follows: Sect. 2 introduces the return on response investment metric. Section 3 describes our proposed dynamic risk management response system. Section 4 details the tool implementation and validation. Section 5 depicts a case study to automate the response in a critical infrastructure system. Related work are presented in Sect. 6. Finally, conclusions and perspective for future work are presented in Sect. 7.

2   Dynamic Return on Response Investment ($RORI$)

The Return On Response Investment (RORI) is a cost sensitive metric used to assess, rank and select security countermeasures from a pool of candidates. The process undertaken by the DRMRS extends initial work reported in [4]. The approach proposes the combination of authorization models and quantitative metrics, for the selection of mitigation actions. The actions, modeled in terms of contextual rules, are prioritized based on a cost-sensitive metric that extends the return on investment (ROI) concept and all its variants [5–7]. The goal is finding an appropriate balance between the financial damages associated to a given threat, and the benefits of applying some mitigation actions to handle the threat, with respect to the loss reduction. The RORI metric is calculated for each mitigation action, according to Eq. 1.

$$RORI = \frac{(ALE \cdot RM) - ARC}{ARC + AIV} \cdot 100 \tag{1}$$

In theory, all parameters composing the RORI metric should be given by expert knowledge, historical data, and/or a risk assessment methodology that evaluates all possible system's threats and gives directions about the most suitable mitigation actions to reduce risk levels down to acceptable values. In practice, however, the estimation of such parameters represents a big challenge and a time consuming task to security administrators. Depending upon the type of órganizations, the RORI parameters can be more or less complex to estimate. For small and medium size organizations, the quantification of such parameters, is a process that could be performed within hours of discussions with use case providers and simple simulation runs [4]. For large and critical organizations, the process can take several weeks (and even months).

Based on the previous shortcomings, a first improvement has been made in the RORI expression to enhance the Risk Mitigation (RM) function. [8] extends the concept of attack surface used in previous versions of the RORI metric. It identifies authorization and contextual dimensions that may directly contribute to the exposition of system vulnerabilities. New properties associated to the vulnerabilities, such as temporal conditions (e.g., granted privileges only during working hours), spatial conditions (e.g., granted privileges when connected within the company premises), and historical conditions (e.g., granted privileges only if previous instances of the same equivalent events were already conducted) can now be included and combined with the RORI cost-sensitive metric.

An adaptation of the selection process, based on financial and operational assessment functions, has been presented in [9], which reports the combination of both assessment approaches, over a representative set of mitigation actions. The combination, based on a multi-dimensional minimization approach, proposes the choice of semi-optimal responses that, on the one hand, bear the highest financial attractiveness on return on investment; and, on the other hand, bear the lowest probability of conflicting with the organization's missions. This is seen as beneficial for its application in scenarios where highly critical missions and resources must be protected, without sacrificing missions in favor of security.

The remaining of this section details the parameters of the RORI metric and describes the process to automatically compute them in a dynamic system.

2.1 Description of the Dynamic *RORI* Model

Annual Loss Expectancy, *ALE* expresses the amount of money, e.g., €/year, that an organization may lose if a threat is realized on the system. It includes loss of assets, loss of data, loss of reputation, etc. *ALE* depends directly on the threat and it is independent on the mitigation actions and the policy enforcement points.

Annual Infrastructure Value, *AIV* depends directly on the policy enforcement point, and expresses the monetary value of the infrastructure, e.g., €/year, regardless of the threat and the implemented mitigation actions.

AIV is greater than zero, i.e., $AIV > 0$, and includes costs of equipment, personal, service, etc.

Annual Response Cost, ARC provides the information about the amount of money (e.g., €) associated to the implementation of a mitigation action against a threat. ARC is always greater than or equal to zero, i.e., $ARC \geq 0$, and includes direct costs, such as cost of implementation, cost of maintenance, other direct and indirect cost, such as potential collateral damages. ARC depends on the mitigation action and the policy enforcement point, but it is independent on the threat.

Risk Mitigation, RM represents the level of reduction that is obtained after the implementation of a mitigation action. RM takes values between zero and one hundred, i.e., $0 \leq RM \leq 100$. RM depends on the threat, the mitigation action, and the policy enforcement point.

Each parameter depends on at least one of the following entities: (i) the threat affecting the system, (ii) the type of mitigation action to be implemented, and (iii) the type of policy enforcement point. Table 1 summarizes this information and details the level of complexity on the estimation of each parameter.

Table 1. Complexity level on the estimation of the RORI parameters

Parameter	Threat	MA_Type	PEP_Type	Complexity
AIV			✓	Low
ALE	✓			Low
ARC		✓	✓	Medium
RM	✓	✓	✓	High

2.2 Computation of the Dynamic *RORI* Parameters

In a dynamic environment, nodes can be active or inactive. Each snapshot of the system may provide a list of different nodes involved in the attack scenario. The evaluation process is therefore unique for each system's snapshot, and is discussed in the following definitions.

Definition 1 (ALE Computation). *Since the ALE parameter is associated to the threat, its value remains unchanged for each snapshot of the system. ALE is assessed first qualitatively, and then transformed into quantitative values. We follow the approach proposed in [10] that defines six qualitative levels of severity, and seven qualitative levels of likelihood with their corresponding quantitative values. ALE is calculated as the product of the severity transformed into probabilistic costs and the likelihood transformed into probabilistic frequency.*

Definition 2 (AIV Computation). *The AIV is computed as the sum of the Annual Equipment Cost (AEC) of all policy enforcement points that appears in the system's snapshot, as shown in Eq. 2.*

$$AIV = \sum_{i=0}^{n} AEC_i \tag{2}$$

Each PEP has an associated AEC that is estimated based on historical information and expert knowledge. Contrary to the ALE, the value of the AIV changes at each snapshot of the system. More details on its estimation can be found in [4].

Definition 3 (ARC Computation). *The ARC is associated to the implementation of a given mitigation action. The value depends directly on the type of mitigation action (e.g., reboot, shutdown, patching), and the PEP responsible of its implementation. More details on its estimation can be found in [4].*

Definition 4 (RM Computation). *The RM of an action is computed as the product of the effectiveness EF and the threat coverage COV, using Eq. 3.*

$$RM = EF \cdot COV \tag{3}$$

Effectiveness (EF) of a mitigation action represents the level at which a given action reduces the risk and/or consequences of an attack on the system. EF is intrinsic to the mitigation action type regardless of the threat it mitigates. For instance, a reboot action by itself provides a very low mitigation of a given threat, whereas a patching action provides a very high protection against it. Table 2 summarizes default values associated to mitigation action types. Each value has been assigned based on statistical data and expert knowledge. Coverage (COV) of a given mitigation action represents the number of nodes to which a mitigation action is being executed over the total number of vulnerable nodes, i.e.,

$$COV = \frac{Q_i \cdot WF_i}{\sum_{j=0}^{n} QT_j \cdot WF_j} , \tag{4}$$

where Q_i is the number of nodes from a PEP_type that are affected by a given mitigation action, WF_i is the weighting factor associated to the affected PEP_type, QT_j is the total number of active node types in the system, and WF_j is the weighting factor associated to each node type.

Table 2. Default effectiveness values associated to mitigation action types.

Mitigation action type	Protection	EF
Reboot	Very Low	1.00 %
Shutdown	Low	10.00 %
Backup	Medium	50.00 %
Change configuration	High	80.00 %
Patching	Very High	100.00 %
Install software/hardware	Very High	100.00 %

3 Dynamic Risk Management Response System

The Dynamic Risk Management Response System (DRMRS) handles identified threats, authorized mitigation actions and strategic policies (i.e., default and contextual policy rules, as well as contextual definitions). It extracts concrete entities from reported threats, and infers concrete policy instances to eventually guide the system into new updates and reconfigurations. These are provided as concrete response plans on a long-term proactive perspective. Response plans are validated by human operators, prior final enforcement. The goal of the DRMRS is the automated administration of policy-related activities, including addition of new rules, removal of unnecessary conditions, and activation of strategic responses (i.e., activation of new mitigation and response plans).

The DRMRS is a dynamic process that involves information coming from different sources of an environment, which are notated and defined as follows.

Abstract Security Policies contain the security policies of the target organization. They include details of the threat (e.g., threatID, attack vector, severity, frequency); details of the Policy Enforcement Point (e.g., name, annual equipment value, PEPType, quantity); and details of the mitigation actions (e.g., ID, ARC, coverage, nodeID, restrictions, effectiveness).

Proactive Risk Profile includes information about assets, supporting assets, attack scenarios and detrimental events. These latter are defined as the fact of harming the accomplishment of an organization's objective or mission.

Network Inventory contains information of all active devices of the emulation environment providing various attributes, e.g., the PEP_Type.

Mission Dependency Model contains information about business processes and devices, consequences and requirements. It contains information about entry points, critical resources, and their dependencies and impact to the mission of the organization.

Network Dependency Model contains information about direct dependencies between individual resources of an organization or mission. The model is used to identify indirect dependencies and cover transitive impacts to the mission of the organization from widespread events.

Attack Graph contains information about all possible attack scenarios. The information includes details of the target and source nodes, as well as the attack paths and its associated likelihood.

Authorized Mitigation Actions contain a list of mitigation actions that are authorized to be executed as a reaction to a given threat.

Based on these input data, response plans are generated and evaluated as elaborated in the following sections.

3.1 Response Plan Generation Process

The process, as depicted in Fig. 1, starts by obtaining information of the threat scenarios coming from the Abstract Security Policies (ASP) and the information

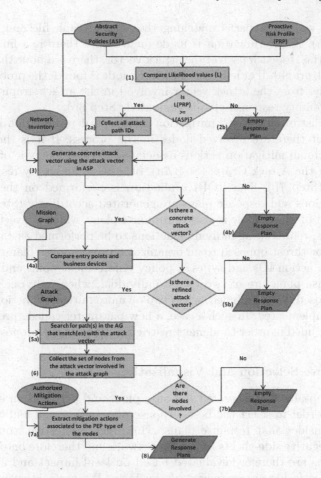

Fig. 1. Workflow for generating potential response plans.

of Detrimental Events (DE) coming from the Proactive Risk Profile (PRP). We compare predefined conditions in both input files. We compare, e.g., if the likelihood of the threat scenario is greater than or equal to the likelihood of the detrimental event (Step 1). In such a case, we collect all attack path IDs that will be used in the attack graph parsing process (Step 2a). If the condition is not met, the process generates án empty response plan (Step 2b).

Given the most updated information of the network inventory and the attack vector from the ASP, we generate a concrete attack vector (Step 3). A determination is made on whether there is a partial concrete attack vector (i.e., for each path of the attack vector, we search all active nodes from the network inventory). If at least one concrete attack vector is found, the process searches for a match of entry points and business devices from the obtained attack vector and the mission dependency model (Step 4a). Otherwise, an empty response plan is generated (Step 4b).

Following, we search paths matching the attack graph file and the attack vector (Step 5). A determination is made on whether there is a final concrete attack vector (i.e., for each path of the attack vector, there is a node that matches with the attack graph). If at least one matching node is found, the process collects the set of nodes from the attack vector involved in the attack graph (Step 6a), otherwise, an empty response plan is generated (Step 6b).

Given the list of authorized mitigation actions, a determination is made on whether or not there are involved nodes in the process. If it is the case, the process extracts all mitigation actions associated to the PEP type of the nodes obtained from the Attack Graph (Step 7a), otherwise, an empty response plan is generated (Step 7b). The RORI evaluation is performed on the extracted mitigation actions and response plans are generated accordingly (Step 8).

The output of this module is a set of response plans, which are vectors of mitigation actions, representing individual actions to be performed as a response to an adversary or threat opposed to an organization. A response plan contains an ID, mitigation action IDs and types, a policy enforcement point and the RORI index. Response plans are of two types: individual, when only one mitigation action is proposed; and combined, when two or more mitigation actions are proposed to be implemented. In such a case, a new parameter called "probability of conflict" is included in order to manage restrictions among the proposed actions.

3.2 Response Selection and Visualization

This module obtains the generated response plans and performs an operational evaluation in order to select the best response plan in financial and operational terms. We consider that response plans, while highly effective, could lead to operational negative side-effects inside the network and therefore onto a mission. Response plans are therefore evaluated based on local impact and assessments of dependencies inside an organization's business. We perform such an operational impact assessment based on a locally validatable probabilistic approach as proposed by Motzek et al. in [11]. The operational impact assessment is based on a probabilistic graphical model obtained from a mission- and network dependency model through probabilistic inference and is detailedly discussed in [11] and [9]. As a result, response plans are enriched with operational information that indicates the impact over the organizational mission(s) in three dimensions: a short-term impact (OI_0), mid-term (OI_1) and long-term impact (OI_2). Based on [9], the number of response plans is reduced to a single response plan that is optimal in each dimension: the financial and the operational impact. Their method searches for a semi-optimal response plan with the lowest operational impact assessment and the highest RORI index.

A response plan is said to be semi-optimal since it might not be the best solution neither in financial nor in operational terms, but it proposes a set of mitigation actions that on the one hand, bear the highest financial attractiveness on return on investment, and, on the other hand, bear the lowest probability of conflicting with a company's mission. This is beneficial for applications, where highly critical missions and resources must be protected, without sacrificing missions in favor of security.

The approach searches for a boundary of acceptable elements (acceptable as a compromise). This boundary is a numerical value representing a normalized deviation (ε) of the optimum. For instance, with $\varepsilon = 0.1$, we accept 10 % deviation of the optimum in each dimension based on the dimensions absolute scale. The acceptance criteria for the financial and operational impact are different. For the financial impact, we keep response plans whose RORI index are greater or equal to 90 % of the highest (best) RORI value. For the operational impact, we keep response plans whose OI_i are up to 10 % of the lowest (best) OI_i value. Then, we check if there is a match in all evaluated response plans. If there is a match, we stop the process; otherwise, we increase the ε value until we find a tuple that matches. In particular, we search the ε where we obtain the smallest set of values. Once a semi-optimal response plan is found, the information is sent to the visualization module, which depicts such results to the security operator.

4   System Testing and Experimentation

Testing and experimentation consists of demonstrating accomplishment of different functional and non-functional requirements defined for the DRMRS. More specifically, we focus on defining a set of tests that are conducted to verify that each requirement is covered by the component implementation. In summary, functional requirements are used to test the syntactical and semantical correct behavior to input data, i.e., correct computation of ALE, ARV, AIV and RM values. All tests have been conducted by manual code inspection, as well as automatically performed tests on artificial data testing syntactical errors, as well as, real data (see Sect. 5) testing correct semantic behavior. In summary all tests were executed without errors or exceptions.

Additionally, several test cases are executed in order to evaluate the computation time in the combined evaluation of mitigation actions. The number of combination for a set of non-restrictive candidates is given by the expression $X = (2^N) - (N+1)$. Since the total number of combinations grows exponentially, we measure the time at which the system is able to perform the evaluation of multiple candidates. An existing non-functional requirement demands the evaluation of multiple response plans in the range of minutes. Results plotted in Fig. 2 show that a combination of 12 restrictive mitigation actions results into 796 combinations that are obtained in less than one second. For 12 non-restrictive mitigation actions, a total of 4082 combinations exists, which are performed in less than 10 s. Given 24 restrictive mitigation actions, 590 464 combinations are evaluated in almost three hours. Therefore, to keep the evaluation process within a reasonable time (less than one minute), the system processes up to 14 non-restrictive mitigation actions (16 369 combinations). Beyond this threshold more than one minute is required, but the approach scales linearly with the number of processed combinations as evident from Fig. 2.

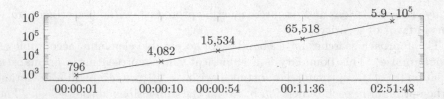

Fig. 2. Computation time (abscissa) to evaluate all combinations of mitigation actions is linear in the number of combinations (ordinate) *(double logarithmic plot)*.

In addition, several integration tests have been performed to verify and validate the appropriate communication of all the components of the DRMRS framework. Such tests rely on the generation of response plans. The communication between the financial and the operational impact assessor modules is an example of integration among the system's components. The set of response plans generated by the financial impact module is sent for evaluation to the operational impact module, making it possible to generate a single response plan that best satisfies the financial and operational impact assessments.

5   Case Study: Automated Response in a Critical Infrastructure System

We study the infrastructure environment of an Energy Distribution organization. The environment consists of a distributed network of Remote Terminal Units (RTU) in energy stations of medium voltage (MV) and high voltage (HV), that acquire data from electrical devices (e.g., PLC, sensors, etc.), and send them to the Supervisor Terminal Unit (STU) of the headquarters. The system uses Supervisory Control and Data Acquisition (SCADA) protocols.

5.1   Threat Scenario

The threat to analyze is a denial of service against a high voltage node of the C&C infrastructure with the objective of taking the C&C offline. More precisely, the threat will cause an out of service condition on Front End Servers (e.g., FE-X1) which breaks communication path from SCADA Servers to RTUs. There exists an attack vector via ICT Network (via VR-08) targeting first the file server (i.e., File-SRV), second, the archive server (i.e., Archive-SRV), and third, the high voltage Front End devices (i.e., FE-X1, FE-X2). This threat has a severity defined as "grave," which corresponds to a single loss expectancy $SLE = 10\,000\,000$ €, and a likelihood defined as "medium," equivalent to an annual rate of occurrence $ARO = 2$. The Annual Loss Expectancy is therefore equivalent to $ALE = 20\,000\,000$ €/year.

5.2 Input Information

After receiving input information, the system checks for active PEPs in the simulation environment in order to obtain the AIV. For this threat scenario, the current snapshot shows that there are 17 active PEPs with an AIV equivalent to 6 925 555€, as shown in Table 3. Note that AIV corresponds to the value obtained out of the sum of all PEP's cost, i.e., AEC, that are active at the time of the snapshot. The AIV parameter is a variable value that depends on the time of the evaluation and the PEP that are detected by the system.

Table 3. Input values of the AIV parameter

PEP	PEP_Type	Description	AEC
PEP16	FWCEDET	Logical Firewall and IPS working in CEDET	105 000
PEP2	SRVMSCADA	Medium Voltage Server	355 000
PEP1	SRVXSCADA	High Voltage Server	355 000
PEP3	FEXSCADA	High Voltage Front End	1 320 000
PEP13	FTPSRV	FTP Server	3 000
PEP11	HMISCADA	Human-Machine Interface	80 000
PEP15	NTPSRV	NTP Server	2 000
PEP20	VRTX	Edge Router on Remote Sites	206 796
PEP14	USERPC	User PC	1 000
PEP5	GWMSCADA	Medium Voltage Gateway	410 532
PEP6	GWXSCADA	High Voltage Gateway	615 800
PEP17	FWDR	Firewall IPS/DR	105 000
PEP10	WEBCADA	Web Server	45 000
PEP18	MGMSRV	Management Server	3 000
PEP9	RTUSCADA	Remote Terminal Unit	2 621 927
PEP4	FEMSCADA	Medium Voltage Front End	660 000
PEP7	VGROUTER	Virtual Router	36 500
Annual Infrastructure Value (AIV)			6 925 555

Following, the system compares the likelihood values of detrimental events in the proactive risk profile against the threat scenario threshold values. For this threat scenario, three detrimental events have greater likelihood values than those associated to the threat scenario, the system therefore retrieves a concrete attack vector for Threat $AS01HV$: 'EntryPoint = VGROUTER; Target1 = WEBSCADA; Target2 = FTPSRV; BusinessDevice = FEXSCADA'

Based on the information from the mission dependency model, we have retrieved the nodes in paths pointing to Business Devices for threat $AS01HV$. Each node has a unique identifier, a host name that corresponds to an instantiated device, a PEP_Type which corresponds to the abstraction class of the

Table 4. Retrieved node information.

Node identifier	Host name	PEP_Type	Node_Type
b992e600-0de2-496c-kkk0-...	mferp1	FEXSCADA	Business Device
718bc323-9d78-4ada-9629-...	dorete	FTPSRV	Target2
e06496d2-6120-4c9d-a310-...	LANGUARD	MGMSRV	Intermediate Node
94d37c8d-bc68-47bf-ad60-...	ARCHIVESRV	FTPSRV	Target2
19b2bb1e-9f23-4fe8-902e-...	KALI	MGMSRV	Intermediate Node
e470baab-5d88-4b20-ac28-...	FTPSRV01	FTPSRV	Target2
876hhezq-77tg-4897-665g-...	xferp2	FEXSCADA	Business Device
d3480ddc-fe4a-4b94-9dc5-...	mferp2	FEXSCADA	Business Device
b54b235d-116a-49b4-9052-...	xferp1	FEXSCADA	Business Device
c9fa4086-d979-4794-9b6e-...	STWEB	WEBSCADA	Target1
c6dd8687-c791-4f91-bf58-...	TPT2000-T2	RTUSCADA	Intermediate Node

PEP, and a Node_Type, which indicates whether the node is an entry point, an intermediate node, a target node or a business device. Please note that business devices are the most critical node types from the emulation environment. They are required to accomplish a business process within the organization. Table 4 summarizes this information.

As shown in Table 4, the PEP types of nodes involved in paths leading to critical devices are: WEBSCADA, FEXSCADA, MGMSRV, RTUSCADA, and FTPSRV. Note that none of the nodes are defined as entry points, and those associated to the PEP_Type MGMSRV do not have pre-defined authorized mitigation actions. In such a case, they are discarded from our analysis.

5.3 Dynamic *RORI* Evaluation

For the RORI evaluation, we obtain the list of authorized mitigation actions associated to threat AS01HV. Table 5 summarizes this information.

As shown in Table 5, each PEP_type has an associated weighting factor (WF) that indicates the level of priority or criticality inherent to the type of PEP in the execution of a mission. For instance, management servers (e.g., MGMSRV) are assigned a $WF = 1$, FTP servers (e.g., FTPSRV) are assigned a $WF = 2$, Web servers (e.g., WEBSCADA) are assigned a $WF = 3$, Front End devices (e.g., FEXSCADA) are assigned a $WF = 4$, and Remote Terminal Units (i.e., RTU) are assigned a $WF = 5$. The COV value is computed using Eq. 4.

To each PEP_type none, one or more of the following mitigation actions can be applied: (**1**) Patching, refers to a piece of software designated to update a computer program or its supporting data, to fix or improve it. This includes fixing or removing security vulnerabilities and other bugs and improving the usability or performance. (**2**) Reboot, refers to the process of restarting a device or a

Table 5. Authorized mitigation action information.

PEP_Type	WF	Affected node	Q	COV	MA_Type	EF	ARC (€)
WEBSCADA	3	STWEB	1	0.09	Shutdown	0.15	15.00
					Reboot	0.01	15.00
					Patching	1.00	25.00
FEXSCADA	4	mferp1, mferp2, xfep1, xferp2	4	0.50	Shutdown	0.15	200.00
					Reboot	0.01	200.00
MGMSRV	1	LANGUARD, KALI	2	0.00	No action	0.00	0.00
RTUSCADA	5	TP2000-T2	1	0.16	Shutdown	0.15	15.00
					Reboot	0.01	15.00
FTPSRV	2	ARCHIVESRV, FTPSRV01, dorete	3	0.19	Shutdown	0.15	15.00
					Reboot	0.01	15.00
					Patching	1.00	25.00

computer program. **(3)** Shutdown, refers to completely remove any possibility to access a device by powering off a device.

Each type of mitigation action has an associated effectiveness (EF) and cost (ARC). The EF value is assigned automatically using the information from Table 2, whereas the ARC value is assigned by expert knowledge and statistical data. Using Eq. 1, we compute the RORI value for individual and combined mitigation actions in Table 6. Each response considers the ARC and EF to calculate the risk mitigation value (RM), using Eq. 3, and take into account restrictions among the candidates (e.g., shutdown a given device is totally restrictive to all other actions that could be executed to such device).

The mitigation action with the highest RORI index is MA_{10}, which requires to install a patch for the PEP_Type "FTPSRV". More specifically, the node "dorete" requires a patching against two vulnerabilities (i.e., CVE-2008-4250,

Table 6. RORI evaluation results for individual mitigation actions.

MA	MA_Type	PEP_Type	RM	Restrictions	RORI
MA_1	Shutdown	WEBSCADA	0.0141	MA_2, MA_3	4.07
MA_2	Reboot	WEBSCADA	0.0009	MA_1	0.26
MA_3	Patching	WEBSCADA	0.0937	MA_1	27.09
MA_4	Shutdown	FEXSCADA	0.0750	MA_5	21.66
MA_5	Reboot	FEXSCADA	0.0050	MA_4	1.44
MA_6	Shutdown	RTUSCADA	0.0234	MA_7	6.76
MA_7	Reboot	RTUCADA	0.0016	MA_6	0.46
MA_8	Shutdown	FTPSRV	0.0281	MA_9, MA_{10}	8.11
MA_9	Reboot	FTPSRV	0.0019	MA_8	0.55
MA_{10}	Patching	FTPSRV	0.1875	MA_8	54.15

Table 7. RORI evaluation results for combined mitigation actions.

MA	ARC	RM	RORI
$MA_{2,3,4,6,9,10}$	295.0	0.3085	89.07
$MA_{3,4,6,9,10}$	280.0	0.308	88.94
$MA_{2,3,4,6,10}$	280.0	0.3075	88.80
$MA_{3,4,6,10}$	265.0	0.3071	88.67
$MA_{2,3,4,7,9,10}$	295.0	0.2975	85.91

and CVE-2006-3439). Considering the previous information about mitigation actions, a total of 214 combinations have been performed to evaluate the RORI metric. Table 7 presents the top 5 combination results.

As shown in Table 7, the highest RORI index corresponds to the combination of mitigation actions MA_2, MA_3, MA_4, MA_6, MA_9, and MA_{10} which proposes the following six concrete actions: *(1) Reboot node STWEB. (2) Install patches to the node STWEB against CVE-2008-4250, and CVE-2006-3439. (3) Shutdown the node mferp2. (4) Shutdown the node TPT2000-T2. (5) Reboot nodes ARCHIVESRV and FTPSRV01 (6) Install patches to the node dorete against CVE-2008-4250, and CVE-2006-3439.*

5.4   Response Plan Generation

For each evaluated mitigation action (including all possible combinations), a response plan has been generated. Each response plan contains the identification of the mitigation action(s), the PEP responsible for its enforcement, and the associated RORI index. The Response Plans contain mitigation actions applied only to the nodes obtained in the Attack Graph parsing (e.g., STWEB, ARCHIVESRV, FTPSRV01, dorete, etc.). For the previous scenario, a total of 224 response plan were generated.

5.5   Response Plan Selection and Visualization

To select a semi-optimal response plan, all proposed response plans based on RORI values are evaluated based on their short-, mid-, and long-term impacts onto the company from an operational perspective, i.e., operational impacts OI_0, OI_1, OI_2. These values are derived as described in [11], where a mission dependency model was created by business experts to the company, and a network dependency model was automatically learned from network traffic analyzes. Table 8 shows a comparison of a selected subset of all 224 evaluated response plans.

The semi-optimal response plan that matches the criteria is RP_{46}, with a deviation of $\epsilon = 0.2$, a RORI index equivalent to 71.34 %, and the following operational impacts: $OI_0 = 0.2724$, $OI_1 = 0.2161$, and $OI_2 = 0.1781$. As a result, the selected response plan is displayed in the visualization module, proposing

Table 8. Financial and operational impact comparison.

MA	RORI	OI_0	OI_1	OI_2
RP_1	4.07	0.1407	0.1407	0.1407
RP_2	0.26	0.137	0.0799	0.0
RP_3	27.09	0.0247	0.0	0.0
RP_4	21.66	0.0989	0.0989	0.0989
RP_5	1.44	0.9995	0.8247	0.0
RP_6	6.76	0.1855	0.1855	0.1855
RP_7	0.46	0.1745	0.1051	0.0
RP_8	8.11	0.0756	0.0756	0.0756
RP_9	0.55	0.0731	0.0478	0.0
RP_{10}	54.15	0.038	0.0	0.0

the enforcement of mitigation actions MA_3, MA_6, MA_9, and MA_{10} which correspond to the following four concrete actions: *(1) Install patches to the node STWEB against CVE-2008-4250, and CVE-2006-3439. (2) Shutdown the node TPT2000-T2. (3) Reboot nodes ARCHIVESRV and FTPSRV01. (4) Install patches to the node dorete against CVE-2008-4250, and CVE-2006-3439.*

6   Related Work

Dynamic systems that automatically evaluate and select the actions to mitigate complex attack scenarios is an open research that represents a big challenge to critical infrastructures. Some research works has been conducted in the assessment of security measures. Kotenko et al. [12,13], e.g., propose a framework for cyber attack modeling and impact assessment based on attack graph generation, real-time event analysis techniques, prognosis of future malefactor steps, attack impact assessment, and anytime approach for attack graph building and analysis. We differ from these research as we do not propose new algorithms or methods of attack graph construction, instead, we propose a novel framework that processes input data to generate response plans for pre-defined threat scenarios.

Agosta et al. [14] propose a software countermeasure framework based on the combination of a cryptographic algorithm implementation with a polymorphic engine which dynamically and automatically transforms the binary code to be protected. The approach enables the generation of multiple versions of the code, to prevent an attacker from recognizing the exact point in time where the observed operation is executed and how such operation is performed. We differ from the previous work since it can only be applied to an algorithm or to a subset of vulnerable instructions, ours is a modular framework that is applied in a whole network to automatically analyze the impact of possible attacks and provide an appropriate response based on multiple criteria.

Ossenbuhl et al. [15], introduce a response selection model that allows mitigating network-based attacks based on an intuitive response selection process that evaluates negative and positive impacts associated with each countermeasure. The model overcomes several challenges in automated response selection, however, several other challenges are left uncovered (e.g., scalability and performance issues, i.e., no alert correlation mechanism has been developed to handle large amount of alerts, security issues, i.e., lack of secured communication channel among the system's components, and applicability issues, i.e., lack of applying responses in more advanced attack scenarios).

7   Conclusions and Future Work

We introduce a Dynamic Risk Management Response System that evaluates, ranks and selects optimal mitigation actions based on financial, operational and threat impact assessments. The system generates response plans containing mitigation actions and corresponding financial and operational evaluations. There are two main improvements of this approach: (i) the dynamic evaluation performed by the system, and (ii) the automation of the response plan generation.

In terms of dynamicity, the system operates on snapshots of a target system with a regular frequency within minutes. At each snapshot, the current condition are assessed. Upon reception of a risk profile, indicating a possible exploitation of a given threat, the system requests input information and performs corresponding analyses. Input data may vary at each snapshot, indicating, e.g., that one or more PEPs are detected on the system, or that one or more mitigation actions are not authorized for the current snapshot. As a result, every time a system snapshot is performed, values of parameters, such as AIV and RM, dynamically change, which in turn changes RORI indexes for the set of evaluated responses.

In terms of automation, the system performs the process in an automatic chain, from the detection of the threat, to the visualization of the selected response plan. The process is automated to assist security administrators in the decision making process. It does not enforce the mitigation action automatically, but provides an assessment of the current system conditions in order to highlight the appropriate response strategies to administrators. For critical infrastructures, selection of mitigation actions generally requires manual intervention by an operator, an approval by supervisors, or more advanced system operator.

Future work will concentrate on managing conflicts among restrictive actions. It is possible that the best response plan suggests an enforcement of mutually exclusive mitigation actions. In such a case, the system should assign priorities to each action being able to discard those with low priority rate.

Acknowledgements. This work received funding from the PANOPTESEC project, as part of the 7th Framework Programme (FP7) of the European Commission (GA 610416).

References

1. Filiol, E., Gallais, C.: Critical infrastructure: where we stand today? In: 9th International Conference on Cyber Warefare and Security (2014)
2. Gordon, K., Dion, M.: Protection of Critical Infrastructure and the role of investment policies relating to National Security. OECD, Whitepaper (2008)
3. Ben Mustapha, Y., Debar, H., Blanc, G.: Policy enforcement point model. In: Conference on Security and Privacy in Communication Networks, pp. 278–286 (2014)
4. Gonzalez-Granadillo, G., Belhaouane, M., Debar, H., Jacob, G.: RORI-based countermeasure selection using the OrBAC formalism. Int. J. Inf. Secur. 13(1), 63–79 (2014)
5. Schmidt, M. Return on Investment (ROI): Meaning and Use, Encyclopedia of Business Terms and Methods (2011)
6. Sonnenreich, W., Albanese, J., Stout, B.: Return on security investment (ROSI) a practical quantitative model. J. Res. Pract. Inf. Technol. 38(1), 45–56 (2006)
7. Mizzi, A.: Return on information security investment: the viability of an anti-spam solution in a wireless environment. Int. J. Netw. Secur. 10(1), 18–24 (2010)
8. Gonzalez-Granadillo, G., Garcia-Alfaro, J., Debar, H.: A polytope-based approach to measure the impact of events against critical infrastructures. J. Comput. Syst. Sci. 1–19 (2016). http://dx.doi.org/10.1016/j.jcss.2016.02.004
9. Gonzalez-Granadillo, G., Motzek, A., Garcia-Alfaro, J., Debar, H.: Selection of mitigation actions based on financial and operational impact assessments. In: International Conference on Availability, Reliability and Security (2016)
10. Lockstep Consulting: A guide for government agencies calculating return on security investment (2004). http://lockstep.com.au/library/return_on_investment
11. Motzek, A., Moller, R., Lange, M., Dubus, S.: Probabilistic mission impact assessment based on widespread local events. NATO IST-128 Workshop on Cyber Attack Detection, Forensics and Attribution for Assessment of Mission Impact (2015)
12. Kotenko, I., Chechulin, A.: A cyber attack modeling and impact assessment framework. In: 5th International Conference on Cyber Conflict (2013)
13. Kotenko, I., Doynikova, E.: Dynamical calculation of security metrics for countermeasure selection in computer networks. In: 24th Euromicro International Conference on Parallel, Distributed, and Network-Based Processing (2016)
14. Agosta, G., Barenghi, A., Pelosi, G.: A code morphing methodology to automate power analysis countermeasures. In: 49th Annual Design Automation Conference, pp. 77–82 (2012)
15. Ossenbuhl, S., Steinberger, J., Baier, H.: Towards automated incident handling: how to select an appropriate response against a network-based attack? In: Conference on IT Security Incident Management & IT Forensics (2015)

Understanding How Components of Organisations Contribute to Attacks

Min Gu, Zaruhi Aslanyan, and Christian W. Probst[✉]

Technical University of Denmark, Kongens Lyngby, Denmark
s146723@student.dtu.dk, {zaas,cwpr}@dtu.dk

Abstract. Attacks on organisations today explore many different layers, including buildings infrastructure, IT infrastructure, and human factor – the physical, virtual, and social layer. Identifying possible attacks, understanding their impact, and attributing their origin and contributing factors is difficult. Recently, system models have been used for automatically identifying possible attacks on the modelled organisation. The generated attacks consider all three layers, making the contribution of building infrastructure, computer infrastructure, and humans (insiders and outsiders) explicit. However, this contribution is only visible in the attack trees as part of the performed steps; it cannot be mapped back to the model directly since the actions usually involve several elements (attacker and targeted actor or asset). Especially for large attack trees, understanding the relations between several model components quickly results in a large quantity of interrelations, which are hard to grasp. In this work we present several approaches for visualising attributes of attacks such as likelihood of success, impact, and required time or skill level. The resulting visualisations provide a link between attacks on an organisations and the contribution of parts of an organisation to the attack and its impact.

1 Introduction

Modern organisations are complex entities. Understanding the interactions between the organisation's infrastructure, IT system, and human actors is difficult; understanding possible attacks on the organisation even more so. Traditional risk assessment methods describe processes that can be used to identify attacks, and to explain the attacks' potential impact on the organisation. However, the focus of these techniques is often rather technical and ignores the internal structure and functioning of the organisation.

To improve the scope of risk assessment and the level of scrutiny, security researchers have suggested socio-technical security models, which include the physical, virtual, and social layer of organisations. Socio-technical security models acknowledge the need of considering all these levels in assessing the risk faced by an organisation since an increasing number of attacks today do involve attack steps on all three levels. The recent attack on a German steel mill [1], for example, started with a spear phishing campaign, installing malware that gave the attackers access to the office network, and from there to the industrial control

© Springer International Publishing AG 2016
B.B. Brumley and J. Röning (Eds.): NordSec 2016, LNCS 10014, pp. 54–66, 2016.
DOI: 10.1007/978-3-319-47560-8_4

system. Eventually, the attack is said to have caused physical damage to the mill's production system.

To communicate the attacks identified in an organisation, attack trees [2,3] are often used; due to their relatively loose definition, attack trees can be adapted to the requirements in many different settings. Attack trees provide structure to the represented attacks by relating a node representing the goal of an attack with different alternative or required sub-goals, which an attacker may or must perform. This structure makes attack trees also an appropriate target for automated identification of attacks [4–6].

The TRE$_S$PASS project [7] applies attack trees as an intermediate representation of attacks. Attacks are generated from a socio-technical system model [8,9] and are the basis of computing the risk faced by an organisation if one or more of the identified attacks are realised. Properties of interest of these attacks include required resources, such as time or money, likelihood of success, or impact of the attack. The analyses also identify the Pareto frontier of incomparable properties, for example, the likelihood of success of an attack, and the required budget.

When communicating the result of risk assessment, two components are of interest: the actual attacks and the contribution of components of the organisation under scrutiny to these attacks. While properties of attack trees or other attack models can be visualised in enlightening ways [10], the same does not hold for the connection between components of the organisation and the attack. Another limiting factor is the sheer size of attack trees, which easily can contain several thousands of nodes. Manual assessment of the individual attacks in huge attack trees is often impossible.

The generated attacks make the contribution of building infrastructure, computer infrastructure, and humans (insiders and outsiders) to the attack explicit. However, this contribution is only visible in the attack trees as part of the performed steps, for example, as leaf labels. Mapping this back to the system model is in principle not complicated. However, the actions usually involve several elements (attacker and targeted actor or asset) that may be located far apart in the model. Especially for large attack trees, visualising these relations quickly results in a large quantity of interrelations, which are hard to grasp.

In this work we present several approaches for visualising attributes of attacks such as likelihood of success, impact, and required time or skill level. The resulting visualisations provide a link between graphical attack models and graphical system models. After a discussion of visualising properties of attack trees, we present our approach of using metrics to identify the importance or contribution of parts of the attack tree, and mapping it to the system model. Our approach currently only considers contribution of model elements – it not, for example, include information on how assets and actors are used in an attack.

Our approach is independent of the attack model or socio-technical system model used. The only requirement is that all model elements have unique identifiers that establish the link between their occurrences in the attack tree and the model, respectively. While we present them in the setting of the TRE$_S$PASS model, which is similar to ExASyM [11] and Portunes [12], the general approach can be applied to any graphical system model and any attack model. For example, the metrics used for visualising model components can also be output as a text file for sorting and further analysis.

The rest of this article is structured as follows. The next section gives an overview of graphical models for systems and attacks, followed by a description of the visualisation of properties of attack trees in Sect. 3. Based on these properties, we specify in Sect. 4 metrics for identifying the contribution of components of organisations to the attacks, and show their application in visualising the contribution to attacks. Finally, Sect. 5 concludes the paper and discusses future work.

2   System and Attack Models

Before discussing the contribution of components of organisations to attacks, we briefly summarise the system and attack models we consider in our work. As stated above, our approach is not limited to specific models for systems and attacks. We only require system models to provide unique identifiers for model elements, and attack models to use these identifiers in describing attack steps.

2.1   System Models

System models include representations of both the physical and the digital infrastructure of an organisation. Approaches such as ExASyM [11] and Portunes [12] represent relevant elements as nodes in a graph. Nodes represent locations, actors, processes, and items, and can be annotated with policies. Actors, processes, and data are located at locations, items and data can also be contained in another item. In our abstraction of the model, these nodes represent the organisational components that enable and contribute to attacks. All elements in the model provide a unique identifier that can be used to refer to the element and to obtain, for example, information on its concrete type, model, or other relevant properties. This information is used in the attack generation, but it can also provide input to the visualisation of system models, for example, whether two elements should be connected by an edge (*e.g.*, two locations) or one within the other (*e.g.*, two items).

While models such as ExASyM [11] and Portunes [12] also define actions that can be performed by actors and processes, these are not required for our approach. We only expect to be able to extract actors and arguments of actions from leaf nodes in attack trees.

2.2   Attack Models

Similarly, attack models represent possible attacks on the modelled organisation. For the approach in this paper, we only require that attack goals can be divided into sub-goals that can be combined either *conjunctively* (must all be completed) or *disjunctively* (only one sub-goal need to be completed). This is very similar to attack trees [2,3], and just as for these it would be interesting to allow more complex combinations at a later point.

As mentioned before we require the attack model to support extraction of actor and assets from the actions in an attack tree. In our current work, actions are contained in the attack-tree leafs. The leaf labels contain words from a regular language that provides, for example, information about type of action, performing actor, which asset is obtained, and where the asset is obtained from. The arguments to the action or exactly the identifiers that connect the attack tree with the system model. We do not need to impose other assumptions that are often found, *e.g.*, about the ordering of sub goals from left to right; this is due to the flow-insensitive nature of our visualisation.

2.3   Running Example

We use the same running example in this paper as in [5], which is based on a case study in the TRE$_S$PASS project [7] centred around an actor Alice, who receives some kind of service, *e.g.*, care-taking, provided by an actor Charlie. Charlie's employer has a company policy that forbids him to accept money from Alice or to steal money. Figure 1 shows a graphical representation of the example

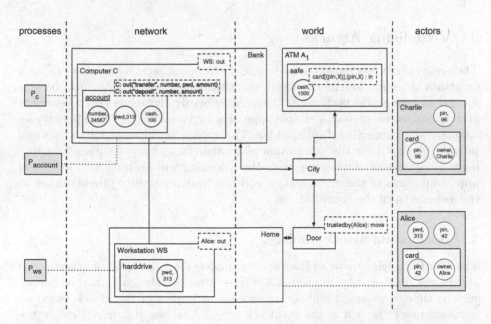

Fig. 1. Graphical representation of the example system. The white rectangles represent locations or items, the gray rectangles represent processes and actors; actors contain the items or data owned by the actor. The round nodes represent data. Solid lines represent the physical connections between locations, and dotted lines represent the present location of actors and processes. The dashed rectangles in the upper right part of some nodes represent the policies assigned to these nodes.

scenario, consisting of Alice's home, a bank with an ATM, and a bank computer. Alice owns a card and a concomitant pin code to obtain money from an ATM, and a password to initiate transfers from her workstation via the bank computer. Some of the nodes are labelled with policies in dashed boxes; for example the money at the ATM requires a card with a pin code, as well as that very pin code in order to obtain money (modelled as input).

Figure 1 shows a graphical representation of the model of our running example. The locations, represented by small rectangles, are connected through directed edges. Actors are represented as rectangles with a location, *e.g.*, Alice is at home and Charlie is in the city. Both actor nodes and location nodes can contain data and items represented as circles. In our example, Alice has a card that contains a pin code and Alice also has (knows) the pin code for her card. Actor nodes can also represent processes running on the corresponding locations. The processes at the workstation and the bank computer represent the required functionality for transferring money; they initiate transfers from Alice's home (P_{WS}), and check credentials for transfers (P_C).

Note that all elements have either a unique name or a unique value, which serve as their identifiers. If an element occurs more than once, for example, the password ($pwd, 313$) or the Alice's pin ($pin, 42$), these occurrences represent copies of the same artefact.

3   Visualising Attacks

The analytic risk assessment based on socio-technical security models operates on attack trees and judgments about quantitative properties of the actions performed and the actors performing them. After briefly discussing how to evaluate attack models, we present a simple approach for visualising several, potentially incomparable properties of such models. The approaches discussed in this section provide the input for the attribution of contribution of organisational components to attacks in the next section: the colouring will be used for identifying important parts of the organisation, and the analyses results provide input to the assessment of the contributions.

3.1   Evaluating Attack Models

The attack models generated from system models form the basis of analytic risk assessment. Properties of interest [13] of these attacks include required resources, such as time or money, likelihood of success, or impact of the attack based on annotations of the leaf nodes in attack trees. Analyses [14] also identify the Pareto frontier of incomparable properties, for example, the likelihood of success of an attack, and the required budget.

The mapping of actions to metrics can again be achieved by mapping the action and its arguments to a specific value. These metrics can represent any quantitative knowledge about components, for example, likelihood, time, price, impact, or probability distributions. The latter could describe behaviour of actors

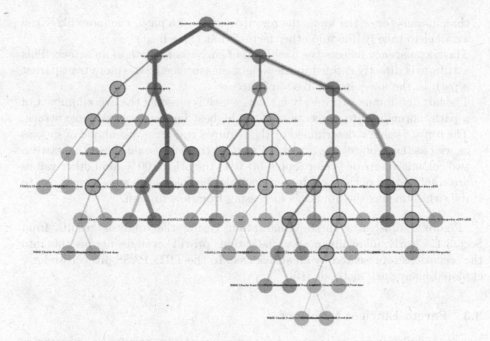

Fig. 2. Attack tree visualisation plot. Nodes with border represent conjunctive nodes, nodes without border disjunctive nodes. The two red paths represent the two attacks with the biggest likelihood of success. The left hand path, however, has a higher chance of success, which is represented by a higher saturation of the colours. The illegible labels for even so small an attack tree document the inapplicability of this concept to showing risk for organisations; attack trees tend to grow so large that they become unhandy and require different visualisation approaches. (Color figure online)

or timing distributions. For the visualisation described in this article the mapping of leaf nodes to metrics and the analyses performed are irrelevant; we assume an attack tree and a mapping from its nodes to an analysis result. For the purpose of this work we have implemented simplified versions of [13,14].

3.2 Attack Tree Visualisations

While not at the core of our work, we briefly discuss the mapping from attack tree analysis results to visualisations, since these map directly to the visualisation of the contribution of components of organisations to the risk faced by the organisation.

We have applied three visual styles to illustrate the influence of paths in the attack tree on the overall result for the tree:

– The line width of edges implies the resource usage of a specific path, that is, how resource demanding an attack path is. We assumed attackers always choose the path with lowest cost, lowest time consumption, and lowest difficulty to apply attacking. Thus the line width is inversely proportional to these three parameters – the lower the resource usage of a path, the more likely the attacker to take it (modulo other factors that come next).

- The transparency reflects the likelihood of success of a path in an attack. This attribute is directly defined in the weight measurement: the more transparent a path is, the lower its likelihood of success.
- The last and foremost property is color, which represents the overall impact of a path, normalised to percentage of the highest impact for the whole attack. The impact value is determined by the required resources, likelihood of success as well as the profit of the attack. In general the color scale chosen is between two colours, where one color represents 0 %, the other 100 %, and other values are combination of the two. In our example the color scale goes from green to red, which means the impact is increasing from low to high.

Figure 2 illustrates these visualisations using the analysis results from Sect. 3.1. Clearly, more advanced visualisations provide even deeper insights into the scenarions represented by an attack tree. In the TRE$_S$PASS project we have explored many such methods [10].

3.3   Pareto-Efficient Solutions

In case of multiple parameters most analytical methods optimise one parameter at a time, *e.g.*, minimise cost or maximise probability of an attack. Such methods may lead to sub-optimal solutions when optimising conflicting parameters, *e.g.*, minimising cost while maximising probability; in this scenario it may not be possible to identify the attack that will result in the biggest gain for the attacker.

Pareto-efficient solutions [14] result in combinations of these conflicting parameters, and can be used to approximate the results for comparable values. Figure 3 shows an example of a Pareto-efficient solutions for an attack tree that results in

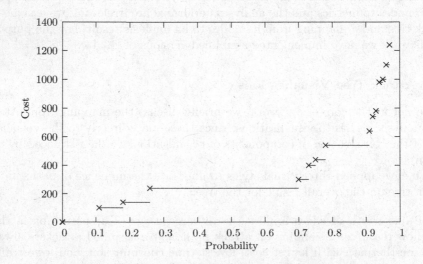

Fig. 3. Pareto efficient solutions for the attack tree [14].

probability of a successful attacks ranging from 0 to 0.97 and the corresponding cost ranging from 0 to 695. Assuming that the attacker has a fixed budget or a rational attacker who will not launch an attack if the cost is higher than the expected gain, we can identify the optimal Pareto-efficient solution from this set.

We are currently experimenting with approaches for visualising this directly on the attack tree to indicate how close a path in the attack tree is to the most Pareto-efficient solution. The approach of scaling between two colours, which we applied for unary predicates as discussed above, does not carry over to binary predicates, where we, *e.g.*, have worse attacks (for the attacker) with higher probability. We are currently considering three colours, *e.g.*, green – red – blue, or stretching of lines, where the colours have the same meaning as discussed above, but the path lengths are scaled depending on how close they are to the Pareto-efficient solution. The scaling would make identification of the most Pareto-efficient attack (and the ordering on attacks) straightforward, since the longer paths are more efficient.

4   Contribution of Components of Organisations to Attacks

Now we put the different elements described above together to visualise the relation between attack trees and system models. Remember that we require all elements in the model to have unique identifiers; we use this identifier to associate model components and attack tree actions.

As for attack trees we need a measure for how much a model element contributes to a given attack. We apply techniques similar to our earlier work on insiderness [15].

4.1   Measuring Impact

Computing the actual impact of a model component on an attack is as difficult as computing the impact of an attack; the results can be used for ordering attacks or influence, but they should not be taken as absolute answers. With this in mind we have applied several techniques for measuring the impact of components on attacks.

As mentioned before we require the attack model to support extraction of actor and assets from the actions in an attack tree, and actions are contained in the attack-tree leafs. Leaf labels provide information about type of action, performing actor, which asset is obtained, and where the asset is obtained from. All this information is provided through the identifiers that connect the attack tree with the system model.

4.2   Counting Occurrences

The simplest concept of measuring impact is that of *counting occurrences* of identifiers. It computes for a given entity in how many places it contributes to the whole attack tree or a path. The occurrence-based ranking ignores analysis results such as impact or likelihood. It is either measured as absolute number or as percentage of occurrences of identifiers in the path or tree being analysed. It is computed per identifier id for a set of nodes in a subtree of the attack tree that represents an attack, assuming that $id \in S$ returns 1 if true, and 0 otherwise, and that node n has successors $c \in succ(n)$:

$$\mathcal{I}(id, n) := \begin{cases} [x, x] & x = (id \in actor(n)) + (id \in assets(n)), \text{ if } n \text{ is a} \\ & \text{leaf node} \\ [l, u] & l = min(\mathcal{I}(id, c)), u = max(\mathcal{I}(id, c)), \text{ if } n \text{ is a} \\ & \text{disjunctive node} \\ [l, u] & l = \Sigma_c\{l'|[l', \_] = \mathcal{I}(id, c)\}, u = \Sigma_c\{u'|[\_, u'] = \\ & \mathcal{I}(id, c)\}, \text{ if } n \text{ is a conjunctive node} \end{cases} \quad (1)$$

As a first crude measure, this impact provides a defender with a quick overview of which components of the organisation actually occur in the attack tree.

The occurrence-based impact provides for every identifier a lower and an upper bound of occurrences; for conjunctive nodes these will be the same, for disjunctive nodes the lower bound is the minimum of the lower bounds, and the upper bound is the maximum of the upper bounds of the child nodes. The combination of lower and upper bounds provides a measure for how reliable the numbers are. It also allows to identify, whether certain elements occur in all attacks: if $\mathcal{I}(id, r) = [x, \_]$ for some identifier id, the root of the attack tree, and $x > 0$, then the element with id contains in every attack in the tree.

4.3 Weighted Sum

The impact factor based on occurrences in the generated attacks is a rather crude approximation, since every occurrence of an identifiers is assigned the same impact independent on the *actual* contribution to the attack. Given that the analyses of attack trees described in Sect. 3.1 provide us with quantitative information about attacks, we can improve over the occurrence-based ranking by weighting occurrences of identifiers with the impact of the attack they occur in. The factors we can choose from are limited by available analyses only, but include, for example, the likelihood of success, required time, difficulty, and cost.

In contrast to the occurrence-based impact we now *include* one of the analysis results, by weighting the count for an identifier with the weight of the path, and potentially normalising it. As before, it is either measured as absolute number or as percentage of occurrences of identifiers in a subtree of the tree being analysed.

For defining the impact, we assume for identifier id for a node n on a path in the attack tree:

- the set-membership test $id \in S$ returns 1 if id is in S, and 0 otherwise,
- $succ(n)$ returns the successors of node n in the attack tree, and
- $val(n, p)$ returns the result of the attack tree analysis for a node n in the (sub-)tree p.

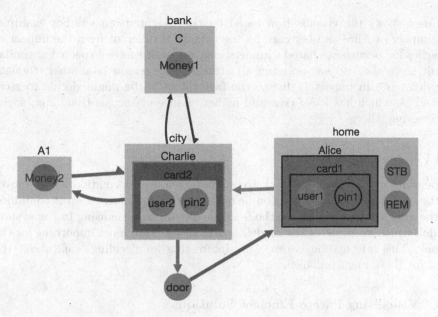

Fig. 4. Visualisation of the weighted impact of an attack tree on the physical infrastructure part of the example model from Fig. 1. Charlie is identified as the major culprit as he occurs in every single attack step. Alice is less involved, since Charlie in some attacks might steal money from the ATM directly (or the ATM altogether). It is also clear from the visualisation that the user tag on Alice's card is not used in the attack, and neither is, *e.g.*, the bank computer C.

Using these functions, we compute the contribution of an asset or actor with identifier id, at node n with subtree p rooted at n based on the following cases. If n is a leaf node, we obtain the result of the attack tree analysis for n and p. If n is a disjunctive node, we compute the minimal impact for successors of n. If n is a conjunctive node, the computation depends on the analysis result val we are using. If we measure difficulty, time, or cost, we value the impact to be the sum of the impact of all successors. If we measure likelihood of success, we assume the impact to be the minimal impact:

$$\mathcal{I}(id, n, p) := \begin{cases} v_l = val(n,p) \cdot (id \in actor(n) + id \in assets(n)) \\ \quad \text{if } n \text{ is a leaf node} \\ v_d = min_{c \in succ(n)}(\mathcal{I}(id, c, p)) \\ \quad \text{if } n \text{ is a disjunctive node} \\ v_{ca} = \Sigma_{c \in succ(n)} \mathcal{I}(id, c, p) \\ \quad \text{if } n \text{ is a conjunctive node and we} \\ \quad \text{measure difficulty, time, or cost} \\ v_{cm} = min_{c \in succ(n)}(\mathcal{I}(id, c, p)) \\ \quad \text{if } n \text{ is a conjunctive node and we} \\ \quad \text{measure likelihood of success} \end{cases} \tag{2}$$

Figure 4 shows the visualisation based on the weighted impact. For example, the impact of Alice and her card on the attacks is different from the impact of Charlie; for occurrence-based visualisations we would have expected a similar result since they do not occur in all attacks. The reason is another, though: the difference in impact is due to the fact that Charlie might decide to steal the ATM, which has lower cost and higher chance of success than, *e.g.*, social engineering Alice.

4.4   Visualising Paths

Depending on the kind of attack trees, they contain information about moves of the attacker in the organisation or not. If the move information is contained in the attack tree, then the methods above extend to visualising in the system model, which locations of the modelled organisation are most important for the attack. This information is especially interesting for deciding, *e.g.*, about the need for (better) surveillance.

4.5   Visualising Pareto-Efficient Solutions

As mentioned in Sect. 3.3, visualising Pareto-efficient solutions requires special approaches due to the fact that the best solution may be in the middle of the spectrum of possible attacks. Therefore, it may be important to visualise not only the best solution, but also identifying solutions that are worse or better, but are not chosen due to the efficiency criterion. The three-colour option discussed above is also applicable in the model setting; other approaches such as the scaling of edges do not carry over since different attacks with differing quantitative valuations must be visualised on the same model.

4.6   Visualising Different Components

There exist many different analyses on attack trees, and it may be interesting to investigate and visualise several values combined on a system model. For many interesting counting approaches, *e.g.*, the ones discussed here, one can combine different values into a vector, and apply for each value the targeted counting operation. Since the values generally may not be comparable directly, one then can either apply Pareto-based techniques, visualise the different values simultaneously, or apply a summation function that combines the individual values.

5   Conclusion

Modern organisations are complex socio-technical systems. Understanding the interactions between the organisation's infrastructure, IT system, and human actors is difficult; understanding possible attacks on the organisation even more so. While attack trees are a natural approach to communicate risks and possible attacks, it is often hard to estimate, which parts of an organisation contribute to these attacks. Even worse, attack trees tend to be so huge that they are hard to understand. Visualising the attack trees directly eases the treatment, but still leaves defenders with large trees; what is needed is an approach that relates the model to attacks.

In this article we have presented a systematic approach for such a mapping of the results of attack generation back to system models. The visualisation can be based on arbitrary counting of occurrences of model elements in the generated attacks. We have presented two such approaches based on simple occurrence and weighted occurrence. More complex ones could, *e.g.*, also take the role of actors into account, such as attacker, victim, or social engineered.

In the TRE$_S$PASS project [7], visualisations such as our approach contribute to the attack navigator [16, 17]. Beyond this, the techniques presented here are widely applicable. Our approach is agnostic to the underlying system and attack models. The only requirement is the ability to associate actions and the involved artefacts in the attack model with elements in the system model, and to obtain quantitative judgments about the attacks. While the techniques discussed in this work especially target IT security attacks, the techniques are applicable to any kind of attacks and risks.

We are currently working on further refinement of the visualisations, *e.g.*, for Pareto-efficient solutions, and on more advanced counting functions. As mentioned above, it would be interesting to take the role of an actor into account. We are also investigating how to extend our approach to attack-defence trees [18], which combine actions by attackers with mitigating actions by defenders.

Acknowledgment. Min Gu is an Erasmus Mundus student and receives funding from NordSecMob – Master's Programme in Security and Mobile Computing. Part of the research leading to these results has received funding from the European Union Seventh Framework Programme (FP7/2007-2013) under grant agreement no. 318003 (TRE$_S$PASS). This publication reflects only the authors' views and the Union is not liable for any use that may be made of the information contained herein.

References

1. BBC News: Hack attack causes 'massive damage' at steel works (2014). http://www.bbc.com/news/technology-30575104. Accessed 15 Oct 2015
2. Schneier, B.: Attack trees: modeling security threats. Dr. Dobb's J. Softw. Tools **24**(12), 21–29 (1999)
3. Kordy, B., Piètre-Cambacédès, L., Schweitzer, P.: Dag-based attack and defense modeling: don't miss the forest for the attack trees. Comput. Sci. Rev. **13–14**, 1–38 (2014)
4. Vigo, R., Nielson, F., Nielson, H.R.: Automated generation of attack trees. In: Proceedings of the 27th Computer Security Foundations Symposium (CSF), pp. 337–350. IEEE (2014)
5. Ivanova, M.G., Probst, C.W., Hansen, R.R., Kammüller, F.: Transforming graphical system models to graphical attack models. In: Mauw, S., Kordy, B., Jajodia, S. (eds.) GraMSec 2015. LNCS, vol. 9390, pp. 82–96. Springer, Heidelberg (2016). doi:10.1007/978-3-319-29968-6_6

6. Ivanova, M.G., Probst, C.W., Hansen, R.R., Kammüller, F.: Attack tree generation by policy invalidation. In: Akram, R.N., Jajodia, S. (eds.) WISTP 2015. LNCS, vol. 9311, pp. 249–259. Springer, Heidelberg (2015). doi:10.1007/978-3-319-24018-3_16

7. The TRE$_S$PASS Consortium: Project web page. http://www.trespass-project.eu. Accessed Apr 2016

8. Kammüller, F., Probst, C.W.: Invalidating policies using structural information. In: 2nd International IEEE Workshop on Research on Insider Threats (WRIT 2013). IEEE Co-located with IEEE CS Security and Privacy 2013 (2013)

9. Kammüller, F., Probst, C.W.: Combining generated data models with formal invalidation for insider threat analysis. In: 3rd International IEEE Workshop on Research on Insider Threats (WRIT 2014). IEEE Co-located with IEEE CS Security and Privacy 2014 (2014)

10. Li, E., Barendse, J., Brodbeck, F., Tanner, A.: From A to Z: developing a visual vocabulary for information security threat visualisation. In: Graphical Models for Security (2016)

11. Probst, C.W., Hansen, R.R.: An extensible analysable system model. Inf. Secur. Techn. Rep. **13**(4), 235–246 (2008)

12. Dimkov, T., Pieters, W., Hartel, P.: Portunes: representing attack scenarios spanning through the physical, digital and social domain. In: Armando, A., Lowe, G. (eds.) ARSPA-WITS 2010. LNCS, vol. 6186, pp. 112–129. Springer, Heidelberg (2010). doi:10.1007/978-3-642-16074-5_9

13. Lenin, A., Willemson, J., Sari, D.P.: Attacker profiling in quantitative security assessment based on attack trees. In: Bernsmed, K., Fischer-Hübner, S. (eds.) NordSec 2014. LNCS, vol. 8788, pp. 199–212. Springer, Heidelberg (2014). doi:10.1007/978-3-319-11599-3_12

14. Aslanyan, Z., Nielson, F.: Pareto efficient solutions of attack-defence trees. In: Focardi, R., Myers, A. (eds.) POST 2015. LNCS, vol. 9036, pp. 95–114. Springer, Heidelberg (2015). doi:10.1007/978-3-662-46666-7_6

15. Probst, C.W., Hansen, R.R.: Reachability-based impact as a measure for insiderness. In: 5th International Workshop on Managing Insider Security Threats (MIST 2013) (2013)

16. Probst, C.W., Willemson, J., Pieters, W.: The attack navigator. In: Mauw, S., Kordy, B., Jajodia, S. (eds.) GraMSec 2015. LNCS, vol. 9390, pp. 1–17. Springer, Heidelberg (2016). doi:10.1007/978-3-319-29968-6_1

17. Pieters, W., Barendse, J., Ford, M., Heath, C.P.R., Probst, C.W., Verbij, R.: The navigation metaphor in security economics. IEEE Secur. Priv. **14**(3), 14–21 (2016)

18. Kordy, B., Mauw, S., Radomirović, S., Schweitzer, P.: Attack-defense trees. J. Log. Comput. **24**(1), 55–87 (2014)

A Stochastic Framework for Prediction of Malware Spreading in Heterogeneous Networks

Sandra König[1]([✉]), Stefan Schauer[1], and Stefan Rass[2]

[1] Digital Safety and Security Department, Austrian Institute of Technology GmbH, Klagenfurt, Austria
{sandra.koenig, stefan.schauer}@ait.ac.at
[2] System Security Group, Institute of Applied Informatics, Universität Klagenfurt, Klagenfurt, Austria
stefan.rass@aau.at

Abstract. The infection of ICT systems with malware has become an increasing threat in the past years. In most cases, large-scale cyber-attacks are initiated by the establishment of a botnet, by infecting a large number of computers with malware to launch the actual attacks subsequently with help of the infected victim machines (e.g., a distributed denial-of-service or similar). To prevent such an infection, several methodologies and technical solutions like firewalls, malware scanners or intrusion detection systems are usually applied. Nevertheless, malware becomes more sophisticated and is often able to surpass these preventive actions. Hence, it is more relevant for ICT risk managers to assess the spreading of a malware infection within an organization's network. In this paper, we present a novel framework based on stochastic models from the field of disease spreading to describe the propagation of malware within a network, with an explicit account for different infection routes (phishing emails, network shares, etc.). This approach allows the user not only to estimate the number of infected nodes in the network but also provides a simple criterion to check whether an infection may grow into a epidemic. Unlike many other techniques, our framework is not limited to a particular communication technology, but can unify different types of infection channels (e.g., physical, logical and social links) within the same model. We will use three simple examples to illustrate the functionalities of the framework.

1 Introduction

In the last years, information and communication technology (ICT) systems have faced an increasing amount of infections and attacks stemming from malware. This ranges from simple adware like DeskAd, bringing annoying content onto the system, over bots, making the infected system part of a bot network, later on used, e.g., for spaming or distributed denial of service (DDoS) attacks, up to ransomware like CryptoLocker, which is used to blackmail an organization. In fewer

B.B. Brumley and J. Röning (Eds.): NordSec 2016, LNCS 10014, pp. 67–81, 2016.
DOI: 10.1007/978-3-319-47560-8_5

cases, more sophisticated malware, e.g., rootkits, is used to gain foothold in the system and start an advanced persistent threat (APT) attack. Whereas simple forms of malware might have minimal effects on an organization's infrastructure, more sophisticated ones, especially ransomware, can cause a significant damage within an organization, with APTs potentially having the biggest effects, as past and current examples like Stuxnet [1] or the hack of the Ukranian power grid [2] show. In both cases, Stuxnet and the Ukranian power grid, the attack has been established for a long time, with the malware carefully and stealthy probing and learning the infrastructure characteristics to manifest itself in vital parts of the system. It was reported that the malware remained unnoticed for a long time in the system, and went over quite a variety of different technical and logical links. While Stuxnet and the Ukranian power grid are just two rather public incidents based on APT attacks, claims of successful attacks or related attempts (that did not cause damage so far) are continuously reported (see, e.g., [3–5]).

Currently, several technologies and numerous applications exist which are used to prevent the infection of an ICT system by malware. Among these are classical applications like firewalls, virus or malware scanners, but also more advanced methodologies like intrusion detection systems (IDS), security incident and event management (SIEM) as well as anomaly detection systems. Although these preventing technologies become more and more advanced, in many cases an infection is triggered by "soft" and non-technological factors, e.g., by following links in phishing emails or drive-by infections. As described in [6], almost 50 % of examined malware requires user interaction for propagation. Hence, the infection of an organization's ICT system cannot be ruled out just due to technological reasons, but the user awareness becomes a core aspect.

From a security managers' point of view, it is important not only to perform preventive actions but also to estimate and assess the potential damage of a malware infection within an organization's ICT infrastructure. In particular, when it comes to critical infrastructures or utility providers (such as power, water or gas providers), a failure of a small number of systems or even a single system might have significant effects on the organization as well as the population and the entire society. Thus, it is crucial to estimate the number of infected systems or whether the infection will turn into an epidemic (i.e., a significant fraction of all nodes in the network will be infected). Currently, there are only a few approaches in the literature modeling the propagation of malware in ICT networks.

In this article, we present a novel framework for modeling and assessing the propagation of malware within a network after one node has been infected (the case where an infection simultaneously originates from multiple nodes, say by a spamming email infection, is covered by our model under suitable changes, e.g., by introduction of an artificial node which infects all neighbors with probability one). In our approach, we treat the spreading of malware in an ICT network as a similar process to spreading of an epidemic in a human network. Existing epidemic models are often based on percolation theory [7] to describe how single events trigger other events in a network [8,9]. Accordingly, we also use percolation theory to describe how malware can spread in an ICT network. Therefore, we model the ICT infrastructure as a graph representing a network of inter-connected components. Further, we use characteristics of a malware to estimate the probability that an infected node also infects the neighbor nodes. As we will show later on, our approach is not restricted to the physical network but can integrate also additional information, e.g., logical links between the nodes or the social network of the employees using the ICT systems. In addition to the network infrastructure, we use the properties of a malware to estimate the probability that a node becomes infected given that one of the neighbor nodes is already infected. Hence, the two main questions that can be answered using our framework are:

(a) How many nodes will be affected by a specific malware on average?
(b) How likely is it that a significant part of the network is affected by the mal-ware? In this context "significant" means an expectedly unbounded number of nodes.

The remainder of this paper is structured as follows: After a quick overview on the related work in Sects. 2, 3 presents a general propagation model for hetero-geneous networks, both for the situation of bounded and unbounded spreading and illustrates it with an example. Section 4 shows how the general model can be helpful in describing a malware infection. Section 5 illustrates the implementa-tion of the model for the case of phishing emails and, finally, Sect. 6 summarizes our approach.

2 Related Work

In the past, there have been only a limited number of approaches describing malware propagation. Some early models are based on random scanning schemes [10, 11], which assume that malware randomly selects new target systems and infects them. More sophisticated malware takes the specific network topology into account, i.e., topological scanning functionalities are determining the prop-agation of the malware [12, 13].

During the last years, several epidemic models have been used to describe the spreading of a malware [14–19]. While these and similar models are quite complex due to being formulated with differential equations, they assume the networks to be homogeneous and thus they are not very flexible. One approach taking into account some heterogeneities in the transmission is [20].

Looking at malware spreading in a more abstract way, we want to understand how certain events trigger other events in a network. Percolation theory [7, 21] has evolved into an indispensable tool for answering this question, especially in physics. Further, models describing disease spreading using percolation theory [8, 9, 22–24] have become popular over the last decades. Most of these models are built for a specific class of networks, such as scale-free networks [25, 26] or lattices [22].

Although percolation models are rather prevalent in the field of disease spreading, they are only rarely used in the fields of security and risk manage-ment so far. A potential reason for this might be the common assumption that all contacts are equally likely to transmit the disease, i.e., that the network is homogeneous in this regard [21,27–30]. Whereas this might represent a reasonable simplification for some problems in disease spreading, such assumptions are inappropriate when modeling ICT security. In this context, it is preferable to distinguish different components (e.g., stemming from different subnetworks) as this might significantly influence how an infection in one component can (or cannot) affect other components. Such heterogeneity has for example been recognized in Industrial Control Systems (ICS) [31], allowing a more detailed analysis of such systems. Therefore, we will relax this assumption by allowing connections between two nodes to be of diverse nature (e.g., email contact, wireless layer 2 connection, etc.), each of which may have its own and distinct characteristics defining how a malware can spread over the network. A model that accounts for both directed and undirected edges has been presented in [32] and has further been generalized in [33] to the situation of several different types of connections. For example, if a network is divided into several subnets, one edge class may be defined to model the cross-connections between the subnets. Consequently, bridges, firewalls or similar may all constitute their own edge class, whereas connections among the nodes of the subnet may belong to different edge classes. Examples may include (but are not limited to) shared network drives, email communication and similar.

3   A Model for Spreading in Heterogeneous Networks

As our focus in this work is on presenting an application-oriented model, we put our upcoming efforts on the modeling. Details of the underlying theory (including formal proofs) can be found in [33], where the interested reader can look up the background of our upcoming considerations.

Let an ICT network be modeled as a graph $G(V, E)$, where V is a finite set of nodes and E is the set of directed edges between them. Since we consider the spreading process being influenced by the different nature of connections between nodes, we partition the full edge set E into n *classes* of edges, i.e., we say that an edge is "of type i", to characterize it. While edges of the same type are indistinguishable, edges of different types have distinctive properties related to the spreading process. Thus, each class i has a specific probability p_i of transmitting the considered malware. (Note that these probabilities do not have to sum to one as they do not represent a distribution but rather represent different characteristics.)

3.1   Formal Description of the Network

Throughout the paper, we will denote sets, matrices and random variables by uppercase letters while vectors are printed in bold. Functions are denoted by calligraphic letters. The topology of a network will be described by its *degree distribution* $P(j, k)$, giving the probability of a node having exactly j ingoing and k outgoing edges.

Over the evolution of the outbreak, we will distinguish the "infected network", consisting of nodes infected by the malware together with the edges connecting them, from the "original network", in which no incident has yet occurred. Since edges within the infected network have been vehicles for malware, we will call them "infected edges". Throughout the remainder of this work, we add the superscript "o" (for "original") to quantities corresponding to this original network while variables describing the network after the infection have no superscript.

Generally, a random network is conveniently described through its degree distribution, i.e., the relative frequencies of occurring degrees of nodes. For a network with n different edge classes, each having probability of transmission p_i, the degree distribution of the infected network is [33]

$$P(\mathbf{j}, \mathbf{k}) = \sum_{\mathbf{j}^o \geq \mathbf{j}} \sum_{\mathbf{k}^o \geq \mathbf{k}} P^o(\mathbf{j}^o, \mathbf{k}^o) \prod_{i=1}^{n} \binom{j_i^o}{j_i} p_i^{j_i}(1 - p_i)^{j_i^o - j_i} \cdot \prod_{i=1}^{n} \binom{k_i^o}{k_i} p_i^{k_i}(1 - p_i)^{k_i^o - k_i} \quad (1)$$

where $\mathbf{j}^o \geq \mathbf{j}$ is a shorthand for the component-wise inequalities $j_i^o \geq j_i$ for all i. This distribution is conveniently represented by its generating function, see [34, 35] for details. The above distribution is described by

$$\mathcal{G}(x_1, \ldots, x_n; y_1, \ldots, y_n) = \sum_{\mathbf{j}, \mathbf{k} \geq \mathbf{0}} P(\mathbf{j}, \mathbf{k}) \prod_{i=1}^{n} x_i^{j_i} y_i^{k_i}, \quad (2)$$

where j_i and k_i represent the number of incoming and outgoing edges of type i, respectively. This representation simplifies the upcoming analysis.

A difficile part of this model is the determination of the probabilities p_i characterizing each type of edges. These values need to be estimated by experts or are based on some kind of vulnerability assessment (preferably, an expert may base an opinion on past reported incidents, combined with own experience; in any case, probabilities may nonetheless remain subjective estimates, and a careful fine-tuning by combining input from multiple domain experts may be advisable to get a robust parameterization). Potential uncertainty in such assignments can be captured by allowing these probabilities to be random themselves [36].

Essentially, our network model is a weighted directed graph $G = (V, E)$, where the (finitely many) weights $w : E \rightarrow \{p_1, \ldots, p_n\}$ represent the different edge classes. The topology of G is random, and described by degree distributions (or generating functions thereof), but not further restricted to obey any particular shape of the distribution (e.g., power-law or similar).

3.2   Predictions for a Bounded Outbreak

Based on the model presented in the previous section, we can predict the degree of damage for a network due to an infection originating from a single node. To measure this damage, we compute the expected number S of components affected by the infection.

Whether an infection is conveyed to another node heavily depends on the types of the incoming edges. If those are not likely to transmit the infection, there is a smaller chance it becomes infected than compared to the situation where the incoming links are more susceptible. Differentiating between the possible types of the edge, over which we arrive at a node yields the expected number of infected nodes

$$\mathsf{E}[S] = 1 + \sum_{j=1}^{n} \frac{\partial}{\partial y_j} \mathcal{G}(1, \ldots, 1; 1, \ldots, 1) \cdot H_j'(1), \tag{3}$$

where $H_i'(1)$ is a solution

$$H_i'(1) = 1 + \sum_{j=1}^{n} \frac{\partial}{\partial y_j} \mathcal{H}_i(1, \ldots, 1; H_1(1), \ldots, H_n(1)) \cdot H_j'(1). \tag{4}$$

The linear equation system (4) to be solved can be written in the form $\mathbf{Ax} = \mathbf{b}$ with $\mathbf{x} = (H_1'(1), \ldots, H_n'(1))$, $\mathbf{b} = (1, \ldots, 1)^T$ and the coefficient matrix $\mathbf{A}$ with entries

$$a_{ij} = -\frac{\partial}{\partial y_j} \mathcal{H}_i(1, \ldots, 1; 1, \ldots, 1) = -\frac{\partial}{\partial y_j} \mathcal{H}_i^o(1, \ldots, 1; 1, \ldots, 1) \cdot p_j$$

for $i \neq j$ and

$$a_{ii} = 1 - \frac{\partial}{\partial y_i} \mathcal{H}_i(1, \ldots, 1; 1, \ldots, 1) = 1 - \frac{\partial}{\partial y_i} \mathcal{H}_i^o(1, \ldots, 1; 1, \ldots, 1) \cdot p_i$$

on the diagonal. It can be solved numerically and the solution is then be plugged into Eq. (3) to receive the desired expected value.

Example 1. *If we assume the network to be modeled by the well known Erdős-Rényi model [37] in which an edge of type i exists with probability q_i, the system (4) is described by the matrix*

$$a_{ij} = \begin{cases} -np_j q_j & \text{if } i \neq j \\ 1 - np_j q_j & \text{if } i = j \end{cases}$$

where p_i again denotes the probability of transmission for an edge of type i. Rearranging terms and using some algebra, we find

$$H_i'(1) = \frac{1}{1 - np_1 q_1 - \ldots - np_n q_n}$$

and thus the expected number of infected nodes is

$$\mathsf{E}[S] = \frac{1}{1 - np_1 q_1 - \ldots - np_n q_n}.$$

From the above computations the following criterion can be deduced (see [33] for a detailed proof):

Theorem 2. *Let a network with n different types of edges be described by the Erdős-Rényi model in which an edge of type i exists with probability q_i and assume it transmits a malware with probability p_i. Then, an epidemic will not occur if*

$$1 - np_1q_1 - \ldots - np_nq_n > 0$$

is fullfilled.

In other words, the expected value of the amount of infected nodes remains finite in this situation.

3.3   Predictions for an Unlimited Outbreak

If an epidemic is possible, e.g., if the criterion given by Theorem 2 is violated, we are interested in the probability P_{ep} of an epidemic, i.e., the probability that an extensive number of nodes is infected. In case an epidemic occurs, we further want to compute the fraction f of affected nodes. These quantities can be computed based on percolation theory [32] with the help of the so called *dual* network consisting of the same nodes as the original one but with all edges pointing in opposite direction [33]. Adapting our notation described in Sect. 3.1, we use a superscript "d" for all objects that relate to the dual network.

Similar to (2) above, we denote the generating function for the degree distribution by $\mathcal{G}$ and we write

$$z_i = \frac{\partial}{\partial x_i}\mathcal{G}(1,\ldots,1;1,\ldots,1)$$

for the average degree of edges of type i. Similar computations as in Sect. 3.2 show that the fraction of affected nodes in case of an epidemic is

$$f = 1 - \mathcal{G}(H_1^d(1),\ldots,H_n^d(1);1,\ldots,1),$$

where $H_i^d(1)$ is the solution of the (nonlinear) equation system

$$H_i^d(1) = \frac{\partial}{\partial y_i}\mathcal{G}(H_1^d(1),\ldots,H_n^d(1);1,\ldots,1)/z_i \qquad (5)$$

for all i. If the system does not admit an analytical solution, numerical approximations can do sufficiently well.

Additionally, the probability of an epidemic is found to be [33]

$$P_{ep} = 1 - \mathcal{G}(1,\ldots,1;H_1(1),\ldots,H_n(1)),$$

where $H_i(1)$ is determined by

$$H_i(1) = \frac{\partial}{\partial x_i}\mathcal{G}(1,\ldots,1;H_1(1),\ldots,H_n(1))/z_i$$

for all i. Again, this system can be solved numerically.

Example 3. *Assume an Erdős-Rényi model for all kind of edges so that an edge of type i exists with probability q_i in the original network before infection. Further, assume that each of the n classes has a specific probability p_i of transmitting a malware. Working out the corresponding generating functions shows that the infected network can again be described by an Erdős-Rényi model with reduced (joint) probability $q_i p_i$ for existence of an infected edge of type i. In order to find the fraction f of affected nodes, one needs to solve the system*

$$H_i^d(1) = \exp\left\{ n \sum_{j=1}^n q_j p_j (H_j^d(1) - 1) \right\}$$

for $H_i^d(1)$ for all i, which is identical to the system that determined the probability P_{ep} for an epidemic. As the right hand side does not depend on i, all H_i^d are equal and be denoted by H. If the condition from Theorem 2 is not fulfilled, i.e. if $s := n \sum_{i=1}^n q_i p_i > 1$, there exists a unique solution $H(s)$ in the open interval $(0, 1)$, namely [33]

$$H(s) = -\frac{W(-se^{-s})}{s}$$

where $W(z)$ denotes the principal branch of the Lambert W-function [38]. Thus,

$$P_{ep} = f = 1 - \exp\{s(H-1)\} = 1 - H = 1 + \frac{W(-se^{-s})}{s}.$$

However, the equality of f and P_{ep} is generally not valid.

4   Modeling Malware Spreading in Networks

At present, there are numerous ways known, how a malware spreads within an ICT network. Nevertheless, only a few means of propagation account for most malware infections, as described in [6]. The biggest part, around 44.8%, is represented by malware which requires user interaction for propagation, e.g., downloading and installing some software or simply clicking on a link. A similarly large part, around 43.2%, uses the "Autorun" functionality provided by Windows, i.e., malware is automatically installed on a system as soon as a USB stick is plugged in or a network storage is mounted (here, we combined the values for "Autorun: USB" and "Autorun: Network" given in [6]). A comparably small amount, around 5.6%, exploits vulnerabilities in software and operating systems to propagate from one system to another (here, we combined the values for the categories "Exploit: Update Long Available", "Exploit: Update Available" and "Exploit: Zero-Day" given in [6]), while the reamining 6.4% comprise File Infector, Password Brute Force and Office Macros.

To illustrate the flexibility of our model, we focus on these three most common means of propagation and describe, how our framework can be applied on the following scenarios

(1) Propagation using phishing emails sent to all contacts of a user
(2) Propagation over an infected network drive shared by several users
(3) Propagation based on (known) vulnerabilities of physically connected computers

Each of the described scenarios uses a different part of the ICT network to attack, but all of them share the following feature: malware that starts spreading in one node does not affect all neighbors with the same likelihood but the probability of transmission is influenced by other factors. In the following subsections, we will demonstrate which factors influence the transmission probability and in Sect. 5 we will visualize the spreading process for one specific scenario.

4.1 Propagation Using Phishing Emails

Among the means of propagation requiring user interaction, the most prominent example is based on phishing emails [6]. In short, an employee finds a message in his mailbox from a seemingly reliable organization (especially names of well known banks or insurance companies are frequently used). In this message, the user is requested to click on a link or open a document to get further information. Clicking on such a link will typically guide the user to a website and start a drive-by download, hence installing a malware without the user being aware of it. In the context of our scenario, we will assume that this malware then forwards the forged link or document to all email contacts of the infected employee. Accordingly, the process starts all over again.

Such a process is conveniently modeled as a spreading over the network of email contacts, which can be interpreted rather as a social than a technical network. However, assuming that every employee is equal likely to click on such a link is far from realistic, in particular when people have different background and knowledge. This heterogeneity of the email contact network can be captured by grouping employees into different classes depending on how likely the are to follow the instructions of a forged message. A nominal categorization (e.g., into classes of "low", "medium" and "high" likelihood) can be performed based on, e.g., a survey among the employees or the experience from awareness trainings.

For this kind of infection, such a categorization directly yields a decomposition of the links in the contact network (corresponding to the classes described described in Sect. 3.1): if an employee is highly likely to install the malware on his computer, all his contacts are highly likely to receive the corresponding email (similarly for the classes "medium" and "low"). Thus, all connections are characterized by their starting point. Additionally, the likelihood of a successful propagation, i.e., an employee following a link received by email from a co-worker, depends to a certain amount on how much the receiver trusts the sender of the email. In other words, if two employees exchange an extensive amount of emails, one of them is more likely to click on a link or open a document, if the email is coming from the other colleague. On the contrary, receiving an email with the request to follow a link from a co-worker with whom little or no previous email contact exists looks suspicious. Thus, the receiver is less likely to click on the link and the malware is less likely to successfully propagate. Such information can also be included in the classification of the links by modeling the respective transmission probability as a random variable.

After classifying all edges, it is further necessary to assign a specific probability to each type to fully apply the percolation model. As mentioned above, such assessments are typically based on either experts' opinions or questionnaires filled out by the employees (e.g., by asking how often they have clicked on such links in the past). We want to point out that such empirical data has a tendency to be biased as employees tend to underestimate the number of incidents. However, using a median can mitigate this effect [39]. A complete simulation of such a scenario to illustrate the application of our stochastic model is described in Sect. 5 below.

4.2   Propagation Over Shared Network Drives

As already mentioned above, the second very common way of propagation for a malware is to use the Windows' autorun functionality [6], which is activated when a USB stick is plugged in or a shared network drive is mounted. In this case, the relevant system files implementing the autorun functionality are changed by the malware such that malicious code is executed whenever the device (USB stick or shared network drive) is mounted. The initial infection of a system can be realized in several ways: either by a drive-by download or by an infected USB stick, e.g., given as a present to an employee or placed at some public area within the organization.

Whereas the spreading process via phishing emails relates more to the organization's social network (cf. Sect. 4.1), the propagation over shared network drives is based on the technical network. In particular, we can model the malware propagation over the logical links in the organization's network, i.e., taking into account the shared network drives and the systems (user) having access to them. Usually, numerous users have access to these shared network drives. Thus, once the shared network drive is infected, a larger number of systems becomes infected in a shorter time, compared to the phishing email scenario described in Sect. 4.1.

Similarly to the propagation via phishing emails, we can distinguish in this scenario between different classes of links in the logical network. In more detail, if an employee frequently connects to an infected shared network drive, the probability that the employee's system becomes infected can be categorized as "high". Accordingly, the less frequent a user mounts a network drive, the lower the probability for the malware to propagate to this system (the links are then corresponding to classes "medium' and "low"). After assigning a specific probability to each of these classes (using empirical data as already discussed in Sect. 4.1), we can apply our percolation model and simulate the malware propagation for this scenario similarly as described in Sect. 5.

4.3   Propagation by Exploiting System Vulnerabilities

In the third scenario, we look at malware spreading based on the exploitation of software vulnerabilities representing the third major category for propagation techniques according to [6]. Compared to the usage of phishing emails or autorun functionalities, this scenario requires less user interaction and is based more on the technical networks structure, i.e., the physical links between the systems. Accordingly, a malware using this propagation technique has to be more sophisticated than in the previous scenarios, since it has to identify and adapt to the individual vulnerabilities present in an organization's network.

Modeling the spreading process of the malware has a strong focus on an organization's physical network structure as well as the individual systems operating in that network. In short, the malware scans for vulnerabilities in adjacent systems and exploits them to firstly gain access to these systems and then obtain administrator's rights to propagate further. Hence, not all systems within the network are equally likely to be infected by the malware. Thus, based on the existence of vulnerabilities in the different systems within the network, the links between these systems can be divided in the three classes "low", "medium" and "high", like in the previous scenarios. In this case, not only the number of vulnerabilities of a system is relevant but also the severity of those vulnerabilities has to be taken into account. In more detail, a system with a large number of vulnerabilities has a "high" chance of being infected with malware, but also a system with fewer but more severe vulnerabilities might fall into the same class (similar considerations can be done for classes "medium" and "low").

Furthermore, the assignment of probabilities to each of the three classes is more complex compared to the other scenarios. As pointed out in Sects. 4.1 and 4.2, the probabilities can be chosen based on experts' opinions but this empirical data can be extended and enhanced due to the availability of detailed information on existing vulnerabilities, e.g., coming from external repositories like NIST's National Vulnerability Database. Although accessing this information is quite easy, integrating it to estimate a probability might be difficult. Nevertheless, when a representative value is defined for each class, our framework can be applied to simulate the propagation within the network using percolation theory.

5   Implementation

A feature of the presented model is that it can be implemented quite easily. The effect of an infection on a network $G(V, E)$ after T time units can be determined with the following algorithm (pseudo-code taken from [39]).

```
1:  t ← 0
2:  while t < T
3:     for each infected node v in V, set N(v) ← {u ∈ V : (v, u) ⊆ E}
4:        for each neighboring node u ∈ N(v)
5:           let k be the class in which the edge v → u falls into,
6:           with likelihood p_k, infect u,
```

```
7:          t ← t + 1.
8:      endfor
9:    endfor
10: endwhile
```

This algorithm assumes a synchronous hopping of the infection from one node to the next and a time-discrete infection. Although this may appear as an over-simplification, we stress that real infections being able to jump at any time from one node to the other, discretizing the continuous process into sufficiently small time-steps provides a useful approximation of the true percolation. The theoretical model, however, is making assertions about the expected outbreak after in an unlimited time-horizon, and is as such not making assumptions on discrete or continuous time, and discrete only to the extent as the network graph is discrete.

Figure 1 shows a simulation of malware spreading based on phishing emails in a heterogeneous (left side) and a homogeneous (right side) network. As defined in the model (cf. Sect. 3.1), in the heterogeneous network users are divided into three classes, labeled "low", "medium" and "high" depending on how likely they are to click on a link. The class of the node influences the probability of forwarding the malware (as described in Sect. 4.1) and therefore also determines the class of the links originating from this node. In our scenario, infected nodes are colored red to facilitate visualization of the malware spreading. Regarding the propagation, we assume the following probabilities: a person of the class "high" has a chance of 0.6 forwarding the malware (plotted as solid links), for the class "medium" the chance is 0.3 (dashed links) and for the class "low" the chance is 0.1 (dotted links).

For our scenario, these values are chosen arbitrarily, since we just want to illustrate the mechanism, whereas in practice, such values can be obtained from empirical data (cf. Sect. 4.1). We compare our scenario to the standard situation of a homogeneous network where all users are assumed to behave similarly and thus a propagation over all edges is equally probable. In order to make this comparison as decent as possible, we choose the uniform probability of transmission to be the (weighted) average of the probabilities used for the heterogeneous case, which yielded $p_{av} = 0.3$ exactly.

Figure 1 illustrates a core feature of our approach: taking into account the structure in the network influences the prediction of the number of affected nodes. In this simulation, we select a node of the class "low" to be infected first (i.e., the user received a malicious email). Thus, the malware had a smaller chance to propagate further than in the homogeneous case such that less nodes are infected after 50 time units. Analogously, if we choose a node within the class "high" as starting point, more nodes will be infected.

However, there the simulation reveals even more information than can be displayed in a single plot. It further shows that the speed of infection changes with the model. As the infection started in a node of class "low", the number of infected nodes grows slower than in the homogeneous case. For this realization,

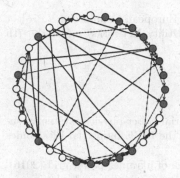 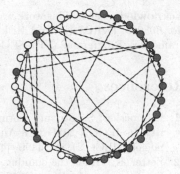

Fig. 1. Situation after 50 time units in a heterogeneous (left) and in a homogeneous (right) network

we observed the following values: in the heterogeneous case it took 38 time units to have 17 infected nodes, while in the homogeneous case this amount was reached after only 14 steps due to the higher likelihood of transmission of edges starting from the first infected node. Thus, a more precise view on the structure of the network yields a more accurate description of the spreading process.

6 Conclusion

Percolation appears as a quite powerful technique to describe spreading of an infection through a network with an arbitrary topology and is heavily applied in the field of disease spreading. In this article, we showed how percolation theory can be used to model the propagation of malware within an ICT network. Our stochastic model allows an analysis of non-uniform spreading by different probabilities of transmission representing different types of connections. Further, we provided linear equation systems for the expected size of an outbreak and discussed the probability of an epidemic. Additionally, we showed that simulations are extremely simple, and can quickly be used to verify the results and described explicit solutions for the Erdős-Rényi model.

To underline the relevance to realistic propagation mechanisms, we discussed three scenarios dealing with the major techniques of malware spreading: phishing emails, autorun functionalities and exploitation of vulnerabilities. All three scenarios are working on different types of networks within an organization, i.e., the social, logical and physical network, respectively, and we showed that our model is applicable on all three of those networks. Furthermore, we discussed the results for one scenario (propagation using phishing emails) in detail and to demonstrate the implementation of the algorithm.

While our stochastic framework captures the diversity of real life ICT networks, other aspects such as the impact of potential countermeasures are still open. This issue can be captured using novel methodologies like game theory to preserve the well-formulated mathematical basis of the approach [40,41]. Additional future work will also deal with an analysis of dynamic networks.

Acknowledgment. This work was supported by the European Commission's Project No. 608090, HyRiM (Hybrid Risk Management for Utility Networks) under the 7th Framework Programme (FP7-SEC-2013-1).

References

1. Karnouskos, S.: Stuxnet worm impact on industrial cyber-physical system security. In: IECON 2011–37th Annual Conference of the IEEE Industrial Electronics Society (IECON), pp. 4490–4494. IEEE (2011)
2. Zetter, K.: Inside the cunning, unprecedented hack of ukraines power grid (2016). https://www.wired.com/2016/03/inside-cunning-unprecedented-hack-ukraines-power-grid/
3. Gosk, S., Winter, T., Connor, T.: Iranian hackers claim cyber attack on New York dam (2015). http://www.nbcnews.com/news/us-news/iranian-hackers-claim-cyber-attack-new-york-dam-n484611
4. Francescani, C.: U.S. infrastructure can be hacked with google, simple passwords (2016). http://www.nbcnews.com/news/us-news/u-s-infrastructure-can-be-hacked-google-simple-passwords-n548661
5. SCADAhacker: Cyber security for critical infrastructure protection - scadahacker (2016). https://www.scadahacker.com/
6. Microsoft: Zeroing in on malware propagation methods (2011)
7. Grimmett, G.: Percolation. Springer, New York (1989)
8. Newman, M.E.J.: The spread of epidemic disease on networks. Phys. Rev. E **66**, 016128 (2002)
9. Poggi, S., Neri, F., Deytieux, V., Bates, A., Otten, W., Gilligan, C., Bailey, D.: Percolation-based risk index for pathogen invasion: application to soilborne disease in propagation systems. Phytopathology **103**(10), 1012–1019 (2013)
10. Zou, C.C., Gong, W., Towsley, D.: Code red worm propagation modeling and analysis. In: Proceedings of 9th ACM Conference on Computer and Communication Security, pp. 138–147 (2002)
11. Moore, D., Shannon, C., Voelker, G.M., Savage, S.: Internet quarantine: requirements for containing self-propagating code. In: Proceedings of INFOCOM 2003, vol. 3, pp. 1901–1910 (2003)
12. Ganesh, A., Massoulie, L., Towsley, D.: The effect of network topology on the spread of epidemics. In: Proceedings of INFOCOM 2005, vol. 2, pp. 1455–1466 (2005)
13. Zou, C.C., Towsley, D., Gong, W.: Modeling and simulation study of the propagation and defense of internet e-mail worms. IEEE Trans. Dependable Secure Comput. **4**(2), 105–118 (2007)
14. Chen, Z., Ji, C.: Spatial-temporal modeling of malware propagation in networks. IEEE Trans. Neural Netw. **16**(5), 1291–1303 (2005)
15. Miller, J.C.: Bounding the size and probability of epidemics on networks. Appl. Probab. Trust **45**, 498–512 (2008)
16. Sellke, S.H., Shroff, N.B., Bagchi, S.: Modeling and automated containment of worms. IEEE Trans. Dependable and Secure Comput. **5**(2), 71–86 (2008)
17. Yan, G., Eidenbenz, S.: Modeling propagation dynamics of bluetooth worms (extended version). IEEE Trans. Mob. Comput. **8**(3), 353–368 (2009)
18. Gao, C., Liu, J.: Modeling and restraining mobile virus propagation. IEEE Trans. Mob. Comput. **12**(3), 529–541 (2013)

19. Yu, S., Gu, G., Barnawi, A., Guo, S., Stojmenovic, I.: Malware propagation in large-scale networks. IEEE Trans. Knowl. Data Eng. **27**(1), 170–179 (2015)
20. Miller, J.C., Volz, E.M.: Incorporating disease and population structure into models of SIR disease in contact networks. PLoS ONE **8**(8), 1–14 (2013)
21. Callaway, D.S., Newman, M.E.J., Strogatz, S.H., Watts, D.J.: Network robustness, fragility: percolation on random graphs. Phys. Rev. Lett. **85**(25), 5468 (2000)
22. Sander, L.M., Warren, C.P., Sokolov, I.M., Simon, C., Koopman, J.: Percolation on heterogeneous networks as a model for epidemics. Math. Biosci. **180**, 293–305 (2002)
23. Kenah, E., Robins, M.: Second look at spread of epidemics on networks. Phys. Rev. E **76**, 036113 (2007)
24. Slathe, M., Jones, J.H.: Dynamics and control of diseases in networks with community structure. PLoS Comput. Biol. **4**(6), e1000736 (2010)
25. Schwartz, N., Cohen, R., ben-Avraham, D., Barabasi, A.L., Havlin, S.: Percolation in directed scale-free networks. Phys. Rev. E **66**, 015104 (2002)
26. Cohen, R., ben Avraham, D., Havlin, S.: Percolation critical exponents in scale-free networks. Phys. Rev. E **66**, 036113 (2002)
27. Cohen, R., Erez, K., ben Avraham, D., Havlin, S.: Resilience of the internet to random breakdowns. Phys. Rev. Lett. **85**(21), 4626 (2000)
28. Cohen, R., Erez, K., ben-Avraham, D., Havlin, S.: Breakdown of the internet under intentional attack. Phys. Rev. Lett. **86**, 3682–3685 (2001)
29. Newman, M.E.J., Ferrario, C.R.: Competing epidemics on complex networks. Phys. Rev. E **84**, 036106 (2011)
30. Newman, M.E., Ferrario, C.R.: Interacting epidemics and coinfection on contact networks. PLoS ONE **8**(8), e71321 (2013)
31. Green, B., Prince, D., Roedig, U., Busby, J., Hutchison, D.: Socio-technical security analysis of industrial control systems (ICS). In: 2nd International Symposium for ICS and SCADA Cyber Security Research 2014 (ICS-CSR 2014), vol. 9 (2014)
32. Meyers, L.A., Newman, M.E.J., Pourbohloul, B.: Predicting epidemics on directed contact networks. J. Theoret. Biol. **240**(3), 400–418 (2006)
33. König, S.: Error propagation through a network with non-uniform failure (2016). arXiv: 1604.03558
34. Wilf, H.S.: Generatingfunctionology. Academic Press, Cambridge (1994)
35. Newman, M.E.J., Strogatz, S.H., Watts, D.J.: Random graphs with arbitrary degree distributions and their applications. Phys. Rev. E **64**, 026118 (2001)
36. Beck, A.: Entwicklung einer Metrik zur automatisierten Analyse und Bewertung von Bedrohungsszenarien mit Hilfe neuraler Netzwerke (2016)
37. Erdős, P., Rényi, A.: On random graphs. Publicationes Mathematicae **6**, 290–297 (1959)
38. Corless, R.M., Gonnet, G.H., Hare, D.E.G., Jeffrey, D.J., Knuth, D.E.: On the Lambert W function. Comput. Math. **5**, 329–359 (1996)
39. König, S., Rass, S., Schauer, S., Beck, A.: Risk propagation analysis and visualization using percolation theory. Int. J. Adv. Comput. Sci. Appl. (IJACSA), **7**(1) (2016)
40. Rass, S.: On Game-Theoretic Risk Management (Part One) - Towards a Theory of Games with Payoffs that are Probability-Distributions. ArXiv e-prints, June 2015. http://arxiv.org/abs/1506.07368
41. Rass, S.: On game-theoretic risk management (part two) - algorithms to compute nash-equilibria in games with distributions as payoffs (2015). arXiv: 1511.08591

Network Security

Creating and Detecting IPv6 Transition Mechanism-Based Information Exfiltration Covert Channels

Bernhards Blumbergs[1]([envelope]), Mauno Pihelgas[1], Markus Kont[1], Olaf Maennel[2], and Risto Vaarandi[2]

[1] NATO Cooperative Cyber Defense Center of Excellence, Tallinn, Estonia
{bernhards.blumbergs,mauno.pihelgas,markus.kont}@ccdcoe.org
[2] Tallinn University of Technology, Tallinn, Estonia
{olaf.maennel,risto.vaarandi}@ttu.ee

Abstract. The Internet Protocol Version 6 (IPv6) transition opens a wide scope for potential attack vectors. IPv6 transition mechanisms could allow the set-up of covert egress communication channels over an IPv4-only or dual-stack network, resulting in full compromise of a target network. Therefore effective tools are required for the execution of security operations for assessment of possible attack vectors related to IPv6 security.

In this paper, we review relevant transition technologies, describe and analyze two newly-developed IPv6 transition mechanism-based proof-of-concept tools for the establishment of covert information exfiltration channels. The analysis of the generated test cases confirms that IPv6 and various evasion techniques pose a difficult task for network security monitoring. While detection of various transition mechanisms is relatively straightforward, other evasion methods prove more challenging.

Keywords: IPv6 security · IPv6 transition · Covert channels · Computer network operations · Red teaming · Monitoring and detection

1 Introduction

In this work we explore possible uses of IPv6 transition technologies for creation of covert channels over dual-stack and native IPv4 connectivity to exfiltrate information for red teaming [6] purposes. An analysis in Sect. 2 shows that this approach is novel and no implementations of such newly-developed tools have been identified previously.

The main contributions of this paper are:

1. two novel approaches for covert channel creation with IPv6 transition mechanisms;
2. fully self-developed proof-of-concept tools that implement the proposed methods (nc64 and tun64);

© Springer International Publishing AG 2016
B.B. Brumley and J. Röning (Eds.): NordSec 2016, LNCS 10014, pp. 85–100, 2016.
DOI: 10.1007/978-3-319-47560-8_6

3. commonly-used protocol tunneling and developed proof-of-concept tool detection comparison table (Appendix A); and
4. a reproducible virtual lab environment providing detection results using opensource network security monitoring tools.

The Internet is in a period of tremendous growth, currently evolving toward the Internet of Anything (IoA). The more widely-deployed IPv4 standard and IPv6 are incompatible, and they can communicate only via transition mechanisms and technologies [38,44]. This introduces an additional layer of complexity and inherent security concerns for the transition and co-existence period [1]. The adoption of IPv6, and availability per the core backbone of the Internet infrastructure and edge networks, varies [10,12]. IPv6 launch campaigns rapidly increased the number of autonomous systems (AS) announcing IPv6 prefix[1,2]. Nevertheless, connecting to the IPv6 Internet while maintaining scalability and minimal overall complexity often means that edge networks deploy various transition mechanisms [36,44], possibly meaning that local area networks (LANs) will continue to use primary IPv4 for an undefined period.

IPv6 protocol implementations and security solutions are relatively new, already supported by default by modern operating systems, and have not yet reached the level of acceptable quality and maturity [15,44]. The lack of expertise and technological maturity result in IPv6 being considered in most cases as a "back-door" protocol, allowing evasion of security mechanisms [21,23]. This is important particularly when an attack originates from inside the network, as network security devices are commonly configured and placed on the perimeter under the assumption that intruders will always come from outside [39].

In the age of advanced high-profile targeted attacks executed by sophisticated and resourceful adversaries, IPv6 is seen as an additional vector for persistent and covert attacks [29,41]. The length of the transition period cannot be estimated, and it can be assumed that even once the entire Internet is native IPv6, there will still be systems running deprecated IPv6 functionality specifications, or heritage transition mechanisms.

Our research shows that current Network Intrusion Detection System (NIDS) solutions have serious drawbacks for handling IPv6 traffic. Addressing these shortcomings would require redevelopment of the principles how NIDSs reassemble packet streams, and correlation of distinct sessions. The described IPv6 transition-based methods (i.e. nc64 and tun64) use both IP version implementations in the same protocol stack. Attribution of these connections to a covert channel is therefore difficult. By comparison, common protocol tunneling approaches (e.g. SSH, DNS) would be easier to detect by an automated solution or human analyst since their behavior pattern is well known and understood.

In this paper, Sect. 2 reviews background and related work, evasion mechanisms, and covert channels; Sect. 3 describes common protocol tunneling approaches and newly-developed attack tool implementation and design; Sect. 4

---

[1] IPv6 Enabled Networks, RIPE NCC. http://v6asns.ripe.net/v/6 (Accessed 15/04/2016).
[2] IPv6 CIDR Report. http://www.cidr-report.org/v6/as2.0/ (Accessed 15/04/2016).

describes the attack scenario, simulation environment, and generated test cases; Sect. 5 discusses experiment execution results (presented in Table 1), and additionally gives recommendations for such attack detection and mitigation possibilities; and Sect. 6 offers conclusions and future research directions.

2   Background and Related Previous Work

The aim for IPv6 was to evolve and eliminate the technical drawbacks and limitations of the IPv4 standard. However, IPv6 reintroduced almost the same security issues and, moreover, added new security concerns and vulnerabilities [11,19]. Current IPv6 attack tools, such as the *THC-IPv6* [21], *SI6-IPv6*[3], *Topera*[4], and *Chiron*[5] toolkits, include the majority of techniques for abuse of IPv6 vulnerabilities, and can be utilized for network security assessment and IPv6 implementation verification.

Already in 1998, Ptacek and Newsham in their research paper [33] showed that NIDS evasions are possible and pose a serious threat. A proof-of-concept tool, *v00d00N3t*, for establishment of covert channels over ICMPv6 [28] has demonstrated the potential for such approach, though it has not been released publicly. Techniques for evading NIDS based on mobile IPv6 implementations reveal that it is possible to trick NIDS using dynamically-changing communication channels [9]. Also, it could be viable to create a covert channel by hiding information within IPv6 and its extension headers [26]. Network intrusion detection system (NIDS) and firewall evasions based on IPv6 packet fragmentation and extension header chaining attacks, have been acknowledged [1,2,21]. Although current Requests for Comments (RFCs) have updated the processing of IPv6 atomic fragments [17], discarding overlapping fragments [24] and enforcing security requirements for extension headers [20,25], these attacks will remain possible in the years ahead as vendors and developers sometimes fail to follow the RFC requirements or implement their own interpretation of them. General approaches for NIDS evasions have been described and analyzed [3,7,32,43], with the basic principles behind evasions based on the entire TCP/IP protocol stack. Advanced evasion techniques (AETs) involve creating combinations of multiple atomic evasion techniques, potentially allowing evasion of detection by the majority of NIDS solutions [30]. Evasions are possible due to NIDS design, implementation and configuration specifics, and low network latency requirements [15].

Existing approaches and technologies consider native IPv6 network implementation and connectivity, and do not take into account possible methods for network security device evasions and covert channel establishment over IPv6 transition mechanisms, in order to reach the command and control (CnC) servers

---

[3] SI6 Networks' IPv6 Toolkit. http://www.si6networks.com/tools/ipv6toolkit/ (Accessed 10/11/2015).

[4] Topera IPv6 analysis tool: the other side. http://toperaproject.github.io/topera/ (Accessed 10/11/2015).

[5] Chiron. http://www.secfu.net/tools-scripts/ (Accessed 10/11/2015).

over IPv4 only or dual-stack Internet connectivity. To the best of our knowledge no publicly available tool implements transition technology-based attacks.

3   Covert Channel Implementations

3.1   Protocol Tunneling

Protocol tunneling and IPv6 tunneling-based transition mechanisms pose a major security risk, as they allow bypassing of improperly-configured or IPv4-only network security devices [11,18,22,23,35]. IPv6 tunnel-based transition mechanisms, as well as general tunneling approaches (e.g. HTTP, SSH, DNS, ICMP, IPsec), can bypass network protection mechanisms. However, IPv6 tunnels add to the heap of possible tunneling mechanisms, leading to unmanaged and insecure IPv6 connections [35]. Moreover, dual-stack hosts and Internet browsers favor IPv6 over IPv4 [10]. Various protocol tunneling approaches can be used to set up a covert channel by encapsulating exfiltrated information in networking protocols. Covert channels based on DNS, HTTP(S), ICMP [5], and SSH [13] protocol tunneling implementations are acknowledged here as the most common approaches for eluding network detection mechanisms, due to both their frequent use and standard network policy, which allows outbound protocols and ports for user requirements and remote network administration needs. For the purposes of the test cases we consider mature and publicly available tools for protocol tunneling establishment.

3.2   Proof-of-Concept Nc64 Tool

We have developed a proof-of-concept tool, nc64[6], for the creation of information exfiltration channel over dual-stack networks using sequential IPv4 and IPv6 sessions. The tool's source code is publicly available under MIT license.

Signature-based IDSs reassemble packets and data flows, in order to conduct inspection against a known signature database. This is done on per-session basis (e.g. a TCP session). If the data is fragmented across multiple sessions, then the IDS cannot retrieve the full information to evaluate whether the traffic is malicious. In such scenario NIDS has to be context aware in order to be able to correlate and reconstruct the original stream from multiple sequential ones. This is very challenging due to performance considerations. While any set of networking protocols could be used for a sequential session creation, the security, transition, and immaturity of IPv6 makes it a preferred choice. When considering NIDS separate session correlation possibilities, IP protocol switching would make it harder since destination IPv4 and IPv6 addresses are different. In a dual-stack operating system, IPv4 and IPv6 protocols are implemented side by side, thus adding a layer of separation between the two standards and making it more difficult for IDSs to reassemble data. Additionally, a single host can have multiple global IPv6 addresses, making the correlation to a single host even harder.

---

[6] nc64 https://github.com/lockout/nc64 (Accessed 12/03/2016).

To exfiltrate data from the source host to a destination CnC server over sequential IPv4 and IPv6 sessions, the data must be split into smaller chunks (i.e. up to IPv6 MTU of 1500B). Alternation between IPv4 and IPv6 per session has to be controlled to minimize the amount of information that is sent over a single IP protocol version in successive sessions (e.g. not allowing three or more sequential IPv4 sessions). This control would avoid partial reassembly and deny successful payload inspection by NIDS.

A CnC server has both IPv4 and IPv6 addresses on which it listens for incoming connections. Once the connection is established, the listener service receives sessions and reassembles data in sequence of reception. This can be hard to accomplish if a stateless transport layer protocol is being used (i.e. UDP) or data chunk size exceeds the maximum path MTU (e.g. causing packet fragmentation).

Our proof-of-concept tool, nc64, is written in Python 3 using standard libraries. It implements the aforementioned principles, and additionally:

1. provides both the listener server and client part in one Python module;
2. accepts user-specified data from a standard input, which provides flexibility and freedom of usage;
3. requires both IPv4 and IPv6 addresses for the destination CnC listener, and can have a list of IPv6 addresses in case the CnC server has multiple IPv6 addresses configured;
4. supports UDP and TCP transport layer protocols, as these are the main ones used in computer networks;
5. enables the destination port to be freely selected to comply with firewall egress rules and match the most common outbound protocol ports (e.g. HTTP(S), DNS), and also allows for setting and randomizing of the source port for UDP-based communications;
6. provides an optional payload Base64 encoding for binary data transmission, and to some degree can be treated as obfuscation if the IDS does not support encoding detection and decoding. It has to be noted that Base64-encoded traffic might reveal the exfiltrated data in the overall traffic since it would stand out, which would also apply when using payload encryption;
7. allows for the setting and randomizing of timing intervals between sequential sessions for an additional layer of covertness and to mitigate possible timing pattern prediction and detection by NIDS;
8. implements control over how many sequential sessions of the same protocol can be tolerated before forcing a switch to the other protocol, ensuring that small files are sent over both IP protocols; and
9. supports additional debugging features, exfiltrated data hash calculation, and transmission statistics.

3.3 Proof-of-Concept Tun64 Tool

We have developed a second proof-of-concept tool, tun64[7], which exfiltrates information by abusing tunneling-based IPv6 transition mechanism capabilities

---

[7] tun64 https://github.com/lockout/tun64 (Accessed 12/03/2016).

over the IPv4-only computer network. The tool's source code is publicly available under MIT license.

Most tunneling-based IPv6 transition mechanisms rely on IPv4 as a link layer by using 6in4 encapsulation [31], whereby an IPv6 packet is encapsulated in IPv4 and the protocol number is set to decimal value 41 (the IANA-assigned payload type number for IPv6). Besides 6in4 encapsulation, we also acknowledge GRE (protocol-47) [14] as an applicable encapsulation mechanism for 6in4-in-GRE double encapsulation. When 6in4 (protocol-41) encapsulation is used, duplex connectivity might not be possible if the network relies on strict NAT. However, for the attack scenario considered in this paper (see Sect. 4.1), a one-way communication channel for information exfiltration to the CnC server is sufficient, making UDP the preferred transport layer protocol [34].

Most of the transition techniques cannot solve transition problems and hence are not appropriate for real-world implementation and widespread deployment [44]. Although tunnel-based transition approaches are considered deprecated by the IETF, some of these technologies continue to be supported by modern operating systems and ISPs. The 6over4 [8], ISATAP [37,40], and 6to4 [27,42] transition mechanisms were selected for implementation in our proof-of-concept tool for tunneling-based information exfiltration. Selection of these mechanisms was based upon the tunnel establishment from the target host or network, their support by either operating systems or local network infrastructure devices [37].

Our proof-of-concept tool, tun64, is written in Python 2.7 using the Scapy library[8]. It implements the aforementioned principles and additionally:

1. provides only the client part, thus relying on standard packet capture tools for reception and reassembly (e.g. tcpdump, Wireshark, tshark);
2. supports TCP, UDP, and SCTP as transport layer protocols;
3. emulates 6over4, 6to4, and ISATAP tunneling by assigning source and destination IPv6 addresses according to the transition protocol specification;
4. enables usage of 6to4 anycast relay routers if the tool is being tested in real Internet conditions, although in our simulated network, 6to4 relay routers or agents are not implemented;
5. allows additional GRE encapsulation to create a 6in4-in-GRE double encapsulated packet, which may allow obfuscation if the NIDS is not performing a full packet decapsulation and analysis;
6. gives an option to freely specify source and destination ports, in order to comply with firewall egress rules; and
7. supports sending a single message instead of files or standard input, a functionality designed with proof-of-concept approach in mind.

4   Testing Environment and Test Description

4.1   Attack Scenario

Our testing environment and experiments are designed according to the following scenario. The attack target is a small- to medium-sized research organization

---

[8] Scapy project. http://www.secdev.org/projects/scapy/ (Accessed 10/11/2015).

(up to 100 network nodes). Research organization assumes it is running an IPv4-only network, even though all the network hosts are dual-stack and their ISP just recently started to provide also IPv6 connectivity. Network administrators have implemented IPv4 security policies and only the following most common egress ports and services are allowed through the firewall: DNS (udp/53, tcp/53), HTTP (tcp/80), HTTPS (tcp/443), SSH (tcp/22), and ICMP (echo). All network hosts can establish a direct connection to the Internet without proxies or any other connection handlers. This organization was recently contracted by government to conduct advanced technological research and therefore has sensitive information processed and stored on the network hosts and servers. A red team, assuming the role of reasonably sophisticated attacker with persistent foothold in the research organization's network, is tasked to exfiltrate sensitive information from the target network. The red team has a selection of tools available at its disposal for the establishment of a covert information exfiltration channel, as described in Sect. 3.

4.2   Testing Environment

To ensure reproducibility of the testbed, we created several *bash* scripts that leverage the Vagrant[9] environment automation tool. The scripts are publicly available in a GitHub repository[10]. A network map of the virtual testing environment is presented in Fig. 1.

The host and CnC devices were built on 32-bit Kali Linux 2.0, which comes bundled with several tunneling tools. Router1 served as the gateway for the target organization, and Router2 as an ISP node in the simulated Internet (SINET). Both routers were also built as authoritative DNS servers to facilitate usage of the Iodine tool, which was explicitly configured to query them during the tests. Two monitoring machines were built to provide detection capability. The first node was connected with a tap to the network link between the routers and all packets were copied to its monitoring interface. Second node was created to avoid conflicts between monitoring tools, and was therefore not used for capture.

In order to create identical testing conditions, we decided to store a packet capture (PCAP) file for each combination of the exfiltration tool, destination port number, transport layer protocol, and IP version. Additionally, several distinct operation modes were tested for the nc64 (e.g. both plain-text and base64 encoded payload) and tun64 (e.g. ISATAP, 6to4, and 6over4 tunneling mechanism emulation) tools, as these significantly impact the nature of the network traffic. Overall, 126 packet capture files were generated to be used as test cases. In the next phase we used the same monitoring nodes to run a selection of popular detection tools which would analyze these PCAP files, produce connection logs, and possibly generate alerts for suspicious activity.

---

[9] Vagrant. https://www.vagrantup.com/ (Accessed 07/12/2015).

[10] Automated virtual testing environment. https://github.com/markuskont/exfil-test bench (Accessed 07/12/2015).

We considered a number of open-source monitoring tools that are often used for network security analysis. These include the signature-based NIDSs Snort[11] and Suricata[12], as well as the network traffic analyzers Bro[13] and Moloch[14]. For Suricata, we used the Emerging Threats (ET) ruleset, while for Snort we experimented with rulesets from both SourceFire (SF) and ET signature providers. Furthermore, we consulted with security vendors. In some cases their solutions were based on the same open-source tools, albeit lacking IPv6 support due to small customer demand. Thus, we decided to focus only on evaluating open-source network detection tools. In our tests, the data exfiltrated from the host system comprise the highly sensitive */etc/shadow* file and the *root* user's private *SSH* cryptographic keys. Both of which could be used for gaining unauthorized access to potentially many other systems in the organization.

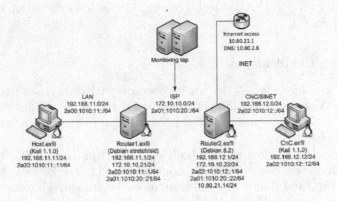

Fig. 1. Testing environment network map

5   Experiment Execution and Discussion of Results

The results of the experiments are presented in an extensive table (see Table 1 in Appendix A). Each row in the table describes a single attack, while the columns represent a detection tool that was used to attempt its detection. In our results, we distinguished four potential outcomes for a test:

1. a positive match (denoted by letter Y and a green cell in the table) was clearly identified as malicious activity with appropriate alerts;
2. a partial or abnormal footprint (P and yellow cell) which raised an alert, but the alert did not describe the activity appropriately;

---

[11] Snort v2.9.8.0. http://manual.snort.org/ (Accessed 07/12/2015).
[12] Suricata v2.1beta4. http://suricata-ids.org/docs/ (Accessed 07/12/2015).
[13] Bro v2.4.1 https://www.bro.org/documentation/index.html (Accessed 07/12/2015).
[14] Moloch v0.12.1. https://github.com/aol/moloch (Accessed 07/12/2015).

3. a potential visible match (V and orange cell) from connection logs which requires human analysis or sophisticated anomaly detection for a positive match; and

4. in the worst case, no visible alerts nor connection logs were generated (N and red cell).

Firstly, we observed that any exfiltration tool utilizing a specific application layer protocol should adhere to its standard port numbers if the malicious user aims to evade detection. For example, a HTTP tunnel on port 22 triggered an *outbound SSH Scan* alert with the ET ruleset, whereas when port 80 was used, only HTTP connection logs were generated such that we classified the attack as being only *visible*. Note that we marked the *outbound SSH Scan* alert for the HTTP tunnel on port 22 only as a *partial* match because it was incorrectly identified as an outbound SSH connection. Additionally, the same rule was responsible for a partial match against the nc64 technique on port 22. Furthermore, an alert was raised if a SSH header was detected on port 443, or if that port was used to send unencrypted HTTP traffic. Similarly, if abnormal (non-DNS) traffic was identified on UDP port 53, the ET ruleset triggered alerts for either *non-compliant traffic to DNS protocol*, or for being *overly aggressive* (i.e., having too many connections). These signatures were easily bypassed if TCP port 53 was used. However, it has to be noted that most server applications can be bound to any applicable port number (e.g. SSH on tcp/2022, HTTPS console over tcp/8443), and thus can potentially be used to avoid or obscure detection.

The difference between SF and ET rulesets, in their default configurations, is significant. The former seems to focus solely on perimeter intrusions, and hence could not detect any malicious outbound traffic in our tests. Furthermore, the ET ruleset produced slightly different results in Snort and Suricata. Most importantly, the former could clearly identify ICMP Ptunnel as the tool used for traffic exfiltration. Bro does not employ any traditional signatures like Snort or Suricata, but does create logs for all identified connections. As such, it was able to produce log records of all test cases. However, although Bro does not generate alerts, it does have an interesting log file named *weird.log* wherein a record of detected anomalous connections is kept. In fact, during our attacks, several *weird.log* records were generated for non-compliant traffic on port 53. Additionally, Bro's SSH connection parser malfunctioned while processing non-standard traffic, and abnormal logs could be observed in the detection system. Moloch provides no alerts, but is designed as a packet capture, indexing and visualization tool. In the most recent release, at the time of conducting the experiment, Moloch does not support IPv6 due to various limitations when indexing 128-bit IP addresses[15]. Therefore, IPv6-only iterations were unnoticed while IPv4 sessions generated by nc64 in dual-stack configuration were *visible*. The *t6to4* mode in tun64 encapsulates the IPv6 packet as payload making it visible in IPv4

---

[15] Moloch 0.14.0 2016/05/08 CHANGELOG specifies a notice that "[IPv6] support is experimental, and will change with ES 5.0." https://github.com/aol/moloch/blob/master/CHANGELOG (Accessed 16/08/2016).

indexing system. This was observed only in cases of TCP connections without additional GRE encapsulation.

From the executed test results, detection of malicious activity by NIDS rules was based predominantly on the direction of network traffic, protocol, and destination port. This detection approach is generally favored because it uses resources (e.g. CPU, RAM) efficiently, with an expensive payload analysis attempted only after the preceding match conditions are achieved. In most cases, the nc64 tool avoided being detected, and Table 1 shows which protocol/port combinations can be used to minimize detection by selected NIDS solutions. In comparison with other exfiltration tools, nc64 performed very well on avoiding rule-based detection, and moreover could potentially elude payload inspection. In contrast, the tun64 tool was detected in the majority of cases, since protocol-41 and protocol-47 triggered the rules and generated warning messages by NIDSs. 6to4 tunneling emulation was detected when TCP or 6in4-in-GRE encapsulation was used, suggesting that double encapsulation is considered more suspicious. However, if an organization relies on IPv6 tunneling-based transition mechanisms utilizing 6in4 or GRE encapsulation, such warnings might be silenced or ignored by network-monitoring personnel. In contrast to other tunneling tools the approach taken by tun64 is feasible only if the network conditions comply with the specific operational requirements.

6   Conclusions

In this paper, the authors addressed a fundamental problem which could allow to bypass NIDSs by using the IPv6 tunneling-based and dual-stack transition mechanisms in a certain way. The proof-of-concept tools were prototyped to further verify under which circumstances the evasion of major open-source and commercial NIDS and monitoring solutions would be possible. Developed tools, tested alongside with other well known protocol tunneling tools, proved to be able to evade detection and addressed certain shortcomings in the core principles of how modern NIDSs work.

It has to be noted, that any reasonably sophisticated method for exfiltrating data will be hard to detect in real-time by existing NIDSs, especially in situations where the data is split into smaller chunks and the resulting pieces use different connections or protocols (e.g. IPv4 and IPv6). Detecting such activity would require the capability to correlate the detection information in near real-time across different connections/flows. And current NIDS solutions typically lack such capabilities. This is theoretically possible, but would most likely incur a significant performance penalty and an increased number of false positives. There are several possibilities to attempt correlating flows using both IPv4 and IPv6 protocols. If the destination host (i.e. CnC) used in multi-protocol exfiltration has a DNS entry for both A and AAAA records, it would be possible to perform a reverse lookup to identify that the connections are going to the same domain name using IPv4 and IPv6 protocols simultaneously. This should not happen under normal circumstances, since IPv6 is usually the preferred protocol on dual-stack hosts. Another option would be to rely on source NIC MAC address for aggregating and correlating flows from both IPv4 and IPv6 which are originating from the same network interface. Note, that this requires capturing the traffic from the network segment where the actual source node resides, otherwise source MAC address might get overwritten by network devices in transit. One caveat still remains — distinguishing the flows which are belonging together, especially on busy hosts with many connections. Finally, behavior based detection (e.g. unexpected traffic, malformed packets, specification non-compliance) would provide a way to detect such evasions, at the same time introducing a significant amount of false positives.

It has to be noted that any commercial product which uses an open-source tool for data acquisition is subjected to same limitations of the respective tool. Also, the lack of knowledge regarding IPv6 exploitation methods translate into low customer demand which leads to insufficient IPv6 support in final products. Finally, commercial tools are often too expensive for small and medium sized organizations. Therefore, we did not consider these products in our final evaluation.

Authors believe, that the tendency of use of IPv6 in attack campaigns conducted by sophisticated malicious actors is going to increase; this is also recognized as an increasing trend by the security reports and articles [4,15,16]. Since IPv6 security aspects are being addressed by protocol RFC updates and deprecation of obsolete transition mechanisms, it would be required to focus on these issues at the security solution developer (i.e. vendor) and implementer (i.e. consumer) levels. Adding IPv6 support to the security devices would not solve this problem, since fundamental changes would be required in the way how network traffic is interpreted and parsed, while being able to trace the context of various data streams and perform their correlation. Also, end-users should know how to properly configure, deploy and monitor security solutions in order to gain maximum awareness of the computer network flows under their direct supervision.

Potential future research directions would include advanced insider threat detection, IPv6 protocol stack implementation analysis in the modern operating system kernels and in embedded device micro-kernels.

Acknowledgements. This research was conducted with the support of NATO Cooperative Cyber Defense Center of Excellence. The authors would like to acknowledge the valuable contribution of Leo Trukšāns, Walter Willinger, and Merike Käo.

A   Appendix

(See Table 1)

Table 1. Protocol tunneling and data exfiltration tool assessment

Iteration	IP Version	Protocol	Port	Snort SF	Snort ET	Suricata	Bro	Moloch
http-22	4	TCP	22	N	P	P	P	V
http-443	4	TCP	443	N	Y	Y	V	V
http-53	4	TCP	53	N	Y	Y	P	V
http-80	4	TCP	80	N	N	V	V	V
Iodine	4	UDP	53	N	N	Y	P	V
nc64-t-22-4-b64	4	TCP	22	N	P	P	V	V
nc64-t-22-4	4	TCP	22	N	P	P	V	V
nc64-t-22-64-b64	4+6	TCP	22	N	P	P	V	V
nc64-t-22-64	4+6	TCP	22	N	P	P	V	V
nc64-t-22-6-b64	6	TCP	22	N	P	P	V	N
nc64-t-22-6	6	TCP	22	N	P	P	V	N
nc64-t-443-4-b64	4	TCP	443	N	N	N	V	V
nc64-t-443-4	4	TCP	443	N	N	N	V	V
nc64-t-443-64-b64	4+6	TCP	443	N	N	N	V	V
nc64-t-443-64	4+6	TCP	443	N	N	N	V	V
nc64-t-443-6-b64	6	TCP	443	N	N	N	V	N
nc64-t-443-6	6	TCP	443	N	N	N	V	N
nc64-t-53-4-b64	4	TCP	53	N	N	N	P	V
nc64-t-53-4	4	TCP	53	N	N	N	P	V
nc64-t-53-64-b64	4+6	TCP	53	N	N	N	P	V
nc64-t-53-64	4+6	TCP	53	N	N	N	P	V
nc64-t-53-6-b64	6	TCP	53	N	N	N	P	N
nc64-t-53-6	6	TCP	53	N	N	N	P	N
nc64-t-80-4-b64	4	TCP	80	N	N	N	P	V
nc64-t-80-4	4	TCP	80	N	N	N	P	V
nc64-t-80-64-b64	4+6	TCP	80	N	N	N	P	V
nc64-t-80-64	4+6	TCP	80	N	N	N	P	V
nc64-t-80-6-b64	6	TCP	80	N	N	N	P	N
nc64-t-80-6	6	TCP	80	N	N	N	P	N
nc64-u-22-4-b64	4	UDP	22	N	N	N	V	V
nc64-u-22-4	4	UDP	22	N	N	N	V	V
nc64-u-22-64-b64	4+6	UDP	22	N	N	N	V	V
nc64-u-22-64	4+6	UDP	22	N	N	N	V	V
nc64-u-22-6-b64	6	UDP	22	N	N	N	V	N
nc64-u-22-6	6	UDP	22	N	N	N	V	N
nc64-u-443-4-b64	4	UDP	443	N	N	N	V	V
nc64-u-443-4	4	UDP	443	N	N	N	V	V
nc64-u-443-64-b64	4+6	UDP	443	N	N	N	V	V
nc64-u-443-64	4+6	UDP	443	N	N	N	V	V
nc64-u-443-6-b64	6	UDP	443	N	N	N	V	N

(continued)

Table 1. (*continued*)

Iteration	IP Version	Protocol	Port	Snort SF	Snort ET	Suricata	Bro	Moloch
nc64-u-443-6	6	UDP	443	N	N	N	V	N
nc64-u-53-4-b64	4	UDP	53	N	Y	Y	P	V
nc64-u-53-4	4	UDP	53	N	Y	Y	P	V
nc64-u-53-64-b64	4+6	UDP	53	N	Y	Y	P	V
nc64-u-53-64	4+6	UDP	53	N	Y	Y	P	V
nc64-u-53-6-b64	6	UDP	53	N	Y	Y	P	N
nc64-u-53-6	6	UDP	53	N	Y	Y	P	N
nc64-u-80-4-b64	4	UDP	80	N	N	N	V	V
nc64-u-80-4	4	UDP	80	N	N	N	V	V
nc64-u-80-64-b64	4+6	UDP	80	N	N	N	V	V
nc64-u-80-64	4+6	UDP	80	N	N	N	V	V
nc64-u-80-6-b64	6	UDP	80	N	N	N	V	N
nc64-u-80-6	6	UDP	80	N	N	N	V	N
netcat-t-22-4	4	TCP	22	N	N	N	V	V
netcat-t-22-6	6	TCP	22	N	N	N	V	N
netcat-t-443-4	4	TCP	443	N	N	N	V	V
netcat-t-443-6	6	TCP	443	N	N	N	V	N
netcat-t-53-4	4	TCP	53	N	N	N	P	V
netcat-t-53-6	6	TCP	53	N	N	N	P	N
netcat-t-80-4	4	TCP	80	N	N	N	V	V
netcat-t-80-6	6	TCP	80	N	N	N	V	N
netcat-u-22-4	4	UDP	22	N	N	N	V	V
netcat-u-22-6	6	UDP	22	N	N	N	V	N
netcat-u-443-4	4	UDP	443	N	N	N	V	V
netcat-u-443-6	6	UDP	443	N	N	N	V	N
netcat-u-53-4	4	UDP	53	N	Y	Y	P	V
netcat-u-53-6	6	UDP	53	N	Y	Y	P	N
netcat-u-80-4	4	UDP	80	N	N	N	V	V
netcat-u-80-6	6	UDP	80	N	N	N	V	N
ptunnel	4	ICMP		N	Y	N	V	V
ssh-4-22	4	TCP	22	N	N	V	V	V
ssh-4-443	4	TCP	443	N	Y	Y	V	V
ssh-4-53	4	TCP	53	N	N	V	V	V
ssh-4-80	4	TCP	80	N	N	V	P	V
ssh-6-22	6	TCP	22	N	N	V	P	N
ssh-6-443	6	TCP	443	N	Y	Y	P	N
ssh-6-53	6	TCP	53	N	N	V	P	N
ssh-6-80	6	TCP	80	N	N	V	P	N
tun64-t-22-isatap	4	TCP	22	N	Y	Y	P	N
tun64-t-22-t6over4	4	TCP	22	N	Y	Y	P	N
tun64-t-22-t6to4	4	TCP	22	N	Y	Y	P	V

(*continued*)

Table 1. (*continued*)

Iteration	IP Version	Protocol	Port	Snort SF	Snort ET	Suricata	Bro	Moloch
tun64-t-443-isatap	4	TCP	443	N	Y	Y	P	N
tun64-t-443-t6over4	4	TCP	443	N	Y	Y	P	N
tun64-t-443-t6to4	4	TCP	443	N	Y	Y	P	V
tun64-t-53-isatap	4	TCP	53	N	Y	Y	P	N
tun64-t-53-t6over4	4	TCP	53	N	Y	Y	P	N
tun64-t-53-t6to4	4	TCP	53	N	Y	Y	P	V
tun64-t-80-isatap	4	TCP	80	N	Y	Y	P	N
tun64-t-80-t6over4	4	TCP	80	N	Y	Y	P	N
tun64-t-80-t6to4	4	TCP	80	N	Y	Y	P	V
tun64-u-22-isatap	4	UDP	22	N	Y	Y	P	N
tun64-u-22-t6over4	4	UDP	22	N	Y	Y	P	N
tun64-u-22-t6to4	4	UDP	22	N	Y	Y	P	N
tun64-u-443-isatap	4	UDP	443	N	Y	Y	P	N
tun64-u-443-t6over4	4	UDP	443	N	Y	Y	P	N
tun64-u-443-t6to4	4	UDP	443	N	Y	Y	P	N
tun64-u-53-isatap	4	UDP	53	N	Y	Y	P	N
tun64-u-53-t6over4	4	UDP	53	N	Y	Y	P	N
tun64-u-53-t6to4	4	UDP	53	N	Y	Y	P	N
tun64-u-80-isatap	4	UDP	80	N	Y	Y	P	N
tun64-u-80-t6over4	4	UDP	80	N	Y	Y	P	N
tun64-u-80-t6to4	4	UDP	80	N	Y	Y	P	N
tun64-t-22-isatap-gre	4	TCP	22	N	Y	Y	P	N
tun64-t-22-t6over4-gre	4	TCP	22	N	Y	Y	P	N
tun64-t-22-t6to4-gre	4	TCP	22	N	Y	Y	P	V
tun64-t-443-isatap-gre	4	TCP	443	N	Y	Y	P	N
tun64-t-443-t6over4-gre	4	TCP	443	N	Y	Y	P	N
tun64-t-443-t6to4-gre	4	TCP	443	N	Y	Y	P	V
tun64-t-53-isatap-gre	4	TCP	53	N	Y	Y	P	N
tun64-t-53-t6over4-gre	4	TCP	53	N	Y	Y	P	N
tun64-t-53-t6to4-gre	4	TCP	53	N	Y	Y	P	V
tun64-t-80-isatap-gre	4	TCP	80	N	Y	Y	P	N
tun64-t-80-t6over4-gre	4	TCP	80	N	Y	Y	P	N
tun64-t-80-t6to4-gre	4	TCP	80	N	Y	Y	P	V
tun64-u-22-isatap-gre	4	UDP	22	N	Y	Y	P	N
tun64-u-22-t6over4-gre	4	UDP	22	N	Y	Y	P	N
tun64-u-22-t6to4-gre	4	UDP	22	N	Y	Y	P	V
tun64-u-443-isatap-gre	4	UDP	443	N	Y	Y	P	N
tun64-u-443-t6over4-gre	4	UDP	443	N	Y	Y	P	N
tun64-u-443-t6to4-gre	4	UDP	443	N	Y	Y	P	V
tun64-u-53-isatap-gre	4	UDP	53	N	Y	Y	P	N
tun64-u-53-t6over4-gre	4	UDP	53	N	Y	Y	P	N
tun64-u-53-t6to4-gre	4	UDP	53	N	Y	Y	P	V
tun64-u-80-isatap-gre	4	UDP	80	N	Y	Y	P	N
tun64-u-80-t6over4-gre	4	UDP	80	N	Y	Y	P	N
tun64-u-80-t6to4-gre	4	UDP	80	N	Y	Y	P	V

References

1. Atlasis, A.: Attacking IPv6 implementation using fragmentation. Technical report, Centre for Strategic Cyberspace + Security Science (2011)
2. Atlasis, A.: Security impacts of abusing IPv6 extension headers. Technical report, Centre for Strategic Cyberspace + Security Science (2012)
3. Atlasis, A., Rey, E.: Evasion of high-end IPS devices in the age of IPv6. Technical report, secfu.net (2014)
4. Blumbergs, B.: Technical analysis of advanced threat tactics targeting critical information infrastructure. Cyber Security Review, pp. 25–36 (2014)
5. Blunden, B.: Covert Channels. In: Blunden, B. (ed.) The Rootkit Arsenal: Escape and Evasion in the Dark Corners of the System, 2nd edn. Jones and Bartlett Learning, Burlington (2013)
6. Brangetto, P., Çalişkan, E., Rõigas, H.: Cyber Red Teaming - Organisational, technical and legal implications in a military context. NATO CCD CoE (2015)
7. Bukač, V.: IDS system evasion techniques. Master's thesis, Masarykova Univerzita Fakulta Informatiky (2010)
8. Carpenter, B., Jung, C.: Transmission of IPv6 over IPv4 Domains without Explicit Tunnels. RFC 2529, IETF Secretariat, standards Track, March 1999
9. Colajanni, M., Zotto, L.D., Marchetti, M., Messori, M.: Defeating NIDS evasion in Mobile IPv6 networks. In: IEEE (2011)
10. Colitti, L., Gunderson, S.H., Kline, E., Refice, T.: Evaluating IPv6 adoption in the internet. In: Krishnamurthy, A., Plattner, B. (eds.) PAM 2010. LNCS, vol. 6032, pp. 141–150. Springer, Heidelberg (2010). doi:10.1007/978-3-642-12334-4_15
11. Convery, S., Miller, D.: IPv6 and IPv4 Threat Comparison and Best-Practice Evaluation. White paper, Cisco Systems, March 2004
12. Czyz, J., Allman, M., Zhang, J., Iekel-Johnson, S., Osterweil, E., Bailey, M.: Measuring IPv6 adoption. In: ACM SIGCOMM14 (2014)
13. Ellens, W., Żuraniewski, P., Sperotto, A., Schotanus, H., Mandjes, M., Meeuwissen, E.: Flow-based detection of DNS tunnels. In: Doyen, G., Waldburger, M., Čeleda, P., Sperotto, A., Stiller, B. (eds.) AIMS 2013. LNCS, vol. 7943, pp. 124–135. Springer, Heidelberg (2013). doi:10.1007/978-3-642-38998-6_16
14. Farinacci, D., Li, T., Hanks, S., Meyer, D., Traina, P.: Generic Routing Encapsulation (GRE). RFC 2784, IETF Secretariat, March 2000. (standards Track. Supplemented with RFC2890)
15. Fortinet: Biting the Bullet: A Practical Guide for Beginning the Migration to IPv6. white paper, Fortinet Inc. (2011)
16. Data SecurityLabs, G.: Uroburos: Highly complex espionage software with Russian roots. Technical report, G Data Software AG, February 2014
17. Gont, F.: Processing of IPv6 "Atomic" Fragments. RFC 6946, May 2013
18. Gont, F.: Security Implications of IPv6 on IPv4 Networks. RFC 7123, February 2014
19. Gont, F., Chown, T.: Network Reconnaissance in IPv6 Networks. Technical report, IETF Secretariat, February 2015. (internet Draft)
20. Gont, F., Liu, W., Bonica, R.: Transmission and processing of IPv6 options. Technical report, IETF Secretariat, March 2015. (best Current Practice)
21. Gont, F., Heuse, M.: Security assessments of IPv6 networks and firewalls. IPv6 Congress 2013 (2013). (presentation)
22. The Government of HKSAR: IPV6 security. Technical report, The Government of the Hong Kong Special Administrative Region, May 2011

23. Hogg, S., Vyncke, E.: IPv6 Security. Cisco Press, Indianapolis (2009)
24. Krishnan, S.: Handling of Overlapping IPv6 Fragments. RFC 5722, IETF Secretariat, December 2009. (standards Track. Updates RFC 2460)
25. Krishnan, S., Woodyatt, J., Kline, E., Hoagland, J., Bhatia, M.: A uniform format for IPv6 extension headers. Technical report
26. Lucena, N.B., Lewandowski, G., Chapin, S.J.: Covert channels in IPv6. In: Danezis, G., Martin, D. (eds.) PET 2005. LNCS, vol. 3856, pp. 147–166. Springer, Heidelberg (2006). doi:10.1007/11767831_10
27. Moore, K.: Connection of IPv6 Domains via IPv4 Clouds. RFC 3056, IETF Secretariat, February 2001. (standards Track)
28. Murphy, R.: IPv6 / ICMPv6 Covert Channels. DEF CON 2014 (2014). (presentation)
29. National Cybersecurity and Communications Integration Center: ICS-CERT Monitor. Technical report, US Dep. of Homeland Security, December 2013
30. Niemi, O.P., Levomki, A., Manner, J.: Dismantling intrusion prevention systems. In: ACM SIGCOMM 2012, August 2012
31. Nordmark, E., Gilligan, R.: Basic transition mechanisms for IPv6 hosts and routers. RFC 4213, IETF Secretariat, October 2005. (standards Track)
32. Pastrana, S., Montero-Castillo, J., Orfila, A.: Evading IDSs and firewalls as fundamental sources of information in SIEMS. In: Pastrana, S., Montero-Castillo, J., Orfila, A. (eds.) Advances in Security Information Management: Perceptions and Outcomes. Nova Science Publishers, New York (2013)
33. Ptacek, T.H., Newsham, T.N.: Insertion, evasion, and denial of service: eluding network intrusion detection. Technica report, DTIC Document, January 1998
34. Sarrar, N., Maier, G., Ager, B., Sommer, R., Uhlig, S.: Investigating IPv6 traffic: What happened at the world IPv6 day? In: Taft, N., Ricciato, F. (eds.) PAM 2012. LNCS, vol. 7192, pp. 11–20. Springer, Heidelberg (2012). doi:10.1007/978-3-642-28537-0_2
35. Degen, S., et al.: Testing the security of IPv6 implementations. Technical report, Ministryof Economic Affairs of the Netherlands, March 2014
36. Skoberne, N., Maennel, O., Phillips, I., Bush, R., Zorz, J., Ciglaric, M.: Ipv4 address sharing mechanism classification and tradeoff analysis. IEEE/ACM Trans. Netw. 22(2), 391–404 (2014)
37. Steffann, S., van Beijnum, I., van Rein, R.: A comparison of IPv6-over-IPv4 tunnel mechanisms. RFC 7059, IETF Secretariat, November 2013. (informational)
38. Tadayoni, R., Henten, A.: Transition from IPv4 to IPv6. In: 23rd European Regional Conference of the International Telecommunication Society, July 2012
39. Taib, A.H.M., Budiarto, R.: Evaluating IPv6 Adoption in the Internet. In: 5th Student Conference on Research and Development. IEEE, December 2007
40. Templin, F., Gleeson, T., Thaler, D.: Intra-site automatic tunnel addressing protocol (ISATAP). RFC 5214, IETF Secretariat, March 2008. (informational)
41. TrendLabs: targeted attack trends 2014 Report. Technical report, TrendMicro (2015)
42. Troan, O., Carpenter, B.: Deprecating the Anycast Prefix for 6to4 Relay Routers. RFC 7526, IETF Secretariat, May 2015. (best Current Practice)
43. Vidal, J.M., Castro, J.D.M., Orozco, A.L.S., Villalba, L.J.G.: Evolutions of evasion techniques aigainst network intrusion detection systems. In: ICIT 2013, The 6th International Conference on Information Technology, May 2013
44. Wu, P., Cui, Y., Wu, J., Liu, J., Metz, C.: Transition from IPv4 to IPv6: a state-of-the-art survey. IEEE Comm. Surv. Tutorials 15(3), 1407–1424 (2013)

ML: DDoS Damage Control with MPLS

Pierre-Edouard Fabre[1,2]([✉]), Hervé Debar[2], Jouni Viinikka[1],
and Gregory Blanc[2]

[1] 6cure, Colombelles, France
{pef,jvi}@6cure.com
[2] Institut Mines-Telecom, Telecom SudParis,
CNRS Samovar UMR 5157, Evry, France
{herve.debar,gregory.blanc}@telecom-sudparis.eu

Abstract. We present a DDoS mitigation mechanism dispatching suspicious and legitimate traffic into separate MultiProtocol Label Switching (MPLS) tunnels, well upstream from the target. The objective is to limit the impact a voluminous attack could otherwise have on the legitimate traffic through saturation of network resources. The separation of traffic is based on a signature identifying suspicious flows, carried in an MPLS label, and then used by a load-balancing mechanism in a router. The legitimite traffic is preserved at the expense of suspcious flows, whose resource allocations are throttled as needed to avoid congestion.

Keywords: Multiprotocol Label Switching · Quality of Service · Volumetric DDoS · Amplification DDoS · Network resilience · Bloom filter

1 Introduction

The past few years have seen the rise in the amount of volumetric Distributed Denial of Service (*DDoS*) attacks [1–3]. These attacks aim at exhausting available bandwidth and/or other networking resources required to reach the victim. Attack traffic causes congestion when flows from distributed sources converge towards the target.

Dedicated mitigation solutions, also known as middleboxes [4,5], are usually positioned close to the target, and are unable to mitigate the attack if the upstream links or the middleboxes themselves are saturated by the attack volume. This drawback has been studied and different methods for the distribution of middleboxes in the network have been proposed [6–8]. The financial costs, however, increase with number of deployed middleboxes. We seek to develop a mitigation mechanism using existing network infrastructure in order to limit the number of required middleboxes.

Even if a majority of volumetric attacks such as amplification DDoS attacks take advantage of traffic spoofing [9], the traffic from the amplifier to the victim is unspoofed. Thus mitigation solutions based on spoofing detection mechanisms, such as reverse path forwarding [10,11], cannot be applied close to the target.

© Springer International Publishing AG 2016
B.B. Brumley and J. Röning (Eds.): NordSec 2016, LNCS 10014, pp. 101–116, 2016.
DOI: 10.1007/978-3-319-47560-8_7

Destination-based filtering such as blackholing [12] will discard all legitimate traffic towards the target as well, completing the DDoS condition for the target.

To overcome these limitations, researchers [13,14] have proposed new approaches to mitigate volumetric attacks that (1) aim to preserve the legitimate traffic, (2) are activated only when network saturation occurs, and (3) forward a part of the suspicious traffic towards the target, as long as the network is not saturated. We share these goals, especially as we aim to couple this in-network defense mechanism with a on-premise defense mechanism, a middle-box, placed right in front of target and which we suppose capable of fine-grained filtering at line rate.

In this paper, we propose the Mitigation Label (*ML*), a special-purpose MPLS label that carries an attack signature encoding knowledge about suspicious flows. For encoding, we use a Bloom filter-like structure called tBF we define in this paper. The ML is generated by an out-of-band component, a Label Computation Agent, upon the reception of a DDoS alert. The ML is propagated to a Load-Balancing Router (*LBR*), upstream of a congestion point, at the edge of the network. The LBR dispatches the suspicious and legitimate traffic into different MPLS tunnels with a load-balancing mechanism using the ML.

Paper Organization: The remainder of this paper is organized as follows, Sect. 2 provides the background of our solution, *i.e.* some definitions, and our assumptions. Section 3 presents the existing works we took inspiration from. Section 4 lays the foundations of our damage control solution. Section 5 describes our experimentations and discusses their results. Section 6 concludes the paper.

2   Background

Our proposal is focused on the mitigation of bandwidth-depleting DDoS attacks using amplifiers. This section first describes the characteristics of the attack our contribution seeks to mitigate. We then define the terms required later in paper and state our underlying assumptions.

2.1   Characteristics of a Distributed Reflective DDoS Attack

Distributed Reflective Denial of Service (*DRDoS*) attacks exploit the fact that the UDP protocol is connectionless, *i.e.* the protocol has no mechanism to verify the origin of traffic. An attacker can issue a request to a service with the source address of the UDP datagram spoofed to the target's address, resulting in the service sending its reply towards the target. If the reply is larger than the request, the server can be used as an amplifier, and the attack is called an *amplification DDoS*.

DNS is an example of such a service, and DNS resolvers can be used as amplifiers. Many resolvers are, however, configured to respond only to legitimate clients, limiting the usability of the resolver as an amplifier. For example, ISPs typically allow requests only from source addresses corresponding to their customers. Resolvers without such limitations are called *open resolvers*, and they can be and are exploited for amplification attacks.

Even if the attacker initially spoofs the source address of the request, the traffic from the amplifier to the target is unspoofed. This means that the number of sources seen in an attack is limited by the number of amplifiers (*e.g.* open resolvers for DNS) the attacker can find and use. In this paper, we position ourselves between the amplifier and the target, not between the attacker and the amplifier.

2.2 Definitions

This section provides definitions of concepts used later in the paper.

Flow is a stream of packets sharing the tuple < source IP, target IP >.

Suspicious flow is a flow that, according a detection mechanism, contains malicious traffic. Given the low granularity of our flow definition, a suspicious flow may also contain legitimate packets.

Legitimate flow refers to flows that are not suspicious.

sFEC stands for a suspicious Forwarding Equivalence Class (FEC). FEC is a MPLS concept of a traffic aggregate receiving similar treatment and sFEC contains flows involved in volumetric attacks. In other words, it is intended to group flows responsible for congestion. Depending on the method used to assign flows within sFEC, it may also end up containing legitimate flows.

2.3 Assumptions

This section states the three assumptions, on which our approach builds, and concerning attack volumetry, identification of suspicious flows, and availability of flow metrics.

Attack Volumetry. The attack traffic volume is expected to be bigger than the volume of legitimate traffic, as we focus on volumetric attacks. We do not consider the congestion caused only by legitimate traffic.

Identification of Suspicious Flows. We expect to obtain alerts indicating suspicious flows, *i.e.* < source IP, destination IP > tuples associated with the attack. In fact, the configuration of the mitigation mechanism requires the description of suspicious flows, where the source and destination IPs respectively refer to the amplifier and target IP addresses. We consider this assumption reasonable, as relevant information exchange formats for example for intrusion detection (IDMEF [15]) and DDoS attack signaling (from IETF DDoS Open Threat Signalling Working Group [16]), allow such information to be carried by the alert messages.

Flow Metrics. Our mitigation mechanism also requires flow metrics, such as volumetries, related to the sFEC. We expect that both suspicious and legitimate volumetries are available. While metrics of suspicious flows may be carried by the alert message, we consider that flow metrics can also be available through network monitoring systems collecting telemetries using, for example, NetFlow [17], sFlow [18] or IPFIX [19]. In fact, if the system monitors traffic at least at the flow granularity, we should be able to collect volumes for both suspicious and legitimate flows.

3   State of the Art

Research on mitigation of bandwidth-depletion attacks broadly falls into two categories: filtering mechanisms and congestion control. Filtering focuses on matching a packet, transaction or queries against either a pattern or a behavior. An action, such as forward or drop, is then assigned to each result. Conversely congestion control mechanisms operate on a macroscopic scale, *i.e.* categories of packets over a period of time. Below we look at both of these categories in more details.

3.1   Traffic Filtering

Middleboxes, as proposed for example by Casado *et al.* [4], Baker *et al.* [20], and Roesch [21] aim at providing traffic filtering functions that routers do not implement. Generally these functions allow a finer-grained filtering and/or are dedicated to mitigate a particular threat. However, the use of middleboxes against volumetric amplification DDoS attacks often shifts the bottleneck from the target to the middlebox. Indeed the saturation would no more occur on the link between the network and the target, but on the link upstream from the middlebox. Qazi *et al.* [8] studied the distribution of such middleboxes to address this particular drawback and to dynamically manage the mitigation resources. However, multiplying middleboxes within the network turns out to be costly.

Current routers allow filtering by means of Access Control Lists (*ACLs*) or via blackholing setups such as described by Cisco [12]. A blackhole is a simple and resource-efficient method [22] to drop a collection of packets based on their destination or source prefix. Compared to the coarse granularity of blackholing, ACLs enable finer-grained traffic filtering. On routers, ACLs may match on IP header fields, for example source and destination IPs, or the protocol number. Formerly, the major drawback of ACLs was performance, as the ACLs tables used to be large. Vendors have fixed the performance issue by implementing filtering in hardware instead of in the router software [23]. Researchers have also worked on the large flow table lookup problem. Dharmapurikar *et al.* [24] proposed to use together a Bloom filter (*BF*) and a Counting Bloom Filter (*CBF*) to match the longest prefix in a prefix table.

Chan *et al.* [25] proposed a counting Bloom filter-based high-packet rate aggregate detection. Packets are added to multiple CBFs and if all counters corresponding to packet's hash exceed a preconfigured and static threshold, packet is classified as suspicious. BFs are reset regularly. According to such definition, the mechanism detects high-rate attacks such as SYN-floods but does not provide a resource-oriented mitigation. Nevertheless the detection does not distinguish between DDoS and flash crowds (a rush in traffic that only involve legitimate users).

Cohen *et al.* [26] introduced Spectral Bloom Filter that supports online query on how many time an element has been added into. Although it may seem similar to our proposed tBF by design, we propose an offline resource-oriented Bloom Filter generation by selecting a subset of flows to filter, which is not based on the same logic nor heuristic.

3.2   Congestion Control

Wang *et al.* [27] presented a router architecture that classifies packets based on the transport layer header, and then applies different Quality of Service (*QoS*) treatments to each class of traffic, in order to prevent flooding attacks from consuming bandwidth. The router aggregates flows according to the transport header fields (limited to UDP, TCP and ICMP protocols) and the IP Differentiated Services field. A bandwidth allocation is assigned to each aggregate. A flooding attack is then constrained by the resources allocated to its QoS aggregate.

Multipath routing/forwarding is the ability to configure on a router multiple next-hops for a certain destination (*e.g.* IP prefix, MPLS label, etc.). Several works use this feature to enhance the network resilience. Menth *et al.* [28] proposed the Self-Protecting Multipath (*SPM*) that consists of several disjoint paths that forward traffic before and after a failure of one of the paths. Traffic is redistributed to remaining paths in case of outages. Kazmi *et al.* [29] developed a model to select path to provide resilience against link failure, with the aim to reduce link utilization. Murphy and Garcia-Lunes-Aceves [30] used destination-based traffic split together with traffic shaping to avoid congestion and ensure acceptable delays. Using weighted Equal Cost MultiPath (ECMP) that load-balances traffic between available paths according to related weights, Zhang *et al.* [31] proposed a model to compute split ratios in order to minimize end-to-end delays by optimizing the bandwidth allocation.

To preserve legitimate traffic from collateral damage caused by attack traffic, Hachem *et al.* [14] proposed HADEGA that uses MPLS support for Differentiated Services and Traffic Engineering. It maps network flows to several Behavior Aggregates (*BA*) based on their level of suspicion, *i.e.* their likelihood of being malicious and their impact. Different QoS levels are assigned to BAs to prioritize less suspicious flows. The QoS assignment to a BA is implemented through MPLS Differentiated Services and per-hop behaviors applied to BAs. Our work makes use of these techniques and provides a new way to classify traffic into two predefined BAs.

While filtering mechanisms allow fine grained classification according to the packet's probability of being suspicious, they lack the ability to shape traffic according to the available network resources. Congestion control is intended to meet this requirement. It also allows to make a distinction in the packet processing with regard to certain classifications and to available network resources, such as bandwidth. The assignation of a packet to a class, however, is not the concern of congestion control mechanisms. As filtering and congestion control mechanisms may be complementary, this paper proposes the combination of both mechanisms to mitigate the bandwidth depletion effect of amplification attacks. We provide details on a new signature-based filter that together with a bandwidth enforcement system is able to achieve this goal.

4   Concepts and Architecture

Our contribution is a damage control system based on a novel load-balancing mechanism, that distributes flows among quality of service-aware LSPs in order to mitigate volumetric DDoS attacks. The overall architecture is depicted in Fig. 1. A monitoring system continuously collects metrics from network equipment. It is also aware of DDoS events in the network, either by detecting itself the attack or by collecting alerts from dedicated sensors. The mitigation is triggered by the monitoring system by sending or transferring a DDoS alert to a Label Computation Agent (LCA). The agent processes the alert and, in order to finalize the mitigation configuration, may ask additional flow metrics (Sect. 2.3) from the monitoring system. Then, the LCA generates a *Mitigation Label* that contains load-balancing parameters (Sect. 4.3) for each network ingress LSR ($iLSR$) involved in the mitigation (only one shown in the figure). The LCA then advertises the ML to each iLSR. The ML is forwarded together with the packet (see Fig. 2) up to the load-balancing router. The LBR distributes the traffic based on information carried in the ML to two LSPs. The two LSPs are called priority and mitigation paths. The *priority* path carries the traffic that should be preserved from congestion as much as possible. The *mitigation* path carries traffic that may be dropped by the network if congestion occurs. For the remainder of paper, we consider that iLSR and LBR functions are provided by the same equipment, located at the network ingress, and we call LBR.

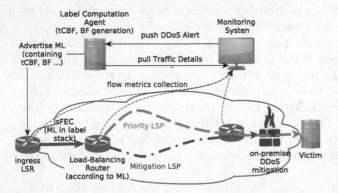

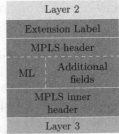

Fig. 1. Load-balancing-based volumetric DDoS mitigation

Fig. 2. MPLS header with ML

4.1   Design Overview

The proposed mitigation solution builds on MultiProtocol Label Switching (*MPLS*) [32]. MPLS allows to define a path (Label Switched Path, *LSP*) from ingress towards egress network for a set of flows belonging to the same FEC. The ingress router maps the packet to a FEC and pushes a label in the MPLS header. Hence, core routers forward packets only by looking at the label. We use MPLS to leverage its existing extensions: (1) Traffic Engineering [33] that allows managing and optimizing network resources, and (2) Differentiated Services [34] that allows classifying traffic. In fact it enables us to forward the flows while prioritizing legitimate traffic and to prevent congestion or resource exhaustion caused by an attack [14]. While these two MPLS extensions are commonly implemented in routers, the proposed load-balancing mechanism requires additional router developments, as described later. Considering the mitigation application, we restrict the load-balancing to the sFEC, which is defined by a minimal length destination prefix that includes the victim IP addresses. As such the sFEC can be mapped to destination based route in the routing table.

We define the mitigation label (*ML*, see Fig. 2) as an extended special purpose MPLS label [32] pushed by the ingress LSR on the MPLS label stack of traffic. It carries information about suspicious flows taking part to an ongoing attack. As noticed in Sect. 3, a few works have made use of Bloom filters to represent set of elements. A Bloom filter [35] is a data structure that represents the elements (flows in our case) of a set S. It supports membership queries on S over a domain D, where responses can be: (1) the queried element is not a member of S, or (2) it may be member of the set S. The probability the element (*e.g.* a flow) is not a member of is named the false positive probability. However, plain BFs are unusable in our context, *i.e.* with thousands of flows (amplifiers towards targets) to insert into a small BF constrained by the ML length. In fact for such case, the false positive probability is 1. To address this issue, we propose in Sect. 4.3 the *threshold-based Bloom filter* (tBF), a BF inferred from a subset of S, which has been chosen by assessing the impact of flows.

4.2   Workflow

This part details the mitigation steps that have been mentioned in the introduction of Sect. 4.

Multipath Reservation. Mitigation and priority LSPs can be established either before the attack detection or during the mitigation set up with the help of the Traffic Engineering MPLS extension. It allows us to define bandwidth allocation for each path at the reservation time, in order to prevent attack traffic from impacting other traffic. These bandwidth constraints should be carefully selected so that the total volume of the traffic going to the priority and mitigation links does not exceed the capacity of the egress router or the on-premise mechanism. One way tho achieve this is to setup bandwidth throttling using MPLS extensions for both priority and mitigation LSPs.

From a business point of view, a network operator can approach the bandwidth allocation in different ways. He can reserve a certain amount of bandwidth for mitigation paths of all customers and dynamically assign a portion for a threatened customer. In another situation, the mitigation path could be permanently allocated to a customer who may have subscribed to the service. In both use cases, the network service provider carefully chooses the mitigation allocation as a tradeoff between the cost of bandwidth and mitigation efficiency. Our experiments address this question.

Traffic Updates. During an attack, both malicious and legitimate traffic vary over time. New flows may appear and existing flows may terminate. The overall flow volumetry is changing. Hence, the mitigation label that depends on inbound traffic, has to be regularly recomputed to take into account the updated traffic data. The recomputation process is similar to the initial computation with updated flow statistics. The minimum possible duration of the computation iteration is constrained by either the mitigation configuration, *i.e.* the label generation and advertisement, or the sampling period of the monitoring system. We found that the mitigation label computation lasts less than a second in our setting. If the mitigation and priority paths have already been established, the ML may be advertised in the range of seconds. The monitoring system refresh period is likely larger and thus defines the shortest ML update interval.

ML-Based Load-Balancing. Once a packet belonging to the sFEC hits a LBR, it reads the ML as well as flow details needed to compute the flow hash. Then the LBR compares the flow hash with the attack signature obtained from the packet ML. The signature consists of a 20-bit field, into which suspicious flows reported by the monitoring system have been inserted (by the LCA). If the packet matches the signature, the LBR forwards it through the mitigation LSP, otherwise, it uses the priority LSP.

4.3   Threshold-Based Bloom Filter

As mentioned earlier, the size limitation of 20-bits imposed by the MPLS label renders plain BF useless for us. We introduce tBF to address this issue.

Threshold. Assume that hash functions map elements of D to an index of the Bloom filter bit array. A BF is constructed by hashing each element of the set S with k hash functions. The array position, which has been initialized to 0, given by the hash result is set to 1. The membership test of an element e is realized with the BF by comparing the result of the k hash functions applied to e. If any of the k array positions obtained among the k hash result is 0, the element e is not a member of S. Conversely, if all the k positions given by the hash results are 1, e may be a member of S.

Counting Bloom filters (*CBF*) [36] use a counter array instead of the Bloom filter bit array. The filter is generated by incrementing array positions given by the hash results of the element to add as member instead of only setting it to 1. The membership query is the same bitwise operation as for Bloom filters.

We use a CBF of size m with a single hash function ($k = 1$) whose values are integers in the range $[0; m - 1]$. Under these circumstances, an element, *i.e.* a flow, is described with only one counter. When we insert a flow into the CBF, the flow volume (in terms of bytes over the monitoring system refresh period) is added to the counter at position i, given by the flow hash result. The flow volumes have been previously retrieved from the monitoring system (Sect. 2.3). The total volume of flows whose hash gives the same result i, is then equal to the CBF counter value at position i, *i.e.* i^{th} counter of the CBF. Considering furthermore the domain S of all flows inserted into the CBF, we define a subset S_i of S as flows f of S that have the same hash result i.

We define the threshold t as a positive integer describing the volume, starting from which a subset is considered as a major subset, *i.e.* the sum of subset's flow volumes has importance compared to the total volume of flows of S. Each counter is compared to the threshold. If the counter is greater or equal to the threshold, the bit of the same position in the tBF is set to 1. Hence the tBF is a Bloom filter inferred from the CBF by applying threshold to each counter (Fig. 3). On the other hand, a counter at a given position, whose value is below the threshold leads to set the tBF bit at this position to 0. As we use tBF in the same manner as a BF, setting the ith tBF bit to 0, implies that all flows whose hash result is i to be considered as not members of S, which in turn induces false negatives for the membership queries made with tBF.

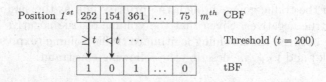

Fig. 3. Threshold-based Bloom filter generation given a threshold of $t = 200$

Constraint-Based tBF Generation. Given that we need to insert a large number of elements in a 20-bit field, we introduced the tBF. This section details the computation of the tBF which aims at preventing the priority link saturation. We use the following definitions:

S The set of elements to be inserted in the tBF (suspicious flows in our case).
D The set of elements that can be tested against the tBF (all possible flows in our case).
L The set of most frequently tested elements that are not in the set S (the most active legitimate flows in our case).

The suspicious flow set (S), retrieved from DDoS alerts received by the Monitoring System, is used to generate the tBF and select a threshold. If elements of

L, *i.e.* frequent legitimate flows, are known, they are also used to compute the threshold. Otherwise L is an empty set ($L = \emptyset$). To rank subsets as major or not, we sort them by taking into account both legitimate and suspicious traffic. First we insert legitimate and suspicious flows into their own CBF with a size of $m = 20$, respectively CBF_L and CBF_S. Second we introduce another 20-bit CBF (CBF_{mixed}) to carry the impact of the volume of subsets:

$$CBF_{mixed}[i] = \frac{CBF_S[i]}{1 + CBF_L[i]}, \forall i \in [0; m-1] \ .$$

This initialization: (1) increases the weight of the mixed counter i along with $CBF_S[i]$ counter (representing the volume of S_i), (2) decreases the weight of the mixed counter i along with $CBF_L[i]$ counter, and (3) allows the case where the set L is empty is assessed. Considering a given tBF, we define the volume of false positive (V_{FP}) as the sum of volumes of flows in subsets L_i given by the position i such that the ith bit of the tBF is set to 1. Conversely the volume of false negative (V_{FN}) is equal to the sum of CBF_S counters given by the position $\bar{i}$ such that the $\bar{i}^{th}$ bit of the tBF is null, *i.e.*:

$$V_{FP} = \sum_i CBF_L[i], \text{ such that } tBF[i] = 1 \ ,$$

$$V_{FN} = \sum_{\bar{i}} CBF_S[\bar{i}], \text{ such that } tBF[\bar{i}] = 0 \ .$$

The generation of the tBF is a constraint-based process. We intend to prevent the priority link, which has allocation A_{pri}, from being saturated. We estimate the volume of the traffic going through the priority link as the sum of volumes for false and true negatives. Given that the volume of true negative is equal to the difference between the incoming legitimate traffic volume (expressed by the $V_{in}leg$ variable) and V_{FP}, we describe the following constraint:

$$V_{in}leg - V_{FP} + V_{FN} < A_{\text{pri}}. \tag{1}$$

The generic idea is to select the threshold by decrementing it from its maximum value (*i.e.* the sum of all mixed counters) to 0 and testing the constraint (Eq. 1). However to avoid decrementing the threshold, we sort subsets S_i of S by their impact, *i.e.* we sort CBF_{mixed} counters in the decreasing order. We then initialize the tBF with 0s and one by one set the bit at position i to 1, where positions are sorted according to their impact. We stop setting bits to 1 when the constraint on the priority link allocation is satisfied (Eq. 1). If all tBF bits have been set to 1 before the constraint has been satisfied, we choose to reset to 0 the tBF bit at position i, such that S_i has the smallest impact. In this way, we prevent all inbound traffic to be load-balanced through the mitigation path.

5   Experimentations

Our mitigation mechanism has been implemented as a software platform. The platform takes as input traffic captures representing the network ingress traffic and outputs two captures representing both priority and mitigation links. The platform load-balances input traffic through a priority and a mitigation buffers. Subsequently, buffers are throttled using a token bucket algorithm [37] to enforce the bandwidth constraints of priority and mitigation output captures (representing links). This section details the simulation platform and the inbound traffic used for experiments. We then describe assessment method and associated variables, as well as a description of the results we obtained. Finally we discuss the results.

5.1 Experimental Approach

Experiments are conducted using a 5 s sliding window: (1) both legitimate and suspicious traffic telemetries are gathered from traffic capture during 5 s, (2) the mitigation label is then computed and applied to the next 10 s, (3) at the 5th s of the second step, we loop to the first step. For evaluation purposes, metrics (Sect. 5.2) are extracted from the mean of measures obtained from each iteration.

We generate input traffic captures by mixing legitimate traffic captures extracted from the MAWI data set [38] and several generated attack captures. We select /24 destination-based aggregates (cf. the sFEC) from MAWI captures as legitimate traffic. The average legitimate traffic bandwidth of each capture is between 14 and 16 Mbits/s. Attack traffic is generated by replaying DNS ANY replies from 40000 randomly chosen source IPs (amplifiers) towards 4 targets selected in the sFEC destination IPs. In fact, although Rossow [3] found up to billions of potential amplifiers, the attack with the highest number of amplifiers reported only involved around 17000 different IP sources.

Figure 4 shows measures used to conduct the evaluation, and their place of collection. We first measure inbound legitimate (green hashed) and malicious (red filled) traffic volumes, respectively named $V_{in}leg$ and $V_{in}mal$. The traffic is load-balanced between priority and mitigation LSPs, which have allocation A_{pri} (Sect. 4.2) and A_{mit} bandwidths, respectively. $V_{pri}leg$ denotes the volume of legitimate traffic forwarded through the priority link. Finally $V_{out}leg$ refers to the outgoing legitimate traffic volume that has been forwarded either through both paths, and that has not been dropped by the QoS mechanisms.

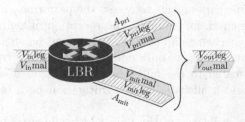

Fig. 4. Load-balancing measures (Color figure online)

5.2 Variables and Metrics

Our solution aims to maintain an acceptable level of Quality of Service for legitimate traffic. In the experiments we simply assess the QoS through its availability aspect by measuring traffic losses. The evaluation does not cover more complex aspects such as delay and jitter. This section provides the metric that is used to assess the Quality of Service. We then describe variables required to carry out the evaluation. They are inferred from traffic measures.

The efficiency is evaluated with a metric we call *Reception* which is the ratio between the outbound and inbound legitimate volumes ($\frac{V_{out}\text{leg}}{V_{in}\text{leg}}$). It evaluates how much legitimate volume our solution is able to preserve.

The volume of attack traffic is controlled by the variable *AttackFactor* which is the ratio of volumes of inbound suspicious and legitimate traffic, $\frac{V_{in}\text{mal}}{V_{in}\text{leg}}$. As we expect the attack volume to be at least equal to the legitimate volume (Sect. 2.3), we generate malicious traffic with attack factor ranging from 1 to 50. Large attack factors allow us to assess the limitations of our solution.

As discussed in Sect. 4.2, we have to find a tradeoff between the allocation for mitigation path and the mitigation efficiency, *i.e.* the value of *Reception* of legitimate traffic. From a network provider's perspective, we express the need for mitigation allocation per client as a percentage of the overall bandwidth allocated to the customer, *i.e.*:

$$BA_{\text{mitigation}} = \frac{A_{\text{mit}} \times 100}{A_{\text{pri}} + A_{\text{mit}}}.$$

We have considered two cases: (1) the overall bandwidth allocation ($A_{\text{pri}} + A_{\text{mit}}$) is fixed, *e.g.* the ISP has already provided an allocation for the mitigation path, (2) only the bandwidth allocation of the priority path is fixed, *e.g.* the mitigation path is provisioned during the mitigation. The cost of mitigation grows with the bandwidth allocated to the mitigation path. We then should find the optimum percentage of mitigation allocation that minimizes the mitigation allocation and maximizes the value of *Reception* of legitimate traffic.

5.3 Results

We conducted multiple experiments to assess the performance of our mitigation mechanism. We compared, for example, the reception of legitimate traffic for a simple load-balancing scheme and our ML-based load-balancing solution. However, due to space constraints, we only report results that correlate performance with bandwidth allocated to the mitigation path. Figures 5a and b show the impact of the bandwidth allocated to the mitigation path on the reception of legitimate traffic.

Figure 5a depicts variations of the bandwidth allocated to mitigation path considering a fixed overall bandwidth allocation ($A_{\text{pri}} + A_{\text{mit}}$). Regardless of the amount of the mitigation path bandwidth being allocated, the mitigation mechanism prevents legitimate traffic from suffering from congestion when the

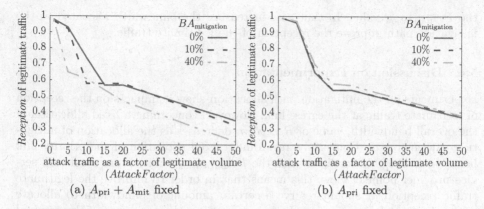

(a) $A_{pri} + A_{mit}$ fixed   (b) A_{pri} fixed

Fig. 5. Impact of the mitigation allocation ($BA_{mitigation}$) on the Legitimate Traffic Reception

attack and legitimate traffic volumes are equal ($AttackFactor = 1$) and guarantee at least 90 % of the legitimate traffic to be forwarded when the attack volume reach 5 times the legitimate volume with a $BA_{mitigation}$ strictly lower than 40 %. Then the *Reception* drastically drops when the attach traffic reaches 5 times the legitimate volume considering a percentage of mitigation path allocation of 40 %. The fall is shifted for $BA_{mitigation}$ of 10 % to an *AttackFactor* of 10 and to an *AttackFactor* of 15 when no bandwidth is allocated to the mitigation path. Indeed, considering larger allocation of mitigation link, more tBF bits are set to 1 to satisfy the priority bandwidth constraint leading more legitimate flows to be load-balanced to the mitigation path. Additionally, the mitigation bandwidth throttling is active from an attack volume that is higher as one time the legitimate traffic volume. From an attack factor of 20 to 50, the reception of legitimate traffic linearly declines from around 55 % to 35 % and 22 % for a ratio of mitigation path allocation of respectively 0 and 40 %.

In conclusion, allocation bandwidth to the mitigation path does not enhance the reception of legitimate traffic at the network egress. This is due to the fact that allocating bandwidth to the mitigation path while the overall allocation remains constant implies the reduction of priority path bandwidth allocation. Hence, in order to satisfying priority bandwidth constraints the number of tBF bits set to 1 is increasing. That implies that more legitimate flows are load-balanced to the mitigation link which is more aggressively throttled than the priority path.

Considering a fixed bandwidth allocation of the priority path, *i.e.* a constant $BA_{mitigation}$ (Fig. 5b), we notice that the value of *Reception* of legitimate traffic rises with the bandwidth allocated to the mitigation path, *e.g.* a $BA_{mitigation}$ of 10 % only add a few percents to the *Reception*, such that curves representing a $BA_{mitigation}$ of 0 % and 10 % are superposed. In fact, as the constraint defined by $BA_{mitigation}$ in Eq. 1 is fixed, we generate the same tBF for all experiments. Hence the traffic forwarded through the priority path is the same regardless the $BA_{\text{mitigation}}$ value. In that case increasing the bandwidth allocated to the mitigation path improve the reception of the legitimate traffic.

5.4   Discussion on Experimentation

Experiments on the mitigation path allocation show it impacts on the reception of legitimate traffic at the egress link. However, concerning a fixed allocation of the overall bandwidth, value of *Reception* decreases as the allocation of mitigation path increases. Conversely, regarding a fixed allocation of the priority link bandwidth, the gain increases with the $BA_{\text{mitigation}}$ value. From a network service provider point of view, this means that in order to improve the legitimate traffic reception, it should reserve a certain amount of bandwidth to allocate mitigation path for a customer. It then cannot be taken as a part of the nominal customer bandwidth. Moreover the choice of the $BA_{\text{mitigation}}$ may be conditioned by both the additional cost of allocating bandwidth for suspicious traffic and the cost of legitimate traffic loss. The cost of both allocating bandwidth for suspicious traffic by increasing the customer bandwidth and dropping legitimate traffic should be studied in order to chose the $BA_{\text{mitigation}}$.

We should point out that for a stateful protocol such as TCP, the impact of a packet loss may be more costly. It will trigger mechanisms such as retransmission and can impact transmission window size, *etc.* It may then induce delays or even session resets. Such aspects were not taken into account in our experiments. In addition, in our simulated environment, due to the static behavior of capture replays, sources seem to continue to send consecutive TCP packets in the stream despite any packet losses. In a real network, following a number of successive packet drop inducing the destination not to acknowledge, the session may end withing a timeout period.

We compared our solution to a weighted load-balancing scheme, *i.e.* a packet hash is used to map the packet to either mitigation or priority LSPs according to weights associated to LSP bandwidths. For the sake of brevity, we have omitted the resulting figure. However we provide outlines for a fixed allocation of the overall bandwidth ($A_{\text{mit}} + A_{\text{pri}}$) below. Considering a given value of $BA_{\text{mitigation}}$, our solution has better results regardless the attack factor. For example, with a $BA_{\text{mitigation}}$ of 0 %, 10 % and 20 %, we found that our solution increases the reception of legitimate traffic up to 50 % for an attack factor of 20. In fact, as the simple load-balancing scheme does not prioritize legitimate traffic, the value of *Reception* quickly drops with the attack factor.

6   Conclusion

We presented a resource-oriented in-MPLS label filter that tends to mitigate the impact of massive DDoS attacks on the network, while preserving legitimate flows and forwarding suspicious traffic to a middlebox for finer grained filtering. It can be used on Traffic Engineering enabled MPLS networks where routers implement the mitigation label forwarding scheme. We run experiments with real legitimate and generated attack traffic to validate our mechanism. Results highlight the need to allocate additional bandwidth to forward suspicious traffic towards an on-premise mechanism. Future work aims at catering the need for overprovisioning the bandwidth allocation to forward suspicious flows. We then plan to evaluate and reduce our mitigation mechanism impact on connection-oriented protocols such as TCP. Finally we will study finer flow classification to decrease the number of legitimate flows forwarded through the mitigation path.

Acknowledgement. This research is supported by the European Seventh Framework Programme (FP7) and by the Japanese Ministry of Internal Affairs and Communication (MIC) during the project NECOMA under grant agreement No 608533, and by the French research program Programme d'Investissements d'Avenir (PIA) during the project SIEM+ under grant agreement P111271-3583256.

References

1. Cisco Security Intelligence Operations: Cisco 2014 Annual Security Report. Technical report, Cisco (2014)
2. Prince, M.: Technical details behind a 400gbps NTP amplification DDoS attack
3. Rossow, C.: Amplification hell: revisiting network protocols for DDoS abuse. In: NDSS. The Internet Society (2014)
4. Casado, M., Cao, P., Akella, A., Provos, N.: Flow-cookies: using bandwidth amplification to defend against DDoS flooding attacks. Quality of Service - IWQoS 2006, pp. 286–287 (2006)
5. Greenhalgh, A., Handley, M., Huici, F.: Using routing and tunneling to combat DoS attacks. In: SRUTI. USENIX Association (2005)
6. Abujoda, A., Papadimitriou, P.: Midas: middlebox discovery and selection for on-path flow processing. In: COMSNETS, pp. 1–8. IEEE (2015)
7. Mahimkar, A., Dange, J., Shmatikov, V., Vin, H.M., Zhang, Y.: dFence: transparent network-based Denial of Service mitigation. In: NSDI. USENIX (2007)
8. Qazi, Z.A., Tu, C.C., Chiang, L., Miao, R., Sekar, V., Yu, M.: SIMPLE-fying middlebox policy enforcement using SDN. In: ACM SIGCOMM 2013 Conference
9. Paxson, V.: An analysis of using reflectors for distributed Denial-of-Service attacks. Comput. Commun. Rev. **31**(3), 38–47 (2001)
10. Cisco, I.: Unicast reverse path forwarding (1999)
11. Ferguson, P., Senie, D.: Network Ingress Filtering: Defeating Denial of Service Attacks which employ IP Source Address Spoofing. RFC 2827, May 2000
12. Systems, C.: Remotely triggered black hole filtering - destination based and source based. Technical report, Cisco Systems (2005)
13. Fung, C.J., McCormick, B.: VGuard: a distributed denial of service attack mitigation method using network function virtualization. In: Network and Service Management (CNSM), pp. 64–70, November 2015
14. Hachem, N., Debar, H., García-Alfaro, J.: HADEGA: a novel MPLS-based mitigation solution to handle network attacks. In: IPCCC, pp. 171–180. IEEE (2012)
15. Debar, H., Curry, D., Feinstein, B.: The Intrusion Detection Message Exchange Format (IDMEF). RFC 4765 (Experimental), March 2007
16. Teague, N.: Open threat signaling using RPC API over HTTPS and IPFIX. Internet-Draft draft-teague-open-threat-signaling-01, IETF Secretariat, July 2015

17. Cisco, I.: Netflow (2008)
18. Traffic monitoring using sflow (2003)
19. Sadasivan, G., Brownlee, N., Claise, B., Quittek, J.: Architecture for IP Flow Information Export. RFC 5470, March 2009
20. Baker, Z.K., Prasanna, V.K.: Time and area efficient pattern matching on FPGAs. In: Tessier, R., Schmit, H. (eds.) FPGA, pp. 223–232. ACM (2004)
21. Roesch, M.: Snort: lightweight intrusion detection for networks. In: Parter, D.W. (ed.) LISA, pp. 229–238. USENIX (1999)
22. Vordos, I.: Mitigating distributed denial of service attacks with multi-protocol label switching-traffic engineering (MPLS-TE). Ph.D. thesis, Naval Postgraduate School (2009)
23. Understanding ACL on catalyst 6500 series switches. Technical report, Cisco
24. Dharmapurikar, S., Krishnamurthy, P., Taylor, D.E.: Longest prefix matching using bloom filters. IEEE/ACM Trans. Netw. 14(2), 397–409 (2006)
25. Chan, E.Y.K., et al.: IDR: an intrusion detection router for defending against distributed denial-of-service (DDOS) attacks. In: ISPAN, pp. 581–586. IEEE Computer Society (2004)
26. Cohen, S., Matias, Y.: Spectral Bloom filters. In: Proceedings of the 2003 ACM SIGMOD International Conference on Management of Data, SIGMOD 2003, pp. 241–252. ACM, New York (2003)
27. Wang, H., Shin, K.G.: Transport-aware IP routers: a built-in protection mechanism to counter DDoS attacks. IEEE Trans. Parallel Distrib. Syst. 14(9), 873–884 (2003)
28. Menth, M., Reifert, A., Milbrandt, J.: Self-protecting multipaths — a simple and resource-efficient protection switching mechanism for MPLS networks. In: Mitrou, N., Kontovasilis, K., Rouskas, G.N., Iliadis, I., Merakos, L. (eds.) NETWORKING 2004. LNCS, vol. 3042, pp. 526–537. Springer, Heidelberg (2004). doi:10.1007/978-3-540-24693-0_44
29. Kazmi, N.A., Koster, A.M.C.A., Branke, J.: Formulations and algorithms for the multi-path selection problem in network routing. In: ICUMT, pp. 738–744. IEEE (2012)
30. Murthy, S., Garcia-Luna-Aceves, J.J.: Congestion-oriented shortest multipath routing. In: Proceedings IEEE INFOCOM 1996, pp. 1028–1036. IEEE (1996)
31. Zhang, J., Xi, K., Zhang, L., Chao, H.J.: Optimizing network performance using weighted multipath routing. In: 21st International Conference on Computer Communications and Networks (ICCCN), 2012, pp. 1–7, July 2012
32. Rosen, E., Viswanathan, A., Callon, R.: Multiprotocol Label Switching Architecture. RFC 3031, January 2001
33. Awduche, D., Malcolm, J., Agogbua, J., O'Dell, M., McManus, J.: Requirements for Traffic Engineering Over MPLS. RFC 2702 (Informational), September 1999
34. Faucheur, F.L., et al.: Multi-Protocol Label Switching (MPLS) Support of Differentiated Services. RFC 3270, May 2002
35. Bloom, B.H.: Space/time trade-offs in hash coding with allowable errors. Commun. ACM 13(7), 422–426 (1970)
36. Fan, L., Cao, P., Almeida, J.M., Broder, A.Z.: Summary cache: a scalable wide-area web cache sharing protocol. In: SIGCOMM, pp. 254–265 (1998)
37. Cisco: Cisco IOS Quality of Service Solutions Configuration Guide, Release 12.2 - Policing and Shaping Overview
38. Fontugne, R., Borgnat, P., Abry, P., Fukuda, K.: MAWILab: combining diverse anomaly detectors for automated anomaly labeling and performance benchmarking. In: CoNEXT, p. 8. ACM (2010)

Software Security

Empirical Analysis on the Use of Dynamic Code Updates in Android and Its Security Implications

Maqsood Ahmad[1]([✉]), Bruno Crispo[1,2], and Teklay Gebremichael[1]

[1] University of Trento, Trento, Italy
maqsood.ahmad@unitn.it, teklaigeb@gmail.com
[2] KU Leuven, Leuven, Belgium
bruno.crispo@kuleuven.be

Abstract. Dynamic code update techniques, such as reflection and dynamic class loading (DCL), enable an application (app) to change its behavior at runtime. These techniques are heavily used in Android apps for extensibility. However, malware developers misuse these techniques to conceal malicious functionality, bypass static analysis tools and expose the malicious functionality only when the app is installed and run on a user's device. Although, the use of these techniques alone may not be sufficient to bypass analysis tools, it is the use of reflection/DCL APIs with *obfuscated parameters* that makes the state-of-art static analysis tools for Android unable to infer the correct behavior of the app. To understand the current trends in real apps, it is important to perform a study on the sources of the parameters used in reflection/DCL APIs. In this paper, we describe how malicious apps bypass analysis tools using reflection/DCL with parameters provided by sources, such as network, files, encrypted strings, etc., which are hard to analyze statically. We further develop a tool to analyze a dataset of 3,645 real world malware samples and 16,528 benign apps in order to investigate the sources of the parameters used in reflection/DCL APIs. The results of our analysis indicate the presence of such programming practices in both legitimate and malicious apps. However, malicious apps tend to obfuscate the parameters of reflection/DCL APIs more often. The use of *Crypto* related APIs as sources of the parameters of reflection/DCL APIs is significantly higher in malicious apps, which endorses the fact that malicious apps try to thwart static analysis tools.

Keywords: Android malware · Reflection · Dynamic class loading

1 Introduction

Android reached 82.8 % of smartphone market share in 2015, 1.4 billion active devices worldwide and surpassed 1.6 million apps in July 2015 in Google Play Store alone [8,10,13]. The pervasiveness of mobile devices and their capability to collect and store users' private information makes them very attractive for

© Springer International Publishing AG 2016
B.B. Brumley and J. Röning (Eds.): NordSec 2016, LNCS 10014, pp. 119–134, 2016.
DOI: 10.1007/978-3-319-47560-8_8

malware developers, hence, the number of mobile malware samples increases as the days goes by. In 2014, 97 % of all the mobile malware targeted Android based devices [1].

Malware developers use an array of techniques to evade analysis tools deployed by app markets and execute malicious code on users' devices. Code obfuscation, anti-debugging, emulator detection, time bombs, reflection and DCL are some of the techniques found in modern mobile malware. In this paper, we are particularly interested in the latter two techniques. Reflection and DCL enable development of flexible apps which can change their behavior at runtime after being installed on a user's device. The same feature serves well for malware developers as they develop seemingly benign apps at installation time that can load additional malicious code at runtime using DCL and access it using reflection APIs. Doing so, they evade static analysis tools that rely on the availability of all the information before the analysis starts. Reflection/DCL APIs operate on string parameters representing code files, classes, methods, etc. When these parameters are not readily available in the code at analysis time (i.e., encrypted and only decrypted at runtime, read from a file provided via network), state-of-the-art static analysis tools find it impossible to infer the exact behavior of the app. Therefore, the sources of these parameters become much more important from security point of view as they play a vital role in malicious usage of reflection/DCL APIs. While previous works use various techniques to analyze apps in the presence of dynamic code updates, this dimension of reflection/DCL is most often overlooked [22, 26, 27].

In this work, we analyze the sources of the parameters of reflection/DCL APIs that allow apps to conceal malicious behavior and evade static analysis tools. We develop a tool, based on SAAF [20], to track information flow to reflection and DCL APIs. It uses backward program slicing to determine the sources of the parameters used in reflection/DCL APIs. The tool takes an Android .apk file (or a directory containing .apk files), performs analysis on it and generates statistics about the usage of reflection/DCL APIs and the corresponding sources of their parameters. The results of our analysis on real world apps show that it is more common in malicious apps to take parameters of reflection/DCL APIs from sources, such as *Crypto* related APIs, which help thwart static analysis.

To summarize, the contributions of this work are:

- We develop an automated static analysis tool which can perform analysis on Android apps, detect information flow between given source and sink APIs, and produce statistics about the presence of such information flow paths between source/sink APIs in individual apps as well as the whole market (Sect. 3).
- We collect and analyze a dataset of real world apps containing 16,528 benign and 3,645 malicious apps in order to investigate the sources of the parameters used in reflection/DCL APIs (Sect. 4). To the best of our knowledge, this is first study focusing on the sources of the parameters of reflection/DCL APIs. The analysis results would help in understanding the behavior of apps that

use dynamic code updates and designing more effective analysis procedures and policies to detect malicious apps in the market.

2 Motivating Examples

Evidence of obfuscated parameters of reflection/DCL APIs used in real world malware motivate this work. To explain it further, we consider three concrete samples of mobile malware: BrainTest, Fakenotify and AnserverBot [16,24,28]. In BrainTest, the strings representing the code files to be downloaded, classes to be instantiated and methods to be invoked using reflection/DCL APIs are provided through a file downloaded from the Internet at runtime; in Fakenotify, the strings representing the classes to be instantiated and methods to be invoked are provided as encrypted strings and only decrypted at runtime; and Anserver-Bot is a malware family where strings representing code files to be loaded are provided as encrypted strings.

BrainTest: Check Point Mobile Threat Prevention detected an Android malware in August 2015, which is packaged inside a game app known as BrainTest and has 100,000-500,000 downloads at Google Play Store. As reported, the malware infected up to 1 million users.

The malware uses a number of techniques to bypass Google Bouncer. It conceals its malicious activity if the IP or domain in which the app is being executed is mapped to Google Bouncer. It uses a combination of time bombs, dynamic code loading, reflection, encrypted code files, and malicious code (root exploits) downloaded from the Internet, to harden reverse engineering and evade analysis tools.

Once the app is installed on a user's device, it decrypts an encrypted file `start.ogg` from the app's assets directory and loads it using `DexClassLoader`. The dynamically loaded file starts communicating with a Command&Control (C&C) server. The server responds with a `.json` file that contains a link to a `.jar` file which the app downloads and dynamically loads using `DexClassLoader`. In addition, the `.json` file also contains names of the classes and methods which are to be invoked by the app using reflection APIs. The malware then drops root exploits and installs/uninstalls other APKs as the C&C server directs.

Listing 1.1. FakenotifyA - SMS Trojan

```
1  SmsManager localSmsManager = SmsManager.getDefault();
2  String str2 = paramString1;
3  String str3 = paramString2;
4  localSmsManager.sendTextMessage(str2, null, str3, null, null);
```

Fakenotify: It is noticed that Android malware evolves to harden analysis and reverse engineering. Listing 1.1 shows an excerpt from an SMS trojan named FakenotifyA [16]. The Listing shows how FakenotifyA uses a standard SMS sending procedure to send messages to premium numbers. Although, the message, `paramString2`, and the number, `paramString1`, to which the message is sent are provided at runtime, the SMS sending mechanism is pretty obvious and easy to detect for the analysis tools.

Listing 1.2. `FakenotifyB - Version 2 of FakenotifyA`

```
1  Class class1 = Class.forName(StringDecoder.decode("&nd}D%d.(!x!ejDn5.SmsM&n&g!}"));
2  Object obj = class1.getMethod(StringDecoder.decode("g!(?!f&wx("), new Class[0]).invoke(null, new Object
      [0]);
3  class1.getMethod(StringDecoder.decode("s!ndz!4(M!ss&g!"), new Class[] {java/lang/String, java/lang/String,
      java/lang/String, android/app/PendingIntent, android/app/PendingIntent}).invoke(obj, new Object[]
      {e, null, s1, null, null});
```

After some time, a new version of the same malware, FakenotifyB, surfaced. FakenotifyB is exactly similar to FakenotifyA when it comes to its malicious functionality, however, FakenotifyB makes use of reflection to dynamically create an instance of the `SMSManager` class, retrieves objects of its `getDefault` and `sendTextMessage` methods and invokes them. In addition to using reflection, the parameters representing the names of `SMSManager` class and its methods are provided in encrypted form and only decrypted at runtime. The SMS sending routine is shown in Listing 1.2 and it is much harder for analysis tools to infer its behavior unlike FakenotifyA [16].

AnserverBot: The presence of such evasive usage of reflection/DCL APIs is not an isolated incident in the Android malware. There are many examples where whole malware families rely on loading code dynamically and using encrypted strings in reflection/DCL APIs to evade detection by analysis tools. Listing 1.3 shows a piece of code taken from a sample of the AnserverBot family. It uses an encrypted string (`9CkOrC32uI327WBD7n__`) to hold the file name which is then decrypted (`str2`) at runtime and concatenated with another string (`str1`) to get the file name (`str3`). The absolute path is then retrieved in `str4` and provided to `DexClassLoader` to load the file dynamically.

Listing 1.3. `Excerpt from AnserverBot`

```
1  //9CkOrC32uI327WBD7n__  -> /anserverb.db
2  String str2 = Xmlns.d("9CkOrC32uI327WBD7n__");
3  str3 = str1.concat(str2);
4  for (File localFile = new File(str3); ; localFile = paramFile){
5    String str4 = localFile.getAbsolutePath();
6    String str5 = a.getFilesDir().getAbsolutePath();
7    ClassLoader localClassLoader = a.getClassLoader().getParent();
8    //get the class specified by "paramString1" from anserverb.db
9    Class localClass = new DexClassLoader(str4, str5, null, localClassLoader)
        .loadClass(paramString1);
```

The point worth noticing in these three examples is the use of parameters in reflection/DCL APIs that are not readily available for the analysis tools. Consequently, static analysis tools find it impossible to construct the exact behavior of these apps. Therefore, the focus of this work is not only reflection/DCL APIs, but also the manner in which the parameters are provided to these APIs.

3   Analysis Tool: Design and Implementation

The architecture and workflow of the analysis tool is shown in Fig. 1. It is composed of two main modules represented by the dotted rectangles, i.e., a slice extraction module and a slice analysis module.

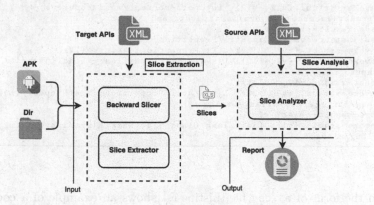

Fig. 1. Analysis tool design

Slice Extraction: Most android app analysis tools transform Android's Dalvik bytecode to Java bytecode or source code in order to use the already available tools for Java program analysis. However, the translation from Dalvik bytecode to Java source code cannot always be accurate, specifically in apps that use some obfuscation techniques. We perform analysis on disassembled Dalvik bytecode, i.e., smali code, which does not suffer from this limitation.

The slice extraction module takes an .apk file or a directory, where .apk files are located, and a list of target APIs as input. A target API along with its specific parameter is the starting point of the analysis. The *Backward Slicer* searches for all the occurrences of the target API in the app's smali code after disassembling the .apk file and backtracks them. The backtracking process starts with the register that stores the value of the parameter used in the target API and tracks backward in the code to find all other registers that have a direct or indirect effect on the value of this register. Consequently, the analysis tool captures the information flow to the target API. The set of code statements involved in the information flow to a target API is called a *Backward Slice*. The *Backward Slicer* is based on SAAF which can perform backward program slicing on smali code [20]. However, original SAAF does not consider the information flow performed through Android Intents and may miss some information flows. Intents are messaging objects used for inter-component and inter-app communication. Typically, they are used to start activities, services or invoke broadcast receivers. In order to extend this functionality, we modified SAAF to track information flow performed through explicit Android Intents. The *Slice Extractor* extracts all the code instructions that form a particular slice, marked by the *Backward*

Listing 1.4. Backward Code Slice. TargetLine: 63, TargetClass: Ljava/lang/Class;, TargetMethod: forName

```
 1 34:  invoke-virtual {p0}, Ldisi/test/app/MainActivity;->getResources()
           Landroid/content/res/Resources;
 2 36:  move-result-object v12
 3 38:  const/high16 v13, 0x7f05
 4 40:  invoke-virtual {v12, v13}, Landroid/content/res/Resources;->
           openRawResource(I)Ljava/io/InputStream;
 5 42:  move-result-object v10
 6 46:  new-instance v9, Ljava/util/Properties;
 7 48:  invoke-direct {v9}, Ljava/util/Properties;-><init>()V
 8 52:  invoke-virtual {v9, v10}, Ljava/util/Properties;->load(Ljava/io/
           InputStream;)V
 9 55:  const-string v12, "class"
10 57:  invoke-virtual {v9, v12}, Ljava/util/Properties;->getProperty(Ljava/
           lang/String;)Ljava/lang/String;
11 59:  move-result-object v1
12 63:  invoke-static {v1}, Ljava/lang/Class;->forName(Ljava/lang/String;)Ljava
           /lang/Class;
```

Slicer, in the form of a `.csv` file. Listing 1.4 shows an example of a code slice for the method `forName` of the class `Ljava/lang/Class;`. Once the slices are extracted, the analysis process moves to the next module, i.e., slice analysis.

Slice Analysis: The next step in the analysis is to detect information flow from a source API to the target API. This module takes the slice files generated in the previous step and a list of source APIs as input. It consists of a set of Python scripts, which we call *Slice Analyzer*, collectively. The *Slice Analyzer* traverses through each code instruction in the slices corresponding to the target APIs and locates the presence of source APIs. The purpose of such traversal is to infer a source/sink relationship between the source and the target APIs. The *Slice Analyzer* not only reveals such source/sink relationships, but also provides statistics regarding the number of apps containing the target/source APIs, occurrences of the target/source APIs and their relationship in each individual app and in all the analyzed apps in a market. A report containing these statistics is generated in the form of a `.json` file.

4   Application Analysis

We analyze a dataset of apps for potential dangerous usage of reflection/DCL APIs. Potential dangerous usage refers to the usage of reflection/DCL APIs in conjunction with certain sources of their parameters that complicate the overall analysis and might be used by malware developers to evade static analysis tools. There are two distinct entities in this analysis, i.e., (1) reflection/DCL APIs, (2) source APIs. The purpose of the analysis is to infer the presence of information flow from the source APIs to certain parameters of reflection/DCL APIs. In this section, we describe the target reflection/DCL APIs, the corresponding source APIs of their parameters and the apps dataset.

4.1   API Selection

Reflection and DCL APIs: Table 1 contains a representative list of DCL and reflection APIs that are tracked for analysis and considered as the target APIs. The first two columns represent the class and method names, whereas the last column represents the specific parameters of interest in these API calls. The APIs are divided into three categories. The first category, *Dynamic Code Loading*, contains APIs that are used to load code in the form of .jar/.apk/.dex files at runtime. APIs in the second category, *Class Retrieval*, are used to load classes and create their objects. The last category, *Method Retrieval and Invocation*, contains APIs that are used to retrieve method objects and invoke them.

We have included only those APIs which can potentially help conceal malicious behavior and they require essential parameters when using either DCL or reflection. For instance, loadDex method of the class Ldalvik/system/DexFile is tracked for its first parameter, sourcePathName, which is of type String and represents the path to the .jar/.apk/.dex file to be loaded. A malware developer can obfuscate the parameter provided to the loadDex method and make it hard for analysis tools to determine the location of the code which is loaded dynamically. Similar is the case with the constructors of PathClassLoader and DexClassLoader. Obfuscation of the parameters of these class constructors makes it hard for analysis tools to infer the location of the dynamically loaded code. Here, libraryPath, represents the path to the directory containing native libraries.

Moreover, static analysis can be led to unsound results through the use of obfuscated parameters passed to the loadClass method of the Ljava/lang/ClassLoader class or the forName method of the Ljava/lang/Class class. In both cases, static analysis tools will be unable to know the exact class which is to be loaded at runtime. Using obfuscated parameters in methods, such as getDeclaredMethod, getMethod and invoke, can leave the analysis tool clueless

Table 1. The list of tracked APIs and their parameters

Class	Method	ParamNo	Params
Dynamic Code Loading			
Ldalvik/system/PathClassLoader;	<init>	1,2	dexPath, libraryPath
Ldalvik/system/DexClassLoader	<init>	1,3	dexPath, libraryPath
Ldalvik/system/DexFile;	loadDex	1	sourcePathName
Class Retrieval			
Ljava/lang/ClassLoader;	loadClass	1	className
Ljava/lang/Class;	forName	1	className
Method Retrieval and Invocation			
Ljava/lang/Class;	getDeclaredMethod	1	methodName
Ljava/lang/Class;	getMethod	1	methodName
Ljava/lang/reflect/Method;	invoke	1	methodObject

about the methods being retrieved or called. So, even if the location of the code and class to be loaded is known, the behavior of the app can not be completely determined as static analysis can not correctly identify the method or the order in which the methods are being called, which is pivotal to an app's behavior.

Source APIs: Hard coded strings inside the code are easy to analyze for static analysis tools even if they are used as parameters to reflection/DCL APIs. However, when these strings are not readily available inside the code, static analysis tools are completely ineffective in inferring an app's behavior. To evade static analysis tools, the string parameters to reflection/DCL APIs can be retrieved from various sources at runtime. Table 2 provides a list of APIs that are used to access such sources. The sources are chosen based on their potential capability to evade static analysis tools specifically when they provide parameters which are to be used in reflection/DCL calls. The first column in the table represents the classes and the second column represents the

Table 2. Sources of parameters

Class	Methods
Map, Hashtable	
Ljava/util/Map;	X*
Crypto	
Ljavax/crypto/Cipher;	doFinal
Ljavax/crypto/Cipher;	update
Ljavax/crypto/CipherInputStream;	read
Ljavax/crypto/Mac;	doFinal
Ljavax/crypto/Mac;	update
Ljavax/crypto/SealedObject;	getObject
Telephony	
Landroid/telephony/TelephonyManager;	X
Landroid/telephony/SmsManager;	X
Internet	
Ljava/net/URLConnection;	X
Ljava/net/HttpURLConnection;	X
Ljava/net/ssl/HttpsURLConnection;	X
Ljava/net/JarURLConnection;	X
Input Streams	
Ljava/io/InputStream;	X*
Readers	
Ljava/io/Reader;	X*
Content Resolver	
Landroid/content/ContentResolver;	X

corresponding methods which are considered as potential sources. Classes are grouped in categories, e.g., Crypto, Telephony, etc. X in the second column indicates that there are several methods in the corresponding class which are considered to be potential sources, thus, we simply did not enumerate all of them in the table. Similarly, X* represents that all the subclasses are also considered, e.g., subclasses of InputStream such as FileInputStream, BufferedInputStream, etc.

Some of the categories, such as *Telephony* and *Internet*, are purely dynamic and cannot be analyzed by static analysis tools. A malware developer can use these sources to communicate important parameters to the target APIs from a C&C server and thus a static analysis tool has no way to determine the behavior of the app. Other categories, such as *InputStreams*, *Readers* and *Crypto*, etc., include APIs that access resources which might be available at the time of analysis. However, their use hardens analysis. For instance, an app can retrieve the required parameters, using APIs from *InputStreams/Readers* categories, from a file which can be in any format while the analysis needs to know in advance which format to expect.

In order to test the ability of existing tools to analyze such apps, we developed a set of apps that leak sensitive information. These apps use reflection APIs to call various sensitive APIs where the names of these APIs and their classes are provided as strings by some of the sources listed in Table 2, such as *Hashtable*, *Crypto*, and *InputStream*. We analyzed these apps using Flowdroid [11], IccTa [21], SAAF [20], Androguard [2], SCandroid [18] and Amandroid [25]. We observed that none of these tools were able to successfully detect the concealed malicious functionality. It is worth mentioning here that some of the tools, such as Flowdroid, SAAF, etc., can determine the targets of reflection calls to a certain extent when the parameters used in reflection APIs are string constants provided in the code.

4.2 Dataset Description

For the analysis process, we created a dataset of real world apps containing both benign and malicious samples.

Google Play Store: The dataset consists of 13,223 apps downloaded from the Android official Google Play Store [7]. Although, there are instances of malicious apps been published to the official app store, Google Play Store uses Google Bouncer as a vetting mechanism for the apps submitted to the store. Hence, one can safely assume that the probability of a malicious app at the Google Play Store is considerably lower as compared to other markets.

F-droid: We added 3,305 apps downloaded from an online third party market, i.e., F-droid [6]. F-droid also provides the source code of the apps. Third-party app markets usually contain a higher number of malicious apps as these markets, most of the times, do not analyze the apps before publishing them. However, these samples are assumed to be benign in our work as they are flagged benign by most of the antivirus tools on VirusTotal [9].

To complement the downloaded benign apps, the dataset also consists of 3,645 malware samples, in the form of .apk files.

Genome Project: 1,260 malware samples, divided into 49 families, are taken from the Malware Genome Project [29].

AndroidSandbox: 1,875 of the malware samples in our dataset are downloaded from AndroidSandbox [3]. AndroidSandbox is an online malware analysis service, unfortunately, out of service temporarily.

Contagio Mobile Malware Dump: The rest of the malware samples are downloaded from Contagio Blog [4]. Contagio Blog is a repository for collecting malware samples. These samples are also downloadable for research purposes.

5   Analysis Results and Discussion

Experiment Design: We performed the experiment separately for the various app sources as discussed in the previous section. Doing so, we had more control over when to stop/start the analysis in case there is some problem. Moreover, this design of the experiment later on helped in two ways, i.e., (1) comparing results from different app sources, and (2) aggregating the results into two categories (malicious and benign).

We used two machines for the experiment. The first one is a desktop, Dell Precision T1700, with a Quad-Core Intel(R) Xeon(R) 3.10 GHz CPU and 8 GB memory. The second machine is an HP laptop having an Intel Core i7-2630QM 2.00 GHz CPU and 4 GB of memory. Analyzing all these apps with our tool on the two machines running in parallel took roughly a month.

The analysis provides an idea about the prevalence of reflection/DCL usage, in real world apps, in a manner which can be used to conceal malicious behavior and bypass app vetting process deployed at app markets.

The goal of the analysis is to answer the following research questions:

- **Q1:** What is the distribution of different categories of reflection/DCL APIs (as mentioned in Sect. 4) in both legitimate and malicious apps?
- **Q2:** How often do reflection/DCL APIs receive their parameters from one or more source APIs (as mentioned in Sect. 4)?
- **Q3:** What is the share of individual source APIs among all the mentioned source APIs in providing parameters to the target APIs?
- **Q4:** What is the highlight of the analysis results which is distinguishable in benign and malicious apps?

Q1. Presence of Reflection/DCL APIs: It is important to mention that we are only concerned with the developer's code and do not consider the occurrences of the target APIs in the Android framework itself. Figure 2(a) shows a graphical representation of the prevalence of the three categories of the target APIs, i.e., *Code, Class, Method*, in the analyzed apps. It shows that class loading and method invocation using reflection is widely used in both legitimate as well as malicious apps. At the same time, usage of additional code loading in the form of .jar/.dex/.apk is comparatively lower. The Black bars in the graph show that the use of code loading in the form of .jar/.dex/.apk is negligible in legitimate apps, whereas malicious apps tend to use this feature which helps them evade static analysis tools.

Q2. Parameters from Source APIs: A small fraction of the total occurrences of the target APIs in the analyzed apps receive their parameters from the source APIs, mentioned in Sect. 4, which could potentially hinder static analysis tools. This fraction is less even in malicious apps as shown in Fig. 2(b), except for the Genome malware dataset. The obvious reasoning behind these low numbers (or almost equal numbers in legitimate and malicious apps) can be the fact that most of the malware samples are repackaged versions of benign apps and, therefore, would use reflection/DCL in the same manner in general. This necessarily implies that apps usually provide class names and method names to reflection/DCL APIs as string constants, which is a good news for static analysis tools. However, in order to evade static analysis tools, it is not necessary to obfuscate the parameters of all the reflection/DCL calls, rather obfuscating those calls which perform malicious behavior is enough. Moreover, the trend in malicious apps is to provide a significant amount of benign functionality to lure the user into installing the app and, also, surreptitiously perform some malicious functionality.

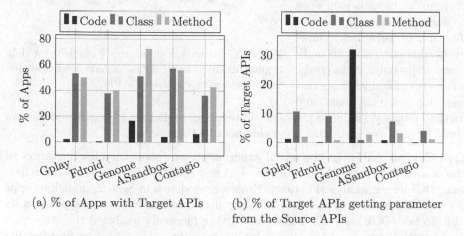

(a) % of Apps with Target APIs   (b) % of Target APIs getting parameter
                                       from the Source APIs

Fig. 2. Prevalence of Target APIs in the analyzed apps and Source APIs providing the parameter passed to Target APIs

Q3. Contribution of Individual Source APIs: Apart from the bar representing the percentage of *Dynamic Code Loading* APIs taking its parameters from the source APIs for the Genome malware dataset in Fig. 2(b), the rest of the bars for all the apps datasets hardly reach 10 %. This behavior is more or less identical at this coarse level in both legitimate as well as malicious apps. However, Fig. 3, which provides a finer view of the contributions of individual sources, reveals more about the behavior of legitimate and malicious samples. Figure 3 shows the graph for the top 5 contributing source API categories in each dataset. It reveals that most of the apps in both datasets, benign and malicious, retrieve class and method names from Map/Hashtable and, therefore, it is the prime contributor in providing parameters to reflection/DCL calls. One reason for the high usage of Map/Hashtable can be the usage of DexGuard (a commercial Android app obfuscator) [5]. Its string encryption mechanism uses byte-arrays and Maps for obfuscating strings.

The other major contributing sources are `Input Streams` and `Readers`, which are used to retrieve class and method names from configuration files either provided along with the `.apk` package or provided at runtime. Both of these categories can be used to conceal behavior and, therefore, their usage in malicious apps is slightly on the higher side. The use of `Telephony`, however, is mostly found in malicious apps only. Apparently, there are not many benign reasons for receiving class and

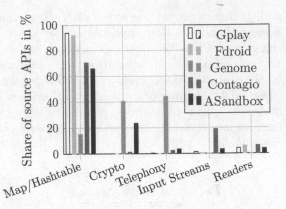

Fig. 3. Contribution of source APIs in providing arguments to Target APIs. X-axis represent the various categories of source APIs.

method names via an SMS message. However, for malicious apps, this mechanism could be used as a communication channel to a C&C server.

Q4. Crypto APIs: In the initial experiment, we found very few instances of the standard `Crypto` APIs being used as the sources of parameters for reflection/DCL in our analyzed dataset. However, as shown in Sect. 2, malicious apps do use encrypted strings, which are only decrypted at runtime, as parameters of reflection/DCL calls. Therefore, we further manually analyzed the *Anserver-Bot* family of the Genome dataset by disassembling the `.apk` files and looking into the Smali code. We found out that *AnserverBot* stores the code file names as encrypted strings and decrypts them at runtime when passing them on to `DexClassLoader`. However, it does not use the standard `Crypto` APIs to decrypt these strings, but rather uses its own logic for decryption. We could not look into all the apps for such encryption/decryption techniques, which could be another interesting study, but understandably, using non-standard encryption/decryption techniques might be more attractive to malware developers.

These results show that a wide range of real world apps, specifically malicious apps, use reflection/DCL in a manner that enables them to bypass state-of-the-art automated analysis tools. The increasing number of apps and the rapid evolution of anti-analysis techniques found in modern day malware demand for more effective and sophisticated automated analysis tools.

6   Considerations on Analysis Tools for Android

The combination of code update techniques along with anti-debugging, emulator detection techniques and the ability to reveal malicious behavior only when particular conditions (i.e., temporal) are met enables malware developers to bypass analysis tools. We propose some recommendations that could be useful in detecting malware even in the presence of evasive techniques.

Modern analysis tools need to have an efficient and effective dynamic analysis part due to some inherent limitations of static analysis. We recommend to push for targeted dynamic analysis where target APIs, such as those of reflection/DCL, are identified and the application is triggered with inputs which make it follow the target paths. A targeted triggering solution coupled with other solutions, such as Stadyna [27], will help in revealing malicious behavior otherwise concealed by a malicious app.

Considering the problem of stimulating apps' behavior during an analysis/debug environment, loadtime analysis of the code other than that contained in the standard .dex file of an app can help detecting malicious code loading. Android framework can have an analysis module which performs some lightweight on-device analysis of the code loaded from arbitrary locations before loading it. [17] provides a library for secure class loading, but they only check for the integrity of the code. Adding other forms of security analysis to their solution would be more helpful.

According to Google's policy, all the apps must use the Google Play Store for their updates. However, this policy is not always enforced, as the BrainTest example shows. An effective enforcement of this policy would result in catering the problem of malicious code updates to an extent. Therefore, any app which downloads code from any location other than the Google Play Store should be deemed malicious and not allowed to do so.

7   Limitations

A non trivial number of apps were analyzed in this work and should provide a fair view of reflection/DCL usage. However, we understand that the same experiment on a much larger scale, possibly performed by app markets such as Google play store, would result in providing a much better picture of the situation regarding how benign and malicious apps use reflection/DCL.

The malware datasets, in particular, the one from the Genome Project, is a bit old now keeping in view the rapid increase in the number of mobile malware samples. The trend towards more obfuscation and sophistication in malware implies that the evasive behavior would be more prevalent in newer malware samples.

We do not analyze native code, therefore, the sources of parameters coming from native code are not considered in the analysis presented in this paper. Moreover, the analysis tool does not capture information flow to reflection/DCL calls obfuscated through other reflective calls.

8   Related Work

Literature shows that there have been efforts to analyze apps in the presence of reflection and DCL in Java as well as in Android. Livshits et al.'s work uses points-to analysis and cast analysis to statically resolve the targets of reflection [22]. Similarly, Christensen et al. use Java string analyzer to statically track the arguments passed to reflection APIs to resolve their targets [15]. A static analysis tool for Android apps, Flowdroid, performs data flow analysis and resolves the targets of reflection only when the parameters are string constants [11]. However, none of them provides an analysis on the sources of the parameters passed to these APIs and their possible contribution in concealing malicious behavior.

Hirzel *et al.* extend pointer analysis to resolve reflection, DCL and native code using online (dynamic) analysis [19]. They instrument the virtual machine service that handles reflection and DCL with handlers, which dynamically updates a constraint database during the program execution. Similarly, Bodden *et al.* propose TamiFlex which complements static analysis of Java apps by resolving DCL and reflection [12]. TamiFlex executes a Java app, which is modified using `java.lang.instrument` API, and logs the information about DCL and reflection. However, similar to dynamic analysis, both these techniques suffer from the triggering problem.

Zhauniarovich *et al.* present Stadyna which is a tool for analyzing Android apps in the presence of reflection and DCL [27]. They combine static and dynamic analysis similar to [12]. They also present an extensive analysis of the presence of reflection and DCL in legitimate and malicious apps. Our work is different as we focus on the sources of the parameters of reflection/DCL APIs that can be used to evade static analysis tools. We also present an extensive analysis of real world apps for possible presence of such dangerous/suspicious usage of reflection/DCL.

Poeplau *et al.* [23] have tried to solve the problem of dynamic code loading, potentially malicious, using a whitelisting approach. Their whitelists are based on hashes of codes to be loaded. They propose that only those pieces of code could be loaded dynamically, which have their hashes available in the mentioned whitelist. They also developed a sample malicious app and practically evaded Google Bouncer using DCL. Similarly, Canfora *et al.* present composition malware where they present a model for evading analysis tools. However, their focus is more on downloading the code from different places and combining them at runtime to create malicious app logic [14]. However, in our work we present a more generic evasion process used by malicious apps focusing on the underlying reflection and DCL APIs and the sources of their parameters.

9   Conclusion

Dynamic code update features, such as reflection and DCL, are widely used in Android apps to make them extensible. These features, however, attract malware developers due to their potential capability of evading analysis tools when their parameters are obfuscated or provided only at runtime. In this work, we developed a tool that analyzes Android apps and finds source/sink relationships between certain potentially dangerous source APIs and reflection/DCL APIs. Moreover, to emphasize the importance of the parameters used in reflection/DCL APIs, we analyzed a dataset of real world apps. The results of our analysis show that malicious apps do try to hide the parameters of reflection/DCL APIs, by encrypting them or receiving them at runtime from the outside world, in order to bypass static analysis tools. The results of our analysis combined with the study of the static analysis tools available today for Android apps highlight the need for further research and development of analysis tools that efficiently combine static and dynamic analysis.

References

1. 2015 mobile threat report published by the pulse secure mobile threat center (MTC). https://www.pulsesecure.net/lp/mobile-threat-report-2014/
2. AndroGuard: Reverse engineering, malware and goodware analysis of Android applications. https://code.google.com/p/androguard/
3. Android Sandbox. http://www.androidsandbox.net/samples/
4. Contagio Mobile Malware Mini Dump. http://www.http://contagiominidump.blogspot.it/
5. Dexguard: The most advanced security software for android applications. https://www.guardsquare.com/dexguard
6. F-Droid – Android market. https://f-droid.org/
7. Google Play – Android official market. https://play.google.com/store/apps
8. Number of available applications in the Google Play Store from December 2009 to July 2015. http://www.statista.com/statistics/266210/number-of-available-applications-in-the-google-play-store/
9. Virustotal - free online malware and url scanner. https://www.virustotal.com
10. Smartphone OS Market Share, 2015 Q2 (2015). http://www.idc.com/prodserv/smartphone-os-market-share.jsp
11. Arzt, S., Rasthofer, S., Fritz, C., Bodden, E., Bartel, A., Klein, J., Le Traon, Y., Octeau, D., McDaniel, P.: FlowDroid: precise context, flow, field, object-sensitive and lifecycle-aware taint analysis for android apps. In: Proceedings of the 35th ACM SIGPLAN Conference on Programming Language Design and Implementation, pp. 259–269 (2014)
12. Bodden, E., Sewe, A., Sinschek, J., Oueslati, H., Mezini, M.: Taming reflection: aiding static analysis in the presence of reflection and customclass loaders. In: Proceedings of the 33rd International Conference on Software Engineering, pp. 241–250. ACM (2011)
13. Callaham, J.: Google says there are now 1.4 billion active Android devices worldwide (2015). http://www.androidcentral.com/google-says-there-are-now-14-billion-active-android-devices-worldwide
14. Canfora, G., Mercaldo, F., Moriano, G., Visaggio, C.A.: Composition-malware: building android malware at run time. In: 2015 10th International Conference on Availability, Reliability and Security (ARES), pp. 318–326. IEEE (2015)
15. Christensen, A.S., Møller, A., Schwartzbach, M.I.: Precise analysis of string expressions. In: Cousot, R. (ed.) SAS 2003. LNCS, vol. 2694, pp. 1–18. Springer, Heidelberg (2003). doi:10.1007/3-540-44898-5_1
16. F-Secure: Trojan: Android/FakeNotify Gets Updated (2011). http://www.f-secure.com/weblog/archives/00002291.html?tduid=f57e2769518f081721ffca586e797b2a
17. Falsina, L., Fratantonio, Y., Zanero, S., Kruegel, C., Vigna, G., Maggi, F.: Grab'n run: secure and practical dynamic code loading for android applications. In: Proceedings of the 31st Annual Computer Security Applications Conference, pp. 201–210. ACM (2015)

18. Fuchs, A.P., Chaudhuri, A., Foster, J.S.: Scandroid: automated security certification of android applications, **2**(3). Univ. of Maryland (2009). http://www.cs.umd.edu/avik/projects/scandroidascaa
19. Hirzel, M., Dincklage, D.V., Diwan, A., Hind, M.: Fast online pointer analysis. ACM Trans. Program. Lang. Syst. (TOPLAS) **29**(2), 11 (2007)
20. Hoffmann, J., Ussath, M., Holz, T., Spreitzenbarth, M.: Slicing droids: program slicing for smali code. In: Proceedings of the 28th Annual ACM Symposium on Applied Computing, pp. 1844–1851 (2013)
21. Li, L., Bartel, A., Bissyande, T.F.D.A., Klein, J., Le Traon, Y., Arzt, S., Rasthofer, S., Bodden, E., Octeau, D., McDaniel, P.: IccTA: detectinginter-component privacy leaks in android apps. In: 2015 IEEE/ACM 37th IEEE International Conference on Software Engineering (ICSE 2015) (2015)
22. Livshits, B., Whaley, J., Lam, M.S.: Reflection analysis for Java. In: Yi, K. (ed.) APLAS 2005. LNCS, vol. 3780, pp. 139–160. Springer, Heidelberg (2005). doi:10.1007/11575467_11
23. Poeplau, S., Fratantonio, Y., Bianchi, A., Kruegel, C., Vigna, G.: Executethis! analyzing unsafe and malicious dynamic code loading in android applications (2014)
24. Polkovnichenko, A., Boxiner, A.: Braintest - a new level of sophistication in mobile malware. Technical report, Check Point Technologies Ltd
25. Wei, F., Roy, S., Ou, X., et al.: Amandroid: a precise and generalinter-component data flow analysis framework for security vetting of androidapps. In: Proceedings of the 2014 ACM SIGSAC Conference on Computer and Communications Security, pp. 1329–1341. ACM (2014)
26. Wognsen, E.R., Karlsen, H.S., Olesen, M.C., Hansen, R.R.: Formalisation andanalysis of dalvik bytecode. Science of Computer Programming (2013)
27. Zhauniarovich, Y., Ahmad, M., Gadyatskaya, O., Crispo, B., Massacci, F.: Stadyna: addressing the problem of dynamic code updates in the security analysis of android applications. In: Proceedings of the 5th ACM Conferenceon Data and Application Security and Privacy, pp. 37–48. ACM (2015)
28. Zhou, Y., Jiang, X.: An analysis of the AnserverBot Trojan. Technical report, Department of Computer Science, NC State University (2013). http://www.csc.ncsu.edu/faculty/jiang/pubs/AnserverBot_Analysis.pdf
29. Zhou, Y., Jiang, X.: Dissecting android malware: characterization and evolution. In: Proceedings of the 2012 IEEE Symposium on Security and Privacy, pp. 95–109 (2012)

Evaluation of Resource-Based App Repackaging Detection in Android

Olga Gadyatskaya[1(✉)], Andra-Lidia Lezza[1], and Yury Zhauniarovich[2]

[1] SnT, University of Luxembourg, Luxembourg, Luxembourg
olga.gadyatskaya@uni.lu, andra.lezza.001@student.uni.lu
[2] Qatar Computing Research Institute, HBKU, Doha, Qatar
yzhauniarovich@qf.org.qa

Abstract. Android app repackaging threatens the health of application markets, as repackaged apps, besides stealing revenue for honest developers, are also a source of malware distribution. Techniques that rely on visual similarity of Android apps recently emerged as a way to tackle the repackaging detection problem, as code-based detection techniques often fail in terms of efficiency, and effectiveness when obfuscation is applied [19,21]. Among such techniques, the resource-based repackaging detection approach that compares sets of files included in apks has arguably the best performance [10,17,20]. Yet, this approach has not been previously validated on a dataset of repackaged apps.

In this paper we report on our evaluation of the approach, and present substantial improvements to it. Our experiments show that the state-of-art tools applying this technique rely on too restrictive thresholds. Indeed, we demonstrate that a very low proportion of identical resource files in two apps is a reliable evidence for repackaging. Furthermore, we have shown that the Overlap similarity score performs better than the Jaccard similarity coefficient used in previous works. By applying machine learning techniques, we give evidence that considering separately the included resource file types significantly improves the detection accuracy of the method. Experimenting with a balanced dataset of more than 2700 app pairs, we show that with our enhancements it is possible to achieve the F-measure of 0.9919.

Keywords: Android security · Repackaging · Resource files

1 Introduction

With more than 1.4 billion active devices and more than 1.6 million of apps only on the official Google Play market, Android is the dominating mobile OS today[1]. Android is an open eco-system, i.e., users can install apps not only from Google Play [6]. This openness led to flourishing third-party markets, e.g., with localized content, or even with stolen apps. Indeed, *application repackaging*, when

---

The work of Olga Gadyatskaya was supported by the Luxembourg National Research Fund (C15/IS/10404933/COMMA).

[1] According to Gartner http://www.gartner.com/newsroom/id/3169417.

© Springer International Publishing AG 2016
B.B. Brumley and J. Röning (Eds.): NordSec 2016, LNCS 10014, pp. 135–151, 2016.
DOI: 10.1007/978-3-319-47560-8_9

a legitimate app is re-published by adversaries, is polluting Android markets worldwide. It is a known vector of Android malware distribution [26], and not even Google Play is immune to this threat [23]. While the recently spotted Trojans hardly included any useful functionality, users still fell victims to their lure because familiar icons and names were used by the badware[2].

App repackaging detection approaches recently turned to the intuition of visual similarity between original apps and their plagiarized copies [10,15–17, 19,20]. Indeed, the users have certain expectations for the "look and feel" of the original apps, and it might be more challenging for malicious repackagers to change the GUI design than to insert, modify or remove some code parts [19]. Among these techniques, arguably the best performance could be achieved by the *resource-based repackaging detection* approach that directly compares the "look and feel" of applications represented by the included images, multimedia, layout and other files. This approach was adopted by, e.g., the FSquaDRA tool [20], the PlayDrone system [17], and the APPraiser framework [10]. These tools compute similarity of two applications based on the number of identical files (resources) included in both packages proportional to the total number of included files (the Jaccard similarity score that ranges in [0,1]).

Although a strong correlation of the resource-based similarity score with the code-based similarity score produced by Androguard [5] was previously reported [20], and manual validation exercises were positive [10,17,20], a thorough assessment of the resource-based repackaging detection approach effectiveness has never been done before. Whether it could show reliable results in a practical setting was an open question.

In this paper we close this gap by empirically evaluating resource-based repackaging detection in experiments on a dataset including repackaged and non-repackaged pairs. In particular, we explore the following research questions:

RQ1: Does the resource-based repackaging detection approach work in practice? Can we identify a definitive threshold for the resource-based similarity score that separates classes of repackaged and not-repackaged app pairs with tolerable false positive and false negative rates?

RQ2: Does the effectiveness of the resource-based repackaging detection tool depend on the similarity metric used (i.e., Jaccard similarity used in [10,17,20])? If yes, which similarity metric suits better to the problem of the resource-based repackaging detection?

RQ3: Can we improve the repackaging detection rates with the help of machine learning algorithms?

RQ4: Can the predictive power be improved if different types of resources will be considered separately?

RQ5: What types of resources are more or less susceptible to modifications during the repackaging process?

---

[2] http://www.welivesecurity.com/2016/02/24/porn-clicker-trojans-google-play-analysis/.

Answering these questions, this work makes the following contributions:

- We practically verified that resource-based approaches [10,17,20] can be indeed used for detection of repackaged applications. We have found the threshold value 0.0629, which can be further used directly in tools [10,17,20] to minimize both false positive and false negative errors.
- Our experiments with several similarity scores showed that the Overlap similarity score achieves the best performance (F-measure 0.9847), while prior works [10,17,20] relied on the slightly less efficient Jaccard similarity.
- We experimented with repackaging detection based on individual scores for distinct resource file types. We used 18 file types as a feature vector, evaluated several classifiers with these features and found that effectiveness of the approach is improved by considering separately different types of files. In the best case, with the non-optimized Random Forest classifier, we achieved F-measure of 0.9919 improving the single score-based approach considerably.
- We investigated the susceptibility to modification in repackaging of the individual resource file types. Our results show that multimedia files, libraries, raw resources and images are least frequently changed in repackaging, while the main dex code file, the manifest file and the compiled resources (e.g., strings) are the most frequently changed resource file types.

Our findings underline that resource-based repackaging detection is a practical enhancement to an on-market triage. To stimulate further investigations and adoption of the method, we release our system open-source[3].

2   Resource-Based Repackaging Detection

Resource Files. Resource files are an integral part of any Android application package (apk). They include graphics, texts, layouts, and multimedia content that will be presented to the user to provide a unique user experience. Other types of files in the apk are code files (classes.dex and library files) and the manifest file. In this paper, we in fact refer to all files composing an apk as resource files. Resource files are typically numerous (an average apk includes more than 300 files [20]), thus they can be considered representative for the apk.

Upon package signing by the developer, SHA1 digests of all included resource files (and other files) are created and stored in the apk within the MANIFEST.MF file. Later, on the device, the hashes are used to verify the integrity of the files constituting the package. The Android application signing mechanism, however, does not protect against integrity violation of the package (repackaging). In malicious repackaging, the adversary strips off the signature of the original developer, decompiles the app, introduces the required changes (e.g., changes the ad library identifier to redirect the revenue streams or injects malicious code), rebuilds the app and signs it again with a new certificate [23].

---

[3] The code is available at https://github.com/zyrikby/FSquaDRA2.

Resource-Based Similarity Score. The basic intuition behind the resource-based similarity score, which is ultimately leveraged for repackaging detection in [10,17,20], is that, in order to maintain the visual similarity of the repackaged app with the original one, the repackager does not change the resource files at all, or only modifies a fraction of them. Thus, resource files can be used to pinpoint visually similar app pairs.

The resource-based similarity score (*ressim* for short) for a pair of apks is computed in [10,17,20] by applying the Jaccard similarity coefficient to sets of resource file hashes. For two apks A and B with file hash sets H_A and H_B, correspondingly, $Jressim(A, B) = |H_A \cap H_B|/|H_A \cup H_B|$, where $Jressim$ stands for Jaccard resource similarity score. With this formula, two apps with completely different sets of files hashes have the $Jressim$ score equal to 0, whereas two apps with completely identical resources have the $Jressim$ score equal to 1.

The tools utilizing resource-based repackaging detection are FSquaDRA [20], PlayDrone [17], and APPraiser [10]. FSquaDRA computes the resource-based similarity score ($Jressim$) and leverages the fact that hashes of all files are already included in the apk [20]. For identifying similar apps, APPraiser utilizes the same $Jressim$ score applied to included files (it computes MD5 hashes of the files and eliminates common libraries), but it is implemented at the market scale and more efficiently than FSquaDRA by leveraging the sparseness of data [10]. PlayDrone also applies the $Jressim$ score for detection of similar apps, and it includes resource file names as features alongside MD5 digests of the files themselves, and excludes common libraries from consideration [17]. PlayDroid operates at the Google Play market scale. Evaluation of the approach conducted with these tools was limited.

Indeed, the reported validation of the resource-based similarity approach is based on manual experiments with a limited number of apps [10,17,20], and the strong correlation discovered between the $Jressim$ score and the similarity score computed by the static analyzer **Androguard**, which measures the apk similarity score based on the included method signatures (i.e., the code) [5]. Thus, the strong correlation of resource-based scores with the code-based ones shown in [17,20] gives justification that the resource-based similarity detection approach is valid. Despite strong suggestions from the literature [10,15–17] and our personal communication with mobile security companies that the approach is applied in practice, the resource-based similarity detection method so far has not been validated on a sufficiently large dataset.

Moreover, without evaluation on the ground truth (a dataset with known repackaged and non-repackaged pairs), it is not possible to estimate a threshold (a value such that all pairs with a higher $Jressim$ score are reliably repackaged, and with a lower score are probably not repackaged) for the $Jressim$ score that can then be used by app markets in their triage. For the FSquaDRA tool the threshold value 0.7 was suggested, but [20] acknowledged that there was no way to confirm the threshold or adjust it without a repackaged dataset. The PlayDroid system applies the threshold value 0.8 and reports experiments with thresholds in range [0.6, 1.0]. (however, it includes resource file names as features in addition to the MD5 hashes of resource files, and excludes common libraries, so we cannot directly compare these threshold values) [17]. The APPraiser tool relies on the threshold value 0.8, and [10] reported that changing it to 0.7 or 0.9 did not affect the experiments significantly. At the same time, the *Jressim* value of 0.7 implies that 70 % of files are the same for two apks. Intuitively, much smaller fraction of identical resource files could already be a sign of repackaging.

Other Repackaging Detection Methods. State-of-art approaches in repackaging detection on Android have a strong focus on code similarity (e.g., [1,3–5,8,9,11,18,25]). To achieve scalability, tools leverage a combination of lightweight app fingerprints (e.g., certificates, package names, method signatures, n-grams of code) for identifying similar apps (e.g., [7,12]).

Recently, techniques that look at visual application similarity emerged. Differently from the resource-based repackaging detection approach evaluated in this paper, these techniques investigate layout files (e.g., [16]) and activity transition graphs (e.g., [15,19]) as means to represent the UI behaviour that is difficult to modify without a good understanding of the code. Among these techniques, DroidEagle [16] follows the same intuition as resource-based repackaging detection, and applies perceptual hashing to image files in order to detect similar pictures. It focuses on representing layout files as tree layout hashes and searching for similar layout structures.

ResDroid [15] utilizes resource files as features for detecting repackaged applications (e.g., it computes the average number of png files per folder in res/drawable). The MassVet system [2] follows a hybrid approach, as it relies on both similarity of UI structures and code similarity.

3   Dataset

We use a dataset of repackaged app pairs received from a fellow research group [11][4]. The dataset contains 2754 apps originally mapped into 1497 repackaged pairs. This dataset is representative of the piggybacking case: all app pairs in it include the original benign app and a repackaged version piggybacking malware (confirmed by VirusTotal[5]) [11]. Notice that for each repackaged app pair, its member apps are signed with different certificates.

As a first step to explore the obtained dataset, we applied the FSquaDRA tool [20] to perform pair-wise comparison of all files. In this experiment, we found that for 38 apps information about file hashes cannot be extracted by the tool. Among these 38 apps, 26 apps could not be installed, because they were not correctly signed: the whole META-INF folder was absent, or this folder was located in a wrong place (e.g., in theassets folder), or the signature file was missing). We received the error message Failure [INSTALL_PARSE_FAILED_NO_CERTIFICATES] during installation of these apps.

---

[4] https://github.com/serval-snt-uni-lu/Piggybacking.
[5] https://www.virustotal.com/.

As a security-aware app market would have discarded these apps anyway, we excluded these apks from consideration.

We were able to install the remaining 12 apps on a device and emulator. 10 of those were functional only on the device; and 2 failed to run on both device and emulator. The 12 apps are all malicious applications that install other apps in the background and show the same ads at startup. The FSquaDRA tool was unable to process them because they were misconfigured, so we excluded these apps from consideration. Overall, 126 repackaged app pairs were excluded from our dataset (for all 126 pairs at least one app was among the 38 non-processable ones). The remaining 1371 app pairs constitute for us the *truly repackaged pairs* dataset. To evaluate the false negative error rate of the approach, we have computed the *Jressim* scores for app pairs in this dataset.

Moreover, in order to evaluate the false positive error rate of the approach, we created a set of *truly non-repackaged pairs* by randomly selecting 1371 app . pairs from the dataset, excluding the broken 38 apps. We matched two apps together only if 3 conditions were satisfied: (1) their pair was not already considered as truly repackaged, (2) they did not belong to a connected component of repackaged apps (if apps a and b are a repackaged pair, and apps b and c are a repackaged pair, then apps a, b and c belong to the same connected component of repackaged apps), (3) they were signed with different certificates. We computed the *Jressim* scores for the selected non-repackaged pairs. Thus, we obtained a balanced labelled dataset for further experiments consisting of 2742 app pairs of two kinds: repackaged and non-repackaged. Notice that similarly to the designers of the original dataset [11], in our experiments we focus on detecting plagiarism (malicious repackaging), not rebranding (repackaging by the same developer).

Table 1. Summary statistics for evaluation of resource-based repackaging results (the *Jressim* scores) on the ground truth

Dataset	Statistics	Value
Truly repackaged app pairs (1371 pairs)	Min	0.0000
	1st Quartile	0.5050
	Median	0.7442
	3rd Quartile	0.9167
	Max	1.0000
	Mean	0.6893
Truly non-repackaged app (1371 pairs)	Min	0.0000
	1st Quartile	0.0000
	Median	0.0000
	3rd Quartile	0.0000
	Max	0.4218
	Mean	0.0022

4   Resource Similarity Evaluation

In this section we address the **RQ1** and empirically evaluate the baseline resource-based similarity detection approach (the *Jressim* score) on the ground truth.

Baseline Results. To answer **RQ1** we started by applying the resource-based repackaging detection method implemented by the open-source tool FSquaDRA [20] to our dataset. Table 1 reports the summary statistics for both repackaged and non-repackaged pairs and it reveals the shape of data. We can see that for the truly repackaged pairs the *Jressim* scores are quite high (with mean value 0.6893 and median 0.7442). At the same time, there are still repackaged app pairs that have 0.0 similarity score. For the truly non-repackaged app pairs the summary statistics are different. We see that more than 75 % of the *Jressim* scores in this case are equal to 0. At the same time, some app pairs in this dataset expose non-zero *Jressim* scores while being non-repackaged.

We can now compute the value (*threshold*) that minimizes the false positive error rate (the number of non-repackaged pairs that will be above the threshold) and false negative error rate (the number of repackaged pairs that will fall below the threshold) using the standard 10-fold cross-validation scheme. For Jaccard similarity, the average threshold in 10-fold cross validation on the dataset at hand is **0.0629**. This threshold might be further used with tools like FSquaDRA and APPraiser [10,20]. We report the accuracy, precision, recall and the F-measure for this threshold in Table 2(a).

At the same time, figures reported in Table 1 show that the baseline resource-based repackaging detection approach produces a number of outliers: some repackaged app pairs have low *Jressim* scores, while some non-repackaged app pairs have relatively high *Jressim* scores (significantly higher than the threshold 0.0629). We have looked at these outliers in order to understand the practical reasons for errors in the approach.

Table 2. Accuracy statistics

(a) *Jressim* accuracy metrics overview with the threshold 0.0629

Metrics	Value
Accuracy	0.9847
Precision	0.9912
Recall	0.9781
F-measure	0.9845

(b) Androguard metrics overview with the threshold 0.4330

Metrics	Value
Accuracy	0.9581
Precision	0.9764
Recall	0.9441
F-measure	0.9600

(a)   (b)

Fig. 1. Icons of apps in a repackaged pair with the *Jressim* score 0.0

False Negatives. Repackaged app pairs with the *Jressim* score less than 0.0629 are false negatives. There are 29 such pairs (out of 1371); all of them were present in the original list of repackaged pairs that came with the dataset [11].

Among the 29 false negatives, 7 pairs have the *Jressim* score equal to 0.0. We have manually reviewed these apps. 4 pairs are visually similar, while 3 pairs are visually different (for 2 pairs even different functionality). 4 visually similar pairs have different hashes of the resource files, and the resource files have been substantially changed in the repackaged apps (new folders were introduced; images were substituted). Figure 1 gives an example of icons of a repackaged pair with *Jressim* = 0.0. As seen from the figure, the repackagers have produced a completely new icon that is still recognizable to a user.

For the other 22 pairs of repackaged apps with *Jressim* greater than 0 but less than 0.0629, the apps in these pairs are visually similar. The large proportion of these are plagiarized apps translated into a different language. Repackagers of these apps changed substantially resource files, thus, the approach failed to classify them correctly.

False Positives. 11 non-repackaged pairs are false positives as they have the *Jressim* score greater than the threshold 0.0629. We manually inspected these apps and checked which resources were shared between the apps in these pairs. We found that the false positives appeared in our results due to usage of the same libraries for app development. E.g., 3 app pairs were developed using the Facebook SDK[6]. These findings show that a prior filtering of resources is useful, as it will allow to considerably reduce the amount of false positives. Such pruning can be done automatically, e.g., by removal of the most popular file hashes in the whole dataset [10,17].

Comparison with Androguard. We applied Androguard [5][7] to our dataset to measure code-based similarity for both repackaged and non-repackaged pairs. The threshold that yields the lowest cumulative error for Androguard on our dataset is 0.4330. Table 2(b) summarizes the accuracy metrics for Androguard achieved with this threshold. Notice that the threshold value 0.4330 minimizes the cumulative error on the whole dataset. In the 10-fold cross-validation scheme the accuracy metrics will be lower.

Tables 2(a) and (b) indicate that the resource-based repackaging detection approach has better effectiveness than the code-based approach. Moreover, resource-based repackaging detection has a much better efficiency. Using FSquaDRA [20], we ran full pairwise comparison (comparing all app pairs for apps in the original dataset [11]) in 165 s (on a laptop with 2.8 GHz processor and 16 GB of RAM). Androguard required more than 10 h only for the truly repackaged and non-repackaged pairs. Androguard is inherently slow on non-repackaged pairs [5], which in practice constitute the vast majority [10].

---

[6] Facebook SDK for Android https://developers.facebook.com/docs/android.
[7] https://github.com/androguard/androguard.

5 Fine-Tuning the Basic Approach

We now analyze how to improve the predictive power of the basic resource-based repackaging detection approach. In particular, we explore the questions **RQ2** and **RQ3** regarding the most suitable similarity metrics and classifier with the best discriminative power.

To answer these questions we used our dataset and machine learning approaches. For machine learning tasks we used the scikit-learn library, version 0.17.1 [13]. Additionally to the provided algorithms, we also developed a basic classifier separating two classes using a threshold obtained by minimizing the cumulative error (as reported in Sect. 4); to avoid over-fitting this classifier was further applied only in the 10-fold cross-validation setting.

Exploring Similarity Metrics. In [10,20] the Jaccard similarity metric was used for the full sets of hashes of resource files in a given pair of apps. In general, any similarity score applied to sets (multisets) of resource file hashes shows to which extent one application is similar to another. In this section we explore if usage of another metrics can improve the discriminative power of the method. To achieve this goal, we extended the open-source FSquaDRA tool [20] with the possibility to calculate similarity scores using different metrics. In particular, we took as a reference the `SimMetrics` Java library[8] and implemented in Python the metrics that compare lists of objects (sets/multisets). In particular, we implemented the following metrics:

Block (Manhattan) Similarity: $similarity(a,b) = 1 - distance(a,b)/(|a| + |b|)$, where $distance(a,b) = ||a - b||_1$ (distance from point a to point b is the sum of of absolute differences of their Cartesian coordinates).

Cosine Similarity: $similarity(a,b) = a \cdot b / (||a|| \times ||b||)$, i.e., it measures $\cos \phi$ of the angle ϕ between vectors a and b. Cosine similarity considers cardinality of elements (number of occurrences).

Sørensen-Dice Similarity: $similarity(a,b) = 2 \times |a \cap b|/(|a| + |b|)$.

Euclidean Similarity: $similarity(a,b) = 1 - distance(a,b)/\sqrt{|a|^2 + |b|^2})$, where $distance(a,b) = ||a - b||$ (distance from point a to point b is Euclidean norm of the vector $a - b$).

Jaccard Similarity: $similarity(a,b) = |a \cap b|/|a \cup b|$. This is the *Jressim* score used in [10,20].

Generalized Jaccard Similarity: follows the same formula as Jaccard similarity, but works over multisets.

Overlap Similarity: $similarity(a,b) = |a \cap b|/min(|a|, |b|)$.

Generalized Overlap Similarity: same as the overlap similarity, but works over multisets.

---

[8] https://github.com/Simmetrics.

Table 3. Predictive power comparison of similarity metrics

Metric	Accuracy	Precision	Recall	F-measure
Block	0.9832	0.9891	0.9774	0.9831
Cosine	0.9832	0.9883	0.9781	0.9831
Dice	0.9836	0.9898	0.9774	0.9835
Euclidian	0.7400	0.9020	0.5383	0.6733
Jaccard	0.9847	**0.9912**	0.9781	0.9845
Generalized Jaccard	0.9836	0.9898	0.9774	0.9835
Generalized overlap	0.9840	0.9855	0.9825	0.9840
Overlap	**0.9847**	0.9856	**0.9840**	**0.9847**
SimonWhite	0.9836	0.9898	0.9774	0.9835
Tanimoto	0.9829	0.9891	0.9767	0.9827

Simon White Similarity: the generalized (quantitative) Sørensen-Dice similarity, else called Simon-White coefficient, works over multisets and considers cardinality of elements.

Tanimoto Similarity: is expressed using the cosine similarity formula, but multiple occurrences of elements are not considered (as it works over sets).

We calculated these metrics for all app pairs in our dataset. For each metric, the average results in 10-fold cross-validation for the basic classifier that discriminates based on the similarity score is reported in Table 3 (same folds partition was applied for all metrics). The result demonstrate that the Overlap similarity metric has better accuracy, recall and the F-measure, while the Jaccard similarity metric shows better precision. The F-measure, which harmonically combines both precision and recall, indicates that generally Overlap similarity is preferable for the repackaging classification task with our dataset. Both previous studies on resource-based similarity detection [10, 20] relied on the Jaccard similarity score, however, experiments show that the Overlap metric can achieve better results. Therefore, in the rest of this paper we rely on this similarity metric.

For the Overlap similarity score (*Oressim* for short) the average *threshold* in 10-fold cross-validation is **0.1188**. This threshold should be further used in resource-based repackaging detection approach with the Overlap similarity score.

Applying Classifiers. In order to answer **RQ3** and assess which classifiers have the best discriminative power in our task, we experimented with 5 general-purpose classifiers: Logistic Regression, Support Vector Machines with a linear kernel, Decision Tree, Random Forest and Gradient Boosting. In this work we used the default values of the algorithm parameters, i.e., we skipped the parameter tuning step. Moreover, these classifiers were instantiated with the same initial state to ensure experiment replicability.

We applied the selected classifiers, including our own, to the dataset using only one feature – the Overlap similarity score *Oressim* calculated on all file

Table 4. Predictive power comparison of classifiers

Classifier	Accuracy	Precision	Recall	F-measure
OurClassifier	**0.9847**	0.9855	**0.9840**	**0.9847**
Logistic Regression	0.9799	**0.9941**	0.9657	0.9796
Linear SVM	0.9814	0.9904	0.9723	0.9812
Decision Tree	0.9756	0.9776	0.9737	0.9755
Random Forest	0.9763	0.9784	0.9745	0.9762
Gradient Boosting	0.9799	0.9840	0.9759	0.9798

hashes. Every classifier was validated in 10-fold cross-validation. Table 4 reports the average results for all classifiers. We can see that the cumulative error minimization classifier (OurClassifier) performs well and shows the best scores for accuracy, recall and the F-measure. In terms of precision, the Logistic Regression classifier has shown better results. Thus, in the task of resource-based repackaging detection with a single feature (the Overlap similarity score for all files), the algorithm classifying app pairs based on the score threshold separating classes of repackaged and non-repackaged app pairs can be used. At the same time, this algorithm cannot be generalized when several features are used for classification.

6   Resource Files Analysis and Improved Classification

We now address the research questions **RQ4** and **RQ5** concerning the exploration of resource file types for fine-tuning repackaging detection.

Exploring Resource File Types. An app package includes different types of files. It is still an open question whether repackagers generally modify all types of files, or only some specific types. Therefore, while previously a cumulative similarity score on all files was used, it might be beneficial to explore different types of resources separately. We now start to explore **RQ4** by dissecting the files constituting Android packages into different types.

Android documentation specifies resource types that can be included in a package[9]. However, during compilation some of them are compiled and placed into the compiled resource file `resources.arsc`. As the `MANIFEST.MF` file only stores paths to files and the hashes of their contents, it is impossible to compute separate similarity scores for these compiled resources. Operating with the `MANIFEST.MF` information, we can only divide files into types based on the common path prefixes and suffixes. In particular, we divide files based on their purpose (e.g., audio-video files) and their location (for instance, under the `res/` folder). The following resource types (features) are identified:

---

[9] http://developer.android.com/guide/topics/resources/available-resources.html.

Location-based file division:

1. `manifest`: the manifest file (`AndroidManifest.xml`)
2. `main_code`: main files with the compiled Android code (`classesN.dex`, where N is either empty or integer number)
3. `resources_arsc`: compiled resources file (`resources.arsc`)
4. `libs`: files located under `lib/` and `libs` folders
5. `assets`: files under `assets/` directory
6. `res_all`: all files located under `res/` folder
7. `res_raw`: files under `res/raw/` directory
8. `res_xml`: files located under `res/xml/` directory
9. `res_drawable`: files under `res/drawables/` folder
10. `res_menu`: files located under `res/menu/` directory
11. `res_layout`: layout files under `res/layout/` directory
12. `res_anim`: files under `res/anim/` folder
13. `res_color`: files in `res/color/` directory

Purpose-based file division:

14. `native_libs`: all files with `.so` extension
15. `code_general`: all files with `.so`, `.bin`, `.dex` and `.jar` extensions
16. `audio_video`: supported audio and video files[10]
17. `image`: all supported image files
18. `all_xml`: all XML files

We extracted the hashes corresponding to the considered types from both packages in an app pair under consideration, and calculated the Overlap similarity score *Oressim* separately for every file type. Thus, for each pair we obtained a feature vector with 18 values. The features are not independent: e.g., `code_general` includes `native_libs` and `main_code`. However, since the classifiers we chose do not assume feature independence, in contrast to e.g., Naïve Bayes, we did not put any restrictions on them. After extracting features, we applied the selected classifiers, excluding our own as it could not be generalized for multiple features, to the dataset using 10-fold cross-validation.

To discover the optimal set of features that drives better results, we applied the sequential forward selection (SFS) algorithm [14]. This algorithm starts with a single feature and sequentially adds the variables with which the classifier shows the highest score, until the size of the feature space specified by the user is reached. Once a feature is added, it cannot be removed from the search space. In our case, we selected the total number of features (18) as the limit. This approach reports not only if the classification can be improved by considering separately different types of files, but also if we can reduce the set of features to be extracted from files, thus, saving time for the feature extraction.

Some apps may lack files of a particular type. The conventional approach in this case is to assign the similarity score equal to 0 (e.g., this is how the

---

[10] http://developer.android.com/guide/appendix/media-formats.html.

SimMetrics library works). However, we also experimented with assigning to such cases a value that is out of the range (-1) to distinguish them.

Table 5 reports the F-measure for all classifiers (the accuracy score shows similar behavior, thus, we do not provide it here). Several important conclusions can be drawn from the results. First, it is now evident that if file types are considered as features, the effectiveness of repackaging detection can be improved. The Random Forest classifier with a combination of 12 features achieves the F-measure score of 0.9919, which is considerably better than our classifier operating on the cumulative similarity score (the F-measure 0.9847). Considering only 2 types of resources (when N/A's are substituted to -1), the Random Forest classifier already outperforms our classifier that minimizes the cumulative error.

Secondly, the classifiers behave differently depending on how the N/A values are treated. When we substitute N/A values to 0, Linear SVM and Logistic Regression classifiers show almost similar scores, outperforming the score of our custom classifier. At the same time, when N/A are equal to -1, even using a number of features, those classifiers cannot beat our classifier trained only on a single feature. At the same time, the Decision Tree algorithm shows the opposite behavior improving its score when N/A values are substituted to -1. This shows that classifiers used in resource-based repackaging detection systems should be selected considering, among all factors, how the N/A values are treated.

Last but not least, Table 5 demonstrates that generally the scores achieved by the Random Forest and Gradient Boosting algorithms in case when N/A values are substituted to -1, are better than using the conventional approach

Table 5. F-measure dependency on the number of features for the classifiers. Values highlighted with **bold** shows best result within a column, with *red* – best result in a row.

Features number	Logistic regression		Linear SVM		Decision tree		Random forest		Gradient boosting	
	$n/a = 0$	$n/a = -1$	$n/a = 0$	$n/a = -1$	$n/a = 0$	$n/a = -1$	$n/a = 0$	$n/a = -1$	$n/a = 0$	$n/a = -1$
1	0.9733	0.9733	0.9734	0.9734	0.9700	0.9700	0.9712	0.9712	0.9745	0.9745
2	0.9842	0.9834	0.9842	0.9820	0.9803	0.9879	0.9792	0.9872	0.9839	0.9868
3	0.9857	0.9838	0.9857	0.9824	0.9813	0.9883	0.9821	0.9886	0.9857	0.9883
4	0.9860	0.9842	0.9868	0.9831	0.9832	**0.9883**	0.9850	0.9897	0.9861	0.9901
5	0.9868	0.9842	0.9872	0.9835	0.9832	0.9883	0.9853	0.9908	0.9861	0.9901
6	0.9871	0.9842	0.9872	0.9838	**0.9835**	0.9883	0.9868	0.9904	0.9857	**0.9901**
7	0.9871	0.9842	0.9872	0.9842	0.9832	0.9879	0.9882	0.9919	0.9861	0.9901
8	0.9871	0.9842	0.9872	0.9846	0.9831	0.9875	0.9886	0.9908	0.9868	0.9901
9	0.9871	0.9842	0.9872	0.9846	0.9835	0.9872	0.9872	0.9901	0.9868	0.9897
10	0.9871	**0.9842**	**0.9872**	0.9846	0.9832	0.9875	0.9879	0.9905	**0.9868**	0.9897
11	0.9875	0.9842	0.9872	0.9846	0.9832	0.9872	0.9875	0.9908	0.9868	0.9897
12	0.9875	0.9842	0.9872	0.9846	0.9824	0.9872	0.9875	0.9919	0.9865	0.9894
13	**0.9875**	0.9842	0.9872	0.9842	0.9824	0.9875	**0.9890**	0.9919	0.9861	0.9897
14	0.9875	0.9842	0.9868	0.9846	0.9824	0.9861	0.9875	0.9919	0.9868	0.9894
15	0.9875	0.9842	0.9868	0.9846	0.9824	0.9857	0.9879	0.9912	0.9858	0.9894
16	0.9875	0.9834	0.9868	0.9842	0.9828	0.9850	0.9872	0.9908	0.9850	0.9890
17	0.9864	0.9831	0.9864	0.9839	0.9820	0.9846	0.9872	0.9908	0.9857	0.9886
18	0.9868	0.9827	0.9864	0.9835	0.9817	0.9858	0.9868	0.9901	0.9846	0.9883

(substitution to 0). Obviously, the absence of files of a particular type is also a feature and thus, it can improve the predictive power of a classifier, as we observed in our experiments.

Susceptibility of File Types to Modification in Repackaging. One of the main questions we would like to answer in this paper is **RQ5**. Obviously, to further improve the method for app plagiarism detection based on resource files, it is important to know which resources are more frequently modified during the repackaging process. To answer this question we performed the following experiment. For every type of files (present in both packages from an app pair) we calculated the average similarity score using only repackaged pairs from our dataset. File types with higher such scores are *less frequently modified* in repackaging. Obviously, if in a repackaged app pair the similarity score for some file type is high, then such files were mostly not modified. The results of this experiment are presented in Table 6(a).

Table 6(a) suggests that multimedia, raw, images, libraries in general, and native libraries are less frequently changed in the repackaging process. Several important conclusions can be drawn from this fact. First, despite the fact that in the recent years several methods were proposed to detect repackaged apps using resource similarity, it seems that adversaries still do not consider them as a threat to their business. Thus, the resource files that are not required to be changed in repackaging are mostly left untouched. Secondly, the mentioned file types are more difficult to change. Clearly, without special tools it is quite difficult to edit multimedia files or native libraries. That can also explain why these file types are mostly left in the original state. These considerations can improve the resiliency of approaches based on resources similarity comparison.

Table 6. Results for different file types in repackaging (on average)

(a) Files modified in repackaging (1 − files never modified; 0 − always modified)

Average Score	Feature
0.9788	audio_video
0.9574	res_raw
0.9269	images
0.9229	libs
0.9199	native_libs
0.9177	assets
0.8202	res_drawable
0.7648	res_all
0.4840	code_general
0.3679	res_xml
0.3503	res_anim
0.3273	res_menu
0.3077	all_xml
0.2802	res_color
0.2557	res_layout
0.1524	resources_arsc
0.0934	manifest
0.0773	main_code

(b) Same files in non-repackaged pairs (1 − always the same; 0 − never the same)

Average Score	Feature
0.0159	res_drawable
0.0130	images
0.0118	res_all
0.0094	libs
0.0087	native_libs
0.0057	res_color
0.0045	code_general
0.0036	res_raw
0.0032	assets
0.0030	all_xml
0.0018	res_layout
0.0	audio_video
0.0	manifest
0.0	res_anim
0.0	resources_arsc
0.0	res_xml
0.0	main_code
0.0	res_menu

According to our analysis, `dex` files, the Android manifest and the compiled resource files are changed quite often. This observation perfectly agrees with the repackaging process logic for the piggybacking scenario, which is the case for our original dataset [11]. If adversaries want to add some malicious functionality, they change the `dex` and Android manifest files to add necessary permissions [22]. There are many tools that can do this automatically for malicious and benign purposes (e.g., for instrumentation in testing [24]). The file containing compiled resources is also often modified in repackaging. This file incorporates information about string resources included in an apk. Evidently, if adversaries repackage an apk with the purpose of publishing it in other national markets, they translate the application. Therefore, an additional locale should be added to string resources, resulting in the compiled resources file change. Secondly, the adversaries often change ads IDs, which are usually defined within the string resources.

Table 6(b) reports similarity scores for the different resource files types for the non-repackaged dataset. This information is also instructive, as it allows to analyze better the false positives discussed in Sect. 4. Indeed, we see that developers reuse images (e.g., "like" buttons) and libraries across different apps.

We should mention that besides modification of the files, the score changes if files of that type are added or removed. Currently, we do not isolate these cases.

7   Discussion

Threats to Validity. We evaluated the resource-based repackaging detection approach on one dataset [11], which was originally collected under assumption of a lazy adversary who does not change a lot during repackaging. On more diverse datasets effectiveness of resource-based similarity detection approaches can be different, and it needs to be further investigated.

The resource-based similarity detection approach is currently not robust against an attacker who takes care to slightly change all files included in the original apk. This is not a challenging task, and minor edits can be automated. However, as we have mentioned in Sect. 4, most of repackaged pairs we failed to detect were either not visually similar, or visually similar to a user, but not to a machine. As Fig. 1 shows, repackagers can be very creative in modifying apps so that the main theme is recognizable, while the included images are very different. Advance AI techniques can be applied to detect such apps, but these techniques are currently not scalable to the on-market setting.

Yet, though the approach is very accurate on our dataset, which is quite recent, its robustness against a casual attacker (who just changes the files a little to modify the hashes) still can be improved, by, e.g., working with perceptual hashes or fuzzy hashes of the files (not the hashes included in the original package). Better understanding which file types are generally not modified in repackaging (e.g., multimedia, libraries and images) suggests that we can apply fuzzy hashing techniques only to those types of files.

Efficiency. We have operated in our experiments in a setting with a full pairwise comparison. This is not actually a scenario applicable to day-to-day app markets operations. Instead, in a practical set-up, a market expects to compare a relatively small set of recently submitted apps to a very large set of already known apps [10]. For a set-up like this, an app market can maintain a database with sorted hashes of already known files (e.g., in a tree-structure) that is efficiently searchable for hashes from the new apps.

8   Conclusions

In this paper we have practically evaluated the resource-based repackaging detection approach. Our experiments show that this technique is very effective with outstanding results for accuracy, precision, recall and the F-measure. Furthermore, we improve the existing tools [10,17,20] by suggesting the Overlap similarity metric to be used with the Random Forest classifier on 12 features. We have also reported which resource file types are less prone to modification in repackaging, and which resource files can coincide in non-repackaged pairs. Our results may be instructive for researchers and practitioners looking into adding the resource-based repackaging detection approach to their app triage schemes.

References

1. Chen, K., Liu, P., Zhang, Y.: Achieving accuracy and scalability simultaneously in detecting application clones on Android markets. In: Proceedings of ICSE. IEEE/ACM (2014)
2. Chen, K., Wang, P., Lee, Y., Wang, X., Zhang, N., Huang, H., Zou, W., Liu, P.: Finding unknown malice in 10 s: mass vetting for new threats at the Google-Play scale. In: Proceedings of USENIX Security Symposium (2015)
3. Crussell, J., Gibler, C., Chen, H.: Attack of the clones: detecting cloned applications on Android markets. In: Foresti, S., Yung, M., Martinelli, F. (eds.) ESORICS 2012. LNCS, vol. 7459, pp. 37–54. Springer, Heidelberg (2012). doi:10.1007/978-3-642-33167-1_3
4. Crussell, J., Gibler, C., Chen, H.: Scalable semantics-based detection of similar Android applications. In: Proceedings of ESORICS (2013)
5. Desnos, A.: Android: static analysis using similarity distance. In: Proceedings of HICSS 2012, pp. 5394–5403 (2012)
6. Gadyatskaya, O., Massacci, F., Zhauniarovich, Y.: Security in the Firefox OS and Tizen mobile platforms. IEEE Comput. **47**(6), 57–63 (2014)
7. Gonzalez, H., Kadir, A., Stackanova, N., Alzahrani, A., Ghorbani, A.: Exploring reverse engineering symptoms in Android apps. In: Proceedings of EuroSec. ACM (2015)
8. Guan, Q., Huang, H., Luo, W., Zhu, S.: Semantics-based repackaging detection for mobile apps. In: Caballero, J., Bodden, E., Athanasopoulos, E. (eds.) ESSoS 2016. LNCS, vol. 9639, pp. 89–105. Springer, Heidelberg (2016). doi:10.1007/978-3-319-30806-7_6
9. Hanna, S., Huang, L., Wu, E., Li, S., Chen, C., Song, D.: Juxtapp: a scalable system for detecting code reuse among Android applications. In: Flegel, U., Markatos, E., Robertson, W. (eds.) DIMVA 2012. LNCS, vol. 7591, pp. 62–81. Springer, Heidelberg (2013). doi:10.1007/978-3-642-37300-8_4

10. Ishii, Y., Watanabe, T., Akiyama, M., Mori, T.: Clone or relative? Understanding the originals of similar Android apps. In: Proceedings of IWSPA. ACM (2016)
11. Li, L., Li, D., Bissyandé, T.F., Lo, D., Klein, J., Le Traon, Y.: Ungrafting malicious code from piggybacked Android apps. Technical report, SnT, University of Luxembourg (2016)
12. Lindorfer, M., Volanis, S., Sisto, A., Neugschwandtner, M., Athanasopoulos, E., Maggi, F., Platzer, C., Zaneró, S., Ioannidis, S.: AndRadar: fast discovery of Android applications in alternative markets. In: Dietrich, S. (ed.) DIMVA 2014. LNCS, vol. 8550, pp. 51–71. Springer, Heidelberg (2014). doi:10.1007/978-3-319-08509-8_4
13. Pedregosa, F., Varoquaux, G., Gramfort, A., Michel, V., Thirion, B., Grisel, O., Blondel, M., Prettenhofer, P., Weiss, R., Dubourg, V., Vanderplas, J., Passos, A., Cournapeau, D., Brucher, M., Perrot, M., Duchesnay, E.: Scikit-learn: machine learning in Python. J. Mach. Learn. Res. **12**, 2825–2830 (2011)
14. Saeys, Y., Inza, I., Larrañaga, P.: A review of feature selection techniques in bioinformatics. Bioinformatics **23**(19), 2507–2517 (2007)
15. Shao, Y., Luo, X., Qian, C., Zhu, P., Zhang, L.: Towards a scalable resource-driven approach for detecting repackaged Android applications. In: Proceedings of ACSAC. ACM (2014)
16. Sun, M., Li, M., Lui, J.: DroidEagle: seamless detection of visually similar Android apps. In: Proceedings of WiSec. ACM (2015)
17. Viennot, N., Garcia, E., Nieh, J.: A measurement study of Google Play. In: Proceedings of SIGMETRICS. ACM (2014)
18. Wang, H., Guo, Y., Ma, Z., Chen, X.: WuKong: a scalable and accurate two-phase approach to Android app clone detection. In: Proceedings of ISSTA. ACM (2015)
19. Zhang, F., Huang, H., Zhu, S., Wu, D., Liu, P.: ViewDroid: towards obfuscation-resilient mobile application repackaging detection. In: Proceedings of WiSec. ACM (2014)
20. Zhauniarovich, Y., Gadyatskaya, O., Crispo, B., La Spina, F., Moser, E.: FSquaDRA: fast detection of repackaged applications. In: Atluri, V., Pernul, G. (eds.) DBSec 2014. LNCS, vol. 8566, pp. 130–145. Springer, Heidelberg (2014). doi:10.1007/978-3-662-43936-4_9
21. Zhauniarovich, Y., Ahmad, M., Gadyatskaya, O., Crispo, B., Massacci, F.: StaDynA: addressing the problem of dynamic code updates in the security analysis of Android applications. In: Proceedings of CODASPY (2015)
22. Zhauniarovich, Y., Gadyatskaya, O.: Small changes, big changes: an updated view on the Android permission system. In: Monrose, F., Dacier, M., Blanc, G., Garcia-Alfaro, J. (eds.) RAID 2016. LNCS, vol. 9854, pp. 346–367. Springer International Publishing, Switzerland (2016). doi:10.1007/978-3-319-45719-2_16
23. Zhauniarovich, Y., Gadyatskaya, O., Crispo, B.: Demo: enabling trusted stores for Android. In: Proceedings of CCS, pp. 1345–1348. ACM (2013)
24. Zhauniarovich, Y., Philippov, A., Gadyatskaya, O., Crispo, B., Massacci, F.: Towards black box testing of Android apps. In: Proceedings of Software Assurance Workshop at ARES, pp. 501–510 (2015)
25. Zhou, W., Zhou, Y., Jiang, X., Ning, P.: Detecting repackaged smartphone applications in third-party android marketplaces. In: Proceedings of CODASPY (2012)
26. Zhou, Y., Jiang, X.: Dissecting Android malware: characterization and evolution. In: Proceedings of S&P. IEEE (2012)

A Survey on Internal Interfaces Used by Exploits and Implications on Interface Diversification

Sampsa Rauti[✉], Samuel Lauren, Joni Uitto, Shohreh Hosseinzadeh,
Jukka Ruohonen, Sami Hyrynsalmi, and Ville Leppänen

University of Turku, 20014 Turku, Finland
{sjprau,smrlau,jjuitt,shohos,juanruo,sthyry,ville.leppanen}@utu.fi

Abstract. The idea of interface diversification is that internal interfaces in the system are transformed into unique secret instances. On one hand, the trusted programs in the system are accordingly modified so that they can use the diversified interfaces. On the other hand, the malicious code injected into a system does not know the diversification secret, that is the language of the diversified system, and thus it is rendered useless. Based on our study of 500 exploits, this paper surveys the different interfaces that are targeted in malware attacks and can potentially be diversified in order to prevent the malware from reaching its goals. In this study, we also explore which of the identified interfaces have already been covered in existing diversification research and which interfaces should be considered in future research. Moreover, we discuss the benefits and drawbacks of diversifying these interfaces. We conclude that diversification of various internal interfaces could prevent or mitigate roughly 80 % of the analyzed exploits. Most interfaces we found have already been diversified as proof-of-concept implementations but diversification is not widely used in practical systems.

1 Introduction

When defending computer systems against attacks, we have to protect a complex environment with several unknown vulnerabilities. Malicious adversaries, on the contrary, simply need one or a few exploitable security holes in order to compromise a system. Most malware attacks depend on predictable and known internal interfaces on the target platform. *Interface diversification* is one promising approach to counter this threat. Today, there are rather few different execution platforms. Because of this so called 'software monoculture', there are myriads of copies of the same execution platform with identical internal structure. As a consequence, one malicious program works on millions of computers. Malware enters in a system using a security hole in the system's external interface, but the actual malicious payload uses knowledge about the internal interface. However, if the internal interfaces would be different on each computer, malware relying on the knowledge about the identical interfaces would be rendered useless [9,11].

The authors gratefully acknowledge Tekes – the Finnish Funding Agency for Innovation, DIMECC Oy and Cyber Trust research program for their support.

B.B. Brumley and J. Röning (Eds.): NordSec 2016, LNCS 10014, pp. 152–168, 2016.
DOI: 10.1007/978-3-319-47560-8_10

Following this reasoning, diversification — unique randomization applied to the target system's internal interfaces — can be used to make the software more resistant against malicious attacks. In a diversified system, malware does not know the secret "language" used in the system anymore and cannot access any critical resources.

The contributions of this paper are as follows. By surveying hundreds of existing vulnerabilities, we study what interfaces are being targeted by the attackers and what are the attack vectors and payloads. This allows us to see which interfaces should be diversified in order to prevent the attacks. The focus on interfaces and the practical analysis of exploits sets our survey apart from other diversification surveys like [23]. Therefore, we contribute to the on-going discussion by an empirical study that analyses the real-world attacks and how they could have been prevented with diversification. Furthermore, we also study where the changes caused by diversification are propagated and how difficult it is to diversify a specific interface. Moreover, based on the set of interfaces usually targeted by attackers, our study also surveys which of these interfaces have already been diversified in the literature and proposes interfaces that are good candidates for diversification in the future. Finally, not every attack can be prevented by using diversification methods, but this study shows that the clear majority of analyzed exploits could be thwarted.

2   Interface Diversification

2.1   The General Idea

By diversifying internal interfaces, we can limit the number of assumptions an attacker can make about the execution environment, without affecting the interfaces exposed to the end-user. That is, diversification modifies applications' or systems' internals in order to make them unpredictable for attackers. Diversification can be implemented through different obfuscation techniques [9]. In interface diversification, even simple obfuscation methods like renaming and changing the order of parameters in function signatures can be employed.

It should be noted that the term *interface* is interpreted quite broadly here. By interface, we do not only mean normal interfaces provided by software modules but also e.g. commands of a language or memory addresses (of services/resources) are seen as interfaces that can be diversified. In this sense, an interface is anything that can be used to gain access to critical resources of a computer.

A practical example illustrating interface diversification is changing the system call numbers of an operating system. System calls are a way for programs to request a service from an operating system's kernel and get access to computer's essential resources. This is why it makes sense to diversify them in order to prevent the adversary from using system calls.

For example, in Linux, this diversification can be performed by replacing the original system call numbers (over 300 system calls) with new ones. Diversification now has to be propagated to the code using the system calls. The system call numbers have to be changed in all libraries and programs that directly invoke system calls. The names of library functions which directly or indirectly use the system calls also have to be replaced so that the malware can not make use of them. In other words, the transitive closure of the system calls has to diversified so that malicious programs cannot exploit them to access the computer's resources. Furthermore, when the diversification of system call numbers is done uniquely for each Linux installation, the attacker cannot utilize the information gained by breaking one system in a wide-spread attack.

2.2   Internal and External Interfaces

Applications expose and consume interfaces. Typically, an application has an *external interface* that it exposes to its users in order to provide the required functionality. For example, for a web server this external interface could be the set of valid HTTP requests and responses.

However, aside from their external interface, applications often expose other details to the outside world, often as a result of their implementation. By definition, these *internal interfaces* are not expected to be consumed by outsiders. They are considered to be implementation details.

What differentiates malware from legitimate users is that malware often depends on these internal interfaces. This is because if malware only use the external interface — that is, it only utilized the functionality an application was designed to provide — its capabilities would be limited to those of an ordinary user.

Applications can also accidentally expose their internal interfaces, or the interfaces of other components that they consume, through their external interface. SQL injections caused by lack of input sanitation are a good example of this category of vulnerabilities. SQL injections work by exploiting the fact that some applications accidentally expose their database back-end's internal interface through the application's external interface. For example, if an SQL injection happened through a web service, the external HTTP interface would in effect act as a gateway to the database.

In what follows, we present a study where vulnerabilities and internal interfaces utilized by them are analyzed. Based on this, we discuss diversifying several types of internal interfaces in order to mitigate and prevent malicious attacks.

3   Study Setup

3.1   The Setting of the Study

In order to study the internal interfaces exploited by attackers — that is, the interfaces that could be diversified in order to prevent the attacks — we studied 500 exploits from Exploit Database[1]. The 500 samples we used were randomly selected from the exploits that were added to the database between the years

---

[1] www.exploit-db.com.

2010 and 2015. This random sample can be argued to be sufficient; it amounts to about four percent of the total number of exploits in the longitudinal sampling interval.

In this study, we follow the guidelines given by Kitchenham [21] for undertaking systematic reviews. Each vulnerability was studied by at least two reviewers independently and all the cases were discussed by the authors in the meetings. The rare disagreement cases were also addressed in these meetings and disputed until an agreement was found. For each exploit, the following questions were answered:

1. What is the type of the payload?
2. What is the execution environment for the exploit?
3. What is the interface (or what are the interfaces) that should be diversified in order to prevent the attack?
4. Where do we need to propagate the changes to as a result of diversification?
5. What is the attack vector? (e.g. an uploaded file)
6. What is the attack type? (e.g. SQL injection)?

Obviously, because we want to study the interfaces, the third question is the most important one. The answer to the fourth question follows directly from it. The other questions are there to help us define the interface that should be diversified, and also to learn the relations between different variables, like the attack type and the interface to be diversified. Exploit Database was chosen because it is a quite well-known vulnerability database that contains detailed proof-of-concept implementations for the attacks. Several other sources listing vulnerabilities, like Common Vulnerabilities and Exposures (CVE), were not describing the vulnerabilities accurately enough for our purposes and were therefore ruled out.

3.2   Variables

For each of 500 exploits, the following variables were determined. These variables correspond to the questions outlined above.

Payload. *Payload* describes the content that the attacker injects to the system through an attack vector. Depending on the type of an attack the payload can be content executed by an interpreter or static content not meant to be executed. For example, a fragment of JavaScript code used in an injection attack is meant to be executed, a file name provided in order to disclose the contents of a file is not. Here, we will mainly concentrate on executable payloads.

Execution Environment. We are also interested what kind of interpreter executes the payload, in case it is meant to be interpreted as executable. For example, if the payload is a malicious piece of JavaScript, the execution environment is the JavaScript interpreter.

Possible execution environments include:

- *Application's address space and operating context.* This is the case where machine code is injected into the process.
- *SQL database engine.* In the case of SQL injection attacks, the injected query will obviously be executed by the receiving databases engine.
- *Web scripts.* The case where JavaScript or VBScript is injected into a page, such as in XSS attacks. The attacker has access to all the usual facilities provided by the browser and the page in question.
- *Shell interpreter.* Command shells can also be used to execute arbitrary code.
- *Interpreters for other scripting languages.* Other scripting environments like PHP and Python are quite similar to the previous case.

Interface to be Diversified. The most important variable for this study is the interface that should be diversified. Once we have identified the executor of the payload and the characteristics of the environment it offers, we can determine the interface that should be diversified in order to prevent the attack. For instance, if the payload contains SQL commands, diversification should be applied to the SQL language. Sometimes there can be several alternative interfaces that can be diversified to prevent the attack. For example, if there is native code in the payload, both instruction set randomization and diversifying the system call numbers of the operating system can usually thwart the attack.

Interface diversification requires changes to be propagated. When we have successfully applied diversification techniques to the interface in question so that an attacker cannot target it, we have to also propagate those changes to the components that rely on the now diversified interfaces. In order to gauge the feasibility of diversification of a specific interface, it is therefore also necessary to identify the software layers where the changes will be propagated to. For example, if we were to diversify a relational database's public facing SQL interface, we would then have to also propagate those changes to the applications and the components using that interface.

Attack Vector. *Attack vector* describes the channel which the malware uses to get its payload into the system. For example, many SQL injections happen through HTTP requests' GET and POST parameters. Later in the study, we will see which kind of attack vectors are mitigated when diversifying a specific interface.

Attack Type. Finally, we also listed the *attack type* for each vulnerability. This provides us with the information on the attack types that are prevented or mitigated by diversifying a specific interface. An example of attack type is Arbitrary code execution. In this study, this attack type implies that arbitrary native code gets executed in the address space of some process.

4   Results

4.1   The Types of Payloads

Of the 500 exploits we studied, 356 had a clearly identifiable executable payload and an interface that could be diversified to prevent the attack. Note that not all the attacks have a clear payload. For example, a cross site request forgery attack — in which unauthorized commands are given from a client that is trusted by a website — does not really have an executable payload. However, this interpretation can be questioned as in complex systems it is difficult to clearly differentiate executable code and data guiding execution.

Every payload is executed in some execution environment. This environment was identified for each payload category. Payload categories and their respective execution environments are shown in Table 1.

Table 1. Payloads and execution environments.

Payload	Occurrences	Execution environment
Native code	112	CPU and OS
SQL	103	SQL engine
JavaScript	65	Browser's script engine
Any	32	Any
Shell script	30	Command shell
PHP	9	PHP interpreter
VBScript	4	VBScript interpreter
Java bytecode	1	Java virtual machine
Python	1	Python interpreter

We can see that because of the popularity of SQL injection attacks, fractions of SQL queries are the most popular payloads in our study. The vulnerabilities including native code are almost equally numerous. This is followed by JavaScript (also possibly including HTML code), a payload usually employed in cross site scripting (XSS) attacks.

The category *any* is for the exploits in which an arbitrary file can be uploaded to the system. In these cases, the executable payload in the file can be practically anything and can not be specified. PHP and JavaScript are popular choices in this case but native code and shell scripts are also viable options.

There are also quite many payloads written in shell script; the attacker often eventually aims to execute shell commands in order the reach his or her goals. Some smaller categories are PHP, VBScript, Perl and Python, all of which are interpreted script languages. One vulnerability has a payload in Java bytecode.

These categories and their execution environments give us ideas of the interfaces that are good candidates for diversification. We will discuss the actual interfaces next.

4.2   The Found Interfaces

The found interfaces are shown in Table 2. It is worth noting that the identified interfaces are more important than their proportions, because as discussed later, the distribution of vulnerabilities in Exploit Database may be somewhat skewed. Still, this analysis gives a good understanding on the popular interfaces that are candidates for diversification.

Table 2. Diversifiable interfaces.

Interface	Occurrences
OS and CPU interfaces	112
SQL	103
JavaScript	64
Command shell language	33
Path or file name	33
Any	31
Parameter names	21
PHP	9
VBScript	2
Java bytecode	1
Python	1

In total, there were 410 exploits that could have been mitigated or prevented with diversification. This is 82.0 % of all vulnerabilities. Note that not all the attacks can be prevented by diversifying interfaces. For example, if the authentication mechanism can be bypassed because of a logic bug in the software, there is often no way to fix this with diversification. In case of 2 vulnerabilities, there was no source code available and the provided descriptions were not accurate enough to reliably deduce an internal interface that would need to be diversified in order to prevent the attack.

It is also noteworthy that the number of exploits that can be prevented or mitigated with diversification is higher than the number of exploits that have an executable payload. This is because there are some attacks that can be defeated with diversification even though they do not possess an executable payload. An example of this kind of exploit is the cross site request forgery attack we mentioned earlier. There attack does not need to contain any executable payload but it can be prevented by using a unique and random secret token that is generated for each HTTP request in a web application and verified on the server side. This can definitely be seen as a diversification technique.

In the forthcoming, we will give a more detailed discussion on each found interface.

In SQL injection attacks, the attacker injects malicious SQL fragments into an SQL query. An apparent way to avoid this is to diversify the commands in the *SQL language*. Diversification would have to be propagated to all programs and libraries using the diversified SQL language of the specific server.

Diversification of *operating system interfaces* or instruction sets can be used against attacks that aim to execute native code payload in the system. Although we have combined the interfaces here for simplicity, there are several interfaces in operating system (and CPU) that could be diversified to render malicious native code useless.

First, as we already discussed in the example in Sect. 2, the *system call interface* of the system can be uniquely diversified. This will prevent malware that invokes system calls directly from operating properly. The diversification has to be propagated to all trusted binaries so that these executables will work normally. Also, the *library functions* that directly or indirectly invoke the system calls have to be diversified (renamed) in binaries containing or calling these functions. Diversification of function names is propagated to all binaries that invoke the library functions leading to system calls.

Second, the whole *instruction set* used in a specific machine language can be diversified. This is a very effective way of preventing malicious binaries (the binaries using a wrong instruction set) from wreaking havoc in the system.

Third, to defeat the exploits that make use of knowledge about memory layout, *address space layout* can be randomized. This technique randomly diversifies the address positions in the important areas of the process.

When a web application has an XSS vulnerability, the attacker can inject JavaScript code (or HTML) into the web page. If the *JavaScript* language were to be diversified, this could be avoided. The changes would have to be propagated to the browser's JavaScript engine on each client machine.

An attacker's goal is also often to open the command shell in order to perform an attack using shell script. In this case, diversifying the *command shell language* will prevent the attack. Diversification has to be propagated to all script files in the system. Additionally, the source code of any program that create scripts dynamically at runtime has to updated.

File paths and names can be made unique on different computers. This would make file disclosure attacks harder. Especially for critical files like the password file, this can be very useful in some cases. This case illustrates how diversification can also prevent information leakage, not only execution of some malicious payload.

When an arbitrary file is uploaded into a system, it can contain *any* executable content (PHP, JavaScript, native code...). Therefore, in these cases the interface to be diversified could be any of the other interfaces presented here.

Sometimes, randomizing GET or POST *parameter names* in web applications provides additional security. This way, it is not that straightforward for an adversary to get the malicious payload into the system and the threat of successful attack is diminished. This also applies to e.g. SQL table names and fields.

In some cases where the attacker gets to upload a file of his or her choosing or has an opportunity for a code injection attack in web environment, the payload is written in *PHP*. To defeat this threat, the most obvious choice would be to diversify the PHP language. Diversification of PHP is a case that is very similar to diversifying other interpreted languages like Bash or Python. The changes would be propagated to all PHP scripts and libraries on a specific server.

There are also a few *Other* rare interfaces. These are VBScript, Python and Java byte code. Diversifying VBScript is likely to be similar to diversification of JavaScript and other interpreted scripting languages. The same also goes for Python; in many ways, it bears a resemblance to shell scripts.

To fend off attacks aimed at the Java Virtual Machine, the instruction set used in Java byte code can be diversified. In this case, the changes would affect the Java compiler and the virtual machine executing the code.

4.3   Attack Types and Attack Vectors

The connections between attack vectors and diversified interfaces are shown in Table 3. In other words, it illustrates which kinds of attack vectors each diversified interface mitigates. Because the number of different attack vectors was large, we have divided them into five abstract categories. *HTTP* includes attack vectors like GET and POST parameters and HTTP headers. *Remote protocol* (RP in Table 3) means payloads delivered through other protocols like TCP, RPC and FTP. *Local configuration* (LC) includes vectors such as application settings, input files, programs arguments and windows registry. *Local executables* (LE)

Table 3. Groups of attack vectors related to diversified interfaces.

Interfaces	Vectors					
	HTTP	LC	LE	RP	Others	Total
OS and CPU	8	53	22	26	3	112
SQL	103					103
JavaScript	61	1		1	1	64
Shell	19	7	1	2	4	33
Path or file name	32					32
Any			30		1	31
Parameter names	21					21
PHP	8		1			9
VBScript			1			1
Python	1					1
Java bytecode					1	1
Total	253	61	55	29	10	408

category is for different kinds of attack vectors in executables, like DLL injection, function call or simply an executable file uploaded to the system. There were also couple of other cases that did not fit to the previous categories.

In Table 3, we can see for example that diversifying the language interface of SQL mainly prevents the attacks using HTTP (GET and POST parameters) as attack vectors, which is not very surprising. On the other hand, the native code exploits, prevented by diversifying the operating system interfaces, infiltrate to the system through many different attack vectors.

In a similar fashion, Table 4 shows the different attack types prevented or mitigated by diversification of a specific interface. The largest categories are SQL injection attacks and attacks including execution of arbitrary native code.

Table 4. The attack types and the corresponding diversified interfaces.

Attack type	Interfaces	Count	Total
SQL injection	SQL	103	**103**
Arbitrary code execution	OS and CPU	95	**97**
	Any	1	
	Java bytecode	1	
XSS	JavaScript	63	**63**
Command injection	Shell	32	**41**
	PHP	8	
	Python	1	
Local file inclusion	Path or file names	27	**34**
	Parameter names	7	
Arbitrary file upload	Any	30	**30**
Cross-site request forgery	JavaScript	1	**11**
	Path or file names	1	
	Parameter names	9	
Privilege escalation	OS and CPU	7	**10**
	Shell	1	
	Parameter names	2	
Denial of service	OS and CPU	7	**10**
	Parameter names	2	
	PHP	1	
Memory alteration	OS and CPU	2	**3**
	VBScript	1	
Directory traversal	Path or file name	3	**3**
Sandbox escape	OS and CPU	2	**2**
Information disclosure	Path or file name	1	**1**
Arbitrary file removal	Parameter names	1	**1**

Both these categories amount for about 20 % of all 500 exploits. As mentioned before, about 20 % of attacks cannot be prevented by diversification and are left out of this discussion.

When it comes to the native code, diversification has usually been advocated as a method to prevent mainly buffer overflow attacks, but based on this study we see it as an even more generic tool that can be used to prevent arbitrary code execution in general. For example, diversification works well against attacks where a malicious executable file has been uploaded into the system and tries to execute arbitrary code based on its knowledge on the known interfaces.

4.4   Evaluation

Even though our sample is chosen randomly and the number of exploits can be deemed sufficient, the sample is unbalanced towards the early 2010s and, rather expectedly, web application exploits (see Fig. 1). As can be observed from Fig. 2, the other three meta-data categories in the database — denial-of-service (DoS), local, and remote exploits — have attained much fewer exploits compared to web exploits. Moreover, it is worth remarking that EDB is a community-based database and the archived exploits presumably reflect the preferences of the security researchers who contribute to this open data archive. Nevertheless, the observed sample does not differ notably from the total amount of exploits archived during the observed time interval; therefore, the sample can be said to generalize towards EDB, although straightforward generalizations towards the whole exploit population are problematic, of course.

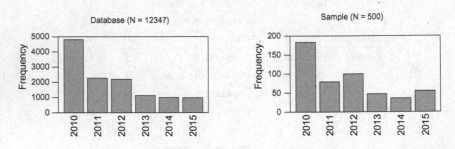

Fig. 1. Annual frequencies (EDB meta-data)

However, while the reported proportions may not perfectly reflect the reality, our data derived from the analysis of 500 exploits still gives a pretty good idea about what kind of interfaces are good targets for diversification. We have also seen many dependencies between interfaces and other variables that do not really depend on their proportions.

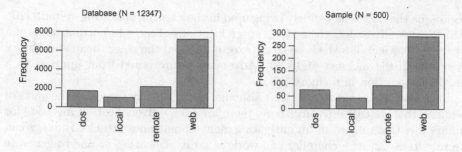

Fig. 2. Categories (EDB meta-data)

5   Existing Interface Diversification Research

In this section, we will briefly survey the diversification methods for different interfaces proposed in the literature. This review is mostly based on the data we have collected while undertaking a systematic literature review on diversification and obfuscation in the field of software security [15]. However, the point of view here (which interfaces have been diversified) is completely novel.

Operating system and CPU. Chew and Song were the first to present the idea of *changing system call mappings and diversifying library APIs* in order to render malware useless [7]. A conceptual scheme and an implementation for this idea was later more accurately described by Jiang et al. [18] and Liang et al. [25]. Rauti et al. have also presented a scheme for system call diversification [28] and diversifying the library function names in binaries [24]. Rauti et al. change the system call numbers and function names before execution, while Jiang et al. perform diversification dynamically at runtime. Runtime diversification allows more flexibility (e.g. some chosen applications can function without diversification) but affects the performance. The techniques altering system call mapping and library function names bear a resemblance to diversification techniques that rename static identifiers in high-level program code [17] in order to get unique instances of programs.

Another method against native code attacks is *Instruction Set Randomization* (ISR). An instruction set can also be seen as an interface known and exploited by malware. Therefore, the machine code instructions can be diversified to prevent execution of any untrusted code [4,5]. The instructions that are used by an application can be randomized using a specific function such as XOR [19]. A problem with instruction set randomization has been the fact that no commercially available CPU supports it. However, with the increasing popularity of cloud environments and virtual machines, we can except this approach to become more usable [32].

Finally, attacks making use of memory's structure can be thwarted by diversifying program's memory layout [8]. This method is usually called *Address Space Layout Randomization* (ASLR). It is used to protect systems from buffer overflow attacks that lead to arbitrary code execution. This is the only diversification technique that is already widely being used in the existing operating systems [20]. ASLR randomly orders the address space locations of most important areas of a process. This includes the base of the executable and the stack, heap and library positions in the memory [1,16,30]. Adversary is prevented from jumping to a particular position in memory.

It is also important to note that although not explicitly targeting the parts of binaries that we call *interfaces* here, there are many diversification methods for binary files that may result in mitigating many of malicious attacks. Binaries can be rewritten [22] or a compiler can work as a diversification engine to generate unique binaries [12]. The diversification methods used include e.g. disassembling and randomizing function blocks [14], breaking application binary to blocks and shuffling them [13], and obfuscating and relocating information [10]. All of these methods result in diverse binaries, making the adversary's job harder.

Shell. Uitto et al. have provided an implementation for a diversified Bash interpreter [31]. All tokens recognized by the Bash interpreter's lexical analyzer are diversified in order to prevent the adversary from writing malicious script fragments. In a very similar way, Kc et al. have previously modified the Perl interpreter to support execution of diversified Perl scripts [19].

Diversifying command shell languages entails some challenges like shared libraries (if many uniquely diversified scripts use a common library, how should the library be diversified?) and programs that generate scripts dynamically at runtime (the source code of these programs has to be changed). Otherwise, the approach works well and only incurs a modest performance penalty [19].

SQL. Diversifying SQL has been proposed by Boyd and Keromytis in [6]. They use a proxy-based solution that decodes the diversified SQL queries before they reach the server. Rauti et al. have proposed a solution that is integrated to the SQL server itself [29]. The latter solution can be argued to provide more security but less flexibility. SQL diversification functionality can also be embedded to database drivers. An example of such scheme is an implementation for PostgreSQL JDBC driver by Locasto and Keromytis [26].

The biggest challenge for this interface diversification scheme is probably the fact that the changes have to be propagated to the applications generating SQL queries. These queries are often created dynamically at runtime which poses a challenge for automatic diversification. Most difficult cases can be handled by providing software developers with a tool that helps them to diversify most difficult queries [20,29].

JavaScript. Athanasopoulos et al. present a JavaScript diversification scheme to prevent cross site scripting attacks and DOM-based attacks in [3]. The proof-of-the-concept implementation was tested against over 1300 XSS and succeeded in preventing them with negligible performance overhead. The apparent challenge with this kind of JavaScript diversification is that JavaScript is generated on the server side but executed on the client machine. Both client (the browser) and server (the component creating JavaScript code) therefore have to be modified in order for this scheme to work. One solution is to implement browser extension on the client side and a proxy on the server side [2]. These components take care of diversification and decoding.

A significant challenge in diversifying JavaScript is sharing the diversification secret between the client and the server. In [2], the key for decoding the diversification is sent in the header of a HTTP message. Therefore, diversification can be unique for each request. The diversification has to be propagated to all external JavaScript files as well, which further complicates matters.

Interfaces not yet diversified. There are some interfaces still to be diversified, though these are not the most interesting ones. Most notably, to the best of our knowledge, there is no diversified implementation of PHP language. However, this problem would most likely be very similar to other interpreted languages that have already been diversified (e.g. Bash and Perl). VBScript is also lacking an implementation of a diversified interpreter. As a web script, it would have the same problem setting as JavaScript.

Based on some exploits we analyzed, some application-specific interfaces and protocols might also be candidates for diversification. As this application-specific security measure is not generic enough, we have not focused on it here. Some application developers might want to beef up their applications' security using this method.

Finally, we have not considered diversifying any network protocols here. This might prevent some attacks and is an interesting topic but does not fall within the scope of this study.

6 Conclusions

This study has shown that the vast majority (80 %) of analyzed exploits can be rendered useless by diversifying some of the most common interfaces the adversaries utilize. We also pointed out that diversification seems to be a useful countermeasure for a larger number of attack categories than usually suggested in the literature.

Our literature review showed that diversification of almost all of the interfaces identified in this study has already been discussed in the literature. However, the practical use of diversification as a security measure is still not widespread and practical diversification tools are missing. Therefore, the challenges and limitations associated with interface diversification approaches still need to be studied more closely and practical solutions to further increase their feasibility and usability are needed. Even though deploying interface diversification schemes is rarely straightforward, it is still a very promising method to defeat many kinds of attacks. With address space layout randomization as a part of several operating systems, applying diversification in larger scale has already begun. In our view, diversification can be seen as a comprehensive protection mechanism that spans all the critical interfaces and software layers in a specific system (see also [27]).

In the future, we hope to see more interface diversification schemes rolled out in practical software systems. Restricted systems with modest code mass and infrequent updates — for instance some small embedded systems with lightweight operating systems — are a good place to begin.

References

1. Abadi, M., Plotkin, G.D.: On protection by layout randomization. ACM Trans. Inf. Syst. Secur. **15**(2), 8:1–8:29 (2012)
2. Athanasopoulos, E., Krithinakis, A., Markatos, E.P.: An architecture for enforcing JavaScript randomization in Web2.0 applications. In: Burmester, M., Tsudik, G., Magliveras, S., Ilić, I. (eds.) ISC 2010. LNCS, vol. 6531, pp. 203–209. Springer, Heidelberg (2011). doi:10.1007/978-3-642-18178-8_18
3. Athanasopoulos, E., Pappas, V., Krithinakis, A., Ligouras, S., Markatos, E.P., Karagiannis, T.: xJS: practical XSS prevention for web application development. In: Proceedings of the 2010 USENIX conference on Web application development, WebApps 2010, pp. 1–12. USENIX Association (2010)
4. Barrantes, E.G., Ackley, D.H., Forrest, S., Stefanović, D.: Randomized instruction set emulation. ACM Trans. Inf. Syst. Secur. **8**(1), 3–40 (2005)
5. Boyd, S.W., Kc, G.S., Locasto, M.E., Prevelakis, V., Keromytis, A.D.: On the general applicability of instruction-set randomization. IEEE Trans. Dependable Secure Comput. **7**(3), 255–270 (2010)
6. Boyd, S.W., Keromytis, A.D.: SQLrand: preventing SQL injection attacks. In: Jakobsson, M., Yung, M., Zhou, J. (eds.) ACNS 2004. LNCS, vol. 3089, pp. 292–302. Springer, Heidelberg (2004). doi:10.1007/978-3-540-24852-1_21
7. Chew, M., Song, D.: Mitigating buffer overflows by operating system randomization. Technical report, CMU (2002)
8. Chongkyung, K., Jinsuk, J., Bookholt, C., Xu, J., Peng, N.: Address space layout permutation (ASLP): towards fine-grained randomization of commodity software. In: 2006 Computer Security Applications Conference, ACSAC 2006, pp. 339–348, December 2006
9. Cohen, F.B.: Operating system protection through program evolution. Comput. Secur. **12**(6), 565–584 (1993)
10. Coppens, B., De Sutter, B., De Bosschere, K.: Protecting your software updates. IEEE Secur. Priv. **11**(2), 47–54 (2013)
11. Forrest, S., Somayaji, A., Ackley, D.: Building diverse computer systems. In: Proceedings of the 6th Workshop on Hot Topics in Operating Systems (HotOS-VI), HOTOS 1997 (1997)
12. Franz, M.: E unibus pluram: massive-scale software diversity as a defense mechanism. In Proceedings of the 2010 Workshop on New Security Paradigms, NSPW 2010, pp. 7–16. ACM (2010)
13. Gupta, A., Kerr, S., Kirkpatrick, M.S., Bertino, E.: Marlin: a fine grained randomization approach to defend against ROP attacks. In: Lopez, J., Huang, X., Sandhu, R. (eds.) NSS 2013. LNCS, vol. 7873, pp. 293–306. Springer, Heidelberg (2013). doi:10.1007/978-3-642-38631-2_22
14. Gupta, A., Kirkpatrick, M.S., Bertino, E.: A secure architecture design based on application isolation, code minimization and randomization. In: 2013 IEEE Conference on Communications and Network Security (CNS), pp. 423–429, October 2013

15. Hosseinzadeh, S., Rauti, S., Laurén, S., Mäkelä, J.-M., Holvitie, J., Hyrynsalmi, S., Leppänen, V.: Using diversification and obfuscation techniques for software security: a systematic literature review (2016)
16. Hovav, S., Page, M., Pfaff, B., Goh, E.-J., Modadugu, N., Boneh, F.: On the effectiveness of address-space randomization. In: Proceedings of the 11th ACM Conference on Computer and Communications Security, CCS 2004, pp. 298–307. ACM, New York (2004)
17. Jackson, T., Salamat, B., Homescu, A., Manivannan, K., Wagner, G., Gal, A., Brunthaler, S., Wimmer, C., Franz, M.: Compiler-generated software diversity. In: Jajodia, S., et al. (eds.) Moving Target Defense. Advances in Information Security, vol. 54, pp. 77–98. Springer, New York (2011)
18. Jiang, X., Wang, H.J., Xu, D., Wang, Y.-M.: RandSys: Thwarting code injection attacks with system service interface randomization. In IEEE International Symposium on Reliable Distributed Systems, SRDS 2007, pp. 209–218 (2007)
19. Kc, G.S., Keromytis, A.D., Prevelakis, V.: Countering code-injection attacks with instruction-set randomization. In: Proceedings of the 10th ACM Conference on Computer and Communications Security, CCS 2003, pp. 272–280. ACM, New York (2003)
20. Keromytis, A.D.: Randomized instruction sets and runtime environments past research and future directions. IEEE Secur. Priv. 7(1), 18–25 (2009)
21. Kitchenham, B.: Guidelines for performing systematic literature reviews in software engineering. Technical report EBSE-2007-01, Keele University, School of Computer Science and Mathematics (2007)
22. Larsen, P., Brunthaler, S., Franz, M.: Security through diversity: are we there yet? IEEE Secur. Priv. 12(2), 28–35 (2014)
23. Larsen, P., Homescu, A., Brunthaler, S., Franz, M.: SoK: automated software diversity. In: 2014 IEEE Symposium on Security and Privacy (SP), pp. 276–291, May 2014
24. Lauren, S., Mäki, P., Rauti, S., Hosseinzadeh, S., Hyrynsalmi, S., Leppänen, V.: Symbol diversification of Linux binaries. In: Proceedings of World Congress on Internet Security (WorldCIS-2014) (2014)
25. Liang, Z., Liang, B., Li, L.: A system call randomization based method for countering code injection attacks. In: International Conference on Networks Security, Wireless Communications and Trusted Computing, NSWCTC 2009, pp. 584–587 (2009)
26. Locasto, M.E., Keromytis, A.D.: PachyRand: SQL randomization for the PostgreSQL JDBC driver. Technical report CUCS-033-05, Columbia University, Computer Science (2005)
27. Portokalidis, G., Keromytis, A.D.: Global ISR: toward a comprehensive defense against unauthorized code execution. In: Jajodia, S., Ghosh, A.K., Swarup, V., Wang, C., Wang, X.S. (eds.) Moving Target Defense, Creating Asymmetric Uncertainty for Cyber Threats. Advances in Information Security, vol. 54, pp. 49–76. Springer, New York (2011)
28. Rauti, S., Lauren, S., Hosseinzadeh, S., Mäkelä, J.-M., Hyrynsalmi, S., Leppänen, V.: Diversification of system calls in Linux binaries. In: Proceedings of the 6th International Conference on Trustworthy Systems (InTrust 2014) (2014)
29. Rauti, S., Teuhola, J., Leppänen, V.: Diversifying SQL to prevent injection attacks. In: Proceedings of Trustcom/BigDataSE/ISPA, pp. 344–351 (2015)
30. Rodes, B.: Stack layout transformation: towards diversity for securing binary programs. In: 2012 34th International Conference on Software Engineering (ICSE), pp. 1543–1546, June 2012

31. Uitto, J., Rauti, S., Mäkelä, J.-M., Leppänen, V.: Preventing malicious attacks by diversifying Linux shell commands. In: Proceedings of the 14th Symposium on Programming Languages and Software Tools (SPLST 2015), vol. 1525. CEUR Workshop Proceedings (2015)
32. Williams, D., Wei, H., Davidson, J.W., Hiser, J.D., Knight, J.C., Nguyen-Tuong, A.: Security through diversity: leveraging virtual machine technology. IEEE Secur. Priv. **7**(1), 26–33 (2009)

A Tale of the OpenSSL State Machine:
A Large-Scale Black-Box Analysis

Joeri de Ruiter[✉]

Institute for Computing and Information Sciences, Radboud University,
Nijmegen, The Netherlands
joeri@cs.ru.nl

Abstract. State machine inference is a powerful black-box analysis technique that can be used to learn a state machine implemented in a system, i.e. by only exchanging valid messages with the implementation a state machine can be extracted. In this paper we perform a large scale analysis of the state machines as implemented over the last 14 years in OpenSSL, one of the most widely used implementations of TLS, and in LibreSSL, a fork of OpenSSL. By automating the learning process, the state machines were learned for 145 different versions of both the server-side and the client-side. For the server-side this resulted in 15 unique state machines for OpenSSL and 2 for LibreSSL. For the client-side, 9 unique state machines were learned for OpenSSL and one for LibreSSL. Analysing these state machines provides an interesting insight in the evolution of the state machine of OpenSSL. Security vulnerabilities and other bugs related to their implementation can be observed, together with the point at which these are fixed. We argue that these problems could have been detected and fixed earlier if the developers would have had the tools available to analyse the implemented state machines.

1 Introduction

TLS (Transport Layer Security) is one of the most widely used security protocols and is used to secure network communications, for example, when browsing the Internet using HTTPS or using email with SMTPS or IMAPS. TLS is the successor of SSL (Secure Socket Layer), originally developed at Netscape. As the name SSL is so widespread, it is often used interchangeably with TLS. The first version of SSL was never released and the second version contained numerous security issues [23]. The third version of SSL was also not without security issues, and these were fixed in the first TLS version [7]. Two more TLS versions were released after this and the fourth one, TLS version 1.3, is currently under development [8,9]. Despite the fact that TLS 1.0 was released in 1999, many servers on the internet today still support SSLv3 and even SSLv2 [2].

Due to its widespread use, the TLS protocol has been the subject of many research projects. For example, it has been analysed using various different formal methods [6,10–14,16,18,19]. These formal analyses focus on the protocol

B.B. Brumley and J. Röning (Eds.): NordSec 2016, LNCS 10014, pp. 169–184, 2016.
DOI: 10.1007/978-3-319-47560-8_11

specifications, while many mistakes are also made in the actual implementation [15]. To counter this, a formally verified TLS implementation has been proposed by combining a formal analysis with an actual implementation [4].

A large proportion of the applications that use TLS to secure their connections use the implementation provided by OpenSSL.[1] The first official release of the OpenSSL project was version 0.9.1c in December 1998, and builds on the code of SSLeay by Young and Hudson. Various forks of OpenSSL exist, such as BoringSSL[2] and LibreSSL[3], which were mainly started with the goal of cleaning up the code and improving its security. Over the years OpenSSL has been plagued with numerous implementation bugs, with sometimes a high security impact. The most well-known example of this is probably the infamous Heartbleed bug.[4]

In this paper we focus on the implementation of state machines of TLS. Every implementation of a protocol needs to implement the corresponding state machine that determines how all the possible messages are handled in different states of the protocol. In [3, 22] the state machines of TLS implementations have been analysed, where for various implementations only recent versions were analysed. In [22] a technique called *state machine inference* was used to extract the state machine from TLS implementations by only interacting with it using valid protocol messages. In this paper we will show how we automated the process of using state machine inference in order to analyse a large number of TLS implementations. We will use this to show how the state machine as implemented in OpenSSL changed over the years and what issues could have been prevented should this technique have been available to the developers. In order to do this we learned the state machine for both the client- and server-side of 145 versions of OpenSSL and LibreSSL. We checked BoringSSL as well, but as it does not seem to use version numbering and it is not really intended for use outside of Google we did not perform a large scale analysis of it. We reported our findings regarding several smaller issues related to the state machine implementation in BoringSSL.

2   TLS

In this section we will provide a short introduction to TLS, necessary to understand the results later on. The goal of TLS is to set up an authenticated confidential channel between two parties. The authentication can be mutual, but in most cases it is only the server that is authenticated to the client.

The protocol starts with a handshake that is used to establish the used parameters, including the cipher suite (a combination of a key exchange, encryption and MAC algorithm), perform the desired authentication and establish shared

---

[1] https://www.openssl.org/.
[2] https://boringssl.googlesource.com/boringssl/.
[3] http://www.libressl.org/.
[4] http://heartbleed.com/.

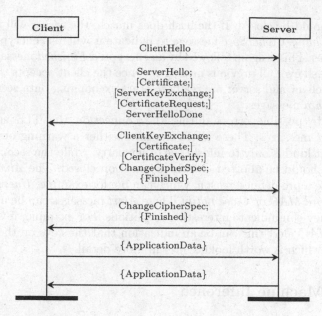

Fig. 1. A regular TLS session. An encrypted message m is denoted as {m}. If message m is optional, this is indicated by [m].

session keys. Different session keys are used for both directions of the communication and for encryption and the computation of the MACs. Once the keys are established, application data can be exchanged, which will be encrypted and authenticated using MACs. In Fig. 1 we provide an overview of a regular TLS session.

To start the handshake, usually the client will send a *ClientHello* message, containing a list of supported ciphersuites and optional extensions. The server will select a ciphersuite and return a *ServerHello* message, as well as other optional messages such as its *Certificate* (used to authenticate the server), the *ServerKeyExchange* message (used in some key exchange algorithms), and a *CertificateRequest* (used to request authentication from the client). The server then indicates it is done by sending a *ServerHelloDone* message. Upon receiving this last message, the client performs the local computations for the key establishment and sends the necessary information to the server in a *ClientKeyExchange* message. If requested by the server, the client also sends the optional *Certificate* and *CertificateVerify* messages to authenticate itself. After this, the client is ready to start encrypting its messages, and it indicates that it will encrypt all following messages by sending the *ChangeCipherSpec* message to the server. This is followed by the *Finished* message, the first encrypted message which is used to provide integrity to the handshake. The *Finished* message contains a keyed hash over all the previous messages that the client sent and received. If this hash does not match the value as expected by the server or the server cannot decrypt the *Finished* message, this can be an indication of a man-in-the-middle attack and the connection should be closed. If the hash does match, the server will respond by sending the *ChangeCipherSpec* message to indicate it will also encrypt all subsequent messages. This is again followed by an encrypted *Finished* message containing a keyed hash over all previous messages. Once the client accepts the *Finished* message, the client and server are ready to start exchanging data securely using *ApplicationData* messages.

To indicate possible errors during the connection the TLS specification includes *Alert* messages. These alerts can have either a warning or fatal level, where the first kind is only to inform the other party, while the second indicates the protocol should be aborted and the connection closed. The *Alert* messages always include a pre-defined reason, which can be, for example, *Unexpected message*, *Bad record MAC* or *Close notify*. These *Alert* messages can be useful in our analysis as they can indicate interesting conditions. For example, if we receive a *Bad record MAC* alert this can be an indication that the keys on the client and server differ, which is worth looking into in more detail.

3   State Machine Inference

To extract the model of a state machines for a protocol from an implementation, a technique known as *state machine inference* can be used. This technique tries to learn the state machine by only sending protocol messages and observing the responses. This makes it a very useful technique for black-box analysis.

As representation of state machines we use Mealy machines. This gives us a non-ambiguous formal way to describe the learned state machines. A Mealy machine consists of a set of states, of which one is the initial state. Additionally, an input alphabet is specified that describes which messages the system accepts as input. Similarly an output alphabet contains the messages that the system can send as responses. For every state, two functions are defined that map every input message to a corresponding output and to a next state respectively.

In state machine inference, two types of algorithms are used. First, a *learning algorithm* is used to come up with a hypothesis for the implemented state machine. To do this it can send protocol messages to the *system under test* (SUT) and receive the corresponding responses. Which messages can be sent is specified in the input alphabet. The algorithm also has the ability to reset the SUT to its initial state. Once the learning algorithm comes up with a hypothesis for the state machine by exchanging messages and resetting the SUT, this hypothesis is passed on to the *equivalence algorithm*. This algorithm determines whether the hypothesis matches the actual state machine. If this is not the case, the equivalence algorithm returns a counter-example. The counter-example is then fed into the learning algorithm, which uses this to update its hypothesis and continues learning until it comes up with another hypothesis. This process is repeated until the equivalence algorithm accepts a hypothesis. As in practice the equivalence algorithm will not know the actual state machine, the equivalence check will need to be approximated. In the next section we will discuss the concrete algorithms we used for the learning and equivalence algorithm.

4   Setup

For the learning of the TLS state machines we use the tool introduced in [22], which makes use of LearnLib [20]. For the learning algorithm we use of Niese's modification of Angluin's well-known L* algorithm [1,17]. The equivalence checking is done using Chow's W-method [5]. Given an upper bound on the number of states, this algorithm is guaranteed to determine correctly whether the correct state machine is found. As this algorithm can be computationally expensive due to the many messages that are sent, we make use of the improvement to the algorithm previously introduced in our tool. This modification makes use of the fact that if a socket is closed, we know that no more messages will be received. Therefore, queries that have a prefix for which we already know the connection will be closed are not performed, thus significantly reducing the number of queries that are send to the implementation. A nice side-effect of this modification is that if there are no loops in the state machine except for one or more sink states where all messages go to the same state with a ConnectionClosed output, we even have the guarantee that we found the correct state machine without having to know an upper bound on the number of states.

In order to get useful results, the abstract input messages, as used by the learning and equivalence algorithms, need to be converted to correctly formatted TLS messages and reversely, the received responses need to be converted to the abstract output messages before they can be used by the algorithms. This translation is done by the *test harness*, which is basically an (almost) stateless implementation of the TLS protocol. In order to successfully finish a TLS handshake, the test harness keeps track of some minimal notion of state by storing essential data such as, for example, the data used in the key exchange.

As input alphabet for our analysis, we made use of a minimal set of TLS messages, that are necessary to establish a successful connection. To test the server-side these are: ClientHello, ClientKeyExchange, an empty client Certificate, ChangeCipherSpec, Finished and two ApplicationData messages, one with a HTTP GET request and one without any data. When sending a ClientHello message, we reset the buffer used to collect all the exchanged messages that need to be hashed for the *Finished* messages. For the client-side testing we use the following messages: ServerHello, Certificate, an empty Certificate, ServerHelloDone, ChangeCipherSpec, Finished and again the same two ApplicationData messages as before.

To be able to learn the state machine for as many implementations as possible we completely automated the learning process. First, a crawler is used to download all versions available on the website or FTP server of a specific implementation. After this the downloaded sources are automatically extracted and compiled. This process is implementation specific and might require some tweaks to be able to build older versions. However, once the required steps are known the building of all downloaded versions is automated. Once we have a binary executable, we perform a sanity check in order to see whether the implementation is able to set up a valid TLS connection with our TLS test framework. Some older implementations are not able to do this, for example, as they do not support TLS yet but only SSLv3 or older. We ignored these older versions in our analysis and focus on only implementations that support at least TLS 1.0. For the versions that do pass the sanity check, the configuration files that are necessary for the actual state machine inference are generated. This is done such that every version uses a unique port so there is no interference between different versions that try to listen on the same port. Once we have the necessary configuration files, the learning is started using our tool from [22]. It is possible to perform the learning in parallel due to the usage of a unique port for each version. Using this process we are able to automatically infer the state machine for many versions of different TLS implementations. All software and models are available online.[5]

5   Analysing the OpenSSL State Machines

Using our automated process we learned the state machine for both the server-side and client-side for 111 different version of OpenSSL and 34 versions of LibreSSL. The latest versions of OpenSSL that we analysed were 1.0.1t, 1.0.2h and 1.1.0-pre4. For LibreSSL the latest version was 2.4.0. For the learning a machine with an Intel Xeon E5-2420 CPU was used. The time required for the learning varied from 3 min for more recent implementations of the server-side to about 2 h for older server-side implementations. These 2 h were exceptional though, and in general the running time per implementation was well below 20 min for both server- and client-side. Below we will discuss our analysis of the state machines we learned for the server- and client-side in Sects. 5.1 and 5.2 respectively.

5.1   Server-Side

For the server-side, the learning process resulted in 15 unique state machines for OpenSSL. The learning of the LibreSSL server-side state machine resulted in only two different state machines. One of these state machines was equal to one of the OpenSSL state machines. In Fig. 2 an overview is given of the different state machines for the server-side and their overlap between different branches of OpenSSL. In this figure we excluded the various beta versions that we learned, leaving 12 different state machines.

The oldest version of OpenSSL for which we learned a state machine is version 0.9.7, released in December 2002. For the server-side this state machines contains 17 states (see Fig. 3), the highest number for all state machines we learned. When analysing the state machine we observe several explanations why the state machine contains so many states. First, it is possible to start a renegotiation after completing a handshake successfully by starting a new handshake. In our case this does not lead to a successful data exchange, and therefore the number of states used for a handshake is already doubled (states 12, 13, 16 and 14).

---

[5] http://www.cs.ru.nl/~joeri/.

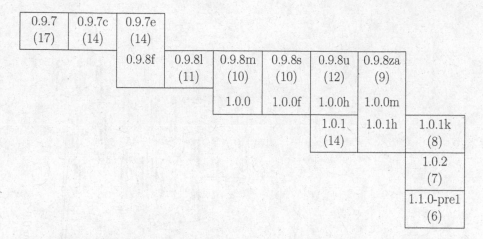

Fig. 2. Overview of the 12 state machines of the server-side for different versions of OpenSSL. The version number indicates the first version in a particular branch that a state machine was used. Per unique state machine the number of states is included.

Secondly, the server accepts empty Certificates from the client after a ClientHello message, which adds an additional state for every handshake attempt (i.e. states 5, 8 and 13).

Though these functionalities can still be seen as genuine, we also observe some clearly erroneous behaviour. For example, when after the initial ClientHello immediately a ChangeCipherSpec message is sent, the connection is not closed and the handshake can still be finished by sending a ClientKeyExchange and Finished message (the path through states 1, 6, optionally via 8, to 9 and finishing in 2). The Finished message is not accepted from state 9 however and instead a *Decrypt error* alert is returned. This additional behaviour is the result of a serious security issue that we will discuss in more detail later.

Other observations include the fact that empty ApplicationData messages are always ignored, except if it is the first message that is sent, in which case the connection is closed. Also, it is possible to send the ClientHello message numerous times at the beginning of a handshake as there is a self-loop with this message after the initial ClientHello message in state 1. A possible explanation for this is support for a feature called *Server-Gated Cryptography*. This is a legacy feature that resulted from the export restrictions on cryptography. Under these restriction strong cryptography was still allowed for financial transactions, so if a client asked for a weak export cipher the server could indicate that it was allowed to use the stronger ciphers and the client could send a new ClientHello message containing the stronger ciphersuites.

If after a successfully completed handshake a ChangeCipherSpec message is sent (from states 10, 12 and 13), all subsequent messages are replied to with a *Bad record MAC* alert.

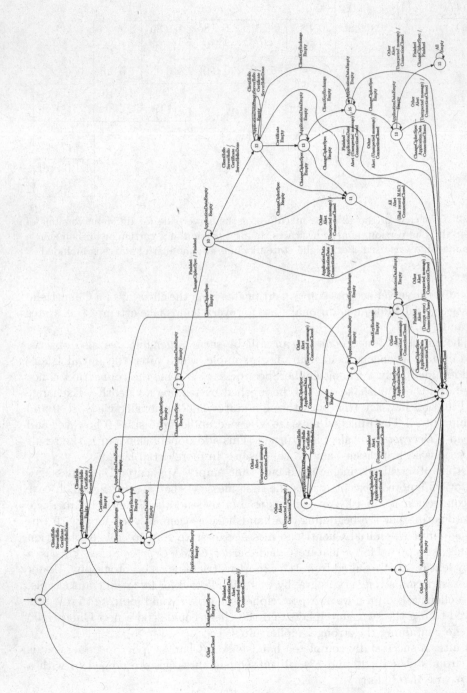

Fig. 3. State machine for the server-side of OpenSSL version 0.9.7.

In version 0.9.7c the state machine is changed and the number of states is reduced to 14. This is due to the fact that the server no longer accepts certificates from the client during the handshake, which results in states 5, 8 and 13 being dropped from the previous state machine. According to the changelog the server now only accepts a certificate if it requested one using a *CertificateRequest* message in order to comply with the official specifications.

The state machine then already changes again in version 0.9.7e. The number of states stays the same though and the only change is that Alert messages are now always sent before the connection is closed after a handshake is initialised. This wasn't the case before for the ChangeCipherSpec and ApplicationData messages (see, for example, state 7 of version 0.9.7). The state machine then stays stable until the end of the branch (version 0.9.7m) and is also the same for the first versions of the 0.9.8 branch that we learned.

Then in November 2009 version 0.9.8l was released, which contains only 11 states. Looking at the learned model, we can see that it is no longer possible to perform a renegotiation after a successfully completed handshake as we previously observed. Around the same time as this release, details are published on a serious vulnerability that is present in many TLS implementations (CVE-2009-3555). This issue made it possible for a man-in-the-middle to inject plaintext data at the beginning of a TLS session. The attacker starts a TLS connection with a server that the victim's client want to speak to. The attacker can then send any data to the server. After this it will start a renegotiation with the server, whereby it forwards the original TLS messages from the victim. The victim does not realise it is performing a renegotiation as it looks the same as the initialisation of a connection. The server will consider it a renegotiation and append the data from the client to the data it initially received from the attacker. The attacker won't be able to eavesdrop on the data that is exchanged between the victim and the server, but by only prepending data it has been shown that, for example, credentials could be stolen.[6] When this issue was reported, developers of different implementations and the IETF came together in "Project Mogul" to find a solution. As the issue is caused by the way renegotiation is performed, OpenSSL initially responded by disabling renegotiation completely, as we observed in the learned state machine.

We also observed some new strange behaviour after the handshake is successfully completed (state 8). Every message, other than ApplicationData or ChangeCipherSpec, is initially ignored, but every following message results in a decryption failure on our side. When analysing the network traffic we noticed that this was due to the fact that the server sent plaintext Alert messages, even though all messages should have been encrypted at this point. We also observe that it is still possible to send a ChangeCipherSpec both directly after the first ClientHello (from state 1) and after a successful handshake (from state 8). As before these paths eventually lead to a *Decrypt error* alert and *Bad record MAC* alert respectively.

---

[6] http://www.securegoose.org/2009/11/tls-renegotiation-vulnerability-cve.html.

In February 2010, RFC 5746 was released [21]. This RFC specifies a secure way to perform renegotiation. This RFC is implemented in the same month in version 0.9.8m. In the state machine multiple ClientHello messages are accepted again, and the strange behaviour that resulted in a decryption error in our framework is no longer present.

At the beginning of 2012, version 0.9.8s was released. The state machine contains 10 states, but we see that a ClientHello is only accepted once now. A second ClientHello is still responded to in the usual way with a ServerHello, Certificate and ServerHelloDone message, though the connection is closed immediately after this. At the end of 2011 it was reported that allowing arbitrary ClientHello messages at the start constitutes a denial-of-service attack as the server has to perform significantly more computations upon receiving a ClientHello than the client (CVE-2011-4619). This issue explains why only one ClientHello is accepted now. However, for Server Gated Cryptography we would still expect to see two ClientHello messages and if a message is rejected it should be responded to with an Alert message and not a valid ServerHello, Certificate and ServerHelloDone message. These issues are fixed in version 0.9.8u, where at most two ClientHello messages are accepted, which increases the number of states again to 12.

Before, we observed the early ChangeCipherSpec, directly after the first ClientHello message, and subsequent messages. This part of the state machine was due to a serious security flaw which was eventually discovered by Kikuchi (CVE-2014-0224).[7] By sending a ChangeCipherSpec message too early, i.e. before the keys have been established, the keys are calculated using an empty master secret and therefore only depend on information known to a possible attacker. Due to the way the Finished message is computed in version 1.0.1, it was vulnerable to decryption of the TLS connection by an attacker who is able to eavesdrop on the connection and even complete hijacking of the connection by a man-in-the-middle. A detailed analysis of this bug is given by Langley on his blog.[8] In version 0.9.8za we see that the ChangeCipherSpec message is no longer accepted directly after the ClientHello message (see Fig. 4). The Change-CipherSpec is however still accepted directly after a successful handshake.

Branch 1.0.0 completely follows the state machine from branch 0.9.8. Branch 1.0.1 starts with a different state machine though, after which it start using the same state machine as 0.9.8za from version 1.0.1h, to finally end with a different state machine again after 1.0.1k. In version 1.0.1 the early ChangeCipherSpec is accepted as with the earlier versions of 0.9.7 and 0.9.8. However, instead of finishing with a *Decrypt error* from the server-side, our framework cannot decrypt any messages it receives from the server.

Version 1.0.1k (see Fig. 5) was released after we reported the issue regarding the ChangeCipherSpec message following a successfully completed handshake. This behaviour was the result of a bug that resulted in the keys being reset to their initial values and the same key being used for both directions (i.e. from client to server and from server to client). This breaks the protection measures in

---

[7] http://ccsinjection.lepidum.co.jp/.
[8] https://www.imperialviolet.org/2014/06/05/earlyccs.html.

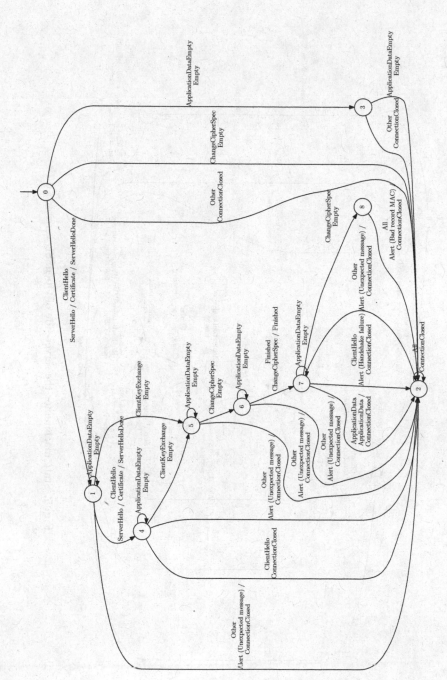

Fig. 4. State machine for the server-side of OpenSSL version 0.9.8za

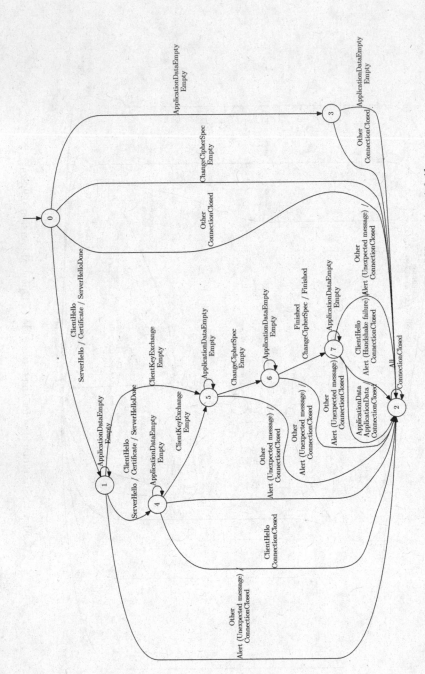

Fig. 5. State machine for the server-side of OpenSSL version 1.0.1k

place against replay attacks. In version 1.0.1k we can see the superfluous Change-CipherSpec message is no longer accepted. At the same time we also checked a development version in which the second ClientHello was replied to with correct messages (ServerHello, Certificate, ServerHelloDone) but immediately after this the connection was closed. This was similar to the behaviour that we observed in version 0.9.8s and was fixed before the code was ever released. From version 1.0.1k the state machine stays stable until the end of the branch.

The state machine for the 1.0.2 branch is stable, except for the beta versions, and contains 7 states. This is one state less than version 1.0.1k, which is due to the fact that Server Gated Cryptography is no longer supported and only one ClientHello is accepted at the beginning of the handshake. In the pre-releases for 1.1.0 the number even drops to 6 states which is caused by the implementation accepting empty ApplicationData messages in every state, even the initial one. In branch 1.1.0, a new implementation is introduced for the state machine.

LibreSSL starts in version 2.0.0 with the same state machine as OpenSSL 0.9.8za. In version 2.2.1 the state machine changes, but the issue we found in OpenSSL with the ChangeCipherSpec message after a successful handshake is still present.

5.2   Client-Side

For the client-side, 9 unique state machines were learned for OpenSSL and one for LibreSSL, which was equal to the latest one from OpenSSL. An overview of the client-side state machines for OpenSSL is given in Fig. 6. Two state machines are again excluded here as they are unique for beta versions.

The first two state machines that we learned did not result in usable state machines. This was due to the fact that these versions did not have extensions enabled by default and therefore rejected our ServerHello messages. In version 0.9.8j, extensions were enabled by default and we get the first model suitable

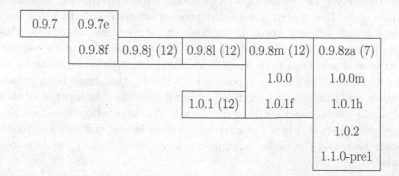

Fig. 6. Overview of the 7 state machines of the client-side for different OpenSSL versions. The version number indicates the first version in a particular branch that a state machine was used. Per unique state machine the number of states is included, except for the first two for which no usable state machine was learned.

for analysis. This state machine contains 12 states and displays some unexpected behaviour. After a successful handshake, most unexpected messages are replied to with a ClientHello message before the connection is closed. It is however possible to send a ChangeCipherSpec message followed by a ServerHello. The ServerHello is responded to with a ClientHello, after which a complete new handshake can be performed. After the ChangeCipherSpec the messages cannot be decrypted any more, indicating that a key is used which is different than expected. The same is the case if a ChangeCipherSpec is sent too early, namely after the ServerHello or the ServerCertificate. This last behaviour matches that of the server-side, which is caused by the vulnerability reported by Kikuchi.

In version 0.9.8l, the number of states stay the same, but the client no longer sends ClientHello messages and renegotiation seems completely disabled. This matches what we observed for the server-side, where renegotiation was disabled to prevent a serious security issue. Renegotiation seems to be re-enabled in version 0.9.8m, as the client sends ClientHello messages again just before closing the connection when receiving an unexpected message after a successful handshake. We are no longer able to perform renegotiations though as our framework does not implement the secure renegotiation as specified in RFC 5746 [21]. From version 0.9.8za, when the bug reported by Kikuchi is fixed, the ChangeCipherSpec message is no longer accepted directly after a successful handshake.

As can be seen in Fig. 6, the next branches implement the same state machines as branch 0.9.8, except for version 1.0.1. This state machine is almost identical to the one from 0.9.8 m though. The only difference is that, upon receiving a Finished message in the initial state, the connection is immediately closed in version 1.0.1, while an alert is sent first in version 0.9.8m. For LibreSSL all versions resulted in the same state machine as OpenSSL version 0.9.8za.

6 Conclusion

By just looking at the state machines, inferred in our automated process, we able to analyse the evolution of OpenSSL, without requiring an analysis of the source code. Due to our automated process we were able to learn the state machine for 145 different versions for both the server- and client-side. Various bugs can be spotted by only analysing the learned models, and indeed we even reported several new bugs to different developers. Observable bugs can be serious security flaws, such as the one reported by Kikuchi, that have been present for many years, and might have been fixed earlier if only the developers had the tools to analyse their state machine implementation. We can see how the state machine improves over time and how the current versions seems quite clean. Would the developers have had the tools, it might not have taken almost 14 years to get to this state.

Having access to the source code, the developers could possibly leverage this fact in their analysis of the implemented state machine. However, language specific tools would be needed for this and the code might need to be instrumented to be able to use these tools. By using a black-box analysis, as used in this paper, developers can use generic tools that work independent of implementation details.

In future work we intend to extend this analysis to other implementations. Next to this, we plan to add automated analysis to our testing framework in order to make it easy for developers to spot unexpected or strange behaviour and observe changes between versions. We expect this can be a helpful tool as currently developers have many tools to perform, for example, analysis of memory usage or even static analysis of their code, but a tool to check exactly what state machine is implemented is currently lacking.

To conclude, state machine inference is a useful technique when analysing implementations and a large-scale analysis of state machines can tell an interesting tale about the evolution of a protocol implementation.

References

1. Angluin, D.: Learning regular sets from queries and counterexamples. Inf. Comput. **75**(2), 87–106 (1987)
2. Aviram, N., Schinzel, S., Somorovsky, J., Heninger, N., Dankel, M., Steube, J., Valenta, L., Adrian, D., Halderman, J.A., Dukhovni, V., Käsper, E., Cohney, S., Engels, S., Paar, C., Shavitt, Y.: DROWN: breaking TLS using SSLv2. In: 25th USENIX Security Symposium (USENIX Security 2016), pp. 689–706. USENIX Association, Austin, August 2016
3. Beurdouche, B., Bhargavan, K., Delignat-Lavaud, A., Fournet, C., Kohlweiss, M., Pironti, A., Strub, P.Y., Zinzindohoue, J.K.: A messy state of the union: taming the composite state machines of TLS. In: 2015 IEEE Symposium on Security and Privacy, pp. 535–552 (2015)
4. Bhargavan, K., Fournet, C., Kohlweiss, M., Pironti, A., Strub, P.: Implementing TLS with verified cryptographic security. In: 2013 IEEE Symposium on Security and Privacy, pp. 445–459 (2013)
5. Chow, T.: Testing software design modeled by finite-state machines. IEEE Trans. Softw. Eng. **4**(3), 178–187 (1978)
6. Díaz, G., Cuartero, F., Valero, V., Pelayo, F.: Automatic verification of the TLS handshake protocol. In: Proceedings of the 2004 ACM Symposium on Applied Computing, SAC 2004, pp. 789–794. ACM (2004)
7. Dierks, T., Allen, C.: The TLS protocol version 1.0. RFC 2246, Internet Engineering Task Force (1999)
8. Dierks, T., Rescorla, E.: The Transport Layer Security (TLS) protocol version 1.1. RFC 4346, Internet Engineering Task Force (2006)
9. Dierks, T., Rescorla, E.: The Transport Layer Security (TLS) protocol version 1.2. RFC 5246, Internet Engineering Task Force (2008)
10. Gajek, S., Manulis, M., Pereira, O., Sadeghi, A.-R., Schwenk, J.: Universally composable security analysis of TLS. In: Baek, J., Bao, F., Chen, K., Lai, X. (eds.) ProvSec 2008. LNCS, vol. 5324, pp. 313–327. Springer, Heidelberg (2008). doi:10.1007/978-3-540-88733-1_22
11. He, C., Sundararajan, M., Datta, A., Derek, A., Mitchell, J.C.: A modular correctness proof of IEEE 802.11i and TLS. In: Proceedings of the 12th ACM Conference on Computer and Communications Security, CCS 2005, pp. 2–15. ACM (2005)
12. Jager, T., Kohlar, F., Schäge, S., Schwenk, J.: On the security of TLS-DHE in the standard model. In: Safavi-Naini, R., Canetti, R. (eds.) CRYPTO 2012. LNCS, vol. 7417, pp. 273–293. Springer, Heidelberg (2012). doi:10.1007/978-3-642-32009-5_17

13. Kamil, A., Lowe, G.: Analysing TLS in the strand spaces model. J. Comput. Secur. **19**(5), 975–1025 (2011)
14. Krawczyk, H., Paterson, K.G., Wee, H.: On the security of the TLS protocol: a systematic analysis. In: Canetti, R., Garay, J.A. (eds.) CRYPTO 2013. LNCS, vol. 8042, pp. 429–448. Springer, Heidelberg (2013). doi:10.1007/978-3-642-40041-4_24
15. Meyer, C., Schwenk, J.: SoK: lessons learned from SSL/TLS attacks. In: Kim, Y., Lee, H., Perrig, A. (eds.) WISA 2013. LNCS, vol. 8267, pp. 189–209. Springer, Heidelberg (2014). doi:10.1007/978-3-319-05149-9_12
16. Morrissey, P., Smart, N.P., Warinschi, B.: A modular security analysis of the TLS handshake protocol. In: Pieprzyk, J. (ed.) ASIACRYPT 2008. LNCS, vol. 5350, pp. 55–73. Springer, Heidelberg (2008). doi:10.1007/978-3-540-89255-7_5
17. Niese, O.: An integrated approach to testing complex systems. Ph.D. thesis, Dortmund University (2003)
18. Ogata, K., Futatsugi, K.: Equational approach to formal analysis of TLS. In: 2005 Proceedings of the 25th IEEE International Conference on Distributed Computing Systems, ICDCS 2005, pp. 795–804. IEEE (2005)
19. Paulson, L.C.: Inductive analysis of the internet protocol TLS. ACM Trans. Inf. Syst. Secur. **2**(3), 332–351 (1999)
20. Raffelt, H., Steffen, B., Berg, T.: LearnLib: a library for automata learning and experimentation. In: Formal methods for industrial critical systems (FMICS 2005), pp. 62–71. ACM (2005)
21. Rescorla, E., Ray, M., Dispensa, S., Oskov, N.: Transport Layer Security (TLS) renegotiation indication extension. RFC 5746, Internet Engineering Task Force (2010)
22. de Ruiter, J., Poll, E.: Protocol state fuzzing of TLS implementations. In: 24th USENIX Security Symposium (USENIX Security 2015). USENIX Association, Washington, D.C., August 2015
23. Turner, S., Polk, T.: Prohibiting Secure Sockets Layer (SSL) version 2.0. RFC 6176, Internet Engineering Task Force (2011)

Cryptography

Speeding up R-LWE Post-quantum Key Exchange

Shay Gueron[1,2(✉)] and Fabian Schlieker[3]

[1] Department of Mathematics, University of Haifa, Haifa, Israel
[2] Intel Corporation, Israel Deveopment Center, Haifa, Israel
[3] Horst Görtz Institute for IT-Security, Ruhr University Bochum, Bochum, Germany
shay@math.haifa.ac.il, fabian.schlieker@ruhr-uni-bochum.de

Abstract. Post-quantum cryptography has attracted increased attention in the last couple of years, due to the threat of quantum computers breaking current cryptosystems. In particular, the key size and performance of post-quantum algorithms became a significant target for optimization. In this spirit, Alkim et al. have recently proposed a significant optimization for a key exchange scheme that is based on the R-LWE problem. In this paper, we build on the implementation of Alkim et al., and focus on improving the algorithm for generating a uniformly random polynomial. We optimize three independent directions: efficient pseudorandom bytes generation, decreasing the rejection rate during sampling, and vectorizing the sampling step. When measured on the latest Intel processor Architecture Codename Skylake, our new optimizations improve over Alkim et al. by up to 1.59× on the server side, and by up to 1.54× on the client side.

Keywords: Post-quantum key exchange · Ring-LWE · Software optimization · AVX2 · AVX512 · AES-NI

1 Introduction

Cryptographic algorithms that are based on number theoretical problems like factorization and discrete logarithm can be broken if and when quantum computers are available. Sufficiently large quantum computers do not exist today, but can be expected to be built in the foreseeable future (e. g., in 10–15 years [1]). Fortunately, lattice theory offers mathematical problems that seem to not be vulnerable to such attacks. Therefore, lattice-based cryptosystems emerge as a viable secure post-quantum alternative.

Lattice-based algorithms have already been proposed for important cryptographic primitives such as digital signatures, encryption, and key exchange. Specifically, Ding et al. introduced a lattice-based key exchange scheme, which was improved by Peikert [4, 13]. A concrete instantiation of this algorithm has been recently proposed by Bos et al. [3]. The work of [3] is quite substantial, and includes a software implementation that can be directly integrated into the

© Springer International Publishing AG 2016
B.B. Brumley and J. Röning (Eds.): NordSec 2016, LNCS 10014, pp. 187–198, 2016.
DOI: 10.1007/978-3-319-47560-8_12

OpenSSL library. The implementation is optimized at the algorithmic level (e. g., uses NTT for polynomial multiplication), but since it relies on generic arithmetic libraries and sampling from the Gaussian distribution, its performance can be improved.

Alkim, Ducas, Pöppelmann and Schwabe [2] addressed the performance issue of the implementation in [3] by using a more optimal parameter choice, and by optimizing the key exchange scheme with hand crafted low level assembly code. In addition, they showed that for key exchange (in contrast to digital signature schemes), it suffices to sample secret random values from a centered binomial distribution rather than from discrete Gaussian distributions. This reduces the associated computational costs significantly. As a result, their implementation (called NEWHOPE) is an order of magnitude faster than [3]. The source code for a C reference implementation and an optimized SIMD version was published online. In this paper, we build on the AVX2 implementation and further improve its performance.

Our Contribution. The work of Alkim et al. focused on optimizing the polynomial arithmetic and error reconciliation parts of the algorithm. As a result, its relative weight in the overall computation time was reduced, compared to the reference code. With that, the pseudorandom polynomial generation (called "parse" in the paper), which only is a small building block in the protocol, becomes ~45 % of the computation time (for both the server and the client sides). We therefore focus our efforts on the parse function, and present optimizations at three independent levels:

- Reduce the rejection rate of pseudorandom candidates during the sampling step from 25 % to 6 %.
- Parallelize the rejection sampling step using AVX2 (and furthermore AVX512) instructions.
- Replace the SHAKE-128 extendable-output function (XOF) [14], for generating pseudorandom bytes, by a faster, parallel implementation of SHA-256. Alternatively, replace the hash based generation with one based on AES256.

We remark that the source code for our optimizations is made available online at https://github.com/fschlieker/newhope.

Organization of This Paper. The paper is organized as follows. In Sect. 2 we give some background on how NEWHOPE works. In particular, we explain the parse function in detail. Section 4 details our proposed optimizations, and the resulting performance is presented in Sect. 5. We conclude and compare to the performance of the standardized ECDH key exchange in Sect. 6.

2   Preliminaries

We follow the notation of [2], so computations are carried out in $\mathcal{R}_q = \mathbb{Z}_q[X]/(X^n+1)$, the ring of integer polynomials modulo the polynomial (X^n+1)

and with coefficients reduced modulo q. The implementation of NEWHOPE is instantiated with $n = 1024$ and $q = 12289$ (a 14-bit prime). We denote polynomials in this ring by boldface characters.

We briefly outline the protocol[1] (consider [2] for details).

Server: The server side creates a random seed (e. g., from /dev/urandom). A hash function, seeded with this seed, defines a stream of pseudorandom bytes. Uniformly distributed coefficients for a public polynomial **a** are then sampled from this stream, using a function called parse. Subsequently, a secret polynomial **s** and an error polynomial **e** (with small coefficients) are sampled from a centered binomial distribution. The server computes **b** = **as** + **e** and sends to the client **b** and the seed.

Client: The client re-generates the same **a** (from the seed) calling the parse function. Polynomials **s'**, **e'** and **e"** are sampled from the binomial distribution. Then, it computes **u** = **as'** + **e'** and **r** = **HelpRec(v)**, and sends these values to the server. Additionally, the client calculates **v** + **bs'** + **e"** = **ass'** + **es'** + **e"**.

Server: The server computes **v'** = **us** = **ass'** + **e's**. Now **v** and **v'** on both sides are "close" though not identical, due to the different error polynomials. The small errors can be corrected by a reconciliation mechanism (for which **r** is needed). Finally, server and client can compute the shared key as the SHA-3 hash over the reconciled data that is identical on both sides.

3 Considerations in Generating the Public Polynomial

The proposal in [3] uses a fixed polynomial **a** as a system parameter. In contrast, [2] recommends to generate a fresh **a** for every key exchange, giving two reasons:

*Fend Off Possible Concerns About a Backdoored Choice of **a**.* The polynomial **a** could be carefully chosen in a way that all the intermediate calculations during the protocol run would have values that are smaller than q. In such case, no reduction takes place, and the secret polynomial **s** can be recovered easily using calculations in $\mathbb{Z}$. This subtle backdoor could potentially allow key escrow to e. g., a standardization body that specified a weak **a**.

Avoid Relying Only on a Single Instance of a Lattice Problem. A fixed **a** gives a powerful attacker the possibility to focus on finding a short basis for that particular lattice (using a lot of computation power). All traffic exchanged under a key that is generated from **a** could then be possibly decrypted. Generating a fresh **a** for every key exchange mitigates this "all-for-the-price-of-one" attack.

The straightforward approach is to let one party generate **a** and send it to the other during the protocol run. This consumes a lot of network bandwidth because a polynomial is stored in 2 KB of data. A better way is to let *both*

---

[1] A comprehensible overview can also be found in a blog post by A. Langley; https://www.imperialviolet.org/2015/12/24/rlwe.html.

parties generate the polynomial independently from pseudorandom bytes that are produced under a shared random seed. With this method, as proposed by Galbraith [5], only the 256-bit seed needs to be transmitted.

When a fresh **a** per session is required, fast pseudorandom generation is obviously needed in order to assure that the generation does not become a performance bottleneck.

Pseudorandom Generation Methods. The authors of [2] argue that a security reduction is (only) possible under the Random Oracle Model (ROM), and therefore instantiate their scheme with SHAKE-128 XOF ([14]) that provides 128 bits of post-quantum security. When this XOF is seeded with a 256-bit random seed, it deterministically defines a stream of pseudorandom bytes. The assumption is that the probability to find a "malicious backdoored" polynomial **a** by sampling from this stream, is negligible. In other words, it is infeasible to try many different seeds until a malicious **a** is found.

We propose two alternatives to using SHAKE-128, both of them offer 128 bits of post-quantum security, and achieve better performance.

1. Parallelized SHA-256. Concatenate the seed with a running counter value, to produce as many hash digests as needed for collecting a sufficient amount of pseudorandom bytes. This procedure can be parallelized, because the digests are computed from independent blocks.
2. Using a block cipher (AES256). First, hash the seed (using SHA-3) and generate a 256-bit value to be used as a key for AES256. Then, produce as many blocks as are needed, by encrypting and incrementing a counter value.

Remark 1. By first hashing the seed before using it directly as a key for a block cipher (AES256), we make sure that crafting a malicious **a** would not be possible by only finding certain AES keys that result in a desired ciphertext (a task, which is, by itself, computationally infeasible). In this scenario, one also needs to find a SHA-3 input that produces the desired key. Therefore, the construction can also be seen as a ROM instantiation.

Remark 2. We show below that the block cipher alternative performs better than hashing. However, if one wishes to operate directly under the same ROM assumption as in [2], it is possible to choose SHA-256 and still enjoy performance improvements.

4   Our Optimizations

This section describes our optimizations and their software implementation.

4.1 Decreasing the Rejection Rate

The function **parse**, that generates **a**, receives a seed and generates (using SHAKE-128 XOF) pseudorandom bytes as "candidates". These pseudorandom bytes are post-processed to sample the $n = 1024$ coefficients for **a**. Every pair of bytes of the pseudorandom stream is viewed as a 16-bit candidate. In [2], the two most significant bits are zeroed to create a 14-bit value. If this value is smaller than q, it is accepted as a coefficient, and otherwise it is discarded. This is the most simple and straightforward way. On average, this process accepts only $\frac{q}{2^{14}} = \frac{12289}{16384} \approx \frac{3}{4} = 75\%$ of the candidates (see Fig. 1(a)). To accumulate $n = 1024$ uniformly distributed (over $\mathbb{Z}_q$) coefficients from two-byte words, **parse** needs to check $1024 \cdot 2 \cdot \frac{4}{3} \approx 2730$ bytes on average.

Ignoring two bits of every sample with a rejection rate of 25 % is not optimal and we propose to use the full 16-bit sample. While we still need to reject some values from the pseudorandom stream (those that are $\geq 5q$ since $\left\lfloor \frac{2^{16}}{q} \right\rfloor = 5$), the overall acceptance probability is now $\frac{5 \cdot q}{2^{16}} = \frac{61445}{65536} \approx 94\%$. However, we need to subtract q up to four times from the accepted candidates to retrieve values in $\mathbb{Z}_q$ (which then remain uniformly random). See Fig. 1(b) for an illustration and Listing 1 for the corresponding pieces of source code.

Note that this small change benefits twice: with less values rejected, we need to generate fewer pseudorandom bytes to begin with. Consequently, less values need to be conditionally checked. On average, the proposed routine needs only $1024 \cdot 2 \cdot \frac{65536}{61445} \approx 2184$ pseudorandom bytes in order to populate the coefficients of **a**.

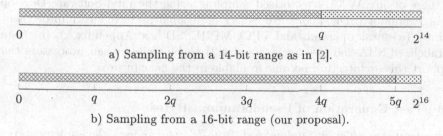

a) Sampling from a 14-bit range as in [2].

b) Sampling from a 16-bit range (our proposal).

Fig. 1. Sampling uniformly random values in $\mathbb{Z}_q$ from different input ranges. Candidates that are accepted are indicated by the crossed area and candidates in the dotted area are rejected. The acceptance rate is significantly higher when sampling from the 16-bit range. In this case, q might have to be subtracted up to four times from an accepted candidate in order to obtain a coefficient in $\mathbb{Z}_q$, but it remains uniformly random.

Remark 3. Note that since the seed and the generated polynomial **a** are meant to be public, the implementation does not need to execute the generation in constant time.

```
1   a) Rejection-sampling from 14 bits:
2
3   candidate = (buf[pos] | ((uint16_t) buf[pos+1] << 8)) & 0x3fff; // take only lower 14 bits
4   if(candidate < PARAM_Q) // accept as coefficient if < q
5     a->v[ctr++] = candidate;
6
7   b) Rejection-sampling from 16 bits (our proposal):
8
9   candidate = (buf[pos] | ((uint16_t) buf[pos+1] << 8)); // take full 16 bits
10  r = candidate / PARAM_Q;
11  if (r < 5) // accept as coefficient if < 5q, since floor(2^16/q) = 5
12    a->v[ctr++] = candidate - r * PARAM_Q; // subtract q up to 4 times to end up in Zq
```

Listing 1. Code snippets for (a) Rejection sampling from two a bytes input, when the two most significant bits are discarded [2]; (b) From the full 16-bit range (our proposal). buf contains the pseudorandom bytes and pos the position in that buffer. a->v points to the coefficients of a and ctr is incremented until we have 1024 accepted coefficients.

4.2   Vectorized Rejection Sampling

The process of filtering pseudorandom 16-bit candidates can be accelerated by using SIMD instructions, just like many other parts of the protocol were accelerated using AVX2. Specifically, it is possible to handle 16 candidates with AVX2 instructions (using 256-bit registers) and 32 candidates with AVX512 (using 512-bit registers) [11,12].

Our AVX2 implementation uses a mixture of vector comparisons and permutations in order to compress and align the accepted candidates ($< q$). An illustrative excerpt of the code is given in Appendix A.

Processors with AVX512 support are not available yet, but we verified correctness of our AVX512-vectorized sampling using the Intel Software Development Emulator (SDE) tool.[2] We expect additional performance improvements due to: (a) mask operands and VPCOMPRESSD (see Appendix A); (b) faster parallelized SHA-256 (see Sects. 3 and 4.3) to be visible when processors that support this architecture become available in the near future.

4.3   Fast Generation of Pseudorandom Bytes

After acquiring a 256-bit random seed (from /dev/urandom), the implementation of [2] uses SHAKE-128 XOF to generate the pseudorandom bytes stream. We investigate two alternatives for such generation.

Using SHA-256 with Modern SIMD Architectures. The AVX2 (AVX512) instructions can be used for computing 8 (16) hashes in parallel [8]. To this end, we built a highly optimized implementation that produces bytes at the rate of 2.75 cycles per byte (C/B) with AVX2 (and much faster on the coming AVX512 architectures).

---

[2] Intel Software Development Emulator (SDE) https://software.intel.com/en-us/articles/intel-software-development-emulator.

Using AES (with AES-NI). We used the pipelined AES implementation of [6,7], which performs at 0.92 C/B on our test platform ("Skylake"). We run it in counter mode (CTR), so incrementing counter values are used as plaintexts and encrypted under a fixed key. This has the advantage that the key schedule only needs to be computed once and ciphertext generation can be efficiently pipelined.

5 Results

This section presents the results of our different optimizations. The performance numbers were obtained by using the test bench included in the implementation of NEWHOPE. The measurements were obtained on a platform with the latest Intel® Core™ Generation processor (Architecture Codename Skylake), with the Intel® Turbo Boost Technology, Intel® Hyper-Threading Technology, and Enhanced Intel Speedstep® Technology disabled. The code was compiled with gcc version 5.2.0 and full optimizations enabled ("-O3"). For consistent comparison, we compiled and measured the baseline implementation [2] on the same system.

Remark 4. During our work, we discovered a bug in this test bench, that leads to somewhat overoptimistic results, presumably due to caching of fixed values across multiple tests. We reported the bug to the authors, together with the appropriate fix. It was corrected in the final version of [2]. The results we report here were measured with the *fixed* version.

The results are presented in Table 1, showing the contribution of the different optimizations. We indicate the distinct optimization methods by abbreviations: reduction of the rejection rate (I), vectorization of rejection sampling (II), pseudorandom bytes generation using SHA-256 (III) and AES256 (IV). Note that the last two optimizations (III and IV) are mutually exclusive. The other optimizations (I, II) are independent, and are therefore combinable. The difference between the cycles count of the server and the client can be explained

Table 1. The performance of the different optimizations, compared to NEWHOPE [2] as the baseline. The numbers represent the cycles counts, measured using the test bench (lower is better) and the speedup factor compared to the baseline that is set to 1 (i. e., higher is better).

	Method	parse cycles	Server cycles	speedup	Client cycles	speedup
Baseline NEWHOPE [2]		59,627	127,712		129,349	
This work	I	47,044	113,361	1.13×	115,909	1.12×
	I, II	38,466	100,343	1.27×	104,120	1.24×
	I, II, III	32,080	94,183	1.36×	97,688	1.32×
	I, II, IV	17,053	80,087	1.59×	84,119	1.54×

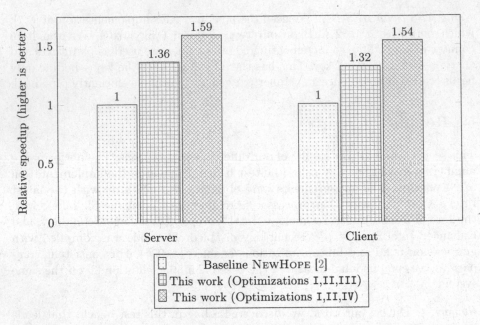

Fig. 2. The highest relative speedup factors on the server and the client sides, achieved by the proposed optimizations (the baseline implementation [2] is set to 1).

as follows. The server needs to obtain a seed from a (typically slow) randomness source, but on the other hand, the client needs to compute one more NTT and polynomial addition during the computations of its part of the exchange.

Figure 2 illustrates our results with all our optimizations enabled, and compares them relatively to the baseline [2] that is set to 1. With the reduced rejection rate method, vectorized rejection sampling and SHA-256 for pseudorandom generation, the speedup factor is 1.36× for the server and 1.32× for the client. The best speedup is achieved when AES-NI are used for generating pseudorandomness. This increases performance by a factor of 1.59× and 1.54×, on the server and the client side, respectively.

6   Conclusion

This paper demonstrated several optimizations that can be used for speeding up R-LWE-based key exchange. Our results show that the server and the client sides can profit from a speedup factor of up to 1.59× and 1.54×, respectively.

For comparison, we also measured the performance of the best available implementation of the standardized ECDH over P-256 key exchange ([9] and its improved version [10]), and found that the key exchange computations consume roughly 223,000 cycles on both sides. With all our optimizations, the R-LWE key exchange takes 80,087 cycles (server) and 84,119 cycles (client) (see Table 1). We point out that the amount of transferred data during the key exchange with

R-LWE (4096 bytes) is higher than with ECDH (64 bytes). Note that the parameters in [2] were chosen quite conservatively. An appropriate level of security would be probably achieved with e. g., $n = 512$, which would halve the amount of transferred data, and speed up computations. The authors justify the choice of $n = 1024$ by being able to thwart possible future advances in cryptanalysis. In any case we can see that, even with the discussed choice of parameters, post-quantum key exchange is already practical on current platforms.

Acknowledgments. This research was supported by the PQCRYPTO project, which was partially funded by the European Commission Horizon 2020 research Programme, grant #645622, and by the ISRAEL SCIENCE FOUNDATION (grant No. 1018/16).

A   Vectorized Rejection Sampling - Code Snippets

The relevant part of our AVX2 optimizations in the source code is shown in Listing 2 . Listing 3 shows the relevant part of our AVX512 optimizations. Note that the AVX512 sampling gets much easier thanks to the new masks feature that gives more targeted data-control in almost all instructions. In particular, the VPCOMPRESSD instruction allows us to write back only specific values instead of a whole vector.

In both these approaches, we incorporate our proposal to reduce the rejection rate as explained in Sect. 4.1. Since we are working on vectors of integers, we do not have a division function in the AVX integer instructions (like in Listing 1) and implement this by repeatedly comparing and subtracting.

```
 1   const __m256i zero = _mm256_setzero_si256();
 2   const __m256i modulus8 = _mm256_set1_epi32(PARAM_Q);
 3   const __m256i modulus16 = _mm256_set1_epi16(PARAM_Q);
 4
 5   uint32_t good = 0;
 6   uint32_t offset = 0;
 7   while(ctr < PARAM_N-16)
 8   {
 9       __m256i tmp0, tmp1, tmp2;
10
11       tmp0 = _mm256_loadu_si256((__m256i *)&buf[pos]);
12
13       // normalize the values in range
14       tmp1 = _mm256_min_epu16(tmp0,modulus16);
15       tmp1 = _mm256_cmpeq_epi16(tmp1,modulus16);
16       tmp2 = _mm256_and_si256(tmp1, modulus16);
17       tmp0 = _mm256_sub_epi16(tmp0, tmp2);
18       tmp1 = _mm256_min_epu16(tmp0,modulus16);
19       tmp1 = _mm256_cmpeq_epi16(tmp1,modulus16);
20       tmp2 = _mm256_and_si256(tmp1, modulus16);
21       tmp0 = _mm256_sub_epi16(tmp0, tmp2);
22       tmp1 = _mm256_min_epu16(tmp0,modulus16);
23       tmp1 = _mm256_cmpeq_epi16(tmp1,modulus16);
24       tmp2 = _mm256_and_si256(tmp1, modulus16);
25       tmp0 = _mm256_sub_epi16(tmp0, tmp2);
26       tmp1 = _mm256_min_epu16(tmp0,modulus16);
27       tmp1 = _mm256_cmpeq_epi16(tmp1,modulus16);
28       tmp2 = _mm256_and_si256(tmp1, modulus16);
29       tmp0 = _mm256_sub_epi16(tmp0, tmp2);
30
```

```
31    tmp1 = _mm256_unpacklo_epi16(tmp0, zero); // transition to epi32
32    tmp2 = _mm256_cmpgt_epi32(modulus8, tmp1); // compare to modulus
33    good = _mm256_movemask_ps((__m256)tmp2);
34    tmp2 = _mm256_permutevar8x32_epi32(tmp1, perm_lut[good]);
35    // ctr includes offset, possible bad values are overwritten
36    _mm256_storeu_si256((__m256i *)&a->v[ctr], tmp2);
37
38    offset = __builtin_popcount(good); // we get this many good (< modulus) values
39    ctr += offset;
40
41    // the very same thing as above, only with unpackhi
42    tmp1 = _mm256_unpackhi_epi16(tmp0, zero); // transition to epi32
43    tmp2 = _mm256_cmpgt_epi32(modulus8, tmp1); // compare to modulus
44    good = _mm256_movemask_ps((__m256)tmp2);
45    tmp2 = _mm256_permutevar8x32_epi32(tmp1, perm_lut[good]);
46    // ctr includes offset, possible bad values are overwritten
47    _mm256_storeu_si256((__m256i *)&a->v[ctr], tmp2);
48
49    offset = __builtin_popcount(good); // we get this many good (< modulus) values
50    ctr += offset;
51
52    pos += 32; // proceed in the pseudorandom buffer
53
54    [...]
```

Listing 2. Vectorized rejection-sampling using AVX2 instructions. First, the candidate values are repeatedly compared to q and q is subtracted up to four times (ll. 14–29). This is the vectorized reduced rejection rate. It is followed by the rejection step, in which the vector is permuted such that the values to be rejected are aggregated in one side of the vector (ll. 31–34, 42–45). A precomputed 8 KB lookup table is needed, in order to hold the 256 possible masks for this permutation. The pointer to the memory destination is increased such that the rejected values are overwritten (ll. 36–39, 47–50).

```
1    const __m512i zero = _mm512_setzero_si512();
2    const __m512i modulus16 = _mm512_set1_epi32(PARAM_Q);
3    const __m512i modulus32 = _mm512_set1_epi16(PARAM_Q);
4
5    uint32_t offset = 0;
6    __mmask16 good = 0;
7
8    while(ctr < PARAM_N-32)
9    {
10       __m512i tmp0, tmp1;
11       __mmask32 mask;
12
13       tmp0 = _mm512_loadu_si512((__m512i *)&buf[pos]);
14
15       // normalize the values in range
16       mask = _mm512_cmple_epu16_mask(modulus32, tmp0);
17       tmp0 = _mm512_mask_sub_epi16(tmp0, mask, tmp0, modulus32);
18       mask = _mm512_cmple_epu16_mask(modulus32, tmp0);
19       tmp0 = _mm512_mask_sub_epi16(tmp0, mask, tmp0, modulus32);
20       mask = _mm512_cmple_epu16_mask(modulus32, tmp0);
21       tmp0 = _mm512_mask_sub_epi16(tmp0, mask, tmp0, modulus32);
22       mask = _mm512_cmple_epu16_mask(modulus32, tmp0);
23       tmp0 = _mm512_mask_sub_epi16(tmp0, mask, tmp0, modulus32);
24
25       tmp1 = _mm512_unpacklo_epi16(tmp0, zero);
26       good = _mm512_cmplt_epi32_mask(tmp1, modulus16);
27       _mm512_mask_compressstoreu_epi32((__m512i *)&a->v[ctr], good, tmp1);
28       offset = __builtin_popcount(good); // we get this many good (< modulus) values
29       ctr += offset;
```

```
30
31      tmp1 = _mm512_unpackhi_epi16(tmp0, zero);
32      good = _mm512_cmplt_epi32_mask(tmp1, modulus16);
33      _mm512_mask_compressstoreu_epi32((__m512i *)&a->v[ctr], good, tmp1);
34      offset = __builtin_popcount(good); // we get this many good (< modulus) values
35      ctr += offset;
36
37      pos += 64; // proceed in the pseudorandom buffer
38
39      [...]
```

Listing 3. Vectorized rejection-sampling using AVX512 instructions. The preparation step is much shorter, due to mask operands providing more control over the data in vector registers (ll. 16–23). With the VPCOMPRESSD, we can selectively write only specific values to memory and save the expensive permutation from our AVX2 approach (ll. 25–35).

References

1. IBM's stunning breakthrough: quantum computing finally 'within reach', February 2012. http://www.foxnews.com/tech/2012/02/28/ibm-quantum-computing-as-little-as-10-years-off.html
2. Alkim, E., Ducas, L., Pöppelmann, T., Schwabe, P.: Post-quantum key exchange-a new hope. IACR Cryptology ePrint Archive 2015/1092 (2015). http://eprint.iacr.org/2015/1092
3. Bos, J.W., Costello, C., Naehrig, M., Stebila, D.: Post-quantum key exchange for the TLS protocol from the ring learning with errors problem. In: 2015 IEEE Symposium on Security and Privacy, pp. 553–570. IEEE Computer Society, May 2015
4. Ding, J., Xie, X., Lin, X.: A simple provably secure key exchange scheme based on the learning with errors problem. IACR Cryptology ePrint Archive 2012/688 (2012). http://eprint.iacr.org/2012/688
5. Galbraith, S.D.: Space-efficient variants of cryptosystems based on learning with errors (2013). https://www.math.auckland.ac.nz/~sgal018/compact-LWE.pdf
6. Gueron, S.: Intel ® Advanced Encryption Standard (AES) new instructions set, September 2012. https://software.intel.com/sites/default/files/article/165683/aes-wp-2012-09-22-v01.pdf
7. Gueron, S.: Intel's new AES instructions for enhanced performance and security. In: Dunkelman, O. (ed.) FSE 2009. LNCS, vol. 5665, pp. 51–66. Springer, Heidelberg (2009)
8. Gueron, S., Krasnov, V.: Simultaneous hashing of multiple messages. J. Inf. Secur. **3**(4), 319–325 (2012)
9. Gueron, S., Krasnov, V.: Fast prime field elliptic-curve cryptography with 256-bit primes. J. Cryptograph. Eng. **5**(2), 141–151 (2015)
10. Gueron, S., Krasnov, V.: Improved P256 ECC performance by means of a dedicated function for modular inversion modulo the P256 group order, April 2015. https://mta.openssl.org/pipermail/openssl-dev/2015-April/001197.html
11. Intel corporation: Intel ® 64 and IA-32 architectures software developer's manual, September 2015. http://www.intel.com/content/dam/www/public/us/en/documents/manuals/64-ia-32-architectures-software-developer-manual-325462.pdf

12. Intel corporation: intel ® architecture instruction set extensions programming reference, August 2015. https://software.intel.com/sites/default/files/managed/07/b7/319433-023.pdf
13. Peikert, C.: Lattice cryptography for the internet. In: Mosca, M. (ed.) PQCrypto 2014. LNCS, vol. 8772, pp. 197–219. Springer, Heidelberg (2014)
14. National institute of standards, technology: FIPS PUB 202-SHA-3 standard: permutation-based hash and extendable-output functions (2015). http://nvlpubs.nist.gov/nistpubs/FIPS/NIST.FIPS.202.pdf

Efficient Sparse Merkle Trees
Caching Strategies and Secure (Non-)Membership Proofs

Rasmus Dahlberg[1]([⊠]), Tobias Pulls[1], and Roel Peeters[2]

[1] Department of Mathematics and Computer Science,
Karlstad University, Karlstad, Sweden
`rasmus.gd.dahlberg@gmail.com, tobias.pulls@kau.se`
[2] KU Leuven, ESAT/COSIC and iMinds, Leuven, Belgium
`roel.peeters@esat.kuleuven.be`

Abstract. A sparse Merkle tree is an authenticated data structure based on a perfect Merkle tree of intractable size. It contains a distinct leaf for every possible output from a cryptographic hash function, and can be simulated efficiently because the tree is sparse (i.e., most leaves are empty). We are the first to provide complete, succinct, and recursive definitions of a sparse Merkle tree and related operations. We show that our definitions enable efficient space-time trade-offs for different caching strategies, and that verifiable audit paths can be generated to prove (non-)membership in practically constant time (<4 ms) when using SHA-512/256. This is despite a limited amount of space for the cache—smaller than the size of the underlying data structure being authenticated—and full (concrete) security in the multi-instance setting.

1 Introduction

Secure HTTPS connections rely on the users' browsers to obtain authentic domain-to-key bindings during set-up. With this in mind, trusted third parties called certificate authorities are used to vouch for the integrity of public keys by issuing X.509 certificates. Though the initial problem of establishing trust might appear to be solved, several new complications arise. Considering that there are hundreds of certificate authorities, all of which are capable of issuing certificates for any domain, it is challenging to concisely observe what has been issued for whom [11]. As such, a misissued or maliciously issued certificate could remain unnoticed forever, or more likely until an attack against a domain has taken place. Naturally this raises an important question: *who watches the watchmen?*

Google's Certificate Transparency (CT) project proposes public logs based on append-only Merkle trees [18]. The basic idea is that an SSL/TLS certificate must be included in some log to be trusted by a browser, and because the infrastructure is public anyone can audit or monitor these logs to ensure correct behavior [6, 16]. Thus, CT allows clients to determine whether a certificate was valid at some point in time, but inclusion in the log cannot guarantee that it is current. For instance, what if a certificate has to be revoked due to a compromised private key

B.B. Brumley and J. Röning (Eds.): NordSec 2016, LNCS 10014, pp. 199–215, 2016.
DOI: 10.1007/978-3-319-47560-8_13

or an entire certificate authority [15,29]? Since the log is both chronological and append-only, effected certificates can neither be removed nor can the absence of a revocation certificate be proven efficiently [12].

Certificate Revocation (RT) is a proposed extension to CT by Laurie and Kasper [17]. The aim is to provide a separate mechanism that proves certificates unrevoked, and requires an authenticated data structure supporting efficient non-membership proofs [34]. As is, there are at least two approaches towards such proofs. One is based on sorted Merkle trees, and the other on tuple-based signed statements on the form "Key k_i has the value v_i; there are no keys in the interval (k_i, k_{i+1})" [9,17]. We consider the former approach in terms of a sparse Merkle tree (SMT), whose scope goes far beyond RT. For example, an SMT can be used as a key building block in a wide area of applications, ranging from persistent authenticated dictionaries to secure messaging applications [10,20,30,32].

After introducing some necessary preliminaries (Sect. 2) and the approach taken here (Sect. 3), our contributions are as follows. First, building on an interesting proposal started by Laurie and Kasper [17], we define efficient caching strategies and complete recursive definitions of an SMT (Sect. 4). Second, we evaluate the security of our definitions in the multi-instance setting, comparing our design decisions with those made in CONIKS [20] (Sect. 5). Third, we examine three caching strategies experimentally for an SMT, showing different space-time trade-offs (Sect. 6). Finally, we discuss related work (Sect. 7) and end with conclusions (Sect. 8).

2 Preliminaries

We start by describing background regarding Merkle trees and audit paths, then cryptographic assumptions that our security evaluation relies on are presented.

2.1 Merkle Trees

A Merkle tree [21] is a binary tree that incorporates the use of cryptographic hash functions. One or many attributes are inserted into the leaves, and every node derives a digest which is recursively dependent on all attributes in its subtree. That is, leaves compute the hash of their own attributes, and parents derive the hash of their children's digests concatenated left-to-right. As further described in Sect. 5, certain digests must also be encoded with additional constants. This is to prevent indistinguishability between different types of nodes [8,20].

Figure1 illustrates a Merkle tree without a proper encoding. It contains eight attributes ρ–ω, and the *root digest* $r \leftarrow d_0^3$ serves as a reference to prove membership by presenting an *audit path* [18]. For instance, dashed nodes are necessary to authenticate the third left-most leaf containing attribute τ. More generally, an audit path comprises all siblings along the path down to the leaf being authenticated. Combined with a retrieved attribute, this forms a proof of membership which is valid if it reconstructs the root digest r' such that $r' = r$. Note that a proof is only as convincing as r, but trust can be established using, e.g., digital signatures or by periodically publishing roots in a newspaper.

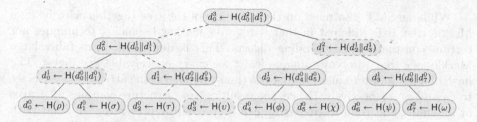

Fig. 1. A Merkle tree containing attributes ρ–ω. The digest rooted at height h and index i is denoted by d_i^h.

2.2 Setting and Cryptographic Assumptions

Inspired by Katz [13] and Melara *et al.* [20], we consider a computationally bounded adversary in the multi-instance setting. This means that there are many distinct SMTs, and the adversary should not gain any advantage in terms of necessary computation if she attempts to attack all SMTs at once. In other words, despite the adversary's multi-instance advantage, the goal is to provide full λ-bit security for each SMT. For security we rely on a collision and pre-image resistant hash function H with digests of size $N := 2\lambda$ bits, and on Lemma 1.

Lemma 1. *The security of an audit path reduces to the collision resistance of the underlying hash function* H.

Proof. This follows directly from the work of Merkle [21] and Blum *et al.* [5].

3 Sparse Merkle Trees

First we introduce non-membership proofs that are based on sorted Merkle trees, then the notion of an SMT and our approach is incrementally described.

3.1 Non-Membership Proofs and High-Level Properties

In RT and like applications, it is crucial to prove certain values absent [17,31,32]. Efficient construction of such non-membership proofs can be enabled by viewing balanced binary search trees, e.g., treaps and red-black trees, as Merkle trees. A lexicographically sorted tree structure serves the purpose of preventing all nodes from being enumerated, involving rules that rotate nodes upon insertion and removal, and the structure of that tree can be fixed by a trustworthy root due to being a Merkle tree. We prove non-membership by generating an audit path through binary search, and a verifying party accepts the proof to be valid if there is no evidence that the tree structure is unsorted or that the root is improperly reconstructed. In other words, the absence of a value is efficiently proven due to a balanced search tree, and the proofs are convincing because the structure of the tree is fixed by a cryptographically derived root.

While an SMT also relies on the structure of the tree together with being a Merkle tree, it is different in that it requires neither balancing techniques nor certain constants when encoding digests. This is due to an intractably large Merkle tree that reserves a unique leaf ℓ for every conceivable key digest. The hash of a key k determines ℓ, and k is a (non-)member if the attribute $a \in \ell$ is set to a_0 and a_1, respectively. Hence, the resulting tree structure contains 2^N leaves at all times, and (non-)membership can be proven by presenting an audit path for leaf $\mathsf{H}(k)$. This set-up also implies *history independence* [25]: a unique set of keys produce a deterministic root digest, regardless of the order in which keys have been inserted or removed. Notably history independence is not necessarily provided by a sorted Merkle tree (e.g., not the case for a red-black tree).

3.2 Tractable Representations

Considering the intractable size of an SMT, it is not without challenges to define an efficient representation. To begin with, the only reason why this is feasible traces back to the key observation that an SMT is *sparse*. This means that the vast majority of all leaves represent non-members, as indicated by a shared attribute a_0, resulting in a construction where the empty subtrees rooted at height h derive identical *default digests*. The basic principle is as follows. An empty leaf computes $d_*^0 \leftarrow \mathsf{H}(a_0)$, a node rooted at an empty subtree with height one derives $d_*^1 \leftarrow \mathsf{H}(d_*^0 \| d_*^0)$, and so forth. Since these default digests can be precomputed, they need neither be associated with explicit nodes nor be derived recursively by visiting all leaves. Instead, referring to Fig. 2, it suffices to process the filled nodes whose digests depend on existing keys.

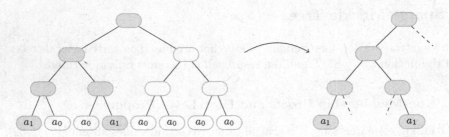

Fig. 2. An illustration of how subtrees with default digest can be discarded to attain a tractable representation of an SMT.

3.3 Earlier Proposals

Different approaches can be used to provide efficient representations of an SMT. Bauer [3] has proposed an explicit pruned tree structure where all the non-empty attributes are elevated upwards through their ancestors. The elevation stops when the root of a subtree containing a single non-empty leaf is reached, and all descendants to such roots are discarded. The original SMT can be reconstructed by recording indices for the non-empty leaves in each subtree, but will require excessive amounts of memory unless they are evenly spread out. Hence, while the proposal is neat, we find the approach started by Laurie and Kasper [17] more generally applicable. It is based on maintaining a collection of keys $\mathcal{K}$, and the collection is authenticated by simulating an SMT. As is, however, their proposal is incomplete and cannot, e.g., derive (non-)membership proofs efficiently. This is due to deriving subtrees' digests over and over again—an issue we solve in the following sections by introducing *relative information*.

3.4   Our Approach

We approach the SMT in terms of a simulation (Definition 1). Let us start by considering the simplest case of no relative information, then why it is necessary.

Definition 1. *A simulated SMT is the composition of (i) a data structure $\mathcal{D}$ containing unique keys k, and (ii) a collection of cached digests, referred to as the relative information δ. Both structures define operations for insertion, removal, and look-up; $\mathcal{D}$ also supports splitting, i.e., dividing it in two based on a key.*

Our SMT is simulated in the sense that there is no explicit tree structure, which is possible because every $k \in \mathcal{D}$ can be mapped to its associated subtrees recursively. For example, as shown in Fig. 3, a root digest can be obtained by simulating a traversal from the root down to all the non-empty leaves. The *base* is initially set to all zeros and refers to the left-most leaf in a subtree. It remains the same on left-traversals, must be updated by setting the appropriate bit to one on right traversals, and is used to determine the *split index*. The split index is the key upon which $\mathcal{D}$ is divided on and refers to the left-most leaf in the right subtree. Thus, as formalized in Sect. 4.3, it is an upper exclusive and lower inclusive bound for the keys in the left and right subtrees, respectively.

Clearly, it is inefficient to obtain a subtree's digest by repeatedly visiting all the non-empty leaves. Therefore relative information is necessary: a collection of cached digests with the sole purpose of preventing such inefficiency. For instance,

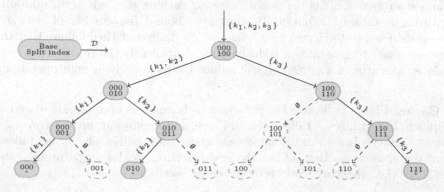

Fig. 3. An illustration of a recursive traversal to obtain the root digest; $k_1 = 000$, $k_2 = 010$, and $k_3 = 111$.

a naïve caching strategy could record every digest that is non-default. Although that requires excessive amounts of memory, it would ensure that all siblings' digests are available upon generating audit paths. Consequently, the number of splits will be constant, and (non-)membership can be proven with the same time complexity as the underlying split operation. Our aim when defining caching strategies is to preserve this property while reducing memory requirements.

4   Efficient Representations

First we define caching strategies that are based on capturing *branches*, then our proposal is formalized by presenting complete recurrences for an efficient SMT.

Definition 2. *A branch is an interior node in a Merkle tree, for which both of the two children derive non-default digests* [27].

4.1   Caching Strategies

During the design of a caching strategy it is important to consider expected and worst case scenarios. The former is somewhat straight forward since the output of H is uniformly distributed, whereas the latter is both strategy and use-case dependent. That is, the non-empty leaves will be evenly spread out in the average case, and a cluster of non-default digests will therefore be formed at the higher $\lceil \log n \rceil + 1$ layers. If these digests are captured by the relative information, the traversals down to the leaves can be prevented. The digests rooted at layers below the dense threshold are of lesser importance due to the sparse property, but can be vital if a worst-case ever occurs. For example, an intuitive caching strategy that we omit is to record the higher $\lceil \log n \rceil + 1$ layers of the SMT. Although the dense part would be captured in the average case, forcing leaves to *clump* at some subtree is trivial for an adversary that selects the keys. Hence, a large majority of the non-default digests cannot be captured, and the resulting cache will be useless if (non-)membership proofs are issued for the clumped subtree. This is the reason why our caching strategies evolve around capturing branches (Definition 2), aiming to bound the number of recursive traversals down to the leaves by a constant. As desired, it then follows that the time necessary to generate an audit path, or equivalently the time necessary to update the status of a single key, will reduce to the underlying split operation.

B Cache. Figure 4a depicts the B cache which captures every digest rooted at a branch. It contains $n - 1$ digests at all times, and requires at most N traversals down to either a branch or leaf upon generating audit paths. The former follows from the observation that all but the first insertion yield a single branch, and the latter (i.e., the worst case) is discussed in Sect. 5.3.

B⁻ Cache. By discarding $f(n)$ branches from the B cache, memory requirements can be reduced at the cost of additional computation. This forms the notion

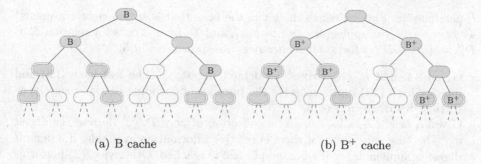

(a) B cache   (b) B^+ cache

Fig. 4. Captured digests as the circled subtrees contain a single non-empty leaf.

of B^-, which provides trade-offs depending on how $f(n)$ is implemented. We examine a probabilistic approach where a branch is captured with probability p, meaning $f(n)$ is roughly $n(1 - p)$. Other variations of $f(n)$ include ignoring every other layer, as well as defining an upper bound for how many branches to ignore.

B^+Cache. The drawback of using a B cache is that, in the average case, only the higher $\lceil \log n \rceil$ layers will be captured. In other words, since the dense part also spans layer $\lceil \log n \rceil + 1$, we are missing out on some performance. B^+ aims to solve this issue by capturing branches together with their children. The resulting cache covers the entire dense part of the SMT, but for the sake of efficiency we also limit the worst case memory requirements by $2n$ due to discarding branches (Fig. 4b). The difference is negligible with regard to time, considering that a branch can derive its digest in constant time from the cached children.

4.2 The Cache Routine

Implementation-wise our caching strategies are convenient. To process an interior digest, a cache function that accepts the left and right child digests can be used. Upon invocation it computes the interior digest d, examines if both children are non-default, deletes the previous branch if applicable, caches in case of a new branch, and outputs d. While this algorithm merely concerns the B cache, it extends perfectly to B^- and B^+. Therefore these caching strategies are practical to mix: start off with B^+, switch to B as memory requirements grow larger, and finally migrate to B^- with shrinking probability p. For instance, this could be interesting in real-world scenarios where memory is a limited resource.

4.3 Recurrences

Let h be the height of a subtree, b the base of a node, and $\mathcal{D}$ a data structure containing unique keys' digests $H(k)$. Further denote by α_i the $i^{th} \geq 0$ left-most bit in α, $\alpha_{i=\beta}$ the assignment of that bit to $\beta \in \{0, 1\}$, and by colon (:) list concatenation. Finally, define the bit in the base that is set on right traversals[1] as $j := N - h$, the split index as $s := b_{j=1}$, and $\mathcal{D}$ divided on s for relation R as $\mathcal{D}_s^R := \{k | k \in \mathcal{D} \wedge kRs\}$. Our recurrences are shown in Fig. 5:

- Given a height h, (1) derives the default digest d_*^h. The leaf hash (LH) and interior hash (IH) functions serve the purpose of encoding digests securely, as further described in Sect. 5.
- Given a height h, a base b, and a collection of keys $\mathcal{D}$, (2) derives the digest d_b^h. The base case occurs if there is relative information available, if a default digest is applicable, or if a non-empty leaf is reached. Otherwise, (2) performs two recursive calls with $\mathcal{D}$ divided on s, b updated in the event of a right traversal, and h reduced by one.
- Given a height h, a base b, a collection of keys $\mathcal{D}$, and a key k for leaf ℓ , (3) generates an audit path for ℓ. Note that the siblings' digests are gathered by list concatenation, repeatedly invoking (2) after reaching ℓ.
- Given a height h, a base b, an audit path P for key k, and an attribute $a \in \{a_0, a_1\}$, (4) reconstructs the root digest by traversing the tree down to the leaf being authenticated. Every sibling's digest is obtained from $P[j]$.
- Given a height h, a base b, a collection of keys $\mathcal{D}$, a subset of keys $\mathcal{K} \subset \mathcal{D}$ where $\mathcal{K} \neq \emptyset$, and an attribute $a \in \{a_0, a_1\}$, (5) outputs the new root digest and updates the relative information. This is achieved by visiting all leaves $\ell \in \mathcal{K}$, also invoking the cache function (C) to compute the interior digest d_b^h and ensure that the relative information is up-to-date.

The size of an audit path is $\mathcal{O}(1)$, but can be further reduced by discarding default digests. This yields a *sparse audit path*, and necessitates encoding of an N-bitmap to determine whether a digest is (non-)default. We omit the details of such a recurrence since it is trivially added when (3)–(4) is provided.

5   Security

Consider a single SMT and assume that the hash function is fixed. Then it follows that the size of an audit path is fixed by N due to the structure of the tree, and consequently we can distinguish between leaves and interior nodes. This means that, for the case of a single SMT with a fixed hash function, no special encoding is necessary to distinguish between nodes, and that the security of an audit path reduces to the collision resistance of the underlying hash function (Lemma 1).

Next, to prevent an adversary from gaining any advantage when attacking several SMTs in parallel, we consider the full (concrete) security of an audit path in the multi-instance setting. Thereafter we relate our encoding of nodes to CONIKS [20], and examine the impact of caching strategies for security.

---

[1] This bit refers to the depth of a subtree.

$$\xi_*^h := \begin{cases} \text{LH}_*^*(a_0) & \text{, if } h = 0 \\ \text{IH}_*^h(\xi_*^{h-1}, \xi_*^{h-1}) & \text{, else .} \end{cases} \tag{1}$$

$$\text{R}_b^h(\mathcal{D}) := \begin{cases} \delta_b^h & \text{, if available} \\ \xi_*^h & \text{, elif } |\mathcal{D}| = 0 \\ \text{LH}_b^*(a_1) & \text{, elif } |\mathcal{D}| = 1 \wedge h = 0 \\ \text{IH}_b^h\big(\text{R}_b^{h-1}(\mathcal{D}_{\bar{s}}^<), \text{R}_s^{h-1}(\mathcal{D}_{\bar{s}}^\geq)\big) & \text{, else .} \end{cases} \tag{2}$$

$$\text{A}_b^h(\mathcal{D}, k) := \begin{cases} \emptyset & \text{, if } h = 0 \\ \text{R}_s^{h-1}(\mathcal{D}_{\bar{s}}^\geq) : \text{A}_b^{h-1}(\mathcal{D}_s^<, k) & \text{, elif } k_j = 0 \\ \text{R}_b^{h-1}(\mathcal{D}_s^<) : \text{A}_s^{h-1}(\mathcal{D}_{\bar{s}}^\geq, k) & \text{, else .} \end{cases} \tag{3}$$

$$\text{B}_b^h(P, k, a) := \begin{cases} \text{LH}_b^*(a) & \text{, if } h = 0 \\ \text{IH}_b^h\big(\text{B}_b^{h-1}(P, k, a), P[j]\big) & \text{, elif } k_j = 0 \\ \text{IH}_s^h\big(P[j], \text{B}_s^{h-1}(P, k, a)\big) & \text{, else .} \end{cases} \tag{4}$$

$$\text{U}_b^h(\mathcal{D}, \mathcal{K}, a) := \begin{cases} \text{LH}_b^*(a) & \text{, if } h = 0 \\ \text{C}_b^h\big(\text{R}_b^{h-1}(\mathcal{D}_s^<), \text{U}_s^{h-1}(\mathcal{D}_{\bar{s}}^\geq, \mathcal{K}, a)\big) & \text{, elif } |\mathcal{K}_s^<| = 0 \wedge |\mathcal{K}_{\bar{s}}^\geq| \neq 0 \\ \text{C}_b^h\big(\text{U}_b^{h-1}(\mathcal{D}_s^<, \mathcal{K}, a), \text{R}_s^{h-1}(\mathcal{D}_{\bar{s}}^\geq)\big) & \text{, elif } |\mathcal{K}_s^<| \neq 0 \wedge |\mathcal{K}_{\bar{s}}^\geq| = 0 \\ \text{C}_b^h\big(\text{U}_b^{h-1}(\mathcal{D}_s^<, \mathcal{K}_s^<, a), \text{U}_s^{h-1}(\mathcal{D}_{\bar{s}}^\geq, \mathcal{K}_{\bar{s}}^\geq, a)\big) & \text{, else .} \end{cases} \tag{5}$$

Fig. 5. Recurrences that derive default digests (ξ), root digests (R), audit paths (A), reconstructed root digests (B), and relative information (U).

5.1   The Merkle Prefix Tree in CONIKS

As described more broadly in Sect. 7, CONIKS is a key verification service that uses a Merkle prefix tree (MPT) to authenticate the users' key bindings [20]. An MPT can be seen as a dynamically sized and explicit SMT where empty subtrees are replaced with empty nodes. Key-bindings are mapped by a hash function H to unique indices i, and every (non-)empty leaf in the tree is associated with a depth ℓ as well as an ℓ-bit unique prefix j of i. The encoding of an empty node is defined in (6).

$$d \leftarrow \text{H}(C_{\text{empty}} \| C_{\text{tw}} \| j \| \ell) \tag{6}$$

C_{empty} is a constant for empty leaves and C_{tw} a tree-wide constant. The encoding of a non-empty node is defined in (7).

$$d \leftarrow \text{H}(C_{\text{leaf}} \| C_{\text{tw}} \| i \| \ell \| p) \tag{7}$$

C_{leaf} is a constant for non-empty leaves and p a payload. Finally, the encoding of an interior node is defined in (8).

$$d \leftarrow \text{H}(d_{\text{left}} \| d_{\text{right}}) \tag{8}$$

The constants C_{empty} and C_{leaf} serve the purpose of preventing indistinguishability between (non-)empty leaves, and the tree-wide constant C_{tw} provides protection against an adversary in the multi-instance setting. In other words, if all MPTs use distinct tree-wide constants, no nodes' pre-images can be valid across different trees. Similarly, no nodes' pre-images can be valid across multiple locations because the leaves' digests are uniquely encoded by $j\|\ell$ and $i\|\ell$ (the location of an interior node is implicit due to the children it commits to). Thus, as opposed to searching collisions across different trees and locations in parallel, an adversary must target a particular tree and location.

We also need to consider different versions of the trees that are generated by updates. To accomplish full λ-bit security for an instance of an MPT, a new tree-wide constant must be selected after each update to prevent parallel attacks through past versions of the same tree structure. This means that for all updates, the entire MPT has to be recomputed from scratch.

5.2   A Secure Encoding for Sparse Merkle Trees

Figure 6 defines a secure encoding for an SMT in the multi-instance setting. We prevent attacks across distinct trees by introducing a tree-wide constant C_{tw}, but we do not protect against attacks on different versions of the same tree structure because C_{tw} is reused between updates. For attacks within a particular tree, we include unique identifiers in every *non-empty subtree*. This differs with respect to MPTs, but is necessary to preserve the sparse property of an SMT: if unique prefixes were included in the empty subtrees, then there would no longer be any default digests. As shown in (10), we solve this issue and retain security by moving the encoding of an empty node into the non-empty parent. An interior node that is non-default will still commit properly to a certain location encoded by base and height[2], and since the digest of an empty node is publicly known even for an MPT no security is lost. Furthermore, note that we do not encode the attributes a_0 and a_1 explicitly in (9). Inclusion of the base suffices to distinguish between (non-)empty leaves, considering that the height of an SMT is implicit.

$$\text{LH}_b^*(a) := \begin{cases} \mathsf{H}(C_{\text{tw}}) & \text{, if } a = a_0 \\ \mathsf{H}(C_{\text{tw}}\|b) & \text{, else .} \end{cases} \qquad (9)$$

$$\text{IH}_b^h\big(d_{\text{left}}, d_{\text{right}}\big) := \begin{cases} \mathsf{H}(d_{\text{left}}\|d_{\text{right}}) & \text{, if } d_{\text{left}} = d_{\text{right}} = \xi_*^{h-1} \\ \mathsf{H}(d_{\text{left}}\|d_{\text{right}}\|b\|h) & \text{, else .} \end{cases} \qquad (10)$$

Fig. 6. Secure node encodings for an SMT.

---

[2] The height is necessary because the base is ambiguous on left traversal, i.e., it has fixed size and is only updated by setting the appropriate bit on right traversals.

5.3   Security Aspects of Caching Strategies

Generally speaking, we often distinguish between best, worst, and average case complexities. For instance, a hash table has amortized constant look-up time, but can degrade to a linear construction if all entries hash to the same bucket. Likewise, a binary search tree that is probabilistically balanced is in danger of breaking down into a linked list. Though critics might claim that attacks based on such degradations are of theoretical interest alone, Crosby and Wallach [7] have already presented denial of service attacks that exploit algorithmic complexities. Thus, within security, it is of great importance to evaluate worst case behavior.

Let us consider the B cache. In the worst case, if there are merely N keys, an adversary could force an almost perfect spine of branches as depicted in Fig. 7. Whenever membership proofs are issued for the leaves on that spine, the large majority of all the non-default digests must be computed because the siblings' digests are not captured by the cache. While this is not an issue for a small SMT, the worst case efficiency actually increases as the tree grows: new insertions yield additional branches, and it is more efficient to stop traversals at a branch than at a leaf. In other words, there are two scenarios each time a sibling's digest is requested. First, the digest is default and can be requested in constant time. Second, the digest is non-default and can be derived by traversing the tree down to a branch or leaf. In either case, regardless of how an adversary selects the keys, *at most N* traversals are necessary (one per layer). A similar analysis applies to B^+, considering that the children of all branches are captured by the relative information. For B^-, one can show that the number of traversals will be bounded by $f(n)$. As such, to prevent an adversary from causing inefficiency, $f(n)$ must be either constant or unpredictable to the adversary.

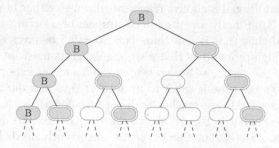

Fig. 7. A branch spine, potentially caused by an adversary.

An almost identical analysis applies for worst case behavior during updates. This follows from the observation that (3) and (5) traverse the tree down to the leaves, invoking (2) on each layer.

6 Performance

We examined performance and space-time trade-offs experimentally using a proof-of-concept implementation in Go[3], selecting SHA-512/256 as the hash function[4], a data structure $\mathcal{D}$ that supports splitting in logarithmic time, and relative information δ that is maintained in constant time (a hash table). Our experiments were executed on an Intel(R) Core(TM) i7-4790 CPU at 3.60 GHz with 2×8 GB DDR4 RAM, and they utilized Go's built-in benchmarking tool. Furthermore, the B^- cache was implemented probabilistically such that a branch is captured with probability p. We tested B^- for $p \in \{0.5 \ldots 0.9\}$, denoted by B_p^-, and included B, B^+, and a hash treap in our experiments. For the relevant operations, i.e., insertion, removal, and look-up, the expected logarithmic time complexity of a hash treap makes it a good representation of other authenticated data structures that are explicitly stored in memory.

Figure 8a shows the size of the authenticated data structure as a function of the data structure being authenticated. There is essentially no distinction between the two for a hash treap[5], and in the case of an SMT this is the relation between δ and $\mathcal{D}$. For 2^{20} keys, the hash treap needs 960 MiB, the B^+ cache 512 MiB, the B cache 256 MiB, and the $B_{0.5}^-$ cache 128 MiB. It is evident that the different caches double in size, and that the size of a hash treap is roughly eight times larger than that of a $B_{0.5}^-$ cache. Furthermore, it should be noted that the B_p^- caches with $p \in \{0.6 \ldots 0.9\}$ have sizes evenly distributed in $[B_{0.5}^-, B]$.

Figure 8b shows the time required to generate an audit path. Since the full structure is in memory for the hash treap, it is just a matter of copying the nodes along the path in negligible time (0.003 ms). Similarly, for B^+ and B, we see consistent results that are less than 1 ms regardless of how large $\mathcal{D}$ is. This is because both caching strategies ensure that the vital non-default digests are cached, whereas additional recursive traversals down to either branches or leaves are necessary for B_p^-. Finally, we observe the impact of selecting p. While $p > 0.6$ gives an expected time that is less than 4 ms, $p = 0.5$ behaves erratically. This follows from the high probability that a sibling's digests must be derived instead of being found in the cache, as is also evident to a smaller extent for $p = 0.6$.

Figure 8c shows the time it takes to update m keys in a data structure containing $n = 2^{15}$ keys. All approaches scale as $\mathcal{O}(m \log n)$, with the hash treap being the fastest. Similarly, Fig. 8d shows the time it takes to update $m = 256$ keys as a function of the size n. The B^+ cache consistently needs less than 20 ms, as opposed to the hash treap which needs 9.5 ms for $n = 2^{20}$. Considering that a hash treap consumes twice as much memory, this is indeed an interesting trade-off. For the remaining caching strategies, p together with the relation between n and m determines the probability of having cache misses. Simplified, larger p yields less variance and greater efficiency in terms of time.

---

[3] Source code available at https://github.com/pylls/gosmt (Apache 2.0).

[4] SHA-512 truncated to 256-bit output, resulting in an SMT with 2^{256} leaves [26].

[5] The size refers to the nodes of the tree together with the children's pointers.

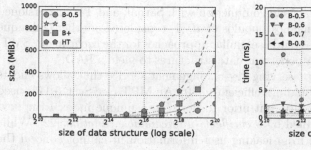

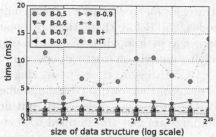

(a) Size of the authenticated data structure.   (b) Time to generate an audit path.

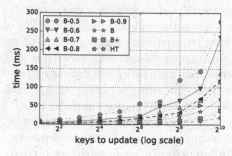

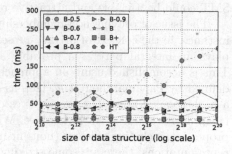

(c) Time to update in a 2^{15} data structure.   (d) Time to update 256 keys.

Fig. 8. Space-time trade-offs for caching strategies and a hash treap (HT).

7   Related Work

Google considers three categories of authenticated data structures when adding transparency to a trust model: verifiable logs, maps, and log-backed maps [12]. While CT relies on verifiable logs to support efficient consistency and membership proofs, verifiable maps based on SMTs are proposed in RT to prove non-membership. This is not without issues, however. All operations must be enumerated to determine whether a map's state is correct. The former two categories are therefore combined into a verifiable log-backed map where consistency issues can be detected by the verifiable log, (non-)membership can be proven by the verifiable map, and full audits can ensure complete correct behavior. As such, using an efficient verifiable map based on our extension of an SMT, the combination of CT and RT can prove whether a certificate's status is current. Other CT-like proposals that an SMT could be applicable to include Distributed Transparent Key Infrastructure [35] and Enhanced Certificate Transparency [32].

Verifiable maps are closely related to persistent authenticated dictionaries (PADs) [10]. While both are dynamic, the difference is that a PAD supports (non-)membership queries to current *and* past versions of the data structure. By extending our representation of an SMT to a secure key-value store, adding some form of persistency yields a PAD. Crosby and Wallach [9] investigated caching strategies for tree-based PADs in conjunction with Sarnak and Tarjan versioned nodes [33]. Before that, Anagnostopoulos *et al.* [1] considered another technique known as path copying. We could use similar approaches for the *cache* in our SMT, relying entirely on existing persistent data structures to yield a PAD.

CONIKS is a privacy-preserving key-management service that allows clients to monitor their own key-bindings efficiently [20]. An MPT (see Sect. 5.1) is used for the purpose of verifiability, but prior to deriving a unique index i the key-bindings are first transformed by a *verifiable unpredictable function* [22]. While that prevents audit paths from leaking user information, it cannot conceal the total number of users. CONIKS solves this issue and others e.g., ensuring *fork consistency* [19], by defining a protocol on top of an MPT. It appears that an SMT could be a viable and attractive replacement if viewed as a dictionary.

The issue of proving non-membership is not only evident in CT and RT. For instance, in the context of privacy-preserving transparency logging [31], Balloon plays an integral part as a provably secure append-only data structure [30]. This is accomplished using an approach towards authenticated data structures defined by Papamanthou *et al.* [28], as well as combining a history tree [8] and a hash treap [10,30]. The former is essentially a verifiable log, and the latter a treap [2,4] viewed as a Merkle tree. While hash treaps and SMTs share many properties, including efficient (non-)membership proofs and history independent representations, there are some striking differences. To begin with, hash treaps store attributes in each node. Unlike in an SMT, information regarding these attributes must be provided in an audit path due to encoding digests differently (possibly leaking valuable information). There will also be exactly n nodes at all times, and efficiency relies on a probabilistic balance. In these regards an SMT is flexible: the variable parameters $\mathcal{D}$ and δ determine if/when efficiency is provided, and memory requirements can be reduced to less than n if need be.

More generally we could compare an SMT to any lexicographically sorted data structure viewed as a Merkle tree, e.g., including certificate revocation trees [14] and subsequent approaches based on 2–3 trees [24]. An SMT is superior to a certificate revocation tree because the update process cannot cause the entire tree structure to be recomputed. When compared to 2–3 trees and other balanced binary search trees, the analysis is similar to that of a hash treap. Note, however, that an SMT should not be confused with authenticated data structures that are unable to prove non-membership efficiently. This means that an SMT is not intended for applications such as Bitcoin [23]: the transactions of separate blocks are grouped together in Merkle trees for the purpose of efficient integrity guarantees, not the ability to prove certain transactions absent.

Finally, this work is an extension of the Bachelor's thesis by Dahlberg [27]. Apart from improving terminology, we defined recursions for batch updates and reconstruction of root digests, as well as caching strategies based on branches. We also added a security evaluation for full (concrete) security in the multi-instance setting, provided a publicly available implementation that uses a memory safe language, and compared our results with a related authenticated data structure.

8   Conclusion

Our definition of an SMT builds upon and extends the principles provided by Laurie and Kasper [17]. The proposal is generic in the sense that an arbitrary data structure supporting insertion, removal, look-up, and splitting can be used, and different caching strategies (B, B$^-$, and B$^+$) provide fine-grained control over consumed space contra run time. In other words, rather than having an explicit tree structure, the resulting SMT is simulated. While this comes at the cost of additional computation when compared to other explicit tree-based data structures, our performance benchmark and worst case analysis show that our definitions are efficient regardless of how an adversary selects the keys. In addition, we prove that these definitions are secure in the multi-instance setting.

There is nothing that prevents further space-time trade-offs as an SMT evolves. In principle, the relation B$^-$ $\subset$ B $\subset$ B$^+$ holds. Therefore, it is simple to go from one strategy to another, e.g., depending on how much memory is available at the time being. This is a major difference with respect to explicit tree structures, which have no previous constructions that are alike. Furthermore, the succinct recursions used to simulate an SMT yield limited implementation complexity, and history independence is a prevalent property if parallelized and distributed solutions are considered for large-scale applications.

Acknowledgements. We would like to thank Stefan Lindskog for his valuable feedback. Rasmus Dahlberg and Tobias Pulls have received funding from the HITS research profile funded by the Swedish Knowledge Foundation.

References

1. Anagnostopoulos, A., Goodrich, M.T., Tamassia, R.: Persistent authenticated dictionaries and their applications. In: Davida, G.I., Frankel, Y. (eds.) ISC 2001. LNCS, vol. 2200, pp. 379–393. Springer, Heidelberg (2001). doi:10.1007/3-540-45439-X_26
2. Aragon, C.R., Seidel, R.: Randomized search trees. In: FOCS, pp. 540–545 (1989)
3. Bauer, M.: Proofs of zero knowledge. CoRR cs.CR/0406058 (2004)
4. Blelloch, G.E., Reid-Miller, M.: Fast set operations using treaps. In: SPAA, pp. 16–26 (1998)
5. Blum, M., Evans, W.S., Gemmell, P., Kannan, S., Naor, M.: Checking the correctness of memories. Algorithmica **12**(2/3), 225–244 (1994)
6. Chuat, L., Szalachowski, P., Perrig, A., Laurie, B., Messeri, E.: Efficient gossip protocols for verifying the consistency of certificate logs. In: CNS, pp. 415–423 (2015)
7. Crosby, S.A., Wallach, D.S.: Denial of service via algorithmic complexity attacks. In: USENIX Security Symposium, pp. 29–44 (2003)
8. Crosby, S.A., Wallach, D.S.: Efficient data structures for tamper-evident logging. In: USENIX Security Symposium, pp. 317–334 (2009)
9. Crosby, S.A., Wallach, D.S.: Super-efficient aggregating history-independent persistent authenticated dictionaries. In: Backes, M., Ning, P. (eds.) ESORICS 2009. LNCS, vol. 5789, pp. 671–688. Springer, Heidelberg (2009). doi:10.1007/978-3-642-04444-1_41

10. Crosby, S.A., Wallach, D.S.: Authenticated dictionaries: real-world costs and trade-offs. ACM TISSEC **14**(2), 17:1–17:30 (2011)
11. Eckersley, P.: How secure is HTTPS today? How often is it attacked? EFF (2011). https://www.eff.org/deeplinks/2011/10/how-secure-https-today
12. Eijdenberg, A., Laurie, B., Cutter, A.: Verifiable data structures. Google Research (2015). https://github.com/google/trillian/blob/master/docs/VerifiableDataStructures.pdf
13. Katz, J.: Analysis of a proposed hash-based signature standard (2014). http://cvs.cs.umd.edu/~jkatz/papers/HashBasedSigs.pdf
14. Kocher, P.C.: On certificate revocation and validation. In: Hirchfeld, R. (ed.) FC 1998. LNCS, vol. 1465, pp. 172–177. Springer, Heidelberg (1998). doi:10.1007/BFb0055481
15. Langely, A.: Enhancing digital certificate security. Google Research (2013). https://security.googleblog.com/2013/01/enhancing-digital-certificate-security.html
16. Laurie, B.: Certificate transparency. ACM Queue **12**(8), 10–19 (2014)
17. Laurie, B., Kasper, E.: Revocation transparency. Google Research (2012). http://www.links.org/files/RevocationTransparency.pdf
18. Laurie, B., Langley, A., Kasper, E.: Certificate transparency. RFC 6962 (2013)
19. Li, J., Krohn, M.N., Mazières, D., Shasha, D.: Secure untrusted data repository (SUNDR). In: OSDI, pp. 121–136 (2004)
20. Melara, M.S., Blankstein, A., Bonneau, J., Felten, E.W., Freedman, M.J.: CONIKS: bringing key transparency to end users. In: USENIX Security Symposium, pp. 383–398 (2015)
21. Merkle, R.C.: A digital signature based on a conventional encryption function. In: Pomerance, C. (ed.) CRYPTO 1987. LNCS, vol. 293, pp. 369–378. Springer, Heidelberg (1988). doi:10.1007/3-540-48184-2_32
22. Micali, S., Rabin, M.O., Vadhan, S.P.: Verifiable random functions. In: FOCS, pp. 120–130 (1999)
23. Nakamoto, S.: Bitcoin: a peer-to-peer electronic cash system (2008)
24. Naor, M., Nissim, K.: Certificate revocation and certificate update. J-SAC **18**(4), 561–570 (2000)
25. Naor, M., Teague, V.: Anti-persistence: history independent data structures. In: STOC, pp. 492–501 (2001)
26. NIST: FIPS PUB 180–4: Secure Hash Standard. Federal Information Processing Standards Publication 180–4, U.S. Department of Commerce (2012). http://csrc.nist.gov/publications/fips/fips180-4/fips-180-4.pdf
27. Östersjö R.: Sparse Merkle Trees: Definitions and Space-Time Trade-Offs With Applications for Balloon. Bachelor's Thesis, Karlstad University (2016)
28. Papamanthou, C., Tamassia, R., Triandopoulos, N.: Optimal verification of operations on dynamic sets. In: Rogaway, P. (ed.) CRYPTO 2011. LNCS, vol. 6841, pp. 91–110. Springer, Heidelberg (2011). doi:10.1007/978-3-642-22792-9_6
29. Prins, R.: DigiNotar certificate authority breach—"operation black tulip". Fox-IT (2011)
30. Pulls, T., Peeters, R.: Balloon: a forward-secure append-only persistent authenticated data structure. In: Pernul, G., Ryan, P.Y.A., Weippl, E. (eds.) ESORICS 2015. LNCS, vol. 9327, pp. 622–641. Springer, Heidelberg (2015). doi:10.1007/978-3-319-24177-7_31
31. Pulls, T., Peeters, R.: Insynd: privacy-preserving transparency logging using balloons. In: ESORICS (2016, to appear)

32. Ryan, M.D.: Enhanced certificate transparency and end-to-end encrypted mail. In: NDSS (2014)
33. Sarnak, N., Tarjan, R.E.: Planar point location using persistent search trees. Commun. ACM **29**(7), 669–679 (1986)
34. Tamassia, R.: Authenticated data structures. In: Battista, G., Zwick, U. (eds.) ESA 2003. LNCS, vol. 2832, pp. 2–5. Springer, Heidelberg (2003). doi:10.1007/978-3-540-39658-1_2
35. Yu, J., Cheval, V., Ryan, M.: DTKI: a new formalized PKI with no trusted parties. CoRR abs/1408.1023 (2014)

Secure Multiparty Sorting Protocols with Covert Privacy

Peeter Laud[✉] and Martin Pettai

Cybernetica AS, Tartu, Estonia
{peeter.laud,martin.pettai}@cyber.ee

Abstract. We introduce the notion of *covert privacy* for secret-sharing-based secure multiparty computation (SMC) protocols. We show how covertly or actively private SMC protocols, together with recently introduced verifiable protocols allow the construction of SMC protocols secure against active adversaries. For certain computational problems, the relative overhead of our protocols, when compared to protocols secure against passive adversaries only, approaches zero as the problem size increases.

We analyse the existing adaptations of sorting algorithms to SMC protocols and find that unless they are already using actively secure primitive protocols, none of them are covertly private or verifiable. We propose a covertly private sorting protocol based on radix sort, the relative overhead of which again approaches zero, when compared to the passively secure protocol. Our results reduce the computational effort needed to counteract active adversaries for a significant range of SMC applications, where sorting is used as a subroutine.

1 Introduction

Secure multiparty computation (SMC) [16] allows a set of mutually distrustful parties to jointly perform computations on the data they have, without anyone of them learning anything beyond the result of the computation. While starting out as a mere theoretical curiosity [10,17,30], both the protocols and the computing infrastructure have improved over the last two decades, such that significant real-world problems may be solved with them [2,3,8]. In these applications, the inputs may come from, and outputs may be learned by many different parties, but the protocols for actual computations are executed by just a small set of *computing parties* (typically two or three), upon which the other parties have to place their trust. The trust has a *threshold* nature: the parties believe that at most a certain fraction of computing parties have been corrupted. E.g. the Sharemind SMC platform [6], which is the basis of the work reported here, has three computing parties, one of which may be passively corrupted.

A passive adversary learns the internal states, the inputs and outputs of corrupted parties, but these parties still follow the prescribed protocol. More desirable is security against an active adversary, which may additionally instruct the parties to change the messages they send out. Security against active adversaries requires significantly more computational effort and/or communication to

© Springer International Publishing AG 2016
B.B. Brumley and J. Röning (Eds.): NordSec 2016, LNCS 10014, pp. 216–231, 2016.
DOI: 10.1007/978-3-319-47560-8_14

be used, either during the protocol execution or at some other time (pre- or post-computation) [13].

For certain computations, the verification of the correctness of the result is simpler than actually performing the computation. For privately performing such computations, we could use a passively secure SMC protocol for computing the result *and the proof of its correctness* and an actively secure protocol for the verification. An existing implementation of this idea for linear programming [14] ensures that the result of the computation is correct and the verification phase does not leak anything to an active adversary. In order to not leak anything at all to an active adversary, the computation protocol has to be *actively private* [4]. This property is stronger than passive security, but weaker than active security which also implies correctness of results. Sharemind's protocols for simple operations are actively private [28] and this property composes [4].

In this paper we study protocols for oblivious sorting, i.e. protocols that transform a vector of private values into another vector of private values that is sorted and is equal to the input vector as multisets. It is easier to verify the sortedness of a vector than it is to sort it. The proof of correctness of sorting is a *private permutation* [27] that transforms the input vector to the output vector; the verification of such proof means applying the permutation and checking the equality of two vectors. Sorting is an important primitive in SMC protocols, used extensively in data analysis and as a "substitute" for operations that cannot be naturally converted into SMC protocols [3,23].

Existing passively secure oblivious sorting protocols either do not naturally produce proofs of correctness, or are not actively private, nor do they seem to be amenable to simple changes which would give active privacy without unduly hampering the performance. To obtain more efficient protocols, but still retain protection against adversaries that deviate from the protocol, intermediate adversarial models have been considered. A *covert adversary* is willing to deviate, but only if it is not caught in the process [1]. One can argue that for many, if not most practical applications of SMC, the protection against a covert adversary is as good as the protection against an active adversary, if detected deviations from the protocol can be brought in front of a court and appropriate punishments levied. Techniques of verifiable computation [15] may be used to turn passively secure SMC protocols into covertly secure protocols [25,26]. These techniques introduce a *post-execution* verification phase to the protocols, where the parties check each other on whether they followed the protocol correctly.

In this paper we define *covert privacy*. A protocol is covertly private if an active adversary may affect its correctness, but if it learns something about the inputs of others, the honest parties will likely be notified of a potential information leak. A covertly private sorting protocol (also producing the proof permutation) together with a verification mechanism is sufficient for dealing with active adversaries only during verification. But it turns out that sorting protocols based on shuffling and data-dependent sorting algorithms are not even covertly private. As the main result of this paper, we propose a sorting protocol based on radix sort, which is covertly private and has complexity similar to the passively secure protocol.

2   Related Work

Let us give an overview of SMC protocols for sorting. Sorting networks were the first tool to be adapted to SMC [20,29]. Shuffling protocols for secret sharing based SMC protocol sets were first proposed in [27] and applied for sorting in [31]. There exist well-engineered SMC sorting protocols based on quicksort [19] and on radix sort [18]. The performance of different sorting protocols in a uniform setting has been evaluated in [5].

This paper also proposes an improved method for certain privacy-preserving computations in a manner that provides security against active adversaries. The current best-performing SMC protocol sets with such security are based on secret sharing over finite fields, making use of message authentication codes to detect misbehaviour [12,22]. Such protocols make use of precomputed shared tuples of values that assist in performing non-linear operations (in particular, multiplication of shared values). This precomputation used to be several orders of magnitude more expensive than the actual execution of the protocol, but recent advances have brought down the cost [21]. An alternative, which we are following in this paper, is to verify the computation parties after the execution [25,26] to make sure that they did not deviate from the protocol.

Our verifiable sorting protocol has similarities to the verifiable SMC protocols for linear programming [14]. Similarly to them, we use passively secure protocols to perform the actual computation and to find the proof of correctness, and higher-security protocols to verify the proof, thereby detecting incorrect results. Differently from them, we also require covert privacy from the actual computation, hence detecting any privacy leaks there may be.

3   Preliminaries

3.1   Universal Composability and Secure Multiparty Computation

We use SMC protocols to build large privacy-preserving applications, for which the security claims can reasonably only be made in compositional manner. Hence we present all our constructions in the *universal composability* (UC) framework [9], which allows us to state that a certain protocol is *at least as secure as* (or *simulates*) a certain ideal functionality.

Let $\mathcal{F}$ be an ideal functionality for n parties, i.e. it is a probabilistic interactive Turing machine with interfaces to communicate with n users, and with an adversary. Let π be an n-party protocol, i.e. it consists of n probabilistic interactive Turing machines $M_1, \ldots, M_n$, each communicating with a user (also called the *environment*), with an adversary and possibly also with some ideal functionalities (which are also part of π).

Definition 1. *An n-party protocol π black-box simulates the ideal functionality $\mathcal{F}$, if there exists a machine* Sim, *such that for all users $H = (P_1, \ldots, P_n)$ and adversaries $\mathcal{A}$, $view_{H\|\pi\|\mathcal{A}}(H) \approx view_{H\|\mathcal{F}\|(\mathsf{Sim}\|\mathcal{A})}(H)$.*

Here the view of H encompasses all messages it exchanges with either π or $\mathcal{F}$, and with $\mathcal{A}$. The probability distribution over such sequences of messages is denoted by $view_{\mathbf{C}}(H)$, where $\mathbf{C}$ is the system that contains H. We use "$\approx$" to denote the similarity of views; this similarity may mean either equality, or statistical or computational indistinguishability.

An adversary may corrupt some machine M_i by sending it a corrupt-message; the machine forwards it to the i-th user (the party P_i). Afterwards, M_i will send to the adversary everything it has seen or will see. Also, the adversary determines which subsequent messages M_i sends to other machines and the user. An adversary is *passive* if it instructs M_i to always send the same messages it would have sent without being corrupted.

Denote $[n] = \{1, \ldots, n\}$. Let f be a *one-shot n-party functionality*, i.e. it is used to compute $(y_1, \ldots, y_n) = f(x_1, \ldots, x_n)$, possibly in randomized manner. The *ideal functionality for f* is an interactive randomized Turing machine $\mathcal{F}_{\text{sec}}^f$ that communicates with n parties and the adversary. It performs by first receiving the set of *corrupted parties* $\mathcal{C} \subseteq [n]$ from the adversary and sending corrupt to each party P_i, where $i \in \mathcal{C}$. The machine then receives x_i from each P_i. If $i \in \mathcal{C}$, then $\mathcal{F}_{\text{sec}}^f$ forwards x_i to the adversary. For each $i \in \mathcal{C}$, the adversary sends x_i' to $\mathcal{F}_{\text{sec}}^f$. For each $i \in [n] \backslash \mathcal{C}$, define $x_i' = x_i$. The machine $\mathcal{F}_{\text{sec}}^f$ computes $(y_1', \ldots, y_n') = f(x_1', \ldots, x_n')$ and sends y_i' to the adversary for $i \in \mathcal{C}$. The adversary responds either with (stop, j) for some $j \in \mathcal{C}$, or with the values y_i for all $i \in \mathcal{C}$. In the first case, $\mathcal{F}_{\text{sec}}^f$ sends (stop, j) to all parties and stops. In the latter case, define $y_i = y_i'$ for all $i \in [n] \backslash \mathcal{C}$. The machine $\mathcal{F}_{\text{sec}}^f$ sends y_i to P_i for all $i \in [n]$ and stops. An adversary for the functionality $\mathcal{F}_{\text{sec}}^f$ is *passive* if it always defines $x_i' = x_i$ and $y_i = y_i'$ for $i \in \mathcal{C}$.

There are a couple of different ways to specify the ideal functionality for SMC. One example of such idealization is the *arithmetic black box* [24], which is convenient to use when constructing higher-level SMC protocols from more basic ones (like addition or multiplication), obtaining the security proof (in sense of Definition 1) of the higher-level protocol almost for free. In this paper, our focus is different, we are discussing different security properties of certain kinds of SMC protocols.

We are interested in SMC protocols based on secret sharing. These protocols are built up from basic protocols for certain operations that turn the sharings of the inputs of that operation into sharing of outputs. If x is a value then we let $[\![x]\!] = ([\![x]\!]_1, \ldots, [\![x]\!]_n)$ denote an arbitrary sharing of x, where $[\![x]\!]_i$ is the i-th share held by the i-th party. A one-shot functionality $f_\otimes$ for an operation $\otimes$ receives as inputs the sharings of the arguments of $\otimes$. It reconstructs the arguments, applies $\otimes$ to obtain the result and returns an arbitrary sharing of it.

In our modeling, there is a particular functionality that we want to securely compute, we consider it as a composition $f_1; f_2; \cdots ; f_k$ of one-shot functionalities (each f_i may also have an arbitrary number of arguments that it simply passes through). The ideal functionality $\mathcal{F}_{\text{sec}}^{f_1; \cdots ; f_k}$ is the sequential composition of $\mathcal{F}_{\text{sec}}^{f_1}; \cdots ; \mathcal{F}_{\text{sec}}^{f_k}$. Here only $\mathcal{F}_{\text{sec}}^{f_1}$ receives its inputs from H and only $\mathcal{F}_{\text{sec}}^{f_k}$ sends its outputs back to it. Otherwise, the inputs are received from previous functionality and passed on to the next one. If $\mathcal{F}_{\text{sec}}^{f_i}$ is securely implemented by the protocol π_i, then the sequential composition of these protocols securely implements $\mathcal{F}_{\text{sec}}^{f_1}; \cdots ; \mathcal{F}_{\text{sec}}^{f_k}$, as implied by the universal composability theorem [9] (which is actually more general than that).

3.2   Privacy vs. Security

Privacy is a security property that for many protocols, including SMC protocols based on secret sharing may be easier to achieve than "full security". For a given one-shot functionality f, privacy is defined as simulating a different ideal functionality $\mathcal{F}_{\text{priv}}^{f}$. The machine $\mathcal{F}_{\text{priv}}^{f}$ works identically to $\mathcal{F}_{\text{sec}}^{f}$ until computing resulting values $(y_1, \ldots, y_n) = f(x_1', \ldots, x_n')$. Afterwards the machine $\mathcal{F}_{\text{priv}}^{f}$ stops, i.e. no other machine actually receives the computed values. A protocol π is a private realization of f if it black-box simulates $\mathcal{F}_{\text{priv}}^{f}$ (Definition 1).

The values computed by $\mathcal{F}_{\text{priv}}^{f}$ are still used when sequentially composing such functionalities. In the composition $\mathcal{F}_{\text{priv}}^{f_1}; \cdots ; \mathcal{F}_{\text{priv}}^{f_k}$, each $\mathcal{F}_{\text{priv}}^{f_i}$ passes the result values to $\mathcal{F}_{\text{priv}}^{f_{i+1}}$ to be used as inputs. The outputs from $\mathcal{F}_{\text{priv}}^{f_k}$ still go nowhere. In addition to that, the inputs received by $\mathcal{F}_{\text{priv}}^{f_2}, \ldots, \mathcal{F}_{\text{priv}}^{f_k}$ are not sent to the adversary, nor can the adversary adjust them. Hence privacy means only that the adversary's view during the protocol, but not necessary after it, can be simulated from just the inputs to the adversarially controlled parties.

Sequential composition of private protocols is again private [4]. In [4], this result is technically shown only for passive adversaries, but nowhere does the proof make use of the passiveness.

3.3   Protocols for Oblivious Sorting

Suppose we are given a vector of secret-shared values $[\![\boldsymbol{x}]\!] = ([\![x_1]\!], \ldots, [\![x_k]\!])$. SMC frameworks, e.g. Sharemind, contain protocols for comparing, adding and multiplying shared values (the results are again shared). These can be combined to an oblivious *compare-exchange node* that computes $[\![\min\{y, z\}]\!]$ and $[\![\max\{y, z\}]\!]$ from $[\![y]\!]$ and $[\![z]\!]$. Such nodes can be used to construct sorting networks for secret-shared data.

Common sorting algorithms are harder to adapt for SMC, because there is no simple means to access an element of a vector by a secret-shared index. Declassifying the accessed indices would leak information about the initial ordering of the vector elements. This can be overcome by first performing a random shuffle of the elements of the vector. The shuffling protocol [27], adapted for Sharemind, works as follows. Let the elements of the vector $[\![\boldsymbol{x}]\!]$ of length k be additively shared (over $\mathbb{Z}_N$ for some integer N) among three parties, two of which are honest and third may be passively corrupted. A permutation $\sigma \in S_k$ is shared as

Data: shared vector $[\![x]\!]$, private permutation $[\![\sigma]\!] = (\sigma_1, \sigma_2, \sigma_3)$
Result: vector $[\![x]\!]$ permuted according to σ

1 **for** $i = 1$ **to** 3 **do**
2   P_i randomly generates $r \in \mathbb{Z}_N^k$
3   P_i sends r to P_{i-1} and $y := [\![x]\!]_i - r$ to P_{i+1}
4   P_{i-1}, P_i, P_{i+1} update
       $([\![x]\!]_{i-1}, [\![x]\!]_i, [\![x]\!]_{i+1}) := ([\![x]\!]_{i-1} + r, (0, 0, \ldots, 0), [\![x]\!]_{i+1} + y)$
5   P_{i-1} and P_{i+1} reorder $[\![x]\!]_{i-1}$ and $[\![x]\!]_{i+1}$ by σ_i
6 $\forall i : P_i$ randomly generates $r_i \in \mathbb{Z}_N^k$ and sends it to P_{i+1}
7 $\forall i : P_i$ updates $[\![x]\!]_i := [\![x]\!]_i + r_i - r_{i-1}$

Algorithm 1. Shuffling protocol of [27]

three random permutations $[\![\sigma]\!] = (\sigma_1, \sigma_2, \sigma_3) \in S_k^3$, satisfying $\sigma_3 \circ \sigma_2 \circ \sigma_1 = \sigma$, such that party P_i knows the permutations σ_{i-1} and σ_{i+1} (the indices are *modulo* 3). The shuffling protocol is given in Algorithm 1. Its main component is for each pair of parties, to turn the additive sharing among three parties into additive sharing among this pair and apply one of the permutations σ_i. The protocol ends with a *resharing* step, after which all shares are random again. A variation of this protocol works for values shared with Shamir's 2-out-of-3 sharing.

After shuffling the vector, the results of comparing its elements may be made public, as long as all elements are different. They can be made different by adding an extra field to the comparison keys, which has the least significance in comparisons and is different for all elements. All pairs of elements may be compared in parallel [31], which has excellent round complexity, but requires $O(k^2)$ of work. Alternatively, comparisons may be made according to some sorting algorithm, e.g. the quicksort [19], moving around the elements of $[\![x]\!]$ as indicated by the comparison results. The private shuffle $[\![\sigma]\!]$ together with the public permutation (that latter can be composed with the last component of $[\![\sigma]\!]$, giving a single private shuffle $[\![\sigma']\!]$) applied during the sorting of shuffled $[\![x]\!]$ provides the proof that the vectors before and after sorting had the same elements. In the rest of the paper, we will assume that all elements of x are different.

Counting sort can also be adapted to SMC, as shown in Algorithm 2. Here private data in y is reordered according to the keys in x. The sorting algorithm computes where each element of x and y would go if the key were equal to 0 (stored in $\bar{c}$) or 1 (stored in c; offset by the number of 0-s in x, which is equal to $\bar{c}_k + 1$). The actual position is computed in line 4, performing an oblivious choice over $[\![x_i]\!]$, selecting either $[\![\bar{c}_i]\!]$ or $([\![c_i]\!] + [\![\bar{c}_k]\!] + 1)$. Note that while $x_i \in \{0, 1\}$, the elements of $[\![x]\!]$ have to be shared over a larger ring (at least $\mathbb{Z}_k$) to make sure that the computations do not overflow; this may require the use of the *share conversion* protocol [7, Algorithm 5]. The positions are randomly shuffled together with $[\![x]\!]$ and $[\![y]\!]$. The declassification returns a random permutation of $\{1, \ldots, k\}$, leaking nothing about $[\![x]\!]$. The composition of $[\![\sigma]\!]$ and o is the proof of sameness of vectors. Counting sort can be extended to radix sort for multi-bit keys as in [5] and the sameness proofs can be composed as in Algorithm 3.

Data: keys $[\![x]\!]$, data $[\![y]\!]$, where $x \in \mathbb{Z}_2^k$, $y \in \mathbb{Z}_N^k$
Result: $[\![x]\!]$, $[\![y]\!]$ stably sorted according to x
1 **foreach** $i \in \{1, \ldots, k\}$ **do** $[\![\overline{x}_i]\!] := 1 - [\![x_i]\!]$
2 $[\![c]\!] := \mathsf{prefixsum}([\![x]\!])$
3 $[\![\overline{c}]\!] := \mathsf{prefixsum}([\![\overline{x}]\!])$
4 **foreach** $i \in \{1, \ldots, k\}$ **do** $[\![o_i]\!] := 1 + [\![\overline{c}_i]\!] + [\![x_i]\!] \cdot ([\![c_i]\!] - [\![\overline{c}_i]\!] + [\![\overline{c}_k]\!] + 1)$
5 Generate a random private permutation $[\![\sigma]\!] \in S_k$
6 Shuffle $[\![x]\!]$, $[\![y]\!]$ and $[\![o]\!]$ according to $[\![\sigma]\!]$
7 $o := \mathsf{declassify}([\![o]\!])$
8 **foreach** $i \in \{1, \ldots, k\}$ **do** $[\![x_i]\!] := [\![x_{o_i}]\!]$; $[\![y_i]\!] := [\![y_{o_i}]\!]$

Algorithm 2. Counting sort as a SMC protocol

Data: Private permutations $[\![\sigma^{(1)}]\!], \ldots, [\![\sigma^{(m)}]\!] \in S_k$
Result: Private permutation $[\![\sigma]\!]$ satisfying $\sigma = \sigma^{(m)} \circ \cdots \circ \sigma^{(1)}$
1 $[\![o]\!] := (1, 2, \ldots, k)$
2 **for** $i = 0$ **to** $m - 1$ **do**
3 $\quad$ Shuffle $[\![o]\!]$ according to $[\![\sigma^{(m-i)}]\!]^{-1}$ (reverse the loop in Algorithm 1)
4 Generate a random private permutation $[\![\sigma']\!] \in S_k$
5 Shuffle $[\![o]\!]$ according to $[\![\sigma']\!]$
6 $o := \mathsf{declassify}([\![o]\!])$
7 **return** the composition of $[\![\sigma']\!]$ and o

Algorithm 3. Composing oblivious shuffles

3.4   Covert Security

Covertly secure protocols are secure against adversaries that may deviate from the protocol, but do not want to get caught [1].

Consider an ideal functionality $\mathcal{F}$ for n parties and a real protocol implementing it. A machine M_i may give a special output accuse_J to the party P_i, indicating that it suspects the parties in $J \subseteq [n]$ of deviating. We require the protocol π to be *detection accurate*, meaning that if for any honest P_i, the machine M_i outputs accuse_J, then $J \subseteq \mathcal{C}$, i.e. only corrupt parties can be caught cheating. We say that a run of π *catches a cheater* (denoted $\pi\Downarrow$) if all honest M_i output accuse_{J_i} to P_i, and the intersection of all the sets J_i is not empty.

Definition 2. *Let $\varepsilon \in [0, 1]$. A detection accurate protocol π black-box simulates the ideal functionality $\mathcal{F}$ in the presence of covert adversaries with ε-deterrent [1] if there exists a machine* Sim, *such that for all users H and adversaries $\mathcal{A}$,*

$$\varepsilon \cdot \Delta(view_{H\|\pi\|\mathcal{A}}(H), view_{H\|\mathcal{F}\|(\mathsf{Sim}\|\mathcal{A})}(H)) \leq \Pr[\pi\Downarrow] .$$

Here $[0, 1]$ is the set of real numbers between 0 and 1, and Δ is the *statistical distance* between probability distributions: $\Delta(\mu, \mu') = \frac{1}{2} \sum_{x \in X} |\mu(x) - \mu'(x)|$, where $\mu, \mu' : X \to [0, 1]$ are two probability distributions over the set X. This form of simulatability with covert adversaries is preserved by sequential composition (taking the minimum of ε-s), as shown by a simple hybrid argument [1].

4   Covertly Private SMC

Covert privacy. The definitions of privacy and covert security can easily be combined. In covert privacy, we let the machines M_i output accuse to the party P_i. Note that we do not specify the set of accused parties here. We define $\pi\Downarrow$ if all honest parties output accuse. We also relax the notion of *detection accuracy*, only requiring that an honest party does not output accuse if $C = \emptyset$.

Definition 3. *Let $\varepsilon \in [0,1]$. A detection-accurate protocol π is a covertly private SMC protocol with ε-deterrent for a functionality f, if there exists a machine* Sim, *such that for all users H, adversaries $\mathcal{A}$,*

$$\varepsilon \cdot \Delta(view_{H\|\pi\|\mathcal{A}}(H), view_{H\|\mathcal{F}^f_{\mathrm{priv}}\|(\mathsf{Sim}\|\mathcal{A})}(H)) \le \Pr[\pi\Downarrow].$$

We see that the covert privacy of a SMC protocol means the following. An active adversary may change the outcome of the protocol without the honest parties noticing it. An active adversary may also learn something about the inputs of honest parties, but if it does so, the honest parties will be notified with significant probability.

Covert privacy composes in the same manner as active or passive privacy. The proof in [4] carries over without modifications.

From Covert Privacy to Covert Security. Consider a covertly private SMC protocol π for a functionality f. Also let π compute for each party P_i a *verification value* v_i; we think of this verification value as not an output to the party P_i, but as input to subsequent protocols. There exist transformations [25,26] that turn passively secure SMC protocols into covertly secure protocols (with 1-deterrent). The transformations perform the following steps:

- binding the parties to the messages they've sent using signatures;
- adding a verification protocol that uses the signed incoming and outgoing messages as verification values.

Given a protocol π, we let $\mathsf{s}[\pi]$ denote the protocol where all outgoing messages are signed. This protocol also outputs the signed messages as verification values. We let $\mathsf{v}[\pi]$ denote the verification protocol for $\mathsf{s}[\pi]$ constructed as in [25] or [26]. The protocol $\mathsf{v}[\pi]$ outputs a set $J_i \subseteq [n]$ of parties to be accused to each honest party P_i. If $J_i = \emptyset$ then no deviations were detected and the result output by π may be used. Note that the execution of $\mathsf{v}[\pi]$ is **much more expensive** (by two or more orders of magnitude) than the execution of π.

Covertly Secure Sorting. Let π_0 be the protocol for checking the correctness of sorting, it is given in Algorithm 4. It performs some simple checks, verifying that the original and the sorted vector are the same, and that the sorted vector actually is sorted. Let π_1 be a covertly private sorting protocol that also outputs the proof of sameness of vectors. The following is one of the main results of this paper.

Data: shared vectors $[\![x]\!]$, $[\![y]\!]$ of length k; private permutation $[\![\sigma]\!] \in S_k$
Result: yes/no, stating whether $[\![\sigma]\!]$ proves that $[\![y]\!]$ is the sorted version of $[\![x]\!]$
1 Shuffle $[\![x]\!]$ according to $[\![\sigma]\!]$
2 **foreach** $i \in \{1, \ldots, k\}$ **do** $[\![b_i]\!] := ([\![x_i]\!] = [\![y_i]\!])$?
3 **foreach** $i \in \{1, \ldots, k-1\}$ **do** $[\![b'_i]\!] := ([\![y_i]\!] \le [\![y_{i+1}]\!])$?
4 **return** declassify$(\bigwedge_{i=1}^{k}[\![b_i]\!] \wedge \bigwedge_{i=1}^{k-1}[\![b'_i]\!])$

Algorithm 4. Protocol π_0: checking the correctness of sorting

Data: shared vector $[\![x]\!]$
Data: Covertly private SMC sorting protocol π_1 (with sameness proof)
Result: sorted $[\![x]\!]$; or accusations against misbehaving parties
1 $([\![x']\!], [\![\sigma]\!], accuse, v) \leftarrow \mathsf{s}[\pi_1]([\![x]\!])$
2 **if** $accuse = \mathsf{true}$ **then go to** 8
3 $(b, v') \leftarrow \mathsf{s}[\pi_0]([\![x]\!], [\![x']\!], [\![\sigma]\!])$
4 $(J_1, \ldots, J_n) \leftarrow \mathsf{v}[\pi_0](x, x', [\![\sigma]\!], b, v')$
5 **each party** P_i **does the following**
6 $\quad |$ **if** $J_i \ne \emptyset$ **then return** accuse$_{J_i}$
7 **if** $b = \mathsf{true}$ **then return** $[\![x']\!]$
8 $(J_1, \ldots, J_n) \leftarrow \mathsf{v}[\pi_1](x, x', [\![\sigma]\!], accuse, v)$ $//$ $\forall i \in [n] \backslash \mathcal{C} : J_i \ne \emptyset$
9 **each party** P_i **returns** accuse$_{J_i}$

Algorithm 5. Covertly secure SMC protocol for sorting

Theorem 1. *The protocol in Algorithm 5 is a covertly secure sorting protocol.*

Proof. Let Sim_0, Sim_1 be simulators for $(\mathsf{s}[\pi_0], \mathsf{v}[\pi_0])$ and $(\mathsf{s}[\pi_1], \mathsf{v}[\pi_1])$, respectively. The simulator Sim for the protocol in Algorithm 5 will receive the shares of $[\![x]\!]$ for corrupted parties and invoke Sim_1 with them. At some point, Sim_1 computes the corrupted parties' shares of $[\![x']\!]$ and $[\![\sigma]\!]$, as well as the accusation bit. At this point Sim invokes Sim_0 with the shares it has computed. It does not return to continue with Sim_1.

The simulator Sim shows that Algorithm 5 black-box simulates the ideal sorting functionality (which receives the shares of the elements of x and returns the shares of the elements of the sorted vector) in the presence of covert adversaries. Indeed, Sim can compute the corrupted parties' shares of $[\![x']\!]$ and $[\![\sigma]\!]$ indistinguishably from the real protocol due to Sim_1 being a simulator for $(\mathsf{s}[\pi_1], \mathsf{v}[\pi_1])$ and these shares belonging to the view of the adversary. If the accusation bit is true in the real protocol then some corrupt party will be accused by all honest parties in line 8 by the security properties of $\mathsf{v}[\pi_1]$. Such accusations do not have to be simulated by Sim according to Definition 2. If the accusation bit is false then Sim will produce a good simulation of the real protocol due to Sim_0 being a simulator for $(\mathsf{s}[\pi_0], \mathsf{v}[\pi_0])$. If the bit b is false in line 7 and the real protocol continues with the invocation of $\mathsf{v}[\pi_1]$, then again some corrupted party will definitely be accused in line 8 and this part of the protocol does not need simulating. $\square$

A conceptually simpler covertly secure sorting protocol would unconditionally jump from line 2 to line 8. But the full protocol in Algorithm 5 is more efficient in executions where no party tries to deviate from the protocol; it is natural to expect most executions to be like that. While the conceptually simpler protocol would always execute $\mathsf{v}[\pi_1]$, the protocol in Algorithm 5 executes $\mathsf{s}[\pi_0]$ and $\mathsf{v}[\pi_0]$ instead. We expect the protocol π_0 which only checks for sortedness to be $O(\log k)$ times cheaper than the sorting protocol π_1. The verification is similarly cheaper.

5 Analysis of Oblivious Sorting Methods

We have discussed SMC protocols based on securely implementing sorting networks and argued that they are actively private. Unfortunately, the sequence of swaps that they produce is not easily converted into a single private shuffle. One can convert the comparison results of each layer of compare-exchange nodes into an oblivious shuffle; these $O(\log^2 k)$ oblivious shuffles (for input vectors of length k) can be composed into a single oblivious shuffle with $O(k \log^2 k)$ work using Algorithm 3. As we show below, at least parts of this algorithm are not covertly private for the same reason as Algorithm 2.

5.1 Methods Based on Shuffling and Comparison

We now show that sorting protocols that first shuffle the vector $[\![x]\!]$ and then declassify the results of comparisons cannot be covertly private, at least for additive secret sharing. For this purpose we present a pair $(H, \mathcal{A})$, such that no simulator Sim can make the sorting protocol π indistinguishable from $\mathcal{F}\|\mathrm{Sim}$, where $\mathcal{F}$ is the ideal sorting functionality.

H and $\mathcal{A}$ first agree on a bit b, followed by $\mathcal{A}$ corrupting one of the parties, and H submitting a vector $[\![x]\!]$ of length 2 to be sorted. The elements of x are $x_1 = 0$ and $x_2 = 1 + 2b$; H additively shares them before submission. In the real protocol, vector $[\![x]\!]$ is shuffled (i.e. perhaps the elements are swapped) and at some moment, $[\![x_1]\!]$ and $[\![x_2]\!]$ are compared to each other. Before the comparison, $\mathcal{A}$ tells the corrupted party to add 2 to its share of $[\![x_2]\!]$. Due to additive sharing, this means that x_2 is increased by 2. The comparison result is declassified. In real execution, the comparison result depends on the bit b. If $b = 0$, then $x_1 < x_2$, because $|x_2 - x_1| = 1$ before the adversary's interference and the increasing of x_2 was sufficient to make it larger than x_1. If $b = 1$ then $|x_2 - x_1| = 3$ before the adversary's interference. In this case the increase of x_2 did not affect the comparison result and either result is possible with 50 % probability. The simulator does not know b and hence does not know, from which probability distribution the simulated result of the comparison should be sampled. Nor can the honest parties in the real execution notice that something is wrong.

5.2 Counting Sort

Most steps of the counting sort protocol (Algorithm 2) are covertly, and even actively private [28], except for the declassification step in line 7. The protocol

Data: Private permutation $[\![\sigma]\!] \in S_{k+1}$, index $x_1 \in \{1, \ldots, k+1\}$
Result: Private permutation $[\![\sigma']\!] \in S_k$, such that $\sigma' = \sigma\!\downarrow_{x_0}$

1 **for** $i = 1$ **to** 3 **do**
2 | P_{i-1} and P_{i+1} send $x_{i+1} = \sigma_i(x_i)$ to P_i
3 | **if** P_i *receives different x_{i+1}-s* **then** P_i outputs accuse
4 **foreach** $i \in \{1, 2, 3\}$ **do** P_{i-1} and P_{i+1} define $\sigma'_i := \sigma_i\!\downarrow_{x_i}$

Algorithm 6. Puncturing a private permutation (in Sharemind)

can be seen as consisting of two parts, the first of them computing the positions for reordering the elements of $[\![x]\!]$ and $[\![y]\!]$, and the second one (lines 5–8) actually performing the reordering. We show that the second part is not covertly secure, if $[\![o]\!]$ is shared over $\mathbb{Z}_k$ (in this case, $0 \equiv k$). We analyse the lines 5–7, because the last line only performs public operations. Note that exactly the same operations are performed in Algorithm 3, lines 4–6. The honest parties may try to detect adversarial interference by noticing that the declassified o is not a permutation of $1, \ldots, k$.

We again present $(H, \mathcal{A})$ for which no simulator Sim exists. H and $\mathcal{A}$ first agree on a bit, after which $\mathcal{A}$ corrupts a party and H shares an arbitrary x and y of length k among the computing parties. It also shares the vector $o = (b, b, \ldots, b)$ (of length k). Even though o should be a permutation in a "normal" execution of the lines 5–7, this does not have to be the case if the previous steps of a larger protocol have also been affected by the adversary. In the execution, $\mathcal{A}$ selects a random permutation $o' \in \mathbb{Z}_k^k$. It lets the shuffling protocol (for $[\![o]\!]$) execute normally, except that during the resharing step (lines 6–7 in Algorithm 1), it tells the corrupted party to add o' to its share. Hence the declassification in line 7 of Algorithm 2 produces a permutation and adversarial interference will not be detected. The declassified permutation is equal to $o' + (b, b, \ldots, b)$. The simulator Sim does not know b, thus cannot simulate this.

6 Covertly Private Reordering

A covertly private reordering protocol (replacing steps 5–7 in Algorithm 2 and steps 4–6 in Algorithm 3) is all that is needed for a covertly private sorting algorithm that can be used in Algorithm 5. We start its presentation by an auxiliary algorithm for *puncturing* a private permutation.

For $i \in \mathbb{N}$, define the mappings $\mathsf{ins}_i, \mathsf{del}_i : \mathbb{N} \to \mathbb{N}$ by $\mathsf{ins}_i(j) = \mathsf{del}_i(j) = j$ if $j < i$ and $\mathsf{ins}_i(j) = j + 1$, $\mathsf{del}_i(j) = j - 1$ for $j \geq i$. Let $\tau \in S_{k+1}$ and $i \in \{1, \ldots, k+1\}$. *Puncturing τ at i gives us the permutation* $\tau\!\downarrow_i = \mathsf{del}_{\tau(i)} \circ \tau \circ \mathsf{ins}_i \in S_k$. A private permutation $[\![\sigma]\!] \in S_{k+1}$ can also be easily punctured while leaking the value $\sigma(i)$ in the process, as shown in Algorithm 6. Clearly, nothing else is leaked, because no other points of σ_i-s are made public. The protocol is covertly private because everything a party receives, it receives from two other parties, one of which has to be honest. Without the last line in Algorithm 6, this protocol covertly securely computes and makes public $x_4 = \sigma(x_1)$.

Data: Shared vectors $[\![x]\!]$, $[\![o]\!]$ of length k, where o is a permutation of $\{1, \ldots, k\}$
Result: $[\![x]\!]$ reordered according to $[\![o]\!]$

1 Generate random $[\![\![y_1]\!]\!], \ldots, [\![\![y_m]\!]\!]$
2 **foreach** $i \in \{1, \ldots, m\}$ **do** $[\![o_{k+i}]\!] := [\![y_i]\!]$
3 Generate a random private permutation $[\![\![\sigma]\!]\!] \in S_{k+m}$
4 Shuffle $[\![o]\!]$ according to $[\![\![\sigma]\!]\!]$
5 $o := \mathsf{declassify}([\![o]\!])$
6 **foreach** $i \in \{1, \ldots, m\}$ **do**
7     $z_i := \sigma(k+i)$ `// Algorithm 6 without last line`
8   **if** $o_{z_i} \neq \mathsf{declassify}([\![\![y_i]\!]\!])$ **then** output accuse
9 Delete positions $z_1, \ldots, z_m$ from o
10 **if** o *is not a permutation of* $\{1, \ldots, k\}$ **then** output accuse
11 Shuffle $[\![x]\!]$ according to $[\![\![\sigma\downarrow_{k+m}\downarrow_{k+m-1}\cdots\downarrow_{k+1}]\!]\!]$
12 **foreach** $i \in \{1, \ldots, k\}$ **do** $[\![x_i]\!] := [\![x_{o_i}]\!]$

Algorithm 7. Protocol for covertly private reordering

The covertly private reordering protocol is given in Algorithm 7. It introduces the *replicated secret sharing* [11] $[\![\![y]\!]\!]$ of a value $y \in \mathbb{Z}_N$. In our case of additive secret sharing with Sharemind security model, $[\![\![y]\!]\!]$ consists of three random elements of $\mathbb{Z}_N$ summing up to y, with each party knowing two of them. Random replicated shared values are generated in the same manner as random private permutations. Conversion from $[\![\![y]\!]\!]$ to $[\![y]\!]$ means just dropping one of the shares. In declassifying $[\![\![y]\!]\!]$, each party sends to both other parties the share they do not yet know. In this manner, each party will learn the missing share from both other parties and the adversary cannot send a wrong share without being detected.

We see that in Algorithm 7 we add extra elements to the index vector $[\![o]\!]$ in order to catch the adversary manipulating many elements of it, the number of added elements m functions as security parameter. After shuffling, we determine where the added elements had to end up, and check that they were not changed by the adversary. Finally, we drop the points $k+1, \ldots, k+m$ from the private permutation σ (this can be done locally after running Algorithm 6 to find $z_1, \ldots, z_m$) and use the result to shuffle $[\![x]\!]$ as before.

Theorem 2. *Let* $c = m/k$. *Algorithm 7 is covertly private with* ε-*deterrent, where* $\varepsilon = 1 - (c+1)^{-c}$.

Proof. We need to construct Sim simulating the view of the corrupted party from this party's input shares. The simulator does not know the honest parties' shares of $[\![x]\!]$ and $[\![o]\!]$, hence it does not know x and o. During the run, it receives all messages the corrupted party sends to honest parties, and must generate honest parties' messages to the corrupt party, thereby learning all these messages. Hence it can still follow Algorithm 7 as follows.

In line 1, Sim will either generate or receive all three shares of $[\![\![y_1]\!]\!], \ldots, [\![\![y_m]\!]\!]$, hence it knows $y_1, \ldots, y_m$. Similarly, in line 3 it learns all three shares of $[\![\![\sigma]\!]\!]$ and therefore σ itself. In line 4, it simulates the invocation of a shuffle (Algorithm 1), which is actively private. In line 5, Sim must simulate the result of declassifying shuffled o. In declassified o, the simulator puts $y_1, \ldots, y_m$ to positions $\sigma(k+1), \ldots, \sigma(k+m)$ and a uniformly random permutation of $\{1, \ldots, k\}$ to the remaining k positions.

The simulator has all information (shares of $[\![\sigma]\!]$ and $[\![y]\!]$) to simulate the lines 6–8. The shuffle in line 11 is actively private and the operations in lines 9,10,12 do not involve communication between parties. We must now justify that the simulation of the declassification in line 5 is sufficiently similar to the real protocol to achieve the claimed deterrent. We make the following claims.

Claim 1. Consider a protocol where first a vector $z \in \mathbb{Z}_N^k$ is generated and shared by an active adversary $\mathcal{A}$ (having corrupted a party), then a private permutation $[\![\sigma]\!]$ is generated and applied to $[\![z]\!]$ using the protocol in Algorithm 1, and finally z is declassified. Any such $\mathcal{A}$ can be emulated by an adversary that selects $z, z' \in \mathbb{Z}_N^k$ and learns $\sigma'(z) + z'$ for an unknown, uniform $\sigma' \in S_k$.

The claim follows from the construction of Algorithm 1. At each resharing and updating of shares in lines 3–4 and 6–7 of Algorithm 1, the adversary can add a known vector to z. The adversary also knows all but one permutations used in line 5. The addition of vectors before the application of the unknown permutation corresponds to selecting a different z in the beginning. The addition after this application corresponds to z'. During declassification, the adversary can add yet another vector to the current z.

Claim 1 explains how much an adversary can affect o in line 5 of Algorithm 7. It can choose some o (not necessarily a permutation of $\{1, \ldots, k\}$) in the beginning and, after it has been permuted, add a known d to it. Assuming that the addition did not affect any elements of y (which would result in an immediate accusation), the adversary hopes to obtain a non-uniformly chosen permutation of $\{1, \ldots, k\}$.

Claim 2. Let $|v| = k$, with v having s different elements. If $\sigma \in S_k$ is uniformly chosen then $\Pr[\sigma(v) = v] \leq (k - s + 1)!/k!$.

Indeed, if $w_1, \ldots, w_s$ are the elements occuring in v with c_i being the count of w_i, then the number of permutations in S_k leaving v in place is $c_1! \cdots c_s! = \prod_{i=1}^{s} \prod_{j=1}^{c_i - 1}(1 + j)$. This product has $k - s$ factors, bounded by $2, 3, \ldots, (k - s + 1)$. Hence it is at most $(k - s + 1)!$. The set S_k has $k!$ elements.

Claim 3. Let $v, d, u \in \mathbb{Z}_N^k$ with u being a permutation of $\{1, \ldots, k\}$. Let $t = \|d\|_0$, denoting the number of non-zero elements (the *Hamming weight*) of d. If $\sigma \in S_k$ is uniformly chosen then $\Pr[\sigma(v) + d = u] \leq (t + 1)!/k!$.

Indeed, if there is no σ_0, such that $\sigma_0(v) + d = u$, then the claim holds. Otherwise, the probability is equal to $\Pr[(\sigma \circ \sigma_0^{-1})(\sigma_0(v)) = \sigma_0(v)]$. By claim 2, this probability as at most $(k - s + 1)!/k!$, where s is the number of different elements in $\sigma_0(v) = u - d$. Vector u has k different elements, hence $u - d$ has at least $k - t$ different elements.

In the following, let $d \in \mathbb{Z}_N^{k+m}$ be the difference in o that the adversary has caused in line 5 of Algorithm 7. Let E be the event that accuse does not occur in the loop in lines 6–8 of the real execution of Algorithm 7. Let $t = \|d\|_0$.

Claim 4. (trivial) $\Pr[E] \leq \binom{k}{t} / \binom{k+m}{t}$.

Claim 5. If $t \leq c$ (i.e. $m \geq tk$) then $\Pr[E] \leq 1/(t+1)!$.

Indeed, we have $\binom{k}{t}/\binom{k+m}{t} = \prod_{i=0}^{t-1} \frac{k-i}{k+m-i} \leq (\frac{k}{k+m})^t$. Applying the inequality $m \geq tk$ gives

$$\Pr[E] \leq \left(\frac{k}{k+m}\right)^t \leq \left(\frac{k}{k+tk}\right)^t = \left(\frac{1}{t+1}\right)^t = \frac{1}{(t+1)^t} \leq \frac{1}{(t+1)!}.$$

Claim 6. If $t \geq c$ then $\Pr[E] \leq (c+1)^{-c}$.

Similarly to previous claim, we get

$$\Pr[E] \leq \left(\frac{k}{k+m}\right)^t = \left(\frac{k}{k+ck}\right)^t = \left(\frac{1}{c+1}\right)^t \leq \left(\frac{1}{c+1}\right)^c = \frac{1}{(c+1)^c}.$$

Claim 7. Let $u \in \mathbb{Z}_N^k$ be a permutation of $\{1, \ldots, k\}$. If $m \geq tk$ then the probability of o being equal to u in line 10 of the real execution of Algorithm 7 is at most $1/k!$.

Indeed, to get to line 10, the event E must occur. If E occurred then all t changes the adversary made to o must have happened to the positions not taken by the elements of y. Hence, if E occurred then by Claim 3, the probability of $o = u$ in line 10 is at most $(t+1)!/k!$. This probability must be multiplied with $\Pr[E]$ and the resulting product is at most $1/k!$.

Claim 7 shows that if m is sufficiently large then no declassification result in the real execution may occur with larger probability than in the simulated execution. This justifies Sim outputting a uniformly random permutation of $\{1, \ldots, k\}$.

Claim 8. If $t \geq c$ then accuse is output in the real execution with probability at least $\varepsilon = 1 - (c+1)^{-c}$.

Indeed, the probability of accuse being output is at least $1 - \Pr[E] \geq \varepsilon$.

The value of t is a random variable determined by the adversary. We have now analysed both the cases $t \leq c$ and $t \geq c$ and shown that in both cases, the adversary cannot get a large difference of views in real and ideal execution. Indeed, if $t \leq c$, then no particular value of o in line 10 can be obtained with greater probability in the real execution than in the simulated execution. Any difference in probabilities is due to accuse being output in the real execution. Thus, if $t \leq c$, we have 1-deterrent against adversaries trying to breach the privacy.

If $t \geq c$ then accuse is output with probability at least ε. As the distance between the views in the real and ideal execution cannot be larger than 1, we have at least ε-deterrent here.   □

7   Conclusions

We have presented a covertly private SMC reordering protocol that may be used to build a covertly private SMC sorting protocol based on the radix sort algorithm. The overhead of the sorting protocol, compared to a passively secure protocol, is only about three times (i.e. $m = 2k$), already giving the probability of ca. 90 % for catching a misbehaving adversary. The resulting covertly secure sorting protocol has only $o(k)$ overhead (over the passively secure protocol) on an input of size k.

It remains to be seen whether the presented reordering protocol is sufficient to construct a covertly private sorting protocol based on the quicksort algorithm.

References

1. Aumann, Y., Lindell, Y.: Security against covert adversaries: efficient protocols for realistic adversaries. J. Cryptology **23**(2), 281–343 (2010)
2. Bogdanov, D., Jõemets, M., Siim, S., Vaht, M.: How the estonian tax and customs board evaluated a tax fraud detection system based on secure multi-party computation. In: Böhme, R., Okamoto, T. (eds.) FC 2015. LNCS, vol. 8975, pp. 227–234. Springer, Heidelberg (2015). doi:10.1007/978-3-662-47854-7_14
3. Bogdanov, D., Kamm, L., Kubo, B., Rebane, R., Sokk, V., Talviste, R.: Students and taxes: a privacy-preserving social study using secure computation. In: Proceedings of Privacy Enhancing Technologies (PoPETS) (2016)
4. Bogdanov, D., Laud, P., Laur, S., Pullonen, P.: From input private to universally composable secure multi-party computation primitives. In: CSF 2014, pp. 184–198
5. Bogdanov, D., Laur, S., Talviste, R.: A practical analysis of oblivious sorting algorithms for secure multi-party computation. In: Bernsmed, K., Fischer-Hübner, S. (eds.) NordSec 2014. LNCS, vol. 8788, pp. 59–74. Springer, Heidelberg (2014). doi:10.1007/978-3-319-11599-3_4
6. Bogdanov, D., Laur, S., Willemson, J.: Sharemind: a framework for fast privacy-preserving computations. In: Jajodia, S., Lopez, J. (eds.) ESORICS 2008. LNCS, vol. 5283, pp. 192–206. Springer, Heidelberg (2008). doi:10.1007/978-3-540-88313-5_13
7. Bogdanov, D., Niitsoo, M., Toft, T., Willemson, J.: High-performance secure multi-party computation for data mining applications. Int. J. Inf. Sec. **11**(6), 403–418 (2012)
8. Bogetoft, P., et al.: Secure multiparty computation goes live. In: Dingledine, R., Golle, P. (eds.) FC 2009. LNCS, vol. 5628, pp. 325–343. Springer, Heidelberg (2009). doi:10.1007/978-3-642-03549-4_20
9. Canetti, R.: Universally composable security: a new paradigm for cryptographic protocols. In: FOCS 2001, pp. 136–145
10. Canetti, R., Lindell, Y., Ostrovsky, R., Sahai, A.: Universally composable two-party and multi-party secure computation. In: STOC 2002, pp. 494–503
11. Cramer, R., Damgård, I., Ishai, Y.: Share conversion, pseudorandom secret-sharing and applications to secure computation. In: Kilian, J. (ed.) TCC 2005. LNCS, vol. 3378, pp. 342–362. Springer, Heidelberg (2005). doi:10.1007/978-3-540-30576-7_19
12. Damgård, I., Keller, M., Larraia, E., Pastro, V., Scholl, P., Smart, N.P.: Practical covertly secure MPC for dishonest majority – Or: breaking the SPDZ limits. In: Crampton, J., Jajodia, S., Mayes, K. (eds.) ESORICS 2013. LNCS, vol. 8134, pp. 1–18. Springer, Heidelberg (2013). doi:10.1007/978-3-642-40203-6_1
13. Damgård, I., Pastro, V., Smart, N., Zakarias, S.: Multiparty computation from somewhat homomorphic encryption. In: Safavi-Naini, R., Canetti, R. (eds.) CRYPTO 2012. LNCS, vol. 7417, pp. 643–662. Springer, Heidelberg (2012). doi:10.1007/978-3-642-32009-5_38

14. Hoogh, S., Schoenmakers, B., Veeningen, M.: Certificate validation in secure computation and its use in verifiable linear programming. In: Pointcheval, D., Nitaj, A., Rachidi, T. (eds.) AFRICACRYPT 2016. LNCS, vol. 9646, pp. 265–284. Springer, Heidelberg (2016). doi:10.1007/978-3-319-31517-1_14

15. Gennaro, R., Gentry, C., Parno, B.: Non-interactive verifiable computing: outsourcing computation to untrusted workers. In: Rabin, T. (ed.) CRYPTO 2010. LNCS, vol. 6223, pp. 465–482. Springer, Heidelberg (2010). doi:10.1007/978-3-642-14623-7_25

16. Goldreich, O.: Foundations of Cryptography. Basic Applications, vol. 2. Cambridge University Press, New York (2004)

17. Goldreich, O., Micali, S., Wigderson, A.: How to play any mental game or a completeness theorem for protocols with honest majority. In: STOC 1987, pp. 218–229

18. Hamada, K., Ikarashi, D., Chida, K., Takahashi, K.: Oblivious radix sort: an efficient sorting algorithm for practical secure multi-party computation. Cryptology ePrint Archive, Report 2014/121 (2014)

19. Hamada, K., Kikuchi, R., Ikarashi, D., Chida, K., Takahashi, K.: Practically efficient multi-party sorting protocols from comparison sort algorithms. In: Kwon, T., Lee, M.-K., Kwon, D. (eds.) ICISC 2012. LNCS, vol. 7839, pp. 202–216. Springer, Heidelberg (2013). doi:10.1007/978-3-642-37682-5_15

20. Jónsson, K.V., Kreitz, G., Uddin, M.: Secure multi-party sorting and applications. Cryptology ePrint Archive, Report 2011/122 (2011)

21. Keller, M., Orsini, E., Scholl, P., Mascot: faster malicious arithmetic secure computation with oblivious transfer. Cryptology ePrint Archive, Report 2016/505 (2016)

22. Keller, M., Scholl, P., Smart, N.P.: An architecture for practical actively secure MPC with dishonest majority. In: CCS 2013, pp. 549–560

23. Laud, P.: Parallel oblivious array access for secure multiparty computation and privacy-preserving minimum spanning trees. Proc. Priv. Enhancing Technol. 2015(2), 188–205 (2015)

24. Laud, P.: Stateful abstractions of secure multiparty computation. In: Laud, P., Kamm, L. (eds.) Applications of Secure Multiparty Computation. Cryptology and Information Security, vol. 13, pp. 26–42. IOS Press, Amsterdam (2015)

25. Laud, P., Pankova, A.: Verifiable computation in multiparty protocols with honest majority. In: Chow, S.S.M., Liu, J.K., Hui, L.C.K., Yiu, S.M. (eds.) ProvSec 2014. LNCS, vol. 8782, pp. 146–161. Springer, Heidelberg (2014). doi:10.1007/978-3-319-12475-9_11

26. Laud, P., Pankova, A.: Preprocessing-based verification of multiparty protocols with honest majority. Cryptology ePrint Archive, Report 2015/674 (2015)

27. Laur, S., Willemson, J., Zhang, B.: Round-efficient oblivious database manipulation. In: Lai, X., Zhou, J., Li, H. (eds.) ISC 2011. LNCS, vol. 7001, pp. 262–277. Springer, Heidelberg (2011). doi:10.1007/978-3-642-24861-0_18

28. Pettai, M., Laud, P.: Automatic proofs of privacy of secure multi-party computation protocols against active adversaries. In: CSF 2015, pp. 75–89

29. Wang, G., Luo, T., Goodrich, M.T., Du, W., Zhu, Z.: Bureaucratic protocols for secure two-party sorting, selection, and permuting. In: ASIACCS 2010, pp. 226–237

30. Yao, A.C.: Protocols for secure computations. In: FOCS 1982, pp. 160–164

31. Zhang, B.: Generic constant-round oblivious sorting algorithm for MPC. In: Boyen, X., Chen, X. (eds.) ProvSec 2011. LNCS, vol. 6980, pp. 240–256. Springer, Heidelberg (2011). doi:10.1007/978-3-642-24316-5_17

Authentication

PASSPHONE: Outsourcing Phone-Based Web Authentication While Protecting User Privacy

Martin Potthast[1], Christian Forler[2], Eik List[1(✉)], and Stefan Lucks[1]

[1] Bauhaus-Universität Weimar, Weimar, Germany
{martin.potthast,eik.list,stefan.lucks}@uni-weimar.de
[2] Beuth Hochschule für Technik Berlin, Berlin, Germany
cforler@posteo.de

Abstract. This work introduces PASSPHONE, a new smartphone-based authentication scheme that outsources user verification to a trusted third party without sacrificing privacy: neither can the trusted third party learn the relation between users and service providers, nor can service providers learn those of their users to others. When employed as a second factor in conjunction with, for instance, passwords as a first factor, our scheme maximizes the deployability of two-factor authentication for service providers while maintaining user privacy. We conduct a twofold formal analysis of our scheme, the first regarding its general security, and the second regarding anonymity and unlinkability of its users. Moreover, we provide an automatic analysis using AVISPA, a comparative evaluation to existing schemes under Bonneau et al.'s framework, and an evaluation of a prototypical implementation.

1 Introduction

Two-factor authentication is an effective means to strengthen user authentication on the Internet. In particular, the use of software-based second-factor tokens is attractive for service providers since it relieves them from considerable costs that come along with developing and delivering custom hardware tokens. For their users, phone-based two-factor solutions have the advantage of employing the nowadays omnipresent smartphone, avoiding the inconvenience of carrying around yet another device for the sole purpose of authentication. However, offering two-factor authentication is not at all the default, yet.

Meanwhile, small and medium enterprises, and especially startups, outsource user verification. This is due to the fact that the proper implementation of a secure authentication solution is a non-trivial task, and that many struggle to get even basic password authentication right [12]. Hence, delegating user verification to a competent trusted third party appears reasonable. In the context password authentication, corresponding infrastructures have been successfully established via OpenID [37] and OAuth [24] (e.g., Google, Yahoo, and Wordpress for OpenID and Twitter, Facebook, and PayPal for OAuth). On the upside, outsourcing user verification is convenient for users and reduces development costs for service providers, mitigating the risks of developing a custom solution from scratch.

© Springer International Publishing AG 2016
B.B. Brumley and J. Röning (Eds.): NordSec 2016, LNCS 10014, pp. 235–255, 2016.
DOI: 10.1007/978-3-319-47560-8_15

On the downside, however, outsourcing authentication has been justly criticized for its impact on privacy: the authentication provider serving as trusted third party gains precise information about a user's preferred services, her usage behavior, as well as the success of a given service. While undesirable for both service providers and their users, the former often choose user convenience and development speed over privacy, whereas most of the latter apparently do not care. Clearly, there is a lot of room for improving the outsourcing of authentication in terms of user privacy. The privacy of phone-based three-party authentication, however, has not been considered until now.

This paper proposes PASSPHONE, a smartphone-based two-factor authentication scheme which outsources user verification to a trusted third party while protecting user privacy. To the best of our knowledge, our scheme is the first smartphone-based one to incorporate anonymity and unlinkability despite employing a trusted third party. We conduct a systematic analysis of our scheme in terms of its security, privacy, feasibility, and competitiveness. In particular, we analyze its security and privacy properties formally, report on a practical implementation, and evaluate its competitiveness under the framework of Bonneau et al. [11]. We also conduct an automatic security analysis using the well-known computer-aided proof system AVISPA [4]. In what follows, after a brief review of related work, Sect. 3 introduces our authentication scheme. Section 4 formally analyzes its authentication security and privacy properties and Sect. 5 reports results from an automatic security analysis. Section 6 discusses insights gained from implementing our scheme, Sect. 7 compares it to a selection of existing phone-based solutions, and Sect. 8 discusses its practical application.

2   Related Work

Privacy in Federated Authentication. Dey and Weis [17] propose PseudoID, which can be considered the complement of our scheme for traditional password authentication. Their scheme also employs blinding to render users unlinkable across service providers. Dey and Weis show the unlinkability of their authentication scheme, but give neither an actual protocol nor an analysis. A proof of concept had been published, but the associated web page has disappeared. Otherwise, the privacy issues of federated authentication services have been highlighted in many contexts: for example, Urueña et al. [44] consider a privacy problem that concerns OpenID and Facebook Connect. They find that the unique identifier assigned to users by both services may leak to third parties, allowing to track users across web services since they encode user identifiers in the GET parameters of URLs. Riesch and Du [38] and Nuñez et al. [33] propose ways to solve the privacy issues of OpenID; Nuñez and Agudo [32] finally proposed a blinded version of OpenID called BlindIdM.

Phone-Based Two-Factor Authentication. Banks have been among the first to roll out two-factor authentication schemes for transactions, whereas online games and Google first deployed this technology at scale for web user authentication [22]. In light of recent security breaches [21,27,28], a shift toward two-factor authentication can be observed since several major companies such as Microsoft, Apple, and Facebook, some of which suffered attacks, rolled out their own implementations [3,31,40].

In the literature, Dodson et al. propose SNAP2PASS [19,20] and van Rijswijk and van Dijk propose TIQR [45]: both are phone-based schemes that use QR codes to transmit a challenge from a service provider via a user's browser to her phone, which responds to the challenge. Dodson et al. also consider outsourcing authentication to a trusted third party (an OpenID provider); though, they do not tackle the privacy issues associated with this approach. The authentication schemes by Aloul et al. [1] and Hallsteinsen et al. [23] are also phone-based challenge-response protocols based on one-time passwords (OTPs) that are generated using a previously shared secret between a user and a key server. This OTP is then transmitted to the device and used as a second means of authentication. In both two-factor authentication schemes, the key server can learn precisely which user tries to authenticate at which service. Karapanos et al.'s SOUNDPROOF [26] aims at increasing the adoption of two-factor authentication by avoiding the need for user interaction with their device. Instead, their authentication detects the physical proximity of the smartphone via matching the ambient sound of their environment. While the approach puts forth usability, it can protect neither against physical nor against man-in-the-middle or phishing attacks, and it is not easily deployable for service providers. Shirvanian et al. [39] categorize smartphone-based two-factor authentication schemes concerning the amount of data transmitted between client and phone. They concern four challenge/response formats: (1) a low-bandwidth variant which uses a PIN as second factor, (2) a mid-bandwidth variant with a QR-code challenge, a full-bandwidth variant which transmits challenge and response via Bluetooth, and another full-bandwidth variant which transmits challenge and response via WiFi. Their protocols are simpler and applicable on a wide range of devices; however, their low-bandwidth variants provide only 20 bits of additional security from a PIN or a low-resolution QR code, and the mid-bandwidth and the full-bandwidth versions require a complex setup with either a webcam, Bluetooth, or WiFi channel controlled by the client.

While the above schemes are those closely related to ours, a number of other schemes concern *transaction* authentication via untrusted devices, such as the ones of Clarke et al. [14], Wu et al. [46], Parno et al.'s PHOOLPROOF [35], Starnberger et al.'s QR-TAN [41], Mannan and van Oorschot's MP-AUTH [29, 30], and Czeskis et al.'s PHONEAUTH [16]. Altogether, however, we are unaware of any phone-based authentication scheme that improves deployability for service providers via outsourcing while incorporating user privacy.

3   The PASSPHONE: Authentication Scheme

This section introduces our authentication scheme. We overview the three parties involved, the devices at their disposal, and how they interact within protocols for bootstrapping and authentication. For completeness, we also introduce protocols for key management.

Parties and their Devices. Our scheme involves the following parties:

- P A prover who wants to use a service provided by S.
- S A service provider, who wants to authenticate P.
- T A trusted third party of prover P and service provider S.

The prover is a human, while the service provider and the trusted third party host server-side services. The prover uses the following means to interact with these services:

- PS The prover's browser to access a service of S.
- PT The prover's phone to authenticate with T.
- PM The prover's mail box.

We assume that servers and the prover's devices have computational power at least comparable to that of current commercial off-the-shelf computer hardware and that they can communicate with each other via the Internet. The prover has all her devices under her full control (i.e., they are not compromised).

3.1 Bootstrapping

To get started, a prover P completes two bootstrapping steps: registration with the trusted third party T, and activation of our authentication scheme at her service provider S.

Registration Protocol. For registration, P installs an authentication App PT on her phone (authenticator, for short). The App may be shipped by T and is ideally available open source. When P launches PT for the first time, PT generates a new key pair (K_{PT}^p, K_{PT}^s), asks for P's mail address ID_{PM}, and then initiates the registration protocol. Table 1 lists the protocol's communication steps; each step is denoted as:

$$(<\text{step}>) <\text{sender}> \rightarrow <\text{receiver}> : <\text{message}>,$$

where a message is optionally encrypted and consists of a header, a payload, and an optional signature:

$$<\text{message}> ::= E_K((<\text{header}>, <\text{payload}>)_{<\text{signature}>}),$$

where E_K denotes an encryption scheme with key K. The <header> contains a domain identifier, step number, protocol version, and sender identifier:

$$<\text{header}> ::= [<\text{domain}>, <\text{step}>, <\text{version}>, <\text{sender}>].$$

In Step (1) of the registration protocol, the authenticator chooses uniformly at random a nonce N_{PT} and derives the hash value $h_{PT} = H(N_{PT})$. Prior, it

Table 1. Protocol to register with the trusted third party.

Protocol 1:	Registration of P at T
Parties:	PT, PM, and T
Pre-conditions:	PT is blank, T is ignorant of PT
Post-conditions:	PT stores (K_{PT}^p, K_{PT}^s) and obtained ID_{PT}, P received tickets for rekeying and key transfer, T verified ID_{PM} and stores $(ID_{PT}, K_{PT}^p, ID_{PM})$

$$
\begin{aligned}
&(1)\ PT \rightarrow\ \ T : \text{TLS}(([\text{REG},1,\text{v},0],\ K_{PT}^p,\ ID_{PM},\ h_{PT})_{PT}) \\
&(2)\ PM \leftarrow\ \ T :\qquad \underbrace{([\text{REG},2,\text{v},ID_T],\ N_T)_T}_{X} \\
&(3)\ PM \rightarrow PT:\qquad X \\
&(4)\ PT \rightarrow\ \ T : \text{TLS}(([\text{REG},3,\text{v},0],\ X)_{PT}) \\
&(5)\ PT \leftarrow\ \ T : \text{TLS}(([\text{REG},4,\text{v},ID_T],\ N_T')_T) \\
&(6)\ PT \rightarrow PM: \text{TLS}(([\text{REKEY},1,\text{v},ID_{PT}],N_{PT},N_T',K_{PT}^p)_{PT})
\end{aligned}
$$

generates a key pair with a secret part K_{PT}^s and a public part K_{PT}^p; the public part, together with ID_{PM} and h_{PT}, is signed by PT and sent to the trusted third party T. Since the identifier ID_{PT} has not been verified by T, yet, we reserve the zero byte value as sender identifier. To verify the prover's mail box PM, the trusted third party sends a signed challenge containing a nonce N_T in Step (2). The prover forwards this message X to her authenticator in Step (3), which responds to the challenge by signing X and sending it back to T in Step (4). After successful verification, the trusted third party generates a new unique nonce N_T', generates $ID_{PT} = H(N_T', h_{PT})$, and sends N_T' to PT in Step (5), which henceforth uses ID_{PT} to identify itself. PT completes the bootstrapping protocol by sending an encrypted key-management ticket for rekeying to its mail account in Step (6). The prover keeps the ticket secret for later recovery of her account. Since T is not aware of N_{PT}, it cannot regenerate the tickets nor be compelled to do so, e.g., by law enforcement.

Activation Protocol. To activate our scheme, the prover P creates an account at S using PS. S initiates the activation protocol shown in Table 2, the purpose of which is to verify that P is capable of authenticating via T, and to learn the blinded identifier h_{PT} of PT.

In Step (1) of the activation protocol, S sends a nonce N_S. Next, PS computes the hash $h_S = H(ID_S \| N_S)$ to hide the identity of S from T. In Step (2), PS sends h_S to T. Note that for messages from PS, we use a constant 1 that is identical for all users. In Step (3), T responds with a signed challenge, consisting of the nonce N_T along with the blinded identifier h_S. In Step (4), PS forwards the entire previous message X to PT along with ID_S and N_S. PT checks the message, and in particular if h_S found in X fulfills $h_S = H(ID_S \| N_S)$. Meanwhile, the prover has to confirm manually that she wants to sign up for the service provider S. In that case, PT responds to T's challenge by sending a copy of the

Table 2. Protocol to activate two-factor authentication.

Protocol 2:	Activation of the second factor for P at S
Parties:	PS, PT, S, and T
Pre-conditions:	S is ignorant of PT, T is ignorant of P using S
Post-conditions:	S has verified that P uses h_{PT}, and S stores h_{PT}
	T stores (ID_{PT}, h_{PT}); T is ignorant of P using S

(1) $PS \leftarrow\ S$: $\text{TLS}([\text{ACTIVATE}, 1, \text{v}, ID_S], N_S)$
(2) $PS \rightarrow\ T$: $\text{TLS}([\text{ACTIVATE}, 2, \text{v}, 1], h_S)$
(3) $PS \leftarrow\ T$: $\text{TLS}((\underbrace{[\text{ACTIVATE}, 3, \text{v}, ID_T], h_S, N_T)_T}_{X}))$

(4) $PS \rightarrow PT$: $([\text{ACTIVATE}, 4, \text{v}, 1], X, N_S, ID_S)$
(5) $PT \rightarrow\ T$: $\text{TLS}(([\text{ACTIVATE}, 5, \text{v}, ID_{PT}], X)_{PT})$
(6) $PS \leftarrow\ T$: $\text{TLS}((\underbrace{[\text{ACTIVATE}, 6, \text{v}, ID_T], h_{PT}, h_S)_T}_{Y})$

(7) $PS \rightarrow\ S$: $\text{TLS}([\text{ACTIVATE}, 7, \text{v}, 1], Y)$

message X in Step (5). After verification, in Step (6), the trusted third party computes $h_{PT} = H(ID_{PT} \| N_T)$ to blind the prover's identity, ID_{PT}, and sends a signed authentication ticket to PS which consists of the blinded identifiers h_{PT} and h_S. Henceforth, the trusted third party maps h_{PT} to ID_{PT}. In Step (7), PS forwards the ticket to S. Finally, if the ticket is valid, S assigns h_{PT} to the prover's user account and activates our authentication scheme.

This protocol ensures the privacy properties of our authentication scheme by two means: first, the identifier ID_S of the service provider is blinded to obtain h_S, so that the trusted third party cannot figure out which service provider the prover uses. Second, the trusted third party blinds ID_{PT} to obtain a provider-specific identifier h_{PT}. This way, colluding service providers cannot identify shared users by comparing authenticator identifiers.

3.2 Authentication

A prover P authenticates herself at her service provider S, e.g., when signing in for a new session. Here, the second factor is checked using the authentication protocol shown in Table 3. While all other protocols of our scheme are invoked only occasionally, this protocol is run on a regular basis.

S initiates the authentication protocol. This protocol is designed similar to the aforementioned activation protocol, with the difference that the prover's provider-specific identifier h_{PT} is carried through all steps. In Step (1), the service provider sends a session nonce N_S to ensure freshness along with h_{PT} to PS. In Step (2), PS blinds the service provider's identifier by computing $h_S = H(ID_S \| N_S)$, and sends it together with h_{PT} to T. In Step (3), T responds with a signed challenge containing N_T, h_{PT}, and h_S. PS forwards the entire previous message X along with ID_S and N_S to PT in Step (4), which verifies the incoming message. The prover then is asked to confirm that she wants

Table 3. Protocol to authenticate the second factor.

Protocol 3:	Authentication of P at S
Parties:	PS, PT, S, and T
Pre-conditions:	S is ignorant of P using PS
Post-conditions:	S has verified that P uses PS

(1) $PS \leftarrow S$: $\text{TLS}([\text{AUTH},1,\text{v},ID_S], h_{PT}, N_S)$

(2) $PS \rightarrow T$: $\text{TLS}([\text{AUTH},2,\text{v},1], h_{PT}, h_S)$

(3) $PS \leftarrow T$: $\text{TLS}(\underbrace{([\text{AUTH},3,\text{v},ID_T], h_{PT}, h_S, N_T)_T}_{X})$

(4) $PS \rightarrow PT$: $([\text{AUTH},4,\text{v},1], X, N_S, ID_S)$

(5) $PT \rightarrow T$: $\text{TLS}(([\text{AUTH},5,\text{v},ID_{PT}], X)_{PT})$

(6) $PS \leftarrow T$: $\text{TLS}(\underbrace{([\text{AUTH},6,\text{v},ID_T], h_{PT}, h_S)_T}_{Y})$

(7) $PS \rightarrow S$: $\text{TLS}([\text{AUTH},7,\text{v},1], Y)$

to authenticate herself at the service provider S. In the affirmative, PT responds to T's challenge by sending a signed copy of the message X in Step (5). After successful verification, in Step (6), T sends a signed authentication ticket consisting of h_{PT} and h_S to PS, which forwards it to the service provider S in Step (7). Finally, if the ticket is valid, S grants P access to her service.

Again, the trusted third party never obtains information about the service provider's identity. Each time the prover logs into her service provider, the provider's identifier is blinded using a fresh nonce. Thus, from the perspective of the trusted third party, every run of the authentication protocol is unique.

3.3 Key Management

The prover's private key is stored on her phone. Losing it locks her out of service providers where she activated our authentication scheme, whereas the lost authenticator may still be used by an adversary to gain access to the prover's accounts. To react in case of such an emergency, corresponding protocols for key revocation and rekeying are provided, which are concerned in the following.

Key-revocation Protocol. As an immediate reaction upon the loss of her authenticator, the prover turns to her service provider and logs in with her first factor. When the service provider initiates the authentication protocol, its first three steps are executed automatically. In Step (4), however, instead of proceeding, the prover initiates the key-revocation protocol shown in Table 4(top). In this case, PS sends a revocation request to T, including the previous message X, and then cancels the login attempt at S. Meanwhile, T revokes the prover's public key if the signature of the revocation request could be verified with the prover's old key. Finally, a confirmation mail is sent to the prover's mail box PM.

Rekeying Protocol. To regain control of her accounts after key revocation, the prover uses a rekeying ticket that was generated during registration (see Table 1,

Table 4. Protocols for key revocation and rekeying.

Protocol 4:	Key revocation via PS

Parties: PS, PM, S, and T
Pre-conditions: T considers K_{PT}^p active; T is ignorant of P using S
Post-conditions: T has revoked K_{PT}^p; T is ignorant of P using S

Steps 1-3 of Protocol 3, the authentication protocol.
(4) $PS \to T$: TLS([REVOKE,1,v,1], X)
(5) $PS \to S$: TLS(Cancel login)
(6) $PM \leftarrow T$: ([REVOKE,2,v,ID_T], $X)_T$

Protocol 5:	Rekeying for PT

Parties: P, PT, PM, and T
Pre-conditions: PT may be blank
Post-conditions: T revoked K_{PT}^p and stores $(ID'_{PT}, K_{PT}^{'p}, ID_{PM})$
P received new tickets for rekeying and key transfer

(1) $P \to PT$: $\underbrace{([REKEY,1,v,ID_{PT}], N_{PT}, N_T, K_{PT}^p)_{PT}}_{X}$
(2) $PT \to T$: TLS(([REKEY,2,v,0], $K_{PT}^{'p}$, h'_{PT}, $X)_{PT}$)
(3) $PT \leftarrow T$: TLS(([REKEY,3,v,ID_T], $N'_T)_T$)
(4) $PT \to PM$: TLS(([REKEY,1,v,ID'_{PT}], $N'_{PT}, N'_T, K_{PT}^{'p})_{PT}$)

Step (6)). Using this ticket, the prover initiates the rekeying protocol shown in Table 4(bottom) to exchange her revoked public key with a new one at the trusted third party. To do so, the prover orders a new, blank authenticator PT from T and forwards the rekeying ticket to PT in Step (1). PT checks the ticket's validity by verifying that $ID_{PT} = H(N_T \| H(N_{PT}))$ and then generates a new key pair $(K_{PT}^{'s}, K_{PT}^{'p})$. PT samples a new nonce N'_{PT} at random and computes $h'_{PT} = H(N'_{PT})$. In Step (2), the new public key $K_{PT}^{'p}$ is sent along with the ticket and h'_{PT} to T. The message is signed using the new secret key $K_{PT}^{'s}$. From the ticket, T extracts ID_{PT}, and verifies if $ID_{PT} = H(N_T\|H(N_{PT}))$ holds and if ID_{PT} corresponds to K_{PT}^p in T's database. If successful, T registers $K_{PT}^{'p}$ as P's new public key and generates a new unique identifier $ID'_{PT} = H(N'_T\|h'_{PT})$, using a fresh nonce N'_T. In Step (3), N'_T is sent to PT, which also computes ID'_{PT} and uses it as its new identifier. Rekeying is completed by sending a new rekeying ticket to the prover's mail box PM in Step (4).

Altogether, from a prover's perspective, the infrequently invoked key-management protocols provide for a consistent experience since manual actions (i.e., passing challenges to the authenticator) are unified with those of registration and authentication.

4 Formal Security Analysis

This section summarizes the results of an in-depth analysis of the security and privacy of the PASSPHONE scheme when employed as second factor in a two-factor-authentication setup. Due to space limitations, we omit the proofs to our theorems in this section and provide them in the full version of this paper [36].

4.1   Authentication-Attack Resistance

Notation. The quality of an adversary $\mathcal{A}$ against a security notion sec is measured by its success probability $\Pr[\mathsf{Succ}_{\mathsf{sec}}]$ in winning a game $\mathcal{G}_{\mathsf{sec}}$ that models sec. Let $x \leftarrow \mathcal{X}$ denote the sampling of x uniformly at random from a distribution $\mathcal{X}$ and let $\{0,1\}^n$ denote the set of all n-bit strings. We consider a set of provers $\mathcal{P}$ and a set of service providers $\mathcal{S}$, where we define that each prover $P^i \in \mathcal{P}$ has a browser instance PS^i and her authenticator PT^i under her control. The set $\mathcal{U}$ denotes the union of $\mathcal{P} \cup \mathcal{S} \cup \{T\}$.

Assumptions. We follow the standard assumption that legitimate parties (provers and service providers in our case) behave *honestly*: they do not understand the semantics of a message before a protocol run completed successfully. We assume that provers, service providers, and the trusted third party communicate over the open Internet, relying on the existing Public-Key Infrastructure (PKI) of TLS for establishing a secure channel with one-sided authentication of S and T towards the prover (PS, PT). This means, we assume that all service providers S and the trusted third party T possess a public key encoded in a valid TLS certificate. The PKI trust assumption is a current best practice for securing the communication between web services and their users. Further, our cryptographic model assumes that the client PS does not manage any permanent state, which is reasonable for a web browser, and that PS executes a correct version of the protocols (e.g., code that was signed by T).

We recommend that all honest parties employ certificate or public-key pinning for the trusted third party and for service providers (i.e., mapping the hosts to their expected X.509 certificate or public key by explicit whitelisting). Moreover, we propose to bind TLS connections to specific channels by employing a fixed version of either the *tls-unique* approach from RFC 5929 [2] or Google's *Channel ID* [6] (see [8,9,25] for attacks and fixes).

Adversarial Model. The goal of the probabilistic polynomial-time (PPT) adversary $\mathcal{A}$ is to authenticate as some honest prover P^i at some honest service provider S^j. $\mathcal{A}$ is aware of the behavioral limitations of honest parties and tries to exploit them. The adversary can eavesdrop, intercept, insert, modify, or delete all communication that is transmitted over the network, but cannot modify the communication transmitted from the prover's browser to her authenticator, which is a fair assumption when using, e.g., scanned QR codes. $\mathcal{A}$ can impersonate a prover, a service provider, or both. The use of TLS prevents it from acting as T or as an honest S in the view of the prover. Moreover, we assume that the cryptographic primitives used are secure. So, $\mathcal{A}$ cannot recover a secret key, predict a random value, find a hash-value's preimage, a collision, or forge a signature with significant advantage. Prior to registration and activation, all parties agree on a security parameter τ,[1] so that all signatures are of length at least τ bits, all nonces and hash values created by H have 2τ bits, and all symmetric and asymmetric secret keys for encryption (again, for TLS) and signing have an effective key length of at least τ bits.

We define an authentication game denoted $\mathcal{G}^{Auth}$, which takes as input a tuple $(\tau, q_{exe}, q_{send}, q_{test})$, and provides $\mathcal{A}$ with access to the following queries:

- Setup(1^τ): The registration and activation steps are executed once to generate the secrets of all involved parties.
- Execute(P^i, S^j, T): Models a *passive* adversary $\mathcal{A}$ who eavesdrops a correct execution of the authentication protocol between a prover P^i, a service provider S^j, and T. The output is given by the transcript of the protocol between P^i, S^j, and T.
- Send(U, U', m): Models an *active* attack, wherein the adversary $\mathcal{A}$ intercepts, modifies, replays, forwards, or creates a message m in the name of party U to party U', where $U, U' \in \mathcal{U}$. The output of such a query is the message that U' would generate after receiving m. A special message Start can be sent in the name of a prover to a service provider to initiate a session between them with the trusted third party.
- Corrupt(P^i, S^j): Models that the secret for the first factor $pwd^{i,j}$ of P^i at S^j has been compromised. The output of this query is $pwd^{i,j}$.
- Test(P^i, S^j): Models an authentication request of $\mathcal{A}$ in the name of P^i at service provider S^j. The output is a bit b, which is 1 if and only if the authentication succeeds and P^i and S^j are honest; otherwise b is 0.

For all inputs, the output bit b of Test(P^i, S^j) after a correct execution of the authentication protocol between honest P^i and S^j will always be 1. We define that any honest party immediately aborts a protocol run if it detects an invalid message, i.e., an incorrect signature, unexpected service provider, incorrect ID, non-matching hash, or invalid message format.

Theorem 1. *Let the employed public-key signature scheme be EUF-CMA-secure and H be a random oracle. Then, for any PPT adversary $\mathcal{A}$ whose run time is bounded by t and whose number of execute, send, and test queries are bounded by q_{exe}, q_{send} and q_{test}, respectively, it holds for a random execution of $\mathcal{G}^{Auth}$ on our protocol $\mathbb{P}$ that $\Pr[Succ_{Auth}] \leq q \cdot 4/2^\tau$, where $q = q_{exe} + q_{send} + q_{test}$.*

4.2 Anonymity

In the context of an outsourced three-party protocol, user anonymity refers to the goal that an honest but curious trusted third party is unable to learn which service provider(s) an individual prover has registered with and wants to authenticate to. We model this goal by a game $\mathcal{G}^{Anon}$ and an adversary $\mathcal{A}$ who plays the role of T, i.e., $\mathcal{A}$ has access to IDs, public keys, and blinded IDs $\langle ID^i_{PT}, K^p_{PT^i}, \langle h^j_{PT^i} \rangle \rangle$ of all provers P^i. We define that at least one honest prover

---

[1] In practice, $\tau \geq 128$ is fixed a-priori by the protocol (version).

P and two honest service providers S^0 and S^1 exist in the game. At setup, the challenger tosses a fair coin to obtain a bit b. Depending on b, P registers with S^b, and generates a secret pwd for the first factor. We define a special service provider $\widehat{S}$ which wraps S^0 and S^1 and appears as a black box to $\mathcal{A}$. So, every time S^0 or S^1 are involved in an execution of our protocols, the game models it as an execution with $\widehat{S}$ in the view of $\mathcal{A}$.

$\mathcal{A}$ is given access to the queries $\mathsf{Setup}(1^\tau)$, $\mathsf{Execute}(\pi, P^i, S^j, T)$, $\mathsf{Send}(\pi, U, U', m)$, which work similarly to their equivalents in the authentication game above. As a difference, $\mathcal{A}$ must provide a parameter $\pi \in \{$REG, ACTIVATE, AUTH, REKEY, REVOKE$\}$ to execute the different protocols. $\mathcal{A}$ is not given access to $\mathsf{Corrupt}$ queries, assuming an honest but curious adversary. Wlog., we assume that $\mathcal{A}$ asks no Send queries to T since it can always answer them without interaction from other parties with the help of T's private key. Moreover, we define that $\mathcal{A}$ is prohibited from using S^0 or S^1 in its send or execute queries, and may only use $\widehat{S}$ instead. At the end of the game, $\mathcal{A}$ makes a $\mathsf{Test}(b')$ query, to which it must provide a bit b'. $\mathcal{A}$ wins the game $\mathcal{G}^{\mathsf{Anon}}$ if and only if $b' = b$, i.e., if it successfully guesses which service provider P has registered with. We denote this event by $\mathsf{Succ_{Anon}}$ and define the anonymity advantage of $\mathcal{A}$ against a protocol scheme $\mathbb{P}$ as

$$\mathbf{Adv}_{\mathbb{P}}^{\mathsf{Anon}}(\mathcal{A}) = 2 \cdot |\Pr[\mathsf{Succ_{Anon}}] - 0.5|.$$

Theorem 2 (Anonymity). *Let the employed public-key signature scheme be EUF-CMA-secure and H be a random oracle. Then, for any PPT adversary $\mathcal{A}$ whose run time is bounded by t and which asks at most q_{exe} execute and q_{send} send queries, respectively, it holds for a random execution of $\mathcal{G}^{\mathsf{Anon}}$ on our protocol $\mathbb{P}$:*

$$Adv_{\mathbb{P}}^{\mathsf{Anon}}(\mathcal{A}) \leq (q_{exe} + q_{send}) \cdot 1/2^{2\tau}.$$

4.3 Unlinkability

For authenticated key-exchange schemes, Tsudik and Xu [42] define unlinkability as the property that no adversary $\mathcal{A}$ can associate two handshakes involving the same honest party even if $\mathcal{A}$ participated in both executions. In the context of web authentication, unlinkability means that no set of colluding service providers is able to link a prover registered with multiple of their services. Clearly, there must be at least two uncorrupted users to prevent the adversary from deducing trivially which two executions involve the same party.

We define a third game $\mathcal{G}^{\mathsf{Unlink}}$ wherein $\mathcal{A}$ plays the role of two disjoint service providers S^0 and S^1. The challenger plays the role of two honest provers P^0 and P^1 and T. At the beginning, the challenger tosses a fair coin to obtain a bit b; if $b = 1$, the challenger registers P^0 with both S^0 and S^1, and P^1 with none of them. If $b = 0$, the challenger registers P^0 with S^0 but not with S^1, and P^1 with S^1 but not with S^0. Likewise to the anonymity game, we define a special prover $\widehat{P}$ which wraps P^0 and P^1 and appears as a black box to $\mathcal{A}$. So, every time P^0 or P^1 is involved in an execution of a protocol, the game models this as an execution with $\widehat{P}$ instead of P^0 or P^1 in the view of $\mathcal{A}$. As before, this configuration can be augmented by many more honest provers and service providers. Additionally, $\mathcal{A}$ can control a set of malicious provers $\mathcal{E}_P$ as well as malicious service providers $\mathcal{E}_S$.

$\mathcal{A}$ is given access to queries of the types $\mathsf{Setup}(1^\tau)$, $\mathsf{Execute}(\pi, P^i, S^j, T)$, and $\mathsf{Send}(\pi, U, U', m)$, for parties $U, U' \in \mathcal{U}$, which work similar to their equivalents in the anonymity game above. This time, $\mathcal{A}$ is prohibited from using P^0 or P^1 in its queries, and must use $\widehat{P}$ as a replacement. When $\mathcal{A}$ uses $\widehat{P}$ and either of S^0 and S^1 in an execute or send query, the challenger uses the prover as a replacement for $\widehat{P}$ that can process the execution of the protocol correctly. Moreover, if $\mathcal{A}$ invokes the registration, activation, rekeying, or revocation protocol for $\widehat{P}$, the challenger executes it for both P^0 and P^1. At the end of the game, $\mathcal{A}$ makes a $\mathsf{Test}(b')$ query and has to provide the bit b'. $\mathcal{A}$ wins the game $\mathcal{G}^{\mathsf{Unlink}}$ if and only if $b' = b$. We denote this event by $\mathsf{Succ}_{\mathsf{Unlink}}$ and define the unlinkability advantage of an adversary $\mathcal{A}$ against a protocol scheme $\mathbb{P}$ as

$$\mathbf{Adv}_{\mathbb{P}}^{\mathsf{Unlink}}(\mathcal{A}) = 2 \cdot |\Pr[\mathsf{Succ}_{\mathsf{Unlink}}] - 0.5|.$$

Theorem 3 (Unlinkability). *Let the employed public-key signature scheme be EUF-CMA-secure and H be a random oracle. Then, for any PPT adversary $\mathcal{A}$ whose run time is bounded by t and which asks at most q_{exe} execute and q_{send} send queries, it holds for a random execution of $\mathcal{G}^{\mathsf{Unlink}}$ on our protocol $\mathbb{P}$:*

$$\mathbf{Adv}_{\mathbb{P}}^{\mathsf{Unlink}}(\mathcal{A}) \leq (q_{exe} + q_{send}) \cdot 1/2^{2\tau}.$$

5   Automatic Security Analysis

Besides the formal security analysis, we also conducted an automatic security analysis of PASSPHONE using the well-known computer-aided proof system AVISPA. After a brief overview of AVISPA's capabilities, we describe the HLPSL implementations of our protocols and the results obtained from feeding them to AVISPA. Moreover, we conduct experiments by deliberately removing security features from our protocols and observing the results from the proof system.

Background. AVISPA provides four backends for protocol verification: a Constraint-Logic-based ATtack SEarcher (CL-ATSE) [43], an On-the-Fly Model Checker (OFMC) [7], a SAT-based Model Checker (SAT-MC) [5], and a Tree-Automata-based backend (TA4SP) [10]. We rely on the widespread CL-ATSE, OFMC, and SAT-MC backends; TA4SP does not support our setup. As input to AVISPA, protocols must be implemented in the High-Level Protocol Specification Language (HLPSL) [13]. HLPSL is a role-centric language well-suited for software engineers and protocol designers.

Implementation Details. All of PASSPHONE's protocols have been implemented in HLPSL. The full version of this paper lists the protocol implementations, and the source code is also available via PASSPHONE's web page at http://www.passphone.org. Special care was taken to align the implementation

Table 5. Results from AVISPA when omitting TLS in individual protocols. A • indicates that TLS is mandatory to uphold security, and a ○ that TLS is optional.

Protocol	Communication step						
	(1)	(2)	(3)	(4)	(5)	(6)	(7)
Registration	•	n/a	n/a	•	•	n/a	
Activation	•	•	•	n/a	○	•	•
Authentication	•	•	•	n/a	○	•	•
Key revocation	•	•	•	•	•		
Rekeying	n/a	•	•	n/a			

as closely as possible with the protocol specifications found in this paper so as to ensure that the results obtained from AVISPA allow for drawing conclusions about them. For consistency and where the syntax allowed it, variable names have been chosen to correspond with those used in the formal specification as well. The two communication channels send (SND) and receive (RCV) are defined in terms of the Dolev-Yao model (dy).

Since our protocols make use of TLS, this has to be reflected in our HLPSL implementation. However, at present, neither AVISPA nor HLPSL support modularization of protocol implementations, so that the implementation of the TLS protocol in HLPSL cannot be invoked from ours. When mixing both protocol implementations into one file, this severely affects legibility. Therefore, for simplicity, we model TLS by means of public keys assigned to each party, which ensure both encryption and sender authenticity. This approach is sound and has been applied in several other high-level protocol implementations using TLS.

Experiments and Results. We fed each protocol's HLPSL implementation to AVISPA and found that all of the aforementioned backends report that they cannot identify any attacks. However, since implementations can be erroneous and since there is currently no standardized unit-testing framework for HLPSL protocol implementations, we conduct experiments and sanity checks in order to verify that our implementation meets our expectations from the manual security analysis. First, we changed each protocol's implementation in a deliberate attempt to make it insecure. The flaws introduced include the removal of TLS for data-origin authentication, signatures, and nonces which opened various attack vectors. We then fed the flawed versions to AVISPA in order to check whether it picks up the vulnerabilities. Without fail, AVISPA identified them. This experiment serves to raise confidence both that the authentication scheme comprises little redundancy and that our implementation reflects well our scheme's formal specification. Second, we were particularly interested whether and to what extent TLS is required to secure our protocols. We employ TLS mainly as a means for data-origin authentication, whereas message encryption is optional. Since TLS is the de facto standard in secure web communications, using a different protocol would severely limit the applicability and acceptance of our authentication scheme in practice. We systematically disabled TLS in a given step of a protocol, re-running AVISPA each time to identify potential attacks that result from doing so. Table 5 summarizes the results for each protocol. As expected, turning TLS off allows for man-in-the-middle attacks in most steps that result from missing data-origin authentication.

6   Prototype Implementation

We implemented all of PASSPHONE's protocols as a proof-of-concept prototype, which is freely available at https://www.passphone.org. This section discusses a selection of implementation details.

Trusted Third Party T. The trusted third party is a web service that offers an API used by authenticators and the prover's browser PS. We implemented it as a Java Servlet to share the implementations for message encoding and cryptography between T and that from our current smartphone implementation. To protect the signing key, we recommend the use of a cryptographic module—e.g., according to the FIPS-140 standard [34]—which protects the signing key of the trusted third party from being copied and which would accelerate cryptographic computations for scalability. This would render compromising the trusted third party's key much more difficult compared to keeping it on hard disk.

Service Provider S **and Client** PS. For our prototype, we implemented two service provider stacks: one as a Ruby-based service running on an nginx server with a MySQL database, and a similar second service provider as a Java Servlet. The trusted third party provides plugins for the most widely-used web software stacks (LEMP/LAMP, Ruby on Rails, etc.), authentication libraries, and web applications. However, given the large number of possible configurations, it is difficult to provide a plugin for each one right away. To minimize the development overhead, we divide plugins into a major, canonical part, and a lightweight, stack-specific part. The major components may be deployed into a virtual machine or on a dedicated server to be run next to an existing service. The lightweight plugins offer the stack-specific API to handle our authentication scheme so that the required changes to existing services are minimally invasive.

Authenticator PT. We implemented the prover's mobile authenticator as a smartphone App for Android devices with SDK 16 and above which currently supports more than 96 % of Android smartphones on the market.[2] The widespread distribution of Android smartphones made this design decision straightforward in terms of usability since they are among the few things many people carry with them at all times. We employed the BouncyCastle library[3] for cryptographic primitives, using SHA-256 as hash function and 256-bit EC-DSA as signature scheme, and the ZXing library[4] for handling QR codes.

---

[2] https://developer.android.com/about/dashboards, State of Aug 1, 2016.

[3] http://bouncycastle.org/.

[4] https://github.com/zxing/zxing.

Challenge Encoding and Transmission. We resort to QR codes for encoding challenges to reduce the typing effort for the user [20,39,41,45]. QR codes exploit the physical proximity of the prover's devices by changing the communication medium in a way so that an adversary cannot intercept a transmitted message unless looking over the prover's shoulder. In general, the more coarse-grained a QR code can be made, the more robust it is with regard to legibility in various situations of screens, lighting, and camera quality. In our setup, we keep the messages that are transmitted via QR codes small by the use of EC-DSA instead of, for example, RSA-based signatures. Our tests show that scanning QR codes is a robust channel when employing version-10 codes (which can encode up to 213 bytes) and medium-level error correction (15 % of codewords can be restored).

Performance and Usability. To estimate the performance of our implementation, we evaluate the run times needed for the authentication protocol. We use two dual-core mobile phones with 1.2 GHz (Samsung-Intrinsity Exynos S5PV310) and 1.7 GHz (Qualcomm Snapdragon 400) processors and cameras with resolutions of eight megapixels. We conduct 20 authentication processes. Besides logging in with the first factor, the majority of time was spent to align the QR code, which took trained smartphone users about 3–5 seconds on average, whereas the ZXing library picks up a QR code as soon as it is in view.

In terms of usability, our implementation adopts the current best practices—e. g., scanning of QR codes—employed in phone-based authentication. Since the required user actions do not differ from those of other authentication schemes employed in practice, we omit a detailed discussion of usability. Nevertheless, we have tested and used our implementation on human test subjects. Our prototype has been deployed as an exhibit at a recent open house presentation. On that occasion, laymen from the general public as well as interested colleagues from other universities for a total of 55 people have tried our prototype. We observed that all visitors expressed concern for their own security, and understood the concept and importance of privacy preservation in authentication. All regular smartphone users among our testers had little to no difficulty in following the instructions given by our App, as all of them said they occasionally scan QR codes, and, with little explanation (i.e., within less than three minutes), all interested visitors also managed to perform a test run of the rekeying protocol. Altogether, in terms of usability, our prototype is on par with the state of the art in that it adopts their best practices, but of course a lot has still to be done to achieve maturity.

7   Comparative Evaluation

This section compares PASSPHONE to others from the literature under the framework of Bonneau et al. [11]. Table 6 summarizes the results of comparing our scheme to 10 other smartphone-based two-factor authentication schemes with respect to 25 common features an authentication scheme can offer.[5] The features have been collected by Bonneau et al., and while their names may seem self-explanatory, some of their definitions are intricate. For many features, Bonneau et al. also specify a *quasi*-variant, where an authentication scheme offers a feature with some reservations. In what follows, we discuss PASSPHONE's rating in comparison to that of the others.

Usability. As outlined above, PASSPHONE is on par with previously published schemes in terms of usability since it adopts their best practices (i.e., transmitting QR codes via smartphones has been studied already). Therefore, we consider our scheme *Quasi-Scalable-for-Users* since it reduces the risks of password reuse similar to PHONEAUTH, and *Quasi-Nothing-To-Carry*, based on the assumption that smartphones will continue to spread. Likewise, our scheme is quite *Easy-to-Learn* since scanning QR codes is a daily routine for regular smartphone users. During authentication, the user has to enter only her password as a first factor, which results in *Quasi-Infrequent-Errors*, and which makes it *Quasi-Efficient-to-Use*. More generally, our scheme provides equivalent usability compared to GOOGLE 2-STEP, but performs better than PHOOLPROOF, CRONTO, and TIQR, because it features *Easy-Recovery-From-Loss* based on our extensive key management protocols. Arguably, key management may be added to these schemes, but corresponding research is still missing.

Deployability. Concerning deployability, PASSPHONE outperforms most other solutions. PHONEAUTH and TIQR have the highest ratings with respect to Bonneau et al.'s framework, whereas TIQR is more mature. Our scheme is *Quasi-Accessible* since it is compatible with screen readers on both desktop and mobile. Moreover, it has *Quasi-Negligible-Cost-per-User* since no SMS need to be delivered. Our scheme requires only small changes at service site (i.e., the integration of a plugin), which renders it *Quasi-Server-Compatible*. In this regard, our scheme is comparable to PHOOLPROOF, which has been similarly assessed in [11]. Beyond JavaScript, our scheme has no requirements to the prover's browser, which sets it apart from PHONEAUTH or PHOOLPROOF.

We do not fully agree with the rating of PHONEAUTH provided by its authors regarding *Maturity* as well as *Browser-Compatibility*: currently, the research prototype seems unavailable at any public outlet, and the scheme works only with an experimental version of Google Chrome. Thus, we demoted PHONEAUTH's ratings accordingly, compared to those reported in [16]. Obviously, being a research prototype, our scheme is also not mature, yet.

Security. Concerning security, PASSPHONE is almost on par with the two best-performing schemes PHOOLPROOF and CRONTO, the only difference being that our scheme involves a trusted third party. While resorting to trusted third parties is often avoided in security protocols, we argue that including a trusted third party becomes a lot less detrimental when incorporating user privacy. It

---

[5] Regarding GOOGLE 2-STEP, we adopt the rating from [16] since one of that paper's authors works at Google Security and may have deeper insights into their scheme; regarding the proposals from [39], we consider the mid-bandwidth and the full-bandwidth schemes with a similar security level as ours.

Table 6. Comparison of phone-based two-factor authentication schemes according to the evaluation framework for authentication schemes by Bonneau et al. [11]. The framework considers 25 features an authentication scheme can offer with respect to usability, deployability, and security. Each column names one feature, and each scheme is rated based on whether it offers the feature (•), it quasi offers the feature with reservations (○), or it does not offer the feature (–).

Authentication scheme	Memorywise-Effortless	Scalable-for-Users	Nothing-to-Carry	Physically-Effortless	Easy-to-Learn	Efficient-to-Use	Infrequent-Errors	Easy-Recovery-from-Loss	Accessible	Negligible-Cost-per-User	Server-Compatible	Browser-Compatible	Mature	Non-Proprietary	Res-to-Physical-Observation	Res-to-Targeted-Impersonation	Res-to-Throttled-Guessing	Res-to-Unthrottled-Guessing	Res-to-Internal-Observation	Res-to-Leaks-from-Other-Verifiers	Res-to-Phishing	Res-to-Theft	No-Trusted-Third-Party	Requiring-Explicit-Consent	Unlinkable	#●	#○
CRONTO [15]	–	–	○	–	●	○	○	–	–	○	–	●	●	–	●	●	●	●	●	○	●	●	●	●	●	13	5
FBD-BT-BT/WF-WF [39]	–	○	○	–	●	●	●	–	○	○	–	–	–	●	●	●	●	●	●	●	–	●	●	–	●	13	4
FBD-QR-BT/WF [39]	–	○	○	–	●	●	○	–	○	○	–	–	–	●	●	●	●	●	●	●	–	●	●	●	●	13	5
GOOGLE 2-STEP [22]	–	–	○	–	●	○	○	○	○	–	●	●	●	–	–	○	●	–	–	–	●	●	●	●	●	10	6
MBD-QR-QR [39]	–	○	○	–	○	○	–	–	○	○	–	○	–	●	–	●	●	●	●	●	–	●	–	●	●	9	7
MP-AUTH [30]	–	–	○	–	●	–	○	○	○	○	–	●	●	–	●	–	●	–	–	–	○	–	●	●	–	7	6
PHONEAUTH (opportunistic) [16]	–	○	○	–	●	●	○	–	●	●	●	●	○	○	●	○	○	○	○	○	○	○	●	●	○	9	13
PHOOLPROOF [35]	–	–	○	–	●	○	○	○	○	○	–	●	●	–	●	●	●	●	●	○	●	●	●	–	●	12	7
SOUNDPROOF [26]	–	–	○	–	●	●	○	○	●	●	–	●	–	●	–	●	○	–	●	●	●	●	●	●	–	13	4
TIQR [45]	–	–	○	–	●	○	○	–	○	○	○	●	●	●	○	●	●	–	●	–	○	●	–	●	●	10	8
PASSPHONE (this paper)	–	○	○	–	●	○	○	●	○	○	○	●	–	●	●	●	●	●	–	●	●	●	–	●	●	13	7

is an open question if this consideration merits introducing the feature *Quasi-No-Trusted-Third-Party* into Bonneau et al.'s framework, but we refrained from doing so in our evaluation. In general, our scheme covers all security-related features, but we cannot guarantee *Resilience-to-Internal-Observation*; if an adversary has full control over the prover's device, she might be able to recover the secret key. Our threat model does not cover this case and we leave it for future work. Finally, we would like to point out that our scheme features *Unlinkability* despite the fact that it uses a trusted third party.

For ease of comparison, Column "Summary" in Table 6 gives the counts of features and quasi-features. Altogether, our scheme offers as many full features as the competition despite suffering losses for introducing a trusted third party and for not being mature, yet. This is encouraging since this evaluation demonstrates the potential of our authentication scheme for future research and development as well as for transfer into practice.

8   Practical Application

Choosing the First Factor. Similar to other phone-based two-factor authentication schemes from the literature, PASSPHONE does not aim at replacing the still prevalent password authentication, but at strengthening it in a two-factor setup. The option of outsourcing the verification of the second factor plus the privacy properties of our scheme, however, renders it attractive for small service providers since it enables them to add two-factor authentication with comparably small development overhead to their existing authentication solution. The first factor used in conjunction with our protocols is therefore not at all tied to the use of login and password; for example, it can be based on physical tokens, biometric properties, or another challenge-response protocol. In practice, however, most service providers still employ passwords as a first factor, exchanging passwords over TLS, processing them with a password-hashing function, and storing them at server side as salted password hashes. Nevertheless, PASSPHONE's security does not rest with the first factor employed.

Limitations of Web-based Authentication. Regarding authentication for web services, we concede that privacy-unaware users may still easily be tracked by means not related to our protocol (e.g., by searching for reused mail addresses or credentials). Moreover, users should be aware that their browser and OS configuration is used by many tracking services. Anonymous communication techniques, such as TOR [18], can be combined with PASSPHONE to also provide IP-level anonymity and unlinkability; however, securing the user from all privacy perils is clearly beyond the scope of what a web-based authentication protocol can address. We stress, however, that PASSPHONE does not introduce yet another angle of de-anonymizing users, which is a first in the domain of web authentication.

9 Conclusion

This work introduces PASSPHONE, a new phone-based two-factor authentication scheme, consisting of all protocols necessary for bootstrapping, authentication, and key management. PASSPHONE is designed with a focus on deployability: it allows for easy integration at service providers by outsourcing authentication to a trusted third party. Moreover, it is the first web-based three-party authentication scheme that protects the privacy of its users by minimizing the amount of information shared among the parties involved, hiding the relation of users and service providers from the trusted third party, and rendering users unlinkable among service providers. We analyze PASSPHONE's security, show its privacy properties, and present insights from a proof-of-concept implementation. Under the authentication scheme evaluation framework of Bonneau et al., our scheme competes with the best-performing ones from the literature. In conclusion, with the success of outsourcing first-factor authentication, also outsourcing the second-factor authentication in a two-factor setup is reasonable, albeit, ideally using different trusted third parties for each factor to spread risks. We hope that PASSPHONE's privacy properties will inspire more privacy-awareness in future protocol designs.

Acknowledgments. The authors thank Anne Barsuhn, Thomas Dressel, Paul Christoph Götze, André Karge, Tom Kohlberg, Kevin Lang, Christopher Lübbemeier, Kai Gerrit Lünsdorf, Nicolai Ruckel, Sascha Schmidt, and Clement Welsch for implementing the first prototype within student projects. Our special thanks go to Thomas Dressel and André Karge for their pursuing work, and to Benno Stein and the anonymous reviewers for valuable comments and suggestions.

References

1. Aloul, F.A., Zahidi, S., El-Hajj, W.: Two factor authentication using mobile phones. In: IEEE AICCSA, pp. 641–644 (2009)
2. Altman, J., Williams, N., Zhu, L.: Channel bindings for TLS. RFC 5929 (2010)
3. Apple. Two-factor authentication for Apple ID (2016). https://support.apple.com/en-us/HT204915
4. Armando, A., et al.: The AVISPA tool for the automated validation of internet security protocols and applications. In: Etessami, K., Rajamani, S.K. (eds.) CAV 2005. LNCS, vol. 3576, pp. 281–285. Springer, Heidelberg (2005). doi:10.1007/11513988_27
5. Armando, A., Compagna, L., Ganty, P.: SAT-based model-checking of security protocols using planning graph analysis. In: Araki, K., Gnesi, S., Mandrioli, D. (eds.) FME 2003. LNCS, vol. 2805, pp. 875–893. Springer, Heidelberg (2003). doi:10.1007/978-3-540-45236-2_47
6. Balfanz, D., Hamilton, R.: Transport layer security (TLS) channel IDs, 8 Nov 2013. IETF Internet Draft v01, expired 12 May 2013
7. Basin, D., Mödersheim, S., Viganò, L.: An on-the-fly model-checker for security protocol analysis. In: Snekkenes, E., Gollmann, D. (eds.) ESORICS 2003. LNCS, vol. 2808, pp. 253–270. Springer, Heidelberg (2003). doi:10.1007/978-3-540-39650-5_15
8. Bhargavan, K., Delignat-Lavaud, A., Fournet, C., Pironti, A., Strub, P.: Triple handshakes and cookie cutters: breaking and fixing authentication over TLS. In: IEEE S&P, pp. 98–113 (2014)
9. Bhargavan, K., Delignat-Lavaud, A., Pironti, A.: Verified contributive channel bindings for compound authentication. In: NDSS. The Internet Society (2015)
10. Boichut, Y., Héam, P.-C., Kouchnarenko, O.: Automatic verification of security protocols using approximations. Technical report INRIA-Lorraine - CASSIS Project (2005)
11. Bonneau, J., Herley, C., van Oorschot, P.C., Stajano, F.: The quest to replace passwords: a framework for comparative evaluation of web authentication schemes. In: IEEE S&P, pp. 553–567 (2012)
12. Bonneau, J., Preibusch, S.: The password thicket: technical and market failures in human authentication on the web. In: WEIS (2010)
13. Chevalier, Y., Compagna, L., Cuellar, J., Hankes Drielsma, P., Mantovani, J., Moedersheim, S., Vigneron, L.: A high level protocol specification language for industrial security-sensitive protocols. In: SAPS, p. 13 (2004)
14. Clarke, D., Gassend, B., Kotwal, T., Burnside, M., Dijk, M., Devadas, S., Rivest, R.: The Untrusted Computer Problem and Camera-Based Authentication. In: Mattern, F., Naghshineh, M. (eds.) Pervasive 2002. LNCS, vol. 2414, pp. 114–124. Springer, Heidelberg (2002). doi:10.1007/3-540-45866-2_10
15. Cronto Limited. Cronto. http://www.cronto.com/

16. Czeskis, A., Dietz, M., Kohno, T., Wallach, D.S., Balfanz, D.: Strengthening user authentication through opportunistic cryptographic identity assertions. In: CCS, pp. 404–414 (2012)
17. Dey, A., Weis, S.: PseudoID: enhancing privacy in federated login. In: PETS, pp. 95–107 (2010)
18. Dingledine, R., Mathewson, N., Syverson, P.F.: Tor: the second-generation onion router. In: USENIX, pp. 303–320 (2004)
19. Dodson, B., Sengupta, D., Boneh, D., Lam, M.S.: Secure, consumer-friendly web authentication and payments with a phone. In: Gris, M., Yang, G. (eds.) Mobi-CASE 2010. LNICSSITE, vol. 76, pp. 17–38. Springer, Heidelberg (2012). doi:10.1007/978-3-642-29336-8_2
20. Dodson, B., Sengupta, D., Boneh, D., Lam, M.: Snap2Pass: consumer-friendly challenge-response authentication with a phone (2010). http://prpl.stanford.edu/papers/soups10j.pdf
21. Gemalto. Findings from the 2014 Breach Level Index. http://breachlevelindex.com/pdf/Breach-Level-Index-Annual-Report-2014.pdf
22. Google. 2-step Authentication (2013). http://www.google.com/landing/2step/
23. Hallsteinsen, S., Jorstad, I., Thanh, D.: Using the mobile phone as a security token for unified authentication. In: ICSNC, p. 68 (2007)
24. Hardt, D.: The OAuth 2.0 authorization framework. RFC 6749 (2012)
25. Karapanos, N., Capkun, S.: On the effective prevention of TLS man-in-the-middle attacks in web applications. In: USENIX, pp. 671–686 (2014)
26. Karapanos, N., Marforio, C., Soriente, C., Capkun, S.: Sound-proof: usable two-factor authentication based on ambient sound. In: USENIX, pp. 483–498 (2015)
27. Lord, B.: Keeping our users secure (2013). https://blog.twitter.com/2013/keeping-our-users-secure
28. Lystad, T.: Leaked password lists and dictionaries - the password project (2013). http://thepasswordproject.com/leaked_password_lists_and_dictionaries
29. Mannan, M., Oorschot, P.C.: Using a personal device to strengthen password authentication from an untrusted computer. In: Dietrich, S., Dhamija, R. (eds.) FC 2007. LNCS, vol. 4886, pp. 88–103. Springer, Heidelberg (2007). doi:10.1007/978-3-540-77366-5_11
30. Mannan, M., van Oorschot, P.: Leveraging personal devices for stronger password authentication from untrusted computers. J. Comput. Secur. **19**(4), 703–750 (2011)
31. Meisner, J.: Microsoft account gets more secure (2013). https://blogs.technet.microsoft.com/microsoft_blog/2013/04/17/microsoft-account-gets-more-secure/
32. Nuñez, D., Agudo, I.: BlindIdM: a privacy-preserving approach for identity management as a service. Int. J. Inf. Secur. **13**(2), 199–215 (2014)
33. Nuñez, D., Agudo, I., Lopez, J.: Integrating OpenID with proxy re-encryption to enhance privacy in cloud-based identity services. In: CloudCom, pp. 241–248 (2012)
34. U.S NIST. Validated FIPS 140–1 and FIPS 140–2 cryptographic modules (2013). http://csrc.nist.gov/groups/STM/cmvp/documents/140-1/140val-all.htm
35. Parno, B., Kuo, C., Perrig, A.: Phoolproof phishing prevention. In: Crescenzo, G., Rubin, A. (eds.) FC 2006. LNCS, vol. 4107, pp. 1–19. Springer, Heidelberg (2006). doi:10.1007/11889663_1
36. Potthast, M., Forler, C., List, E., Lucks, S.: Passphone: outsourcing phone-based web authentication while protecting user privacy. In: Cryptology ePrint Archive (2016, to appear)
37. Recordon, D., Reed, D.: OpenID 2.0: a platform for user-centric identity management. In: Digital Identity Management, pp. 11–16 (2006)

38. Riesch, P.J., Du, X.: Audit based privacy preservation for the OpenID authentication protocol. In: IEEE HST, pp. 348–352 (2012)
39. Shirvanian, M., Jarecki, S., Saxena, N., Nathan, N.: Two-factor authentication resilient to server compromise using mix-bandwidth devices. In: NDSS. The Internet Society (2014)
40. Song, A.: Introducing login approvals (2011). www.facebook.com/notes/facebook-engineering/introducing-login-approvals/10150172618258920/
41. Starnberger, G., Froihofer, L., Göschka, K.M.: QR-TAN: secure mobile transaction authentication. In: IEEE ARES, pp. 578–583 (2009)
42. Tsudik, G., Xu, S.: A flexible framework for secret handshakes. In: Danezis, G., Golle, P. (eds.) PET 2006. LNCS, vol. 4258, pp. 295–315. Springer, Heidelberg (2006). doi:10.1007/11957454_17
43. Turuani, M.: The CL-Atse protocol analyser. In: Pfenning, F. (ed.) RTA 2006. LNCS, vol. 4098, pp. 277–286. Springer, Heidelberg (2006). doi:10.1007/11805618_21
44. Urueña, M., Muñoz, A., Larrabeiti, D.: Analysis of privacy vulnerabilities in single sign-on mechanisms for multimedia websites. Multimedia Tools Appl. 68(1), 159–176 (2014)
45. Van Rijswijk, R., Van Dijk, J.: Tiqr: a novel take on two-factor authentication. In: LISA (2011)
46. Wu, M., Garfinkel, S., Miller, R.: Secure web authentication with mobile phones. In: DIMACS Workshop on Usable Privacy and Security Software (2004)

Secure, Usable and Privacy-Friendly User Authentication from Keystroke Dynamics

Kimmo Halunen[(✉)] and Visa Vallivaara

VTT Technical Research Centre of Finland Ltd., Oulu, Finland
{kimmo.halunen,visa.vallivaara}@vtt.fi

Abstract. User authentication is a key technology in human machine interaction. The need to establish the legitimacy of transactions and possibly the actors behind them is crucial for trustworthy operation of services over the internet. A good authentication method offers security, usability and privacy protections for the users and the service providers. However, achieving all three properties with a single method is a difficult task and such methods are not in wide use today. We combine methods from biometrics, secure key exchange algorithms and privacy-protecting authentication to build an authentication system that achieves these three properties. Our system uses keystroke dynamics to authenticate the user and cryptographic methods to protect the privacy of the templates and samples and to extend the authentication to key exchange. The results show that the system can be used for user authentication, but more work is needed to protect against impersonation in some cases. Our work is extensible to many other biometrics that can be measured and compared in a similar manner as keystroke dynamics and with further research to larger classes of authentication methods.

1 Introduction

User authentication is one of the key technologies in human machine interaction. The services provided in many contexts both locally and over the internet require the user to provide assurance that she is authorised to access the service. To this effect, a good authentication method provides security, usability and privacy protection both for users and the service providers alike.

Generally, user authentication is done via three different types of factors. The most common in web authentication is *something you know*, which is manifested in the ubiquitous passwords that users need to type in order to gain access. The second category of factors is *something you have* such as a key to a lock, a list of one time passwords, a USB token or a mobile phone. These can be used to authenticate the user towards services, usually through a challenge-response system. The third factor is *something you are* such as a biometric, e.g., fingerprint or a facial image. These factors are more common also in the identification of individuals and in authentication between humans.

Different factors and methods of authentication offer different levels of security, usability and privacy protection. A great study of various methods used

© Springer International Publishing AG 2016
B.B. Brumley and J. Röning (Eds.): NordSec 2016, LNCS 10014, pp. 256–268, 2016.
DOI: 10.1007/978-3-319-47560-8_16

in web authentication can be found in [6]. However, no single method can offer the best from all of these categories. Thus, new methods and combinations are needed.

To provide a good level of security, privacy and usability there need to be systems that offer protection in all of these categories. For example, a randomly chosen 16 character password is quite secure and offers good privacy, but it is very hard to use. Thus the usability of such a scheme is rather low, although some progress has been made to help people remember random secrets [7]. On the other hand, many biometrics such as fingerprints and facial recognition systems offer good usability and even security. The privacy protection of such systems is often very poor and the templates can be easily used for surveillance and identification in addition to the original authentication use case.

In this work we present a novel combination of known methods that can achieve good performance in all three categories. By measuring the keystroke dynamics of the user (i.e. timings related to keystrokes), when typing her username, we can use this biometric to authenticate the user. We will then combine this with privacy protection mechanisms from [27] to protect the biometric templates and samples and the protocol from [13] to combine all these into a secure key exchange protocol.

The paper is organised in the following way. In the next section, we present previous work on keystroke dynamics and privacy protecting authentication. In Sect. 3 we describe the methods that we have used to build our authentication system in more detail. In the fourth section we present the results of a user study that we conducted with our system and we end the paper with discussion and conclusions on our work.

2 Previous Work

Keystroke dynamics as a biometric have been researched extensively for many years with earliest results already from the 1980s, e.g., [14]. They can be captured both from regular keyboards, e.g., [19–21] or from mobile devices, e.g., [10, 26]. The measurements are usually related to timings between keypresses and these can be used for fairly accurate authentication results. On the other hand, these can also be used for profiling and identifying users, e.g., [9], which causes privacy considerations. For a more thorough survey on different methods of keystroke dynamics see for example [3].

Privacy-friendly authentication, especially with biometrics, has been a topic of research for some time. Some biometric features can be protected either by specific schemes (many of which have been evaluated in [25]) or more generic constructions such as fuzzy vaults [18] or fuzzy extractors [12]. In these ways, the biometric information is either protected at the template level or only used to generate cryptographic keys, which are then used for authentication. However, the generic methods need to be tailored to suit each specific biometric and measurement type and also contain some limitations of their own. This means that applying these methods is not necessarily straightforward to any given biometric and type of measurement.

Another way to protect the privacy of biometrics is to build a privacy protection system specifically for some biometric, e.g., symmetric hash functions for fingerprints [28]. Keystroke dynamics have not been extensively studied from the privacy preserving authentication point of view. In [22], the authors present a method for using keystroke dynamics on mobile phones and trusted computing technologies to provide some guarantees against privacy invasive attacks. Their attack considers the situation, where the user is profiled by her keystroke patterns by some (web) applications, without the user's consent. Our method protects against this type of attack, because the samples are encrypted before sending them to the application or service provider. Furthermore, our methods also protect the templates that are stored at the server both against breaches to the server by malicious parties and from insider in the server end. This is not covered in the threat model of [22].

From the usability perspective, authentication has also received a lot of scrutiny. Security and usability have been seen as contradictory goals and in many cases this can be validated, although it is not an absolute truth [6,8]. In general, the pinnacle of usability would be that the authentication would not impose any extra interaction between the user and the system. This is captured fairly well in the concept of *implicit authentication* in [17]. This type of authentication is possible with many biometrics such as face, speaker or gait recognition. There are also systems that provide privacy-friendly implicit authentication, such as [27], which we will utilise in our constructions. The work in [27] is concentrated on profiling mobile phone users and protecting templates gathered from these and our work adapts their system to the case of keystroke dynamics.

3   Methods

This section describes our methods for measuring the keystrokes, protecting the templates and securing the authentication. We begin by briefly stating our threat models.

3.1   Threat Model

Because our system is designed for both privacy and security, we have two different goals and threat models. For privacy, we consider an *honest-but-curious* adversary at the server end. This is similar to the adversary of [27]. The adversary is bound to respect the protocol, but may try to learn additional information from the content of the messages and the internal computations that it carries out during authentication.

For security, we have a more powerful adversary as described in [13]. To break the security of the authenticated key exchange, the adversary can read, send and modify messages in transit and, if multiple authentication methods and/or factors are used, learn the secrets from these for any given client. The adversary can also learn the secret key of any given server, i.e., corrupt a server, if mutual authentication between the server and the client is provided. The results of [13] show, that the authenticated key exchange protocol is still secure, if at least one factor or method remains unbroken or not corrupted.

3.2   Measuring Keystrokes

As can be seen from Sect. 2, there are many ways to measure the keystroke dynamics of the user. Our approach started with the work from [1], where four different features were measured from the keystrokes: the entered string of characters and down-down, up-down and down-up times of each keystroke. To simplify our approach, we decided to test whether we could achieve good performance with only some of the timing measurements.

We chose to use the down-up times, up-down times and the entered string of characters in our solution. The entered string of characters is an obvious choice as it prevents the adversary from typing in just any combination of characters with correct timings. However, we do not assume that this string of characters is kept secret and thus it is not just another password. The down-up time measures how long each individual character was held down and up-down time measures how long was the difference from letting go of previous key to pressing down the next one. We did not use down-down times since they aren't independent from the down-up and up-down times.

Furthermore, because the methods from [27] measure the distance of the sampled vector to each of the template vectors, we could not use the averaging of the times in our templates, which was done in [1]. In our templates, each measurement was retained, in order to measure the sample against all these values. This then resulted in slightly larger templates than in the original paper, where averages could be used.

3.3   Protecting Privacy

The privacy protection of the templates was done according to the implicit authentication scheme of [27]. Each of the templates was protected with two methods, each component separately with partially homomorphic encryption and with order-preserving symmetric encryption (OPSE). The partially homomorphic part of the template enabled computing the distance from the average absolute deviation (AAD) of the sample from the template values and the OPSE encrypted part enabled comparisons between the sample and some threshold values, which resulted in the final score that was used for deciding the successfulness of the authentication attempt.

Like in [27], we used Paillier encryption [23] for the homomorphic encryption and the results of Boldyreva et al. from [4,5] for the order-preserving encryption. These are needed to protect the privacy of the templates and samples both in transit between the client and server and also at the server end from the honest-but-curious server itself. The details of the application of these are postponed to Sect. 3.5, where our system is described in more detail.

3.4 Providing Security

The security of our authentication is based on the multi-factor authenticated key exchange (MFAKE) protocol from [13]. The protocol specifies three subprotocols, one for each type of factor (passwords, biometrics and tokens). Each of these can be run in parallel as many times as there are different authentication methods. In our work, we used the keystroke dynamic as the first line of authentication. If the biometric measurement was successful, the authentication proceeded with the key exchange. If it was unsuccessful, the user could enter a password and if it was correct the key exchange proceeded with all the information linked to the key. This is the approach that is suggested also in [27] to be utilised with the implicit authentication scheme. In a real world implementation the system could enhance its performance by learning also from the false negatives (i.e. cases where the implicit authentication fails, but password authentication succeeds). If also the password authentication failed, the authentication was considered completely failed.

The security of the MFAKE protocol is based on tag-based authentication from [16] and this required some changes to the privacy-preserving authentication of [27]. These changes were minor and are discussed in more detail later in this paper. The changes did not affect the security of the MFAKE or the level of privacy protection.

3.5 Our Implementation

We implemented the above system using Python 2.7 with the help of some open source libraries for cryptography: pycrypto[1], paillier[2] and pyope[3]. We used the getch[4] and clock[5] Python functions for the keystroke timing measurements and those gave us $0.44\,\mu s$ precision on the timing.

The first part of the program prompted for the user to provide a username. If this was a new username, the system asked the user to type the username in again for 9 times. This resulted in a total of ten vectors of timings that were combined into a template of the user and the username.

All the measured times were then encrypted with both the homomorphic and order-preserving encryptions and then sent for the server to store as the template for this given username just as in [27]. Naturally, only the measurements from the successful replication of the same username were stored.

The testing part was implemented in a way that the user was requested to type their chosen username and the typing pattern was matched against the template. Two thresholds were chosen from the empirical data to provide approximately 90 % acceptance rate. This test was repeated 10 times for each participant. The scores were computed following the methods presented in [27] as follows.

---

[1] https://www.dlitz.net/software/pycrypto/.
[2] https://github.com/mikeivanov/paillier.
[3] https://github.com/psviderski/pyope.
[4] https://pypi.python.org/pypi/getch.
[5] https://docs.python.org/2/library/time.html.

Let $HE = (KeyGen^{HE}, E^{HE}, D^{HE})$ be a homomorphic encryption scheme, such as Paillier, and $OPSE = (KeyGen^{OPSE}, E^{OPSE}, D^{OPSE})$ be an order preserving symmetric encryption scheme. During system setup $KeyGen^{HE}$ and $KeyGen^{OPSE}$ are used to generate the HE key pair (pk, sk) and the $OPSE$ key k.

The user profile is a pair $U = (DU, UD)$, where $DU = (V_1, \ldots, V_n)$ and $V_i = (v_i(1), \ldots, v_i(10))$, where n is the length of the username and $v_i(j)$ is the time for down-up keystroke for the jth measurement of the ith character in the template. Similarly, $UD = (W_1, \ldots, W_n)$ and $W_i = (w_i(1), \ldots, w_i(10))$ is defined as above, but for up-down timings. The accumulated user profiles contain tuples

$$\left(E_{pk}^{HE}(v_i(j)), E_k^{OPSE}(v_i(j)), E_{pk}^{HE}(w_i(j)), E_k^{OPSE}(w_i(j)) \right)$$

for $j = 1, \ldots, 10$ and $i = 1, \ldots, n$.

The server can precompute the AAD, which will be used in the comparisons between the template and the sample. The AAD from the encrypted values can be computed as follows:

$$E_{pk}^{HE}(AAD(V_i) \times n) = \sum_{i=1}^{n} \left| E_{pk}^{HE}(v_i(j)) - E_{pk}^{HE}(\text{Med}(V_i)) \right|$$

From the above it is straightforward to use the homomorphic properties of HE and remove the scalar factor n by multiplying with n^{-1}. The $\text{Med}(V_i)$ denotes the median of the values in V_i and this can be found by comparing the OPSE encrypted values in the templates. This is done similarly to the values in W_i.

The actual scoring algorithm for authentication proceeds in two stages. First, the samples taken by the client are encrypted into tuples

$$e_i(t) = \left(E_{pk}^{HE}(c_{\text{tag}} \times v_i(t)), E_k^{OPSE}(v_i(t)), E_{pk}^{HE}(c_{\text{tag}} \times w_i(t)), E_k^{OPSE}(w_i(t)) \right)$$

for each variable v_i. We extended the system from [27] by multiplying each of the vector components of the measurement with the tag c_{tag} computed by the client. This was included in the computation of the template to provide tag-based authentication, which is the basis for MFAKE and all its subprotocols. The tags are required in order to guarantee the security of the system in MFAKE by binding all the utilised authentication factors and methods to a single session of the MFAKE protocol. To initialise the MFAKE protocol the client and server perform an unauthenticated Diffie-Hellman key exchange [11]. The tag is the hash value of the original Diffie-Hellman key, the identities of the two communicating parties and all the messages exchanged by that time. We computed the tag using the SHA-256 hash function.

In the server end, the server computes its own tag s_{tag} from its view on the key and the transcript of messages. Then it can compute the inverse of s_{tag} and multiply the vector components with that value to get to the "untagged" values that are used for comparison. This could be done in a similar fashion as with the AAD computation described earlier due to homomorphism $(E_{pk}^{HE}(s_{\text{tag}}^{-1} \times$

$c_{\text{tag}} \times v_i(t))$, which equals $E_{pk}^{HE}(v_i(t))$ if the tags agree). After that, the server computes the end points of the allowable interval for up-down times by

$$E_{pk}^{HE}(b_l^i(t)) = E_{pk}^{HE}(v_i(t)) - E_{pk}^{HE}(AAD(V_i))$$
$$E_{pk}^{HE}(b_h^i(t)) = E_{pk}^{HE}(v_i(t)) + E_{pk}^{HE}(AAD(V_i))$$

and similarly $E_{pk}^{HE}(c_l^i(t))$ and $E_{pk}^{HE}(c_h^i(t))$ for down-up times from the values in W_i.

However, the server does not know how these can be compared with the template values it holds. Thus in the second phase the server delivers the values $E_{pk}^{HE}(b_l^i(t)), E_{pk}^{HE}(b_h^i(t)), E_{pk}^{HE}(c_l^i(t))$ and $E_{pk}^{HE}(c_h^i(t))$ to the client. The client decrypts these getting $b_l^i(t), b_h^i(t), c_l^i(t)$ and $c_h^i(t)$. These are encrypted with E_k^{OPSE} and returned to the server. Now the server can count the number of occurrences in the OPSE encrypted template that fall within the interval defined by these two values. This number is then compared to the given threshold values.

If the matching was within the thresholds, the system would immediately compute the authenticated key with the MFAKE [13] protocol. To this end the client and server combined the transcripts of the message contents that had been sent between them and hashed them with SHA-256 to generate the key. If the username typing pattern was not recognised, the system would prompt for a password. This password was tested through the MFAKE protocol and again the authenticated key exchange would be completed, if a correct password was entered. Otherwise, the authentication failed and a common key was not established between the client and the server.

4   Empirical Results

In the user tests, we tested only the keystroke biometric and left the password authentication part out. Thus, the user taught the system for keystroke dynamics without using the secondary password authentication. This was reasonable, because there is a lot of research on the benefits and weaknesses of password authentication and how users perform with them. Our work would not bring new insights on that front and we decided to focus on the effect of privacy protection on the accuracy of the keystroke dynamics.

We tested our implementation with two groups of volunteers in two different locations. Users were volunteers from academic institutions. The first group had 11 participants and the second 9 participants, making the total number of test subjects 20. We ran the tests on both Windows and Linux operating systems on two different laptops (one for each location).

Each of the subjects chose a username of 8–12 characters. Although in [1] it is stated that less than ten characters is not sufficient for good accuracy, we decided to let the subjects use also shorter usernames that might be more familiar to them. The choice was not restricted in any way and the subjects were free to choose completely new usernames or ones that they used in other systems.

The tests were performed on hardware that was not the same in both locations, but that was available for the authors at the time. Some participants asked to use their own keyboards to better reflect their real typing patterns. We allowed this as our method could be used with any keyboard and a real implementation would be used with wide variety of keyboards. Most of the participants used the keyboard on the laptop.

The testing was divided into two parts with first the learning part and then testing users after a short period of time. This interval varied from 2–7 days due to the schedules of some participants not permitting them to participate at a specific time. The results are further analysed and discussed in Sect. 5.

One third of the subjects chose an 8 character username, probably due to legacy reasons from Unix machines. Others chose longer usernames with 10 and 12 characters being in the second place for popularity. The length of the username did not have any significant impact on the accuracy of the measurements, although the sample sizes are very small for reliable statistical analysis.

4.1   Authentication

In Fig. 1 we can see the scores from the first phase, the learning phase. These scores were used to decide what would be feasible thresholds for authentication. We set our target to 90 % accuracy for the authentication. From the data we computed for down-up time 3.5 as the threshold. For up-down time the threshold

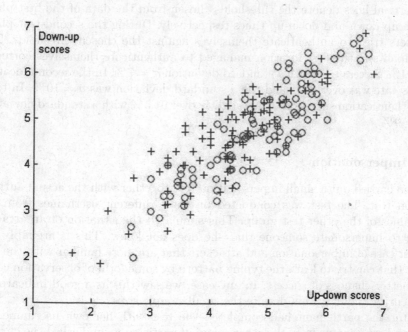

Fig. 1. Scores from the learning phase. Scores from the two different locations are differentiated with crosses and circles.

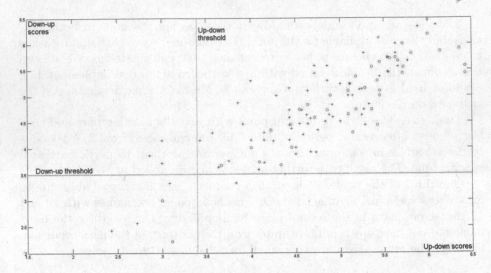

Fig. 2. Scores from the testing phase. Scores from the two different locations are differentiated with crosses and circles. The lines denote the values of the thresholds.

was 3.4 and in order to successfully authenticate the user had to pass both thresholds while typing the correct username.

In Fig. 2 we can see the results from the second phase of tests. The horizontal and vertical lines denote the thresholds chosen from the data of the first phase for the up-down and down-up times respectively. During the second test phase the users tried to authenticate themselves against the chosen thresholds. The participants in the first location managed to authenticate themselves correctly with 91 % success rate with a standard deviation $\sigma = 7\%$. In the second location success rate was over 92 % and the a standard deviation was $\sigma = 10\%$. In total the authentication success rate was slightly over 91.5 % with a standard deviation of $\sigma = 9\%$.

4.2   Impersonation

We also carried out a small impersonation test together with the actual authentication test. The test was conducted on three different usernames from the usernames of the other test group. This simulated the situation of an attacker trying to impersonate someone that she does not know. This is arguably the hardest case of impersonation and attackers that are more familiar with the victim or that can try to learn the typing pattern by some form of observation could have better chances of success. In any case, we saw this as a good indicator of the security of our system despite the small sample sizes.

After the participant had completed the test with her own username, we displayed a username from the other group of participants and asked the current participant to type that username 5 times. After each attempt the scores from that attempt were displayed to the participant attempting the impersonation. We did this for 3 different randomly selected usernames for each participant.

The impersonation challenge succeeded 42 times out of 195 tries so the success rate was little below 22 %. The success probability between different kind of usernames varied greatly. The variance between the results of impersonation attempts usernames is $\sigma^2 = 8.1$ % and thus the standard deviation is $\sigma \approx 28.5$ %. In the best case the impersonation succeeded 9/10 of the time and in the worst case it succeeded with 0/15 attempts.

Because the challenges were selected at random without any effort to balance the occurrences of different usernames, the results are only indicative of the security and not easily comparable. With seven out of 18 usernames there were no successful impersonation attempts (two usernames were not assigned for impersonation at all). On the other hand, none of the three usernames, that were impersonated by four different participants (total of 20 attempts) withstood all attempts. The length of the usernames did not have a significant impact on the security against impersonation.

5   Discussion

Our results show that this type of authentication can be used and it provides usability, security and privacy protection to the user. However, more care needs to be taken to make the impersonation harder for all usernames as the results of Sect. 4.2 clearly show. The weakest usernames were too prone to impersonation to provide any meaningful protection against adversaries. On the other hand, more than half of the usernames were impersonated less than 10 % of the time, when the acceptance threshold was tuned for 90 %.

In any case, our sample of some 20 people is too small to draw definitive conclusions. Especially, if the length of the username would be considered as a factor in both accuracy and security, then a much larger pool of users would be needed. If the increased length would improve security and accuracy, it could act as a positive sign for continuous authentication, where the typing would be measured continuously and authentication would be based on the totality of all things typed. Of course in this type of authentication the content would no longer matter for the authentication unlike in our case with usernames.

One improvement could be to use some more recent methods of measuring keystroke dynamics. This would most likely require readjusting the thresholds to get the same level of accuracy. It might also generate larger templates and decrease the overall performance of the system if more different values need to be stored in the template. Thus, there is a trade-off that needs to be considered, if future work is built upon this system.

Our inclusion of the tag in the keystroke dynamics vectors was necessary to fit the methods of [27] to those of [13]. The tags provide security in the original MFAKE protocol and are based on results of [16]. However, in our case, due to homomorphism, these tags do not protect against a man-in-the-middle tag change. That is, an active attacker could change the original tag t to another tag t' for the keystroke dynamics. The full MFAKE protocol mitigates against this by including in the final computation not only the tag, but also all communications between the server and the client and thus, this change of tag can only lead into a denial of service (i.e. failing authentication), which an active attacker can always do against MFAKE.

Furthermore, the method of [27] also only provides security against honest-but-curious adversaries and as such may constitute even more serious threat. There is a version of the protection method of [27] that is targeted against malicious attackers, but it does not provide much more security for the overhead that it generates and thus we decided not to use it for our work. In a more optimised implementation, the overhead might not become an issue.

The system could be improved also in several other ways. First of all, one could apply more recent partially homomorphic or even fully homomorphic encryption (FHE) schemes, e.g., [15] to provide more versatility to the comparison methods. This would mean that also other biometrics than keystroke dynamics based on simple timing would probably be applicable. Also the order-preserving encryption could be generalised with other property preserving encryption schemes such as [24]. Such a system could offer better privacy protection. Especially with FHE the adversary could not learn even the relative order of the different values in the tempalates and samples. This would make the OPSE encrypted parts of the vector unnecessary and make the comparison much simpler. In this way it would increase the efficiency of the system provided that the FHE is efficient.

Keystroke dynamics provide also an interesting opportunity for continuous authentication while typing. This type of authentication has been discussed for example in [2]. The methods described in this paper are not yet efficient enough for continuous use. This provides an excellent venue for further research, because the system described in [2] does not offer privacy protection at the same level as our work. Also protecting other types of continuous authentication systems such as facial images with privacy safeguards is an important topic. Generalising the results of [27] to this direction would be an interesting topic of research.

Our solution to this privacy-friendly, usable and secure authentication is also generalisable to many other biometrics. Our specific implementation only assumes that the measurements are given in numeric form as a vector and an identification threshold that can be adjusted through experiments or taken from the literature, if such can be found for the biometric method at hand. This makes it suitable to many other biometric authentication applications. The main constraint is that it can only measure the distance of the sample measurement from the template with the AAD metric. This provides a good venue for further research on the topic, e.g., finding ways to use other metrics in a similar manner.

6   Conclusion

In this paper we have shown that it is possible to realise a secure, usable and privacy-friendly authentication from keystroke dynamics. Our method results in fairly good performance even with a simple biometric measurement. The security and privacy features are also provided, although for some usernames the impersonation was very easy.

Further development could make this type of authentication even applicable in a continuous manner, measuring the user constantly while she is typing and still assuring privacy and security. It is fairly straightforward to generalise the system to work with other biometrics that use simple distance metrics for comparison and even more complicated systems can be realised with further research. On the other hand, the overall efficiency of the system should be improved through optimised implementation.

Acknowledgements. We would like to thank Tekes – the Finnish Funding Agency for Innovation, DIMECC Oy, and the Cyber Trust research program for their support of this research. Furthermore, we thank all the volunteers that participated in the experimental study for their time and also the anonymous reviewers for their valuable comments and suggestions that helped in improving this paper.

References

1. Araújo, L.C., Sucupira, L.H., Lizarraga, M.G., Ling, L.L., Yabu-Uti, J.B.T.: User authentication through typing biometrics features. IEEE Trans. Sig. Process. **53**(2), 851–855 (2005)
2. Arias-Cabarcos, P., Almenarez, F., Trapero, R., Diaz-Sanchez, D., Marin, A.: Blended identity: pervasive IdM for continuous authentication. IEEE Secur. Priv. **13**(3), 32–39 (2015)
3. Banerjee, S.P., Woodard, D.L.: Biometric authentication and identification using keystroke dynamics: a survey. J. Pattern Recognit. Res. **7**(1), 116–139 (2012)
4. Boldyreva, A., Chenette, N., Lee, Y., O'Neill, A.: Order-preserving symmetric encryption. In: Joux, A. (ed.) EUROCRYPT 2009. LNCS, vol. 5479, pp. 224–241. Springer, Heidelberg (2009). doi:10.1007/978-3-642-01001-9_13
5. Boldyreva, A., Chenette, N., O'Neill, A.: Order-preserving encryption revisited: improved security analysis and alternative solutions. In: Rogaway, P. (ed.) CRYPTO 2011. LNCS, vol. 6841, pp. 578–595. Springer, Heidelberg (2011). doi:10.1007/978-3-642-22792-9_33
6. Bonneau, J., Herley, C., van Oorschot, P., Stajano, F.: The quest to replace passwords: a framework for comparative evaluation of web authentication schemes. In: 2012 IEEE Symposium on Security and Privacy (SP), pp. 553–567, May 2012
7. Bonneau, J., Schechter, S.: Towards reliable storage of 56-bit secrets in human memory. In: 23rd USENIX Security Symposium (USENIX Security 2014), pp. 607–623 (2014)
8. Braz, C., Robert, J.M.: Security and usability: the case of the user authentication methods. In: Proceedings of the 18th International Conferenceof the Association Francophone d'Interaction Homme-Machine, pp. 199–203. ACM (2006)
9. Brown, M., Rogers, S.J.: User identification via keystroke characteristics of typed names using neural networks. Int. J. Man Mach. Stud. **39**(6), 999–1014 (1993)
10. Clarke, N.L., Furnell, S.: Authenticating mobile phone users using keystroke analysis. Int. J. Inf. Secur. **6**(1), 1–14 (2007)
11. Diffie, W., Hellman, M.E.: New directions in cryptography. IEEE Trans. Inf. Theory **22**(6), 644–654 (1976)
12. Dodis, Y., Ostrovsky, R., Reyzin, L., Smith, A.: Fuzzy extractors: how to generate strong keys from biometrics and other noisy data. SIAM J. Comput. **38**(1), 97–139 (2008)

13. Fleischhacker, N., Manulis, M., Sadr-Azodi, A.: Modular design and analysis framework for multi-factor authentication and key exchange. In: Cryptology ePrint Archive, Report 2012/181 (2012). http://eprint.iacr.org/

14. Gaines, R.S., Lisowski, W., Press, S.J., Shapiro, N.: Authentication by keystroke timing: some preliminary results. Technical report, DTIC Document (1980)

15. Gentry, C.: A fully homomorphic encryption scheme. Ph.D. thesis, Stanford University (2009)

16. Jager, T., Kohlar, F., Schäge, S., Schwenk, J.: Generic compilers for authenticated key exchange. In: Abe, M. (ed.) ASIACRYPT 2010. LNCS, vol. 6477, pp. 232–249. Springer, Heidelberg (2010). doi:10.1007/978-3-642-17373-8_14

17. Jakobsson, M., Shi, F., Golle, P., Chow, R.: Implicit authentication for mobile devices. In: Proceedings of the 4th USENIX Conference on Hot Topics in Security, p. 9. USENIX Association (2009)

18. Juels, A., Sudan, M.: A fuzzy vault scheme. Des. Codes Crypt. **38**(2), 237–257 (2006)

19. Mäntyjärvi, J., Lindholm, M., Vildjiounaite, E., Mäkelä, S.M., Ailisto, H.: Identifying users of portable devices from gait pattern with accelerometers. In: IEEE International Conference on Acoustics, Speech, and Signal Processing, 2005, Proceedings (ICASSP 2005), vol. 2, pp. ii/973–ii/976. IEEE (2005)

20. Monrose, F., Rubin, A.: Authentication via keystroke dynamics. In: Proceedings of the 4th ACM Conference on Computer and Communications Security, pp. 48–56. ACM (1997)

21. Monrose, F., Rubin, A.D.: Keystroke dynamics as a biometric for authentication. Future Gener. Comput. Syst. **16**(4), 351–359 (2000)

22. Nauman, M., Ali, T., Rauf, A.: Using trusted computing for privacy preserving keystroke-based authentication in smartphones. Telecommun. Syst. **52**(4), 2149–2161 (2013)

23. Paillier, P.: Public-key cryptosystems based on composite degree residuosity classes. In: Stern, J. (ed.) EUROCRYPT 1999. LNCS, vol. 1592, pp. 223–238. Springer, Heidelberg (1999). doi:10.1007/3-540-48910-X_16

24. Pandey, O., Rouselakis, Y.: Property preserving symmetric encryption. In: Pointcheval, D., Johansson, T. (eds.) EUROCRYPT 2012. LNCS, vol. 7237, pp. 375–391. Springer, Heidelberg (2012). doi:10.1007/978-3-642-29011-4_23

25. Rathgeb, C., Uhl, A.: A survey on biometric cryptosystems and cancelable biometrics. EURASIP J. Inf. Secur. **2011**(1), 1–25 (2011)

26. Saevanee, H., Bhattarakosol, P.: Authenticating user using keystroke dynamics and finger pressure. In: 6th IEEE Consumer Communications and Networking Conference, CCNC 2009, pp. 1–2. IEEE (2009)

27. Safa, N.A., Safavi-Naini, R., Shahandashti, S.F.: Privacy-preserving implicit authentication. In: Cuppens-Boulahia, N., Cuppens, F., Jajodia, S., Abou El Kalam, A., Sans, T. (eds.) SEC 2014. IFIP AICT, vol. 428, pp. 471–484. Springer, Heidelberg (2014). doi:10.1007/978-3-642-55415-5_40

28. Tulyakov, S., Farooq, F., Mansukhani, P., Govindaraju, V.: Symmetric hash functions for secure fingerprint biometric systems. Pattern Recogn. Lett. **28**(16), 2427–2436 (2007)

Author Index

Printed in the United States
By Bookmasters